CHRONICLES

OF THE

BARBARIANS

ALSO BY DAVID WILLIS MCCULLOUGH

Nonfiction

People, Books & Book People
Brooklyn . . . and How It Got That Way

Fiction

Think on Death
Point No-Point

Anthologies

Great Detectives
American Childhoods
City Sleuths and Tough Guys

CHRONICLES
OF THE
BARBARIANS

FIRSTHAND ACCOUNTS OF PILLAGE AND
CONQUEST, FROM THE ANCIENT WORLD
TO THE FALL OF CONSTANTINOPLE

EDITED BY DAVID WILLIS McCULLOUGH

HISTORY BOOK CLUB
NEW YORK

For Patty O'Neill, Celt

Chronicles of the Barbarians is a publication of History Book Club,
1271 Avenue of the Americas, New York, NY 10020.

Acknowledgment of permission to reprint copyrighted materials can be found starting on page 379. All best efforts have been made to contact the owners of copyrighted material reprinted here. The editors would be pleased to hear from copyright holders who could not be found so that the proper acknowledgments might be made.

Printed in the United States of America

ACKNOWLEDGMENTS

Without Leslie Pockell, this book would not exist. Without the hard work of Liza Miller, it would not be in the form it is. And without the New York Public Library and the Westchester County Library System, the contents would be much different. The editor thanks them all most sincerely.

DWMcC

CONTENTS

Illustrations follow pages 168 and 296

CHRONICLES

OF THE

BARBARIANS

Cattle die, kin die,
The man dies too.
But good fame never dies,
For the man who earns it.

Cattle die, kin die,
The man dies too.
One thing I know that never dies,
The good name of the dead.

—from the Viking poem "Havamal"

INTRODUCTION

"THEY CAME LIKE LOCUSTS"

There was nothing new about the barbarian threat in A.D. 376, or so most Romans probably thought. Rome had been battling unruly tribes at its borders for centuries, and for centuries the Celts, the Gauls, and the Goths had pretty much been kept in their places. True, the year before, Emperor Valentinian had become so enraged over the rude and uncivilized behavior of a delegation of barbarian envoys from across the Danube that he had a fit and died; but dealing with barbarians—through either military force or bribery—was something Romans were thoroughly accustomed to.

Then something happened, something new. According to the fourth-century historian Ammianus Marcellinus, "a race of men, hitherto unknown, had suddenly descended like a whirlwind from the lofty mountains, as if they had risen from some secret recess of the earth, and were ravaging and destroying everything which came in their way."

The Huns were invading from the east, and their fury was felt at first not by the Romans but by other barbarians, the Germanic Goths, who were driven from their lands. One of the first great European floods of refugees was soon under way, and Rome—uncharacteristically—agreed to take them in, so long as they promised to settle in the wastelands of Thrace and their leaders converted to Christianity. Across the Danube they came by the tens of thousands. Because of heavy rains, the river was too flooded to swim, so enterprising Romans set up impromptu ferry services—boats, rafts, even hollowed-out log canoes—and charged outrageous tolls.

The starving Goths were said—and this was the sort of thing "civilized" people often said about barbarians—to trade their children for dogs that they then killed and ate. An even trade was one dog for one child.

Rome and Europe were never again the same. The rampaging Huns moved erratically westward, and soon the Goths safely within the empire were at war with the Romans, for they had come not in disorganized bands, as it had seemed, but as a nation with leaders and generals. Two years later, they routed the eastern emperor Valens's army at Hadrianople and killed him. The fall of the city of Rome was only decades away. Europe was about to become a barbarian continent.

No one calls himself a barbarian. That's what your enemy calls you. For Greeks in the time of Herodotus, in the fifth century B.C., a barbarian was simply someone who did not speak Greek and was therefore—obviously—an inferior. And since the word "barbarian" itself may have come from the Sanskrit word for "stammering," it could mean anyone who speaks unclearly. To be a barbarian meant you could not communicate.

Barbarians also tended, in the eyes of their beholders, to indulge in strange habits such as incest and cannibalism and were first written about as colorful curiosities an adventurous traveler might encounter far from home. Herodotus noted the Scythians' fondness for collecting their enemies' skulls. Gibbon observed that the ancient Scots were thought by their contemporaries to prefer eating the shepherd to eating the sheep. And the Greek geographer Strabo noted that it was quite common among the Gauls for women to do men's work and men women's.

As time went on, the definition took on darker overtones. The inferior (the stranger, the other) became an enemy who not only did not speak as you did or believe in what you believed but who also sought to destroy all that you valued: your art, your culture, your family, the very house you lived in. The barbarian became a threat, often a very real threat who had already leveled a neighboring city and was said to be at your very gates. And later still, as religions became more codified, more evangelical, and more militant, the inferior barbarian became an enemy of God himself, a henchman of the Devil, or—worse yet—an unwitting instrument of God's wrath. He was there at the gates, ready to rape your wife and daughters, take your gold, and kill your priests because of you yourself, because of your sins. Vile as he was, he was God's avenger scourging a sinful world.

But such tangled theology came later, and perhaps one of the most surprising things about the barbarians is how long they were around. Of course there was no one group called "barbarian" and no ancestral homeland of Barbaria.

The bands, armies, tribes, nations, and hordes that appear in this compilation were all people who were there because their neighbors, enemies, and victims feared them: Scythians, Celts, Goths, Huns, Vandals, Vikings, Mongols, Tartars, Saracens, Christians. The voices heard in these ancient chronicles are, for the most part, the voices of those same neighbors, enemies, and victims, with every now and then a rare surviving example of a barbarian speaking for himself. This book does not attempt to be a complete history of the barbarians but simply glimpses of moments from their long story.

The first impression we receive of the barbarians is one of incredible energy. As described by the classical Roman historians (who more often than not were actually Greek), the various tribes of Celts and Goths that streamed out of the north were creatures of boundless, unfocused chaos. They appeared suddenly out of nowhere. They were noisy. They did not fight the way armies were supposed to fight. They slept with everyone: their sisters, their comrades, anyone. They drank something stronger than wine. They had all those horses. They were blond. Some of them even fought naked. And they were big. The barbarians' size is mentioned so often, it is hard not to suspect that the Romans were really quite short and perhaps self-conscious about it.

Although the Romans got better at it with experience, at first they had no idea how to defeat these northern wild men and lost most of the early encounters. The city of Rome itself fell to the Celts, however briefly, as early as 390 B.C., eight hundred years before the date most people associate with the "sacking" of the city. To read Polybius's descriptions of the Roman-Celtic battles in northern Italy in the century that followed is to experience the Romans' puzzlement—and their titillation——over these exotic, vicious blonds.

For the next eight hundred years, the story of barbarian Europe is one of constant movement. From out of western Germany the Celts, the Saxons, and the Franks moved west; from farther east the Gothic tribes moved south. The Vandals came from Scandinavia to the Balkans, across northern Europe down to Spain, then along north Africa to Carthage, from which, circling still, they invaded Italy. Later, in the fourth century A.D., the Asiatic Huns (their name may come from the Chinese *hsiung-nu* or "nomad") came out of the east, establishing the pattern later followed by the Mongols, and attacked the Goths, which stirred the pot once again. As Ambrose of Milan wrote ca. 380, "The

Huns threw themselves on the Alans, the Alans upon the Goths upon the Taifali and Sarmatae . . . and this is not yet to end." Indeed it was not.

Over the centuries the waves of barbarians became more and more exotic. There were "Asiatic shepherds" from the east, dark Moors from across the Mediterranean, and the great clash with Islam—in which each side saw the other as the barbarian, the infidel—that culminated with the Crusades to rid the Holy Land of unbelievers, and then came the fall of Christian Constantinople to the Turks. In the beginning the various mounted tribes scored brilliantly in battles on open fields but poorly in storming cities. "I do not war with stone walls," said a fourth century Visigothic chief after refusing to storm the city of Hadrianople. One of the most common legends in Europe, the historian J. B. Bury has noted, is the story of the local priest or bishop—in Paris it was a young girl, St. Geneviève—whose prayers kept the approaching heathens from storming the city gates. Later barbarians—the Mongols, Tamerlane—found that they had no trouble at all warring with stone walls and reducing them to rubble.

It is tempting, although probably not strictly accurate, to think of the barbarians as Europe's first immigrants. All were nomadic to begin with, although the Celts seemed quickest to put down roots wherever they paused. The Goths—to separate Visigoths from Ostrogoths and other smaller Gothic subdivisions would get us involved in maddening nit-picking—were slower to move from a nomadic to a pastoral culture. But the Roman army, by successfully barricading them for centuries beyond the Rhine and Danube Rivers, forced the Germanic Goths to become settlers, as a comparison of Caesar's 55 B.C. description of the Germans with Tacitus's of a hundred and fifty years later shows.

Calling the barbarians pastoral, however, should not conjure up images of peaceful flocks and Arcadian shepherds. If there were pacifist barbarians, they are not remembered. The barbarians were gleeful, enthusiastic fighters, and early on the Romans saw that these vulgar enemies could become useful servants and soldiers. Procopius writes about the Eruli tribe, a people he frankly called "beastly," but who nevertheless served the Romans as hired fighters for centuries.

By the time Visigoth Alaric sacked Rome in A.D. 410, barbarians were found in every level of society. There had been Celtic legions in the Roman army since the days of Caligula (who ruled from A.D. 37–41). Stilicho, whose father was a

Vandal who had fought on the side of the Romans at Hadrianople, was married to an emperor's niece and was for years the most powerful political figure in the empire. He was executed in A.D. 408, with some believing he was in league with Alaric, whom he had been alternately bribing and fighting on the battlefield. And there was Galla Placidia (d. A.D. 450), who in her busy life was the daughter, granddaughter, half sister, wife, and mother of a number of Roman emperors and also—by way of marriage to Ataulf—queen of the Visigoths.

Centuries earlier, during the Punic Wars between Rome and Carthage in the third and second centuries B.C., both sides had used barbarian mercenaries. The first-century B.C. historian Diodorus Siculus described an incident in Sicily, in 251 B.C., when Romans arranged with local merchants to slip "a great quantity" of wine to the Celts guarding the Carthaginian general Hasdrubal's elephants. (The Celts' fondness for strong drink was something noted by Roman historians from the very beginning.) Then, when the Celts "were in complete disorder and shouting noisily," the Romans attacked them and made off with sixty elephants, which they shipped back to Rome, where one and all were "struck with great wonder."

One of the dreams of Carthaginian rulers was that the different barbarian tribes would unite behind them and, from all sides, squeeze the Romans into submission. The so-called barbarian conspiracy against Rome was entertained or feared for a thousand years. When Agricola and his Roman legions battled Celts in southern Scotland ca. A.D. 80, the local Caledonian leader predicted that when push came to shove the barbarians in the Imperial army, who outnumbered those who were Roman-born, would side with their Celtic brothers. It didn't happen. Some have argued that in time the "barbarization" of Rome through assimilation did bring about the end of the empire, but there was never a dramatic flash of revolt. For all their love of violence, the barbarians won by simply outlasting and outnumbering their more sophisticated enemies. If there was a conspiracy, it was an invisible one.

On the battlefield, barbarians showed little temptation to conspire. Huns battled Goths across northern Europe, and the army that turned Attila back outside Châlons in France was composed largely of different Gothic tribes. Celts fought Britons; Vikings took on everyone, everywhere; Vandals battled

Goths in Spain. And these squabbles took on domestic implications as well. Hunneric, son of the Vandal king Genseric, married a daughter of Theodoric, king of the Visigoths, probably for political reasons. But when Hunneric suspected that his bride was trying to poison him, he cut off her nose and ears, packed her up, and sent her back to her father, which probably did little to improve relations between the rival kingdoms.

Reading through these accounts—in a very real way, this compilation is as much a history of the writing of history as it is of the barbarians themselves— one is struck by the freshness of the observations, especially in the beginning. There is something very appealing about Strabo's decision to describe the entire world and all the people in it and then, beginning in Iberia and heading eastward, do just that. Herodotus's love of a good story and his curiosity are infectious. The clarity and simplicity of the early Greco-Roman historians are impressive, as is their skill at describing battles vividly but not breathlessly. It is impossible to read Ammianus Marcellinus's account of the Battle of Hadrianople—and the Goths' circle of covered wagons like a scene out of the American West—without visualizing it.

Although perhaps appalled by the habits and personal customs of the Celts or the Germans, the early historians were usually not morally judgmental. The barbarians' religions were noted as another curiosity but rarely criticized (very often, their deities were assigned the same names as the ones the Romans worshipped: Mercury, for instance). Once the Christian era began, however, some leaders and churchmen came to refer to the barbarians in terms that aligned them with the Antichrist. By the time of the invasions of the Mongols, anti-infidel, crusader zealotry was spreading throughout Europe, and barbarians had come to be morally demonized. This was an era in which the writing of history had become the profession of monks, who were all too inclined to see the hand of God—or the Devil—behind all things.

A constant theme throughout the book, however, is surprise. Again and again, the barbarian enemies came from nowhere. They were unexpected. They were people no one had ever heard of. They were perhaps not altogether human. Often they were compared to locusts, or to lava flowing from volcanic Mount Etna: never human, but relentless forces of nature. Living as we do in an age of universal, instantaneous communication, it is impossible for us to fully comprehend a world in which enemies could be utterly new and might even be described in all seriousness—as at least one Western traveler among the Mongols did—as having been descended from a tribe in which all the females were human and all the males shaggy dogs.

Did the barbarians in fact have an ethic that their civilized chroniclers overlooked? Since there was no such thing as a typical barbarian, there can hardly be a single answer, but as a group—the Vikings, perhaps, excepted—they were a land-based people with a sense of the earth's expansiveness that the Greeks and Romans, huddled like frogs—to use Plato's simile—around the palmy shore of the Mediterranean Sea, could probably never comprehend. Although the codes of different groups were obviously different, there was often a sense of military honor. Brennus, who led his Celts into Rome in 390 B.C., did so because he felt the Romans had behaved badly in an earlier battle north of the city and had not followed the proper rules of war. Tamerlane, more than fifteen hundred years later, would cross-examine residents of cities he captured (often on religious matters) before deciding how large the slaughter would be. And for some, being a barbarian was a profitable business and not mindless pillage. Batu Khan's Golden Horde, for example, struck terror throughout Russia largely as a pretext for blackmailing the frightened cities to keep the invaders from their gates.

Many of the historians whose work is collected here are highly sophisticated men (sad to say—blame it on the periods we are covering—there is not a female writer in the book) who created the art of writing history: Herodotus, Julius Caesar, Tacitus, Livy. Edward Gibbon is included at length—even though he breaks one of the rules of the collection by not being a near contemporary of the time he writes about—because perhaps more than any other writer he has shaped the way we think and write about barbarians today.

Other writers are unique in different ways. There is the first barbarian historian, a Goth, whose work has survived (Jordanes); there is someone who was held captive by Tamerlane (Johann Schiltberger), someone who had dinner with Attila (Priscus), someone who witnessed a Viking funeral (Ibn Fadlan), someone who knew someone who had a conversation with the unhappy spirit of St. Andrew on the road to Jerusalem (Raymond, Canon of Le Puy), and someone—an "Arab-Syrian Gentleman and Warrior"—who survived a duel with a Christian crusader (Usamah ibn-Murshid).

Still others might be compared to untrained folk artists or primitive painters, writers such as the unnamed author of *The Secret History of the Mongols*, who described a domestic scene outside Genghis Khan's tent that ends in a beheading; or the monks of Novgorod in Russia, who wrote of the approaching Mongol horde and the bribes paid to save their city; or the British monks who recorded Viking raids in *The Anglo-Saxon Chronicle*; or the Welsh Norman who could find nothing to like about the Irish but their music.

Are these accounts accurate? Can they be relied on? There is an old police saying that no one is less trustworthy than an eyewitness. What they say is full of lies, exaggerations, honest mistakes, myths, misunderstandings, and misinterpretations. Something that can almost never be taken at face value is numbers: how many fought, how many were killed, how many forded a river. Yet if history is as much, if not more, what people *think* happened as what really *did* happen, the stories represented here are history at its richest. In keeping with the spirit of the original source documents, no attempt has been made to enforce consistent spellings for proper names or places. As a result, the reader will find as many spelling variations on "Genghis Khan" or "Tamerlane" as there are people writing about them. Dates can also vary from source to source.

This compilation, like Gibbon's *The History of the Decline and Fall of the Roman Empire*, ends with the fall of Constantinople, the last, tattered remnant of the Roman Empire, to the Ottoman Turks in 1453. Looking around today and asking, "Where are the Greeks? Where are the Romans?," it is difficult not to conclude that the barbarians indeed won. We, surely, are the descendants not of those civilized toga wearers but of the vigorous, trouser-wearing immigrant barbarians from nowhere.

At the outset, I said something about no one calling himself a barbarian. But of course there is an exception. One person did proclaim and celebrate his barbaric freedom. "I am not a bit tamed, I too am untamable," Walt Whitman—the unabashed voice of the New World—wrote, "I spread my barbaric yawp over the roofs of the world."

—DWMcC

A BARBARIAN CHRONOLOGY

ca. 424 B.C. — Herodotus dies.

390 B.C. — Celts, led by Brennus, burn Rome and retreat.

55 B.C. — The Gallic War: Julius Caesar invades Britain.

A.D. 9 — Germans, led by Arminius, massacre Varus's Roman legions in the Teutoburg Forest (in what is now northwestern Germany).

70 — Agricola takes command of the XXth Roman Legion in Britain and pushes barbarians to the west and north.

ca. 125 — Emperor Hadrian builds a wall across the narrow neck of Britain below the Scottish border to fend off northern barbarians.

220 — Goths invade Asia Minor and the Balkan Peninsula.

257 — Goths, divided into Visigoths and Ostrogoths, invade Black Sea area.

268 — Goths sack Athens, Sparta, and Corinth.

286 — Diocletian (ruled 284–305) divides the Roman Empire into East and West.

313 — Emperor Constantine recognizes Christianity.

330 — Constantine founds Constantinople in Byzantium as the new capital of the Eastern Empire.

ca. 360 — Huns begin their invasion of Europe from the East.

376 — Huns invade what is now Russia.

376 — Emperor Valens permits Goths to immigrate into the Empire.

378 — Goths defeat the Romans at Hadrianople in Thrace and kill Emperor Valens.

382 — Emperor Theodosius I (ruled 379–395) resettles Visigoths in the Empire.

395 — Alaric (ruled 395–410) becomes king of the Visigoths.

396 — Alaric invades Greece (396) and plunders Athens and the Balkans (398).

401–403 — Goths invade Italian peninsula.

404 — Honorius (ruled 395–423) makes Ravenna capital of the Western Empire and brings troops south from the Rhine to defend it.

406–428 — Gunderic rules the Vandals.

409 — The Vandals, no longer restrained behind the Rhine by the Romans, sweep across northern Europe and reach Spain.

410 — Alaric and the Goths sack Rome.

416 — Goths, led by Ataulf, conquer Vandal kingdom in Spain.

429 — The Vandals, commanded by Genseric (ruled 428–477), cross from Spain into Northern Africa.

433 — Attila becomes ruler of the Huns.

436 — Huns destroy Burgundian Kingdom of Worms.

439 — Vandals, led by Genseric, take Carthage.

442 — Last Roman legions are withdrawn from Britain, leaving the island to the Anglo-Saxons, Celts, Picts, and Scots.

443 — Attila ravages the Balkans.

451 — Attila's westward invasion is stopped by a mixed army of Romans and Goths on the Catalaunian Fields outside Châlons (in what is now northeastern France).

452 — Attila ravages what is now northern Italy but fails to take Rome.

453 — Attila dies.

455 — Genseric and the Vandals cross the Mediterranean and sack Rome.

470 — Huns withdraw from Europe.

471–526 — Theodoric the Great rules the Goths.

477–484 — Hunneric, king of the Vandals, son and successor of Genseric, rules the Vandals.

534 — Belisarius defeats Vandals, now led by Gelimer, in North Africa.

620 — Vikings invade Ireland.

622 — Muhammad's (ca. 570–632) flight from Mecca to Medina (the hegira) marks the beginning of the Islamic calendar.

793 — Vikings raid the monastery on Lindisfarne in England.

795 — Vikings land in Ireland.

800 — Charlemagne, king of the Franks, is crowned emperor of the West by Pope Leo III.

806 — Vikings sack Monastery of Iona in northwest Scotland.

841 — Vikings plunder Rouen and advance to Paris.

845 — Vikings lay siege to Paris.

859 — Vikings enter the Mediterranean and sack the coast up to Asia Minor.

860 — Rurik the Rus establishes a Viking community at Novgorod in what is now his namesake, Russia.

861 — Vikings sack Paris, Toulouse, Cologne, Aix-la-Chapelle, and Worms.

979 — Vikings defeated in Ireland at the Battle of Tara.

991 — Britons battle Viking raiders at Maldon on the Blackwater River in Sussex.

1095 — At Clermont, in France, Pope Urban II calls for a crusade to rescue the holy places and massacre the Muslims.

1096–99 — First Crusade

1098 — Crusaders defeat Turks at Antioch.

1099 — Crusaders take Jerusalem.

1104 — Crusaders take Acre.

1145 — Pope Eugene III proclaims Second Crusade.

1148 — Crusaders, led by Conrad III and King Louis VII, fail miserably in attack on Damascus.

1155 — Temujin (Genghis Khan), founder of Mongol empire, born.

1183 — Saladin, Sultan of Egypt, takes Aleppo.

1187 — Saladin recaptures Jerusalem from the crusaders.

1190 — King Richard the Lion-Heart of England fails to win back Jerusalem, but encounters Saladin, which becomes a popular subject of medieval chivalric tales.

1204 — Crusaders take Constantinople.

1206 — Temujin is proclaimed Genghis Khan ("Strong Ruler") of the Turko-Mongolian people.

1211 — Genghis Khan invades China.

1214 — Genghis Khan captures Beijing.

1215 — Kublai Khan, grandson of Genghis Khan, born.

1218 — Genghis Khan invades Persia.

1219 — Genghis Khan begins his destruction of Muslim cities in central Asia, including Bukhara, Samarkand, and Herat.

1224 — Novgorod, though never attacked, is terrorized by the threat of Mongol invasion.

1227 — Genghis Khan dies; his empire is divided among his three sons.

1235 — Batu Khan, grandson of Genghis Khan, becomes commander of the Mongol army assigned to the conquest of Europe.

1237 — Batu Khan invades Russia; by 1240 he has Moscow and Kiev.

1241 — Batu Khan defeats Germans at Battle of Liegnitz, Silesia; invades Poland and Hungary (the Tatar Invasion) and is at the gates of Vienna when The Great Khan Ogodei (Genghis's son) dies; Batu is recalled to Karakorum to participate in the election of a grand Khan.

1242 — Batu Khan establishes his warriors—the "Golden Horde"—at Sarai, on the Lower Volga.

1251–59 — Kublai Khan, Genghis's grandson, leads military campaigns in South China.

1255 — Batu Khan dies.

1260 — Kublai Khan succeeds his brother, Mongke (Mangu) as khan of Mongol empire.

1268 — Antioch falls to Muslims.

1274 — Kublai Khan fails to conquer Japan.

1279 — Kublai Khan defeats the Sung Dynasty of China and founds the Yuan Dynasty.

1287 — Kublai Khan invades Burma.

1289 — Tripoli falls to Muslims.

1291 — Fall of Acre, the last Christian stronghold, marks the end of the Crusades.

1292 — Marco Polo returns to Venice after spending seventeen years in Kublai Khan's China.

1294 — Kublai Khan dies.

1346 — The Black Death (bubonic plague) breaks out in Sarai, capital of the Golden Horde; from 1347–1351 it spreads throughout Europe, killing more than 20 million people.

1368 — Tamerlane ascends the throne of Samarkand, a branch of the Mongol Empire.

1380 — Tamerlane begins 35 successful campaigns to Persia, Georgia, Russia, Egypt, etc.

1398 — Tamerlane captures Delhi.

1401 — Tamerlane conquers Damascus, Baghdad, and Haleb.

1402 — Tamerlane defeats Ottoman sultan Beyazid at Ankara and takes him prisoner.

1405 — Tamerlane dies; succeeded by Shah Rokh (who ruled until 1447).

1406 — Mausoleum of Timur (Tamerlane) built in Samarkand.

1453 — The Ottoman Turks, led by Mehmed II, storm and capture Constantinople, putting an end—after 1,100 years—to the Roman Empire of the East.

— I —

BARBARIANS
ON THE LANDSCAPE

By the beginning of the first century A.D., the Greeks and Romans were well aware of the barbarians around them. Before turning back to earlier times to hear about the Scythians and the Thracians and the first encounters with the Celts and the Goths, it is worth taking a quick tour across Europe to see how an early writer placed the barbarians on the landscape.

Strabo (ca. 63 B.C.–ca. A.D. 24), a Greek born in Asia Minor, was not the first classical geographer, but his seventeen-book *Geographica* is regarded as the most important—and complete—description of the world and its people to have survived from ancient times. Drawn from his own travels and acknowledged works by earlier Greek and Roman authorities (although he does not hide his distrust of Romans), as well as from rumor and guesswork, it is an appealing mixture of anecdotes, travelers' tall tales, and scholarship.

This introduction to the first-century world of the barbarians begins on the Iberian Peninsula, moves across Britain and Gaul to northern Europe, and ends with a Scandinavian tribe that was a forerunner of the Vikings. Strabo's interests range from toothbrushing practices to tin mining to the Druids to the paths rivers take to reach the sea, and although he never visited the icy north, his fascination in the last section with stories about dramatic ocean tides probably reflects the curiosity—and wonder—of a southerner accustomed to the more tranquil Mediterranean Sea.

STRABO

FROM *GEOGRAPHY*

A.D. 24

SPAIN

All the Iberians, so to speak, were furnished with light arms for the purposes of robbery, and, as we described the Lusitanians, using the javelin, the sling, and the sword. They have some cavalry interspersed amongst the foot-soldiers, the horses are trained to traverse the mountains, and to sink down on their knees at the word of command, in case of necessity. Iberia produces abundance of antelopes and wild horses. In many places the lakes are stocked. They have fowl, swans, and birds of similar kind, and vast numbers of bustards. Beavers are found in the rivers, but the castor does not possess the same virtue as that from the Euxine, the drug from that place having peculiar properties of its own, as is the case in many other instances. Thus Posidonius tells us that the Cyprian copper alone produces the cadmian stone, copperaswater, and oxide of copper. He likewise informs us of the singular fact, that in Iberia the crows are not black; and that the horses of Keltiberia which are spotted, lose that colour when they pass into Ulterior Iberia. He compares them to the Parthian horses, for indeed they are superior to all other breeds, both in fleetness and their ease in speedy travelling.

Iberia produces a large quantity of roots used in dyeing. In olives, vines, figs, and every kind of similar fruit trees, the Iberian coast next the Mediterranean abounds, they are likewise plentiful beyond. Of the coasts next the ocean, that towards the north is destitute of them, on account of the cold, and the remaining portion generally on account of the apathy of the men, and because they do not lead a civilized life, but pass their days in poverty, only acting on the animal impulse, and living most corruptly. They do not attend to ease or luxury, unless any one considers it can add to the happiness of their lives to wash themselves and their wives in stale urine kept in tanks, and to rinse their teeth with it, which they say is the custom both with the Cantabrians and their neighbours. This practice, as well as that of sleeping on the ground, is common both among the Iberians and Kelts. Some say that the Gallicians are atheists, but that the Keltiberians, and their neighbours to the north, [sacrifice] to a nameless god, every full moon; at night, before their doors, the whole family passing the night in dancing and festival. The Vettones, the first time they came to a Roman camp, and saw certain of the officers walking up and down the roads for the mere pleasure of walking, supposed that they were mad, and offered to show them the way to their tents. For they thought when not fighting, one should remain quietly seated at ease.

What Artemidorus relates concerning the adornment of certain of their women, must likewise be attributed to their barbarous customs. He says that they wear iron collars having crows fixed to them which bend over the head, and fall forward considerably over the forehead. When they wish they draw their veil over these crows, so as to shade the whole face: this they consider an ornament. Others wear a tympanium [a headdress shaped like a drum] surrounding the occiput, and fitting tight to the head as far as the ears, turning over and increasing little by little in height and breadth. Others again make bald the front of the head, in order to display the forehead to greater advantage. Some twist their flowing hair round a small style, a foot high, and afterwards cover it with a black veil.

Of singularities like these many have been observed and recorded as to all the Iberian nations in common, but particularly those towards the north, not only concerning their bravery, but likewise their cruelty and brutal madness. For in the war against the Cantabrians, mothers have slain their children sooner than suffer them to be captured; and a young boy, having obtained a sword, slew at the command of his father both his parents and brothers, who had been made prisoners and were bound, and a woman who had been taken together with them. A man being invited by a party of drunken soldiers to their feast, threw himself into a fire.

These feelings are common both to the Keltic, Thracian, and Scythian nations, as well as the valour not only of their men, but likewise of their women. These till the ground, and after parturition, having put their husbands instead of themselves to bed, they wait upon them. Frequently in their employment they wash and swathe their infants, sitting down by some stream. Posidonius tells us that in Liguria, his host Charmoleon, a man who came from Marseilles, related to him, that having hired some men and women to dig his land, one of the women was seized with the pains of labour, and going to a little distance from where they were at work, she brought forth, and returned immediately to her work, for fear she might lose her pay. He observed that she was evidently working in considerable pain, but was not aware of the cause till towards evening, when he ascertained it, and sent her away, having given her her wages. She then carried her infant to a small spring, and having washed it, wrapped it up in as good swaddling clothes as she could get, and made the best of her way home.

Another practice, not restricted to the Iberians alone, is for two to mount on one horse, so that in the event of a conflict, one may be there to fight on foot. Neither are they the only sufferers in being tormented with vast swarms of mice, from which pestilential diseases have frequently ensued. This occurred to the Romans in Cantabria, so that they caused it to be proclaimed, that whoever would catch the mice should receive rewards according to the number taken, and [even with this] they were scarcely preserved, as they were suffering besides from want of corn and other necessaries, it being difficult to get supplies of corn from Aquitaine on account of the rugged nature of the country. It is proof of the ferocity of the Cantabrians, that a number of them having been taken prisoners and fixed to the cross, they chanted songs of triumph. Instances such as these are proofs of the ferocity of their manners. There are others which, although not showing them to be polished, are certainly not brutish. For example, amongst the Cantabrians, the men give dowries to their wives, and the daughters are left heirs, but they procure wives for their brothers. These things indicate a degree of power in the woman, although they are no proof of advanced civilization.

It is also a custom with the Iberians to furnish themselves with a poison, which kills without pain, and which they procure from a herb resembling parsley. This they hold in readiness in case of misfortune, and to devote themselves for those whose cause they have joined, thus dying for their sake.

GAUL

The entire race which now goes by the name of Gallic, or Galatic, is warlike, passionate, and always ready for fighting, but otherwise simple and not malicious. If irritated, they rush in crowds to the conflict, openly and without any circumspection; and thus are easily vanquished by those who employ stratagem. For any one may exasperate them when, where, and under whatever pretext he pleases; he will always find them ready for danger, nothing to support them except their violence and daring. Nevertheless they may be easily persuaded to devote themselves to any thing useful, and have thus engaged both in science and letters. Their power consists both in the size of their bodies and also in their numbers. Their frankness and simplicity lead them easily to assemble in masses, each one feeling indignant at what appears injustice to his neighbour. At the present time indeed they are all at peace, being in subjection and living under the command of the Romans, who have subdued them; but we have described their customs as we understand they existed in former times, and as they still exist amongst the Germans. These two nations, both by nature and in their form of government, are similar and related to each other. Their countries border on each other, being separated by the river Rhine, and are for the most part similar.

Germany, however, is more to the north, if we compare together the southern and northern parts of the two countries respectively. Thus it is that they can so easily change their abode. They march in crowds in one collected army, or rather remove with all their families, whenever they are ejected by a more powerful force. They were subdued by the Romans much more easily than the Iberians; for they began to wage war with these latter first, and ceased last, having in the meantime conquered the whole of the nations situated between the

Rhine and the mountains of the Pyrenees. For these fighting in crowds and vast numbers, were overthrown in crowds, whereas the Iberians kept themselves in reserve, and broke up the war into a series of petty engagements, showing themselves in different bands, sometimes here, some times there, like banditti.

All the Gauls are warriors by nature, but they fight better on horseback than on foot, and the flower of the Roman cavalry is drawn from their number. The most valiant of them dwell towards the north and next to the ocean.

The Gauls wear the *sagum* [a woolen cloak], let their hair grow and wear short breeches. Instead of tunics they wear a slashed garment with sleeves descending a little below the hips. The wool [of their sheep] is coarse, but long; from it they weave the thick saga called *laines*. However, in the northern parts the Romans rear flocks of sheep which they cover with skins, and which produce very fine wool. The equipment [of the Gauls] is in keeping with the size of their bodies; they have a long sword hanging at their right side, a long shield, and lances in proportion, together with a *madaris* somewhat resembling a javelin; some of them also use bows and slings; they have also a piece of wood resembling a *pilum*, which they hurl not out of a thong, but from their hand, and to a farther distance than an arrow. They principally make use of it in shooting birds. To the present day most of them lie on the ground, and take their meals seated on straw. They subsist principally on milk and all kinds of flesh, especially that of swine, which they eat both fresh and salted. Their swine live in the fields, and surpass in height, strength, and swiftness.

To persons unaccustomed to approach them they are almost as dangerous as wolves. The people dwell in great houses arched, constructed of planks and wicker, and covered with a heavy thatched roof. They have sheep and swine in such abundance, that they supply salted pork in plenty, not only to Rome but to most parts of Italy. Their governments were for the most part aristocratic; formerly they chose a governor every year, and a military leader was likewise elected by the multitude. At the present day they are mostly under subjection to the Romans. They have a peculiar custom in their assemblies. If any one makes an uproar or interrupts the person speaking, an attendant advances with a drawn sword, and commands him with menace to be silent; if he persists, the attendant does the same thing a second and third time; and finally, if he will not obey, cuts off from his *sagum* so large a piece as to render the remainder useless. The labours of the two sexes are distributed in a manner the reverse of what they are with us, but this is a common thing with numerous other barbarians.

Amongst [the Gauls] there are generally three divisions of men especially reverenced: the Bards, the Vates, and the Druids. The Bards composed and chanted hymns; the Vates occupied themselves with the sacrifices and the study of nature; while the Druids joined to the study of nature that of moral philosophy. The belief in the justice [of the Druids] is so great that the decision both of public and private disputes is referred to them; and they have before now, by their decision, prevented armies from engaging when drawn up in battle-array against each other. All cases of murder are particularly referred to them. When there is plenty of these they imagine there will likewise be a plentiful harvest. Both these and the others assert that the soul is indestructible, and likewise the world, but that sometimes fire and sometimes water have prevailed in making great changes.

To their simplicity and vehemence, the Gauls join much folly, arrogance, and love of ornament. They wear golden collars round their necks, and bracelets on their arms and wrists, and those who are of any dignity have garments dyed and worked with gold. This lightness of character makes them intolerable when they conquer, and throws them into consternation when worsted. In addition to their folly, they have a barbarous and absurd custom, common however with many nations of the north, of suspending the heads of their enemies from their horses' necks on their return from battle, and when they have arrived nailing them as a spectacle to their gates. Posidonius says he witnessed this in many different places, and was at first shocked, but became familiar with it in time on account of its frequency. The heads of any illustrious persons they embalm with cedar, exhibit them to strangers, and would not sell them for their weight in gold. However, the Romans put a stop to these customs, as well as to their modes of sacrifice and divination, which were quite opposite to those sanctioned by our laws. They would strike a man devoted as [a sacrificial] offering in his back with a sword, and divine from his convulsive throes. Without the Druids they never sacrifice.

It is said they have other modes of sacrificing their human victims; that they pierce some of them with arrows, and crucify others in their temples; and that they prepare a colossus of hay and wood, into which they put cattle, beasts of all kinds, and men, and then set fire to it.

They say that in the ocean, not far from the coast, there is a small island lying opposite to the outlet of the river Loire, inhabited by Samnite women who are Bacchantes, and conciliate and appease that god by mysteries and sacrifices. No man is permitted to land on the island; and when the women desire to have intercourse with the other sex, they cross the sea, and afterwards return again. They have a custom of once a year unroofing the whole of the temple, and roofing it again the same day before sunset, each one bringing some of the materials. If any one lets her burden fall, she is torn in pieces by the others, and her limbs carried round the temple with wild shouts, which they never cease until their rage is exhausted. They say it always happens that someone drops her burden, and is thus sacrificed.

But what Artemidorus tells us concerning the crows partakes still more of fiction. He narrates that on the coast, washed by the ocean, there is a harbour named the Port of Two Crows, and that here two crows may be seen with their right wings white. Those who have any dispute come here, and each one having placed a plank for himself on a lofty eminence, sprinkles crumbs thereupon; the birds fly to these, eat up the one and scatter the other, and he whose crumbs are scattered gains the cause. This narration has decidedly too much the air of fiction. What he narrates concerning Ceres and Proserpine is more credible. He says that there is an island near Britain in which they perform sacrifices to these goddesses after the same fashion that they do in Samothrace.

The following is also credible, that a tree grows in Keltica similar to a fig, which produces a fruit resembling a Corinthian capital, and which, being cut, exudes a poisonous juice which they use for poisoning their arrows. It is well known that all the Kelts are fond of disputes; and that amongst them pederasty is not considered shameful. Ephorus extends the size of Keltica too far, including within it most of what we now designate as Iberia, as far as Gades. He states that the people are great admirers of the Greeks, and relates many particulars concerning them not applicable to their present state. This is one: that they take great care not to become fat or big-bellied, and that if any young man exceeds the measure of a certain girdle, he is punished.

BRITAIN

The greatest portion of the island is level and woody, although many tracts are hilly. It produces corn, cattle, gold, silver, and iron, which things are brought thence, and also skins, and slaves, and dogs sagacious in hunting; the Kelts use these, as well as their native dogs, for the purposes of war. The men are taller than the Kelts, with hair less yellow; they are slighter in their persons. As an instance of their height, we ourselves saw at Rome some youths who were taller than the tallest there by as much as half a foot, but their legs were bowed, and in other respects they were not symmetrical in conformation. Their manners are in part like those of the Kelts, though in part more simple and barbarous; insomuch that some of them, though possessing plenty of milk, have not skill enough to make cheese, and are totally unacquainted with horticulture and other matters of husbandry. There are several states amongst them.

In their wars they make use of chariots for the most part, as do some of the Kelts. Forests are their cities; for having enclosed an ample space with felled trees, they make themselves huts therein, and lodge their cattle, though not for any long continuance. Their atmosphere is more subject to rain than to snow; even in their clear days the mist continues for a considerable time, insomuch that throughout the whole day the sun is only visible for three or four hours about noon.

Caesar twice passed over to the island, but quickly returned, having effected nothing of consequence, nor proceeded far into the country, as well on account of some commotions in Keltica, both among his own soldiers and among the barbarians, as because of the loss of many of his ships at the time of the full moon, when both the ebb and flow of the tides were greatly increased. Nevertheless he gained two or three victories over the Britons, although he had transported thither only two legions of his army, and brought away hostages and slaves and much other booty. At the present time, however, some of the princes there have, by their embassies and solicitations, obtained the friendship of Augustus Caesar, dedicated their offerings in the Capitol, and brought the whole island into intimate union with the Romans. They pay but moderate duties both on the imports and exports from Keltica; which are ivory bracelets and necklaces, amber, vessels of glass, and small wares; so that the island scarcely needs a garrison, for at the least it would require one legion and some cavalry to enforce tribute from them; and the total expenditure for the army would be equal to the revenue collected. . . .

There are also other small islands around Britain; but one, of great extent, Ierna [Ireland, called by Caesar Hibernia], lying parallel to it towards the north, long, or rather, wide; concerning which we have nothing certain to relate, further than that its inhabitants are more savage than the Britons, feeding on human flesh, and enormous eaters, and deeming it commendable to devour their deceased fathers, as well as openly, to have commerce not only with other women, but also with their own mothers and sisters. But this we relate perhaps without very competent authority; although to eat human flesh is said to be a Scythian custom; and during the severities of a siege, even the Kelts, the Iberians, and many others, are reported to have done the like.

GERMANY

Next after the Keltic nations come the Germans who inhabit the country to the east beyond the Rhine; and these differ but little from the Keltic race, except in their being more fierce, of a larger stature, and more ruddy in countenance; but in every other respect, their figure, their customs and manners of life, are such as we have related of the Kelts. The Romans therefore, I think, have very appositely applied to them the name "Germani," as signifying "genuine"; for in the Latin language "Germani" [means] "genuine."

The first division of this country is the land extending along the Rhine from its source to its mouth. Indeed, the valley of that river extends nearly as far as the whole breadth of Germany on the west. Of the people who occupied this country, some have been transplanted by the Romans into Keltica, the others have retired to the interior, as the Marsi; there are but few remaining, and some portion of them are Sicambri; next to the inhabitants of this valley succeeds the tribe dwelling between the Rhine and the river Elbe, which river flows towards the ocean in a direction nearly parallel with the Rhine, and traversing a country of no less extent. There are also between these other navigable rivers, likewise flowing from south to north, and falling into the ocean; for the whole country rises to the south, and forms a ridge of mountains near the Alps, which extends eastward as though it were a continuation of the Alps; and some have even so described it, as well on account of its position as because it produces the same system of vegetation; nevertheless, the altitude of this ridge in no part equals that of the Alps.

Here is situated the Hercynian Wood [the Black Forest]. . . . As I have previously stated, a portion of the Suevi dwells within the Forest, while another portion occupies the territory beyond, on the frontiers of the Getae; wherefore the nation of the Suevi is the most considerable, as it extends from the Rhine as far as the Elbe . . . but at the present time these tribes, having been defeated, have retired entirely beyond the Elbe. All these nations easily change their abode, on account of the scantiness of provisions and because they neither cultivate the lands nor accumulate wealth, but dwell in miserable huts, and satisfy their wants from day to day, the most part of their food being supplied by the herds as amongst the nomadic races, and in imitation of them they transfer their households in waggons, wandering with their cattle to any place which may appear most advantageous. . . .

The Rhine is distant from the Elbe about 3000 stadia, if one could travel in a direct line; but we are compelled to go a circuitous route, on account of the windings of the marshes and the woods.

The Hercynian Forest is extremely dense, and overgrown with very large trees, covering an immense circuit of country, fortified by nature. In the midst of it is situated the region well suited for habitation, of which we have spoken. Near this forest are the sources of the Danube and the Rhine, and the lake situated between these, together with the marshes formed by the Rhine.

JUTLAND

Some of the accounts which we receive respecting the Cimbri are not worthy of credit, while others seem likely enough: for instance, no one could accept the reason given for their wandering life and piracy, that, dwelling on a peninsula, they were driven out of their settlements by a very high tide; for they still to this day possess the country which they had in former times, and have sent as a present to Augustus the caldron held most sacred by them, supplicating his friendship, and an amnesty for past offenses; and having obtained their request, they returned home. Indeed, it would have been ridiculous for them to have departed from their country on account of a natural and constant phenomenon, which occurs twice every day.

It is likewise evidently a fiction, that there ever occurred an overwhelming flood-tide, for the ocean, in the influences of this kind which it experiences, receives a certain settled and periodical increase and decrease. Neither is it true, as has been related, that the Cimbri take arms against the flood-tides, or that the Kelts, as an exercise of their intrepidity, suffer their houses to be washed away by them, and afterwards rebuild them; and that a greater number of them perish by water than by war, as Ephorus relates. For the regular order the flood-tides observe, and the notoriety of the extent of the country subject to inundation by them, could never have given occasion for such absurd actions. For the tide flowing twice every day, how could anyone think for an instant that it was not a natural and harmless phenomenon, and that it occurs not only on their coasts, but on all others bordering on the Ocean? Is not this quite incredible? Neither is Clitarchus to be trusted, when he says that their cavalry, on seeing the sea flowing in, rode off at full speed, and yet scarcely escaped by flight from being overtaken by the flood; for we know, by experience, that the tide does not come in with such impetuosity, but that the sea advances stealthily by slow degrees. And we should think, besides, that a phenomenon of daily occurrence, which would naturally strike the ear of such as approached it, before even they could see it with their eyes, could not by any means terrify them so as to put them to flight, as if they had been surprised by some unexpected catastrophe.

It is reported that the Cimbri had a peculiar custom. They were accompanied in their expeditions by their wives; these were followed by hoary-headed priestesses clad in white, with cloaks of carbasus fastened on with clasps, girt with brazen girdles, and bare-footed. These individuals, bearing drawn swords, went to meet the captives throughout the camp, and, having crowned them, led them to a brazen vessel containing about 20 amphora, and placed on a raised platform, which one of the priestesses having ascended, and holding the prisoner above the vessel, cut his throat; then, from the manner in which the blood flowed into the vessel, some drew certain divinations; while others, having opened the corpse, and inspected the entrails, prophesied victory to their army. In battle too they beat skins stretched on the wicker sides of chariots, which produces a stunning noise.

As we have before stated, the northernmost of the Germans inhabit a country bordering on the ocean; but we are only acquainted with those situated between the mouths of the Rhine and the Elbe. . . . For any particulars as to Germany beyond the Elbe, or of the countries which lie beyond it in order, whether we should call them the Bastarna, as most geographers suppose, or whether other nations intervene, or any others of the tribes dwelling in waggons, it is not easy to give any account. Neither can we say whether these nations extend as far as the [Northern] Ocean, along the whole distance, or whether there are countries rendered unfit for habitation by the cold or by any other cause; or whether men of a different race are situated between the sea and the most eastern of the Germans.

— I I —

THE GREEKS' BARBARIANS

Even in the fifth century B.C., there was history for a Greek to write. Homer—if indeed there was a single poet named Homer who wrote the *Odyssey* and *Iliad*—had lived at least three hundred years before. There were wars with Persia to describe, as well as the mysteries of Egypt. And there was a whole curious world of people who did not speak Greek and were—perhaps—not quite human.

Herodotus (ca. 484–ca. 424 B.C.), who over the years has been called the "Father of History," combined a number of admirable qualities. He was curious about the past but not awed by it. He loved to travel and tell about what he saw but was always careful to explain what was an eyewitness report and what was hearsay. His love of a good story— a well-told good story—did not exclude gossip, jokes, or a few bedroom scenes.

He seems to have been born in Asia Minor, fought against the Persians, been a friend of Sophocles, and traveled widely—including journeys in Egypt and Scythia—and at the end of his life was probably a citizen of the model city the Greeks had established on the site of ancient Sybaris in southern Italy. There, he probably wrote his *History* and died.

He wrote it, he says in his book's first paragraph, "in order that the actions of men may not be effaced by time, nor the great and wondrous deeds displayed both by Greeks and barbarians deprived of renown."

By barbarians Herodotus simply meant those unfortunates who did not speak Greek. Taken from his *History*, here are his observations on the barbaric customs—including a recipe for how to boil skulls—of the Scythians and Thracians.

HERODOTUS

"SCYTHIANS AND THRACIANS"

424 B.C.

SCYTHIANS

The grass that grows in Scythia is the most productive of bile for cattle of any with which we are acquainted, and when the cattle are opened one may see that such is the case. . . .

Scythian nomads are not accustomed to erect images, altars, and temples, except to Mars; to him they are accustomed. The same mode of sacrificing is adopted to all kinds of victims alike, being as follows: the sacrificed animal stands with its fore feet tied together; he who sacrifices, standing behind the beast, having drawn the extremity of the cord, throws it down, and as the victim falls he invokes the god to whom he is sacrificing; then he throws a halter round its neck, and having put in a stick, he twists it round and strangles it, without kindling any fire, or performing any preparatory ceremonies, or making any libation, but having strangled and flayed it, he applies himself to cook it.

As the Scythian country is wholly destitute of wood, they have invented the following method of cooking flesh. When they have flayed the victims, they strip the flesh from the bones, then they put it into caldrons made in the country, if they happen to have any, which very much resemble Lesbian bowls, except that they are much larger; having put it into these, they cook it by burning underneath the bones of the victims. If they have no caldron at hand, they put all the flesh into the paunches of the victims, and having poured in water, burn the bones underneath; they burn very well, and the paunches easily contain the flesh stripped from the bones; thus the ox cooks himself, and all other victims each cooks itself. When the flesh is cooked, he that sacrifices, offering the first-fruits of the flesh and entrails, throws it before him. They sacrifice both other cattle, and chiefly horses.

In this manner, then, and these victims, they sacrifice to the other gods; but to Mars as follows: in each district, in the place where the magistrates assemble, is erected a structure sacred to Mars, of the following kind. Bundles of fagots are heaped up to the length and breadth of three stades, but less in height; on the top of this a square platform is formed; and three of the sides are perpendicular, but on the fourth it is accessible. Every year they heap on it one hundred and fifty wagon-loads of fagots, for it is continually sinking by reason of the weather. On this heap an old iron cimeter is placed by each tribe, and this is the image of Mars; and to this cimeter they bring yearly sacrifices of cattle and horses; and to these cimeters they offer more sacrifices than to the rest of the gods. Whatever enemies they take alive, of these they sacrifice one in a hundred, not in the same manner as they do the cattle, but in a different manner; for after they have poured a libation of wine on their heads, they cut the throats of the men over a bowl; then, having carried the bowl on the heap of fagots, they pour the blood over the cimeter. This, then, they carry up; but below, at the sacred precinct, they do as follows: having cut off all the right shoulders of the men that have been killed, with the arms, they throw them into the air; and then, having finished the rest of the sacrificial rites, they depart; but the arm lies wherever it has fallen, and the body apart. Such, then, are the sacrifices instituted among them. Swine they never use, nor suffer them to be reared in their country at all.

Their military affairs are ordered as follows. When a Scythian overthrows his first enemy, he drinks his blood; and presents the king with the heads of the enemies he has killed in battle; for if he brings a head, he shares the booty that they take, but not if he does not bring one. He skins it in the following manner. Having made a circular incision round the ears and taking hold of the skin, he shakes it from the skull; then, having scraped off the flesh with the rib of an ox, he softens the skin with his hands, and having made it supple, he uses it as a napkin: each man hangs it on the bridle of the horse which he rides, and prides himself on it, for whoever has the greatest number of these skin napkins is accounted the most valiant man. Many of them make cloaks of these skins to throw over themselves, sewing them together like shepherd's coats; and many, having flayed the right hands of their enemies that are dead, together with the nails, make coverings for their quivers: the skin of a man, which is both thick and shining, surpasses almost all other skins in the brightness of its white. Many, having flayed men whole, and stretched the skin on wood, carry it about on horseback. Such usages are received among them.

The heads themselves, not indeed of all, but of their greatest enemies, they treat as follows: each, having sawn off all below the eye-brows, cleanses it, and if the man is poor, he covers only the outside with leather, and so uses it; but if he is rich, he covers it indeed with leather, and, having gilded the inside, he so uses it for a drinking-cup. And they do this to their relatives if they are at variance, and one prevails over another in the presence of the king. When strangers of consideration come to him, he produces these heads, and relates how, though they were his relatives, they made war against him, and he overcame them, considering this a proof of bravery.

Once in every year, the governor of a district, each in his own district, mingles a bowl of wine, from which those Scythians drink who have captured enemies; but they who have not achieved this do not taste of this wine, but sit at a distance in dishonor; this is accounted the greatest disgrace; such of them as have killed very many men, having two cups at once, drink them together.

Soothsayers among the Scythians are numerous, who divine by the help of a number of willow rods, in the following manner. When they have brought with them large bundles of twigs, they lay them on the ground and untie them; and, having placed each rod apart, they utter their predictions; and while they are pronouncing them, they gather up the rods again, and put them together again one by one. This is their national mode of divination. But the Enarees, or Androgyni, say that Venus gave them the power of divining. They divine by means of the bark of a linden-tree: when a man has split the linden-tree in three pieces, twisting it round his own fingers, and then untwisting it, he utters a response.

When the king of the Scythians is sick, he sends for three of the most famous of these prophets, who prophesy in the manner above mentioned; and they generally say as follows, that such or such a citizen has sworn falsely by the royal hearth, mentioning the name of the citizen of whom they speak; for it is a custom with the Scythians in general to swear by the royal hearth when they would use the most solemn oath. The person who they say has sworn falsely is immediately seized and brought forward, and when he is come, the prophets charge him with being clearly proved by their prophetic art to have sworn falsely by the royal hearth, and for this reason the king is ill. He denies it, affirming that he has not sworn falsely, and complains bitterly. On his denial, the king sends for twice as many more prophets; and if they also, examining into the prophetic art, condemn him with having sworn falsely, they straightway cut off his head, and the first prophets divide his property between them; but if the prophets who came last acquit him, other prophets are called in, and others after them. If, then, the greater number acquit the man, it is decreed that the first prophets shall be put to death.

They accordingly put them to death in the following manner: when they have filled a wagon with fagots, and have yoked oxen to it, having tied the feet of the prophets and bound their hands behind them, and having gagged them, they enclose them in the midst of the fagots; then having set fire to them, they terrify the oxen and let them go. Many oxen, therefore, are burned with the prophets, and many escape very much scorched, when the pole has been burned asunder. In this manner, and for other reasons, they burn the prophets, calling them false prophets. The king does not spare the children of those whom he puts to death, but kills all the males, and does not hurt the females.

The Scythians make solemn contracts in the following manner, with whomsoever they make them. Having poured wine into a large earthen vessel, they mingle with it blood taken from those who are entering into covenant, having struck with an awl or cut with a knife a small part of the body; then, having dipped a cimeter, some arrows, a hatchet, and a javelin in the vessel, when they have done this, they make many solemn prayers, and then both those who make the contract, and the most considerable of their attendants, drink up the mixture.

The sepulchres of the kings are in the country of the Gerrhi, as far as which the Borysthenes is navigable. There, when their king dies, they dig a large square hole in the ground; and having prepared this, they take up the corpse, having the body covered with wax, the belly opened and cleaned, filled with bruised cypress, incense, and parsley and anise-seed, and then sewn up again, and carry it in a chariot to another nation: those who receive the corpse brought to them do the same as the Royal Scythians; they cut off part of their ear, shave off their hair, wound themselves on the arms, lacerate their forehead and nose, and drive arrows through their left hand. Thence they carry the corpse of the king to another nation whom they govern, and those to whom they first came accompany them. When they have carried the corpse round all the provinces, they arrive among the Gerrhi, who are the most remote of the nations they rule over. . . . Then when they have placed the corpse in the grave on a bed of leaves, having fixed spears on each side of the dead body, they lay pieces of wood over it, and cover it over with mats. In the remaining space of the grave they bury one of the king's concubines, having strangled her, and his cup-bearer, a cook, a groom, a page, a courier, and horses, and firstlings of every thing else, and golden goblets: they make no use of silver or brass. Having done this, they all heap up a large mound, striving and vying with each other to make it as large as possible.

When a year has elapsed, they then do as follows: having taken the most fitting of his remaining servants—they are all native Scythians, for they serve him whomsoever the king may order, and they have no servants bought with money—when, therefore, they have strangled fifty of these servants, and fifty of the finest horses, having taken out their bowels and cleansed them, they fill them with chaff, and sew them up again. Then, having placed the half of a wheel, with its concave side uppermost, on two pieces of wood, and the other half on two other pieces of wood, and having fixed many of these in the same manner, then having thrust thick pieces of wood through the horses lengthwise up to the neck, they mount them on the half wheels; and of these the foremost part of the half wheels supports the shoulders of the horses, and the hinder part supports the belly near the thighs, but the legs on both sides are suspended in the air; then, having put bridles and bits on the horses, they stretch them in front, and fasten them to a stake; they then mount upon a horse each, one of the fifty young men that have been strangled, mounting them in the following manner: when they have driven a straight piece of wood along the spine as far as the neck, but a part of this wood projects from the bottom, they fix it into a hole bored in the other piece of wood that passes through the horse. Having placed such horsemen round the monument, they depart.

Thus they bury their kings. But the other Scythians, when they die, their nearest relations carry about among their friends, laid in chariots; and of these each one receives and entertains the attendants, and sets the same things before the dead body as before the rest. In this manner private persons are carried about for forty days, and then buried. The Scythians, having buried them, purify themselves in the following manner: having wiped and thoroughly washed their heads, they do thus with regard to the body: when they have set up three pieces of wood leaning against each other, they extend around them woolen cloths; and having joined them together as closely as possible, they throw red-hot stones into a vessel placed in the middle of the pieces of wood and the cloths. They have a sort of hemp growing in this country, very like flax, except in thickness and height; in this respect the hemp is far superior: it grows both spontaneously and from cultivation, and from it the Thracians make garments very like linen; nor would any one who is not well skilled in such matters distinguish whether they are made of flax or hemp; but a person who has never seen this hemp would think the garment was made of flax.

When, therefore, the Scythians have taken some seed of this hemp, they creep under the cloths, and then put the seed on the red-hot stones; but this being put on smokes, and produces such a steam that no Grecian vapor-bath would surpass it. The Scythians, transported with the vapor, shout aloud; and this serves them instead of washing, for they never bathe the body in water. Their women, pouring on water, pound on a rough stone pieces of cypress, cedar, and incense-tree; and then this pounded matter, when it is thick, they smear over the whole body and face; and this at the same time gives them an agreeable odor, and when they take off the cataplasm on the following day they become clean and shining.

They studiously avoid the use of foreign customs.

THRACIANS

The nation of the Thracians is the largest of any men, except at least the Indians; and if they were governed by one man, or acted in concert, they would, in my opinion, be invincible, and by far the most powerful of all nations. But as this is impracticable, and it is impossible that they should ever be united, they are therefore weak. They have various names, according to their respective regions, but all observe similar customs in every respect, except the Getae, the Trausi, and those who dwell above the Crestonaeans.

Of these, what are the customs of the Getae, who pretend to be immortal, I have already described. [They think themselves immortal in this manner. They imagine that they themselves do not die, but that the deceased goes to the deity Zalmoxis, and some of them think that he is the same with Gebeleleizis. Every fifth year they dispatch one of themselves, taken by lot, to Zalmoxis, with orders to let him know on each occasion what they want. Their mode of sending him is this. Some of them who are appointed hold three javelins; while others, having taken up the man who is to be sent to Zalmoxis by the hands and feet, swing him round, and throw him into the air, upon the points. If he should die, being transfixed, they think the god is propitious to them; if he should not die, they blame the messenger himself, saying that he is a bad man; and having blamed him, they dispatch another, and they give him his instructions while he is yet alive. These same Thracians, in time of thunder and lightning, let fly their arrows toward heaven, and threaten the god, thinking that there is no other god but their own.]

The Trausi, in all other respects, observe the same usages as the rest of the Thracians; but with regard to one born among them, or that dies, they do as follows. The relations, seating themselves around one that is newly born, bewail him, deploring the many evils he must needs fulfill, since he has been born; enumerating the various sufferings incident to mankind; but one that dies they bury in the earth, making merry and rejoicing, recounting the many evils from which being released, he is now in perfect bliss. Those above the Crestonaeans do as follows: each man has several wives; when, therefore, any of them dies, a great contest arises among the wives, and violent disputes among their friends, on this point, which of them was most loved by the husband. She who is adjudged to have been so, and is so honored, having been extolled both by men and women, is slain on the tomb by her own nearest relative, and when slain is buried with her husband; the others deem this a great misfortune, for this is the utmost disgrace to them.

There is, moreover, this custom among the rest of the Thracians: they sell their children for exportation. They keep no watch over their unmarried daughters, but suffer them to have intercourse with what men they choose; but they keep a strict watch over their wives, and purchase them from their parents at high prices. To be marked with punctures is accounted a sign of noble birth; to be without punctures, ignoble. To be idle is most honorable; but to be a tiller of the soil, most dishonorable; to live by war and rapine is most glorious. These are the most remarkable of their customs. They worship the following gods only, Mars, Bacchus, and Diana. But their kings, to the exception of the other citizens, reverence Mercury of all the gods; they swear by him only, and say that they are themselves sprung from Mercury. The funerals of the wealthy among them are celebrated in this manner. They expose the corpse during three days; and having slain all kinds of victims, they feast, having first made lamentation. Then they bury them, having first burned them, or, at all events, placing them under ground; then, having thrown up a mound, they celebrate all kinds of games, in which the greatest rewards are adjudged to single combat, according to the estimation in which they are held. Such are the funeral rites of the Thracians.

—III—

ROME ENCOUNTERS
THE CELTS

A.D. 410: Alaric and the Visigoths sack Rome. It is one of those indelible dates, like 1066 and 1492. But that was not the first time the city was taken by barbarians. Just after 400 B.C., eight hundred years earlier, when Rome was still a republic, a band of exotic newcomers to the Italian peninsula swept south from the Rhine, and after a vicious victory in Umbria (the rivers were described as turning red with blood), swarmed through the city gates. The Celts, led by someone called Brennus (which may have been a title rather than a name, since Brennus is the latinized version of the Celtic *bran*, or "prince") entered Rome without a fight, looted it, and left.

The story of this encounter—complete with the well-known tale of the vigilant Capitoline geese—is begun here by a Greek historian, Diodorus Siculus (Diodorus of Sicily, ca. 80–ca. 20 B.C.). His forty-book *The Library of History*, nearly half of which has survived, combines passages of mythology with sparely told military and social history. Further details of what happened in Rome (and the Romans' eventual triumph) are supplied in a more ornate prose style by the later Roman historian Livy, or Titus Livius (59 B.C.– A.D. 17) in his massive 142-book history of Rome.

The third selection is by Polybius, a Greek who died soon after 118 B.C. from a fall from a horse, a suitably dramatic end for an adventurer who had followed the track of Hannibal across the Alps, witnessed the destruction of Carthage, and sailed in the Atlantic Ocean. His account of the Celtic Wars in northern Italy (225–222 B.C.), included here, is remarkable for its fresh details of Celtic military customs and tactics (with an emphasis on their knack for trickery and deception) and for what it reveals of the combination of fear and titillation the barbarians inspired in the Romans. In all accounts, the names "Celts" and "Gauls" are used interchangably.

DIODORUS SICULUS

"ROMANS AND CELTS BATTLE IN UMBRIA"

ca. 390 B.C.

A t the time [ca. 390 B.C.] that Dionysius was besieging Rhegium [Reggio di Calabria], the Celts who had their homes in the regions beyond the Alps streamed through the passes in great strength and seized the territory that lay between the Apennine mountains and the Alps. . . . Now it happened, when the Celts divided up the territory by tribes, that those known as the Sennones received the area which lay farthest from the mountains and along the sea. But since this region was scorching hot, they were distressed and eager to move; hence they armed their younger men and sent them out to seek a territory where they might settle. Now they invaded Tyrrhenia, and being in number some thirty thousand they sacked the territory of the Clusini.

At this very time the Roman people sent ambassadors into Tyrrhenia to spy out the army of the Celts. The ambassadors arrived at Clusium, and when they saw that a battle had been joined, with more valour than wisdom they joined the men of Clusium against their besiegers, and one of the ambassadors was successful in killing a rather important commander. When the Celts learned of this, they dispatched ambassadors to Rome to demand the person of the envoy who had thus commenced an unjust war. The senate at first sought to persuade the envoys of the Celts to accept money in satisfaction of the injury, but when they would not consider this, it voted to surrender the accused. But the father of the man to be surrendered, who was also one of the military tribunes with consular power, appealed the judgement to the people, and since he was a man of influence among the masses, he persuaded them to void the decision of the senate. Now in the times previous to this the people had followed the senate in all matters; with this occasion they first began to rescind decisions of that body.

The ambassadors of the Celts returned to their camp and reported the reply of the Romans. At this they were greatly angered and, adding an army from their fellow tribesmen, they marched swiftly upon Rome itself, numbering more than seventy thousand men. The military tribunes of the Romans, exercising their special power, when they heard of the advance of the Celts, armed all the men of military age. They then marched out in full force and, crossing the Tiber, led their troops for eighty stades along the river; and at news of the approach of the Galatians they drew up the army for battle. Their best troops, to the number of twenty-four thousand, they set in a line from the river as far as the hills and on the highest hills they stationed the weakest. The Celts deployed their troops in a long line and, whether by fortune or design, stationed their choicest troops on the hills. The trumpets on both sides sounded the charge at the same time and the armies joined in battle with great clamour. The elite troops of the Celts, who were opposed to the weakest soldiers of the Romans, easily drove them from the hills. Consequently, as these fled in masses to the Romans on the plain, the ranks were thrown into confusion and fled in dismay before the attack of the Celts. Since the bulk of the Romans fled along the river and impeded one another by reason of their disorder, the Celts were not behindhand in slaying again and again those who were last in line. Hence the entire plain was strewn with dead. Of the men who fled to the river the bravest attempted to swim across with their arms, prizing their armour as highly as their lives; but since the stream ran strong, some of them were borne down to their death by the weight of the arms, and some, after being carried along for some distance, finally and after great effort got off safe. But since the enemy pressed them hard and was making a great slaughter along the river, most of the survivors threw away their arms and swam across the Tiber.

The Celts, though they had slain great numbers on the bank of the river, nevertheless did not desist from the zest for glory but showered javelins upon the swimmers; and since many missiles were hurled and men were massed in the river, those who threw did not miss their mark. So it was that some died at once from mortal blows, and others, who were wounded only, were carried off unconscious because of loss of blood and the swift current. When such disaster befell, the greater part of the Romans who escaped occupied the city of Veii [an ancient Etruscan city northwest of Rome], which had lately been razed by them, fortified the place as well as they could, and received the survivors of the rout. A few of those who had swum the river fled without their arms to Rome and reported that the whole army had perished.

When word of such misfortunes as we have described was brought to those who had been left behind in the city, everyone fell into despair; for they saw no possibility of resistance, now that all their youth had perished, and to flee with their children and wives was fraught with the greatest danger since the enemy were close at hand. Now many private citizens fled with their households to neighbouring cities, but the city magistrates, encouraging the populace, issued orders for them to bring speedily to the Capitoline grain and every other necessity. When this had been done, both the acropolis and the Capitoline were stored not only with supplies of food but with silver and gold and the costliest raiment, since the precious possessions had been gathered from over the whole city into one place. They gathered such valuables as they could and fortified the place we have mentioned during a respite of three days. For the Celts spent the first day cutting off, according to their custom, the heads of the dead. And for two days they lay encamped before the city, for when they saw the walls deserted and yet heard the noise made by those who were transferring their most useful possessions to the acropolis, they suspected that the Romans were planning a trap for them. But on the fourth day, after they had learned the true state of affairs, they broke down the gates and pillaged the city except for a few dwellings on the Palatine.

After this they delivered daily assaults on strong positions, without, however, inflicting any serious hurt upon their opponents and with the loss of many of their own troops. Nevertheless, they did not relax their ardour, expecting that, even if they did not conquer by force, they would wear down the enemy in the course of time, when the necessities of life had entirely given out.

While the Romans were in such throes, the neighbouring Tyrrhenians advanced and made a raid with a strong army on the territory of the Romans, capturing many prisoners and not a small amount of booty. But the Romans who had fled to Veii, falling unexpectedly upon the Tyrrhenians, put them to flight, took back the booty, and captured their camp. Having got possession of arms in abundance, they distributed them among the unarmed, and they also gathered men from the countryside and armed them, since they intended to relieve the siege of the soldiers who had taken refuge on the Capitoline. While they were at a loss how they might reveal their plans to the besieged, since the Celts had surrounded them with strong forces, a certain Cominius Pontius undertook to get the cheerful news to the men on the Capitoline. Starting out alone and swimming the river by night, he got unseen to a cliff of the Capitoline that was hard to climb and, hauling himself up it with difficulty, told the soldiers on the Capitoline about the troops that had been collected in Veii and how they were watching for an opportunity and would attack the Celts.

Then, descending by the way he had mounted and swimming the Tiber, he returned to Veii. The Celts, when they observed the tracks of one who had recently climbed up, made plans to ascend at night by the same cliff. Consequently about the middle of the night, while the guards were neglectful of their watch because of the strength of the place, some Celts started an ascent of the cliff. They escaped detection by the guards, but the sacred geese of Hera, which were kept there, noticed the climbers and set up a cackling. The guards rushed to the place and the Celts, deterred, did not dare proceed farther. A certain Marcus Mallius, a man held in high esteem, rushing to the defense of the place, cut off the hand of the climber with his sword and, striking him on the breast with his shield, rolled him from the cliff. In like manner the second climber met his death, whereupon the rest all quickly turned in flight. But since the cliff was precipitous they were all hurled headlong and perished. As a result of this, when the Romans sent ambassadors to negotiate a peace, they were persuaded, upon receipt of one thousand pounds of gold, to leave the city and to withdraw from Roman territory.

The Romans, now that their houses had been razed to the ground and the majority of their citizens slain, gave permission to anyone who wished to build a home in any place he chose, and supplied him at state expense with roof-tiles; and up to the present time these are known as "public tiles." Since every man naturally built his home where it suited his fancy, the result was that the streets of the city were narrow and crooked; consequently, when the population increased in later days, it was impossible to straighten the streets. Some also say that the Roman matrons, because they contributed their gold ornaments to the common safety, received from the people as a reward the right to ride through the city in chariots. . . .

The Gauls on their way from Rome laid siege to the city of Veascium which was an ally of the Romans. The dictator attacked them, slew the larger number of them, and got possession of all their baggage, included in which was the gold which they had received for Rome and practically all the booty which they had gathered in the seizure of the city.

LIVY

"THE CELTS ENTER ROME"

ca. 390 B.C.

The very Gauls themselves, stunned by the marvellous victory they had so suddenly gained, at first stood rooted to the spot with amazement, like men that knew not what had happened; then they feared an ambush; after that they fell to collecting the spoils of the slain and erecting piles of arms, as their custom is; then at last having discovered no hostile movement anywhere, they began their march, and a little before sunset reached the environs of Rome. There, when the cavalry had reconnoitred and had reported that the gates were not closed, that no out-guards were watching before the gates, that no armed men were on the walls, astonishment held them spell-bound as before; and fearful of the night and the lie of the unknown City, they went into camp between Rome and the Anio, after sending off patrols about the walls and the rest of the gates, to find out what the enemy in their desperate case could possibly be at. As for the Romans, inasmuch as more, on escaping from the battle, had fled to Veii than to Rome, and no one supposed that any were left alive except those who had found refuge in the City, they mourned for all alike, both the living and the dead, and well nigh filled the City with lamentation.

But presently their personal griefs were overwhelmed in a general panic, with the announcement that the enemy was at hand; and soon they could hear the dissonant howls and songs of the barbarians, as their squadrons roamed about the walls. During all the time that intervened before the following morning their hearts were in such suspense, that each moment they anticipated an immediate attack: on the first arrival of the enemy, because they had come close to the City—for they would have stopped at the Allia, had this not been their design; again, towards sundown, because there was little daylight left, they thought that they would enter the City before nightfall; then they concluded that they had put it off till night, to strike more fear into them. Finally the approach of dawn put them beside themselves, and close upon these restless apprehensions came the evil they were dreading, when the hostile forces entered the city gates. Yet neither that night nor the following day did the citizens at all resemble those who had fled in such consternation at the Allia.

For having no hopes that they could protect the City with so small a force as remained to them, they resolved that the men of military age and the able-bodied senators should retire into the Citadel and the Capitol, with their wives and children; and, having laid in arms and provisions, should from that strong-hold defend the gods, the men, and the name of Rome; that the flamen [priests] and the priestesses of Vesta should remove the sacred objects pertaining to the State far from the bloodshed and the flames, nor should their cult be abandoned till none should be left to cherish it. If the Citadel and the Capitol, where dwelt the gods; if the senate, the source of public wisdom; if the young men capable of bearing arms survived the impending destruction of the City, they could easily bear to lose the crowd of old men left behind them, who were bound to die in any case. And in order that the multitude of commoners might endure it with the more composure, the old men who had triumphed and those who had been consuls declared publicly that they would perish with those others, nor burden with bodies incapable of bearing arms in defence of the country the scanty stores of the fighting men.

Such were the consolations which the old men appointed to die exchanged among themselves; then, directing their encouragement to the band of youths whom they were escorting to the Capitol and the Citadel, they committed to their valour and their young strength whatever fortune might yet be in store for a City that for three hundred and sixty years had been victorious in every war. On the departure of those who carried with them all hope and help, from those who had resolved not to survive the capture and destruction of their City, though the separation was a pitiful thing to see, yet the tears of the women, as they ran distractedly up and down, and following now these, now those, demanded of husbands and sons to what fate they were consigning them, supplied the final touch of human wretchedness. Still, the greater part of them followed their sons into the Citadel, though none either forbade or encouraged it, since what would have helped the besieged to lessen the number of non-combatants would have been inhuman.

Another host—consisting chiefly of plebeians—too large for so small a hill to receive, or to support with so meagre a supply of corn, streamed out of the City as though forming at last one continuous line, and took their way towards Janiculum. Thence some of them scattered through the country-side, and others made for the towns nearby. They had neither leader nor concerted plan; each followed the promptings of his own hopes and his own counsels, in despair of the commonwealth.

Meanwhile the flamen of Quirinus and the Vestal virgins, with no thought for their own belongings, were consulting which of the sacred things they should carry with them, and which, because they were not strong enough to carry them all, they must leave behind, and, finally, where these objects would be safe. They judged it best to place them in jars and bury them in the shrine adjoining the flamen's house, where it is now forbidden to spit; the rest of the things they carried, sharing the burden amongst them, along the road which leads by the Sublician Bridge to Janiculum. As they mounted the hill they were perceived by a plebeian named Lucius Albinius, who had a wagon in which he was conveying his wife and children, amidst the throng of those who, unfit for war, were leaving the City.

Preserving even then the distinction between divine and human, and holding it sacrilege that the priestesses of his country should go afoot, bearing the sacred objects of the Roman People, while his family were seen in a vehicle, he commanded his wife and children to get down, placed the virgins and their relics in the wagon, and brought them to Caere, whither the priestesses were bound.

At Rome meantime such arrangements for defending the Citadel as the case admitted of were now fairly complete, and the old men returned to their homes to await the coming of their enemies with hearts that were steeled to die. Such of them as had held [the title] *curule magistracies*, that they might face death in the trappings of their ancient rank and office, as beseemed their worth, put on the stately robes which are worn by those who conduct the *tensae* [carts used to carry images of the gods] or celebrate a triumph, and, thus habited, seated themselves on ivory chairs in the middle of their houses. Some historians record that Marcus Folius, the *pontifex maximus*, led in the recitation of a solemn vow, by which they devoted themselves to death, on behalf of their country and the Roman Quirites [citizens].

The Gauls found their lust for combat cooled by the night which had intervened. At no point in the battle had they been pushed to desperate exertions, nor had they now to carry the City by assault. It was therefore without rancour or excitement that they entered Rome, on the following day, by the Colline Gate (which lay wide open), and made their way to the Forum, gazing about them at the temples of the gods and at the Citadel, which alone presented some show of war. Thence, after leaving a moderate guard to prevent any attack upon their scattered forces from Citadel or Capitol, they dispersed in quest of booty through streets where there was none to meet them, some rushing in a body into whatever houses were nearest, while others sought out the most remote, as though supposing that only such would be intact and full of plunder. But being frightened out of these by their very solitude, lest the enemy should by some ruse entrap them as they wandered apart, they came trooping back to the Forum and the places near it.

There they found the dwellings of the plebeians fastened up, but the halls of the nobles open; and they hesitated almost more to enter the open houses than the shut, so nearly akin to religious awe was their feeling as they beheld seated in the vestibules beings who, besides that their ornaments and apparel were more splendid than belonged to man, seemed also, in their majesty of countenance and in the gravity of their expression, most like to gods.

While they stood reverentially before them, as if they had been images, it is related that a Gaul stroked the beard of one of them, Marcus Papirius, which he wore long, as they all did then, whereat the Roman struck him over the head with his ivory mace, and, provoking his anger, was the first to be slain; after that the rest were massacred where they sat; and when the nobles had been murdered, there was no mercy then shown to anyone; the houses were ransacked, and after being emptied were given to the flames.

But whether it was that not all the Gauls desired to destroy the City, or that their leaders had resolved to make a certain show of burning, to inspire alarm, in hopes that the besieged might be driven to capitulate by affection for their homes, but not to burn up all the houses, in order that they might hold whatever remained of the City as a pledge to work on the feelings of their enemies—however this may have been, the fire spread by no means so freely or extensively on the first day as is commonly the case in a captured town. As the Romans looked down from their fastness and saw the City full of enemies running up and down in all the streets, while first in one quarter and then in another some new calamity would be occurring, they were unable, I do not say to keep their heads, but even to be sure of their ears and eyes. Wherever the shouting of the invaders, the lamentations of the women and children, the crackling of the flames, and the crash of falling buildings drew their attention, trembling at each sound, they turned their thoughts and their gaze that way, as though Fortune had placed them there to witness the pageant of their dying country. Of all their possessions nothing was left them to defend save their persons alone; and so much more wretched was their plight than that of all others who have ever been beleaguered, that they were cut off from their native City and confined where they could see all that belonged to them in the power of their enemies. Nor was the night more tranquil, after a day of such distress; and the night was followed by a restless day, with never a moment that had not still some fresh calamity to unfold. Yet, oppressed as they were, or rather overwhelmed, by so many misfortunes, nothing could alter their resolve; though they should see everything laid low in flames and ruins, they would stoutly defend the hill they held, however small and naked, which was all that Liberty had left. And now that the same events were occurring every day, like men grown used to grief, they had ceased to feel their own misfortunes, looking solely to their shields and the swords in their right hands as their only remaining hope.

The Gauls likewise, having vainly for some days waged war against only the buildings of Rome, when they saw that there was nothing left amidst the smouldering ruins of the captured City but armed enemies, who for all their disasters were not a jot appalled nor likely to yield to anything but force, took a desperate resolution to attack the Citadel. At daybreak the signal was made; and the entire host, having formed up in the Forum, gave a cheer, and raising their shields above their heads and locking them, began the ascent. The defenders on the other hand did nothing rashly or in confusion. At all the approaches they had strengthened the guard-posts, and where they saw the enemy advancing they stationed their best soldiers, and suffered them to come up, persuaded that the higher they mounted up the steep the easier it would be to drive them down. They made their stand about the middle of the declivity, and there, launching their attack from the higher ground, which seemed of itself to hurl them against the foe, dislodged the Gauls, with such havoc and destruction that they never attempted to attack in that manner again, with either a part or the whole of their strength. So, relinquishing all hope of getting up by force of arms, they prepared for a blockade. Having never till that moment considered such a thing, they had destroyed all the corn in the City with their conflagrations, and what was in the fields had all been hurriedly carried off, within the last few days, to Veii. They therefore arranged to divide their army, and employ part of it to pillage the neighbouring nations and part to invest the Citadel, in order that those who held the lines might be provisioned by the foragers.

When the Gauls departed from the City, Fortune's own hand guided them to Ardea, that they might make trial of Roman manhood. Camillus [a general and statesman who was later to lead the rebuilding of Rome] was languishing there in exile, more grieved by the nation's calamity than by his own; and as he sorrowfully inveighed against gods and men, and asked, with wonder and humiliation, where those heroes were who had shared with him in the capture of Veii and Falerii, and whose gallantry in other wars had ever outrun their success, of a sudden he heard that the army of the Gauls was coming, and that the Ardeates in alarm were deliberating what to do about it.

With an inspiration nothing less than divine, he pushed into the midst of their conference, though before accustomed to avoid these councils, and there, "Men of Ardea," he said, "my ancient friends, and of late my fellow citizens—since your goodness would have it so and my own fortune has made it necessary—let none of you suppose me to have come forward in forgetfulness of my condition; but circumstances and our common peril oblige every man at this crisis to contribute what he can to the general defence. And when shall I show gratitude for your great kindnesses to me, if I am backward now? Or when shall you have need of me, if not in war? 'Twas by this art that I stood secure in my native City: unbeaten in war, I was driven out in time of peace by the thankless citizens. But you, men of Ardea, have now an opportunity of requiting the Roman People for such great benefits as you yourselves are mindful of, nor need I cast up to you things which you remember; and your city has an opportunity to win from our common enemy great renown in war. That people now drawing near in loose array has been endowed by nature with bodily size and courage, great indeed but vacillating; which is the reason that to every conflict they bring more terror than strength. This may be seen in their defeat of the Romans.

"They captured the City, which lay wide open; but a handful of men in the Citadel and the Capitol are holding them at bay; already, oppressed by the tedium of the siege, they are departing and roaming aimlessly through the countryside. They greedily gorge themselves with food and wine, and when night approaches they erect no rampart, and without pickets or sentries, throw themselves down anywhere beside a stream, in the manner of wild beasts. Just now success has rendered them even more careless than they are wont to be. If you have a mind to protect your city and not to suffer all this country to become Gaul, arm yourselves in the first watch, and follow me in force, not to a battle but a massacre. If I do not deliver them up to you fast asleep, to be butchered like cattle, I am ready to submit at Ardea to the same fate that I endured at Rome."

Well-wishers and opponents were alike persuaded that there was no such warrior in those days anywhere. Breaking up the council, they supped, and waited intently for the signal. On its being given, in the silence of the early night, they presented themselves before Camillus at the gates. They had not left the city very far behind them, when they came to the camp of the Gauls, unguarded, just as he had prophesied, and open on every side, and, giving a loud cheer, rushed upon it. There was no resistance anywhere: the whole place was a shambles, where unarmed men, relaxed in sleep, were slaughtered. Those, however, who were farthest off were frightened from the places where they lay, and ignorant of the nature of the attack or its source, fled panic-stricken, and some ran unawares straight into the enemy. The most of them were carried into the territory of Antium, where they wandered about until the townspeople sallied out and cut them off.

POLYBIUS

"THE EARLY CELTIC-ROMAN WARS"

225 B.C.

The Celts, descending on Etruria [Tuscany], overran the country [in 225 B.C.] devastating it without let or hindrance and, as nobody appeared to oppose them, they marched on Rome itself. When they had got as far as Clusium [Chiusi], a city three days' journey from Rome, news reached them that the advanced force which the Romans had posted in Etruria was on their heels and approaching. On hearing this, they turned to meet it, eager to engage it. At sunset the two armies were in close proximity, and encamped for the night at no great distance from each other. After nightfall, the Celts lit their camp-fires, and, leaving orders with their cavalry to wait until daybreak and then, when visible to the enemy, to follow on their track, they themselves secretly retreated to a town called Faesulae and posted themselves there, their intention being to wait for their cavalry, and also to put unexpected difficulties in the way of the enemy's attack.

At daybreak, the Romans, seeing the cavalry alone and thinking the Celts had taken to flight, followed the cavalry with all speed on the line of the Celts' retreat. On their approaching the enemy, the Celts left their position and attacked them, and a conflict, at first very stubborn, took place, in which finally the numbers and courage of the Celts prevailed, not fewer than six thousand Romans falling and the rest taking to flight. Most of them retreated to a hill of some natural strength where they remained. The Celts at first attempted to besiege them, but as they were getting the worst of it, fatigued as they were by their long night march and the suffering and hardships it involved, they hastened to rest and refresh themselves, leaving a detachment of their cavalry to keep guard round the hill, intending the next day to besiege the fugitives, if they did not offer to surrender.

At this very time Lucius Aemilius, who was in command of the advanced force near the Adriatic, on hearing that the Celts had invaded Etruria and were approaching Rome, came in haste to help, fortunately arriving in the nick of time. He encamped near the enemy, and the fugitives on the hill, seeing his camp-fires and understanding what had occurred, immediately plucked up courage and dispatched by night some unarmed messengers through the wood to announce to the commander the plight they were in. On hearing of it and seeing that there was no alternative course under the circumstances, the latter ordered his Tribunes to march out the infantry at daybreak, he himself proceeding in advance with the cavalry towards the hill mentioned above. The leaders of the Gauls, on seeing the campfires at night, surmised that the enemy had arrived and held a council at which the King Aneroëstes expressed the opinion, that having captured so much booty (for it appears that the quantity of slaves, cattle, and miscellaneous spoil was enormous), they should not give battle again nor risk the fortune of the whole enterprise, but return home in safety, and having got rid of all their encumbrances and lightened themselves, return and, if advisable, try issues with the Romans.

It was decided under the circumstances to take the course recommended by Aneroëstes, and having come to this resolution in the night, they broke up their camp before daybreak and retreated along the sea-coast through Etruria. Lucius now took with him from the hill the survivors of the other army and united them with his other forces. He thought it by no means advisable to risk a general battle, but decided to hang on the enemy's rear and watch for times and places favourable for inflicting damage on them or wresting some of the spoil from their hands.

Just at this time, Gaius Atilius, the other Consul, had reached Pisa from Sardinia with his legions and was on his way to Rome, marching in the opposite direction to the enemy. When the Celts were near Telamon in Etruria, their advanced foragers encountered the advance guard of Gaius and were made prisoners. On being examined by the Consul they narrated all that had recently occurred and told him of the presence of the two armies, stating that the Gauls were quite near and Lucius behind them. The news surprised him but at the same time made him very hopeful, as he thought he had caught the Gauls on the march between the two armies. He ordered his Tribunes to put the legions in fighting order and to advance thus at marching pace in so far as the nature of the ground allowed the attack in line. He himself had happily noticed a hill situated above the road by which the Celts must pass, and taking his cavalry with him, advanced at full speed, being anxious to occupy the crest of the hill before their arrival and be the first to begin the battle, feeling certain that thus he would get the largest share of credit for the result. The Celts at first were ignorant of the arrival of Atilius and imagined from what they saw, that Aemilius's cavalry had got round their flank in the night and were engaged in occupying the position. They therefore at once sent on their own cavalry and some of their light-armed troops to dispute the possession of the hill. But very soon they learnt of Gaius's presence from one of the prisoners brought in, and lost no time in drawing up their infantry, deploying them so that they faced both front and rear, since, both from the intelligence that reached them and from what was happening before their eyes, they knew that the one army was following them, and they expected to meet the other in their front.

Aemilius, who had heard of the landing of the legions at Pisa but had not any idea that they were already so near him, now, when he saw the fight going on round the hill, knew that the other Roman army was quite close. Accordingly, sending on his cavalry to help those who were fighting on the hill, he drew up his infantry in the usual order and advanced against the foe. The Celts had drawn up facing their rear, from which they expected Aemilius to attack, the Gaesatae from the Alps and behind them the Insubres, and facing in the opposite direction, ready to meet the attack of Gaius's legions, they placed the Taurisci and the Boii from the right bank of the Po. Their waggons and chariots they stationed at the extremity of either wing and collected their booty on one of the neighbouring hills with a protecting force round it. This order of the Celtic forces, facing both ways, not only presented a formidable appearance, but was well adapted to the exigencies of the situation. The Insubres and Boii wore their trousers and light cloaks, but the Gaesatae had discarded these garments owing to their proud confidence in themselves, and stood naked, with nothing but their arms, in front of the whole army, thinking that thus they would be more efficient, as some of the ground was overgrown with brambles which would catch in their clothes and impede the use of their weapons.

At first the battle was confined to the hill, all the armies gazing on it, so great were the numbers of cavalry from each host combating there pell-mell. In this action Gaius the Consul fell in the mellay fighting with desperate courage, and his head was brought to the Celtic kings; but the Roman cavalry, after a stubborn struggle, at length overmastered the enemy and gained possession of the hill. The infantry were now close upon each other, and the spectacle was a strange and marvellous one, not only to those actually present at the battle, but to all who could afterwards picture it to themselves from the reports.

For in the first place, as the battle was between three armies, it is evident that the appearance and the movements of the forces marshalled against each other must have been in the highest degree strange and unusual. Again, it must have been to all present, and still is to us, a matter of doubt whether the Celts, with the enemy advancing on them from both sides, were more dangerously situated, or, on the contrary, more effectively, since at one and the same time they were fighting against both their enemies and were protecting themselves in the rear from both, while, above all, they were absolutely cut off from retreat or any prospect of escape in the case of defeat, this being the peculiarity of this two-faced formation. The Romans, however, were on the one hand encouraged by having caught the enemy between their two armies, but on the other they were terrified by the fine order of the Celtic host and the dreadful din, for there were innumerable horn-blowers and trumpeters, and, as the whole army were shouting their war-cries at the same time, there was such a tumult of sound that it seemed that not only the trumpets and the soldiers but all the country round had got a voice and caught up the cry.

Very terrifying too were the appearance and the gestures of the naked warriors in front, all in the prime of life, and finely built men, and all in the leading companies richly adorned with gold torques and armlets. The sight of them indeed dismayed the Romans, but at the same time the prospect of winning such spoils made them twice as keen for the fight.

But when the javelineers advanced, as is their usage, from the ranks of the

Roman legions and began to hurl their javelins in well-aimed volleys, the Celts in the rear ranks indeed were well protected by their trousers and cloaks, but it fell out far otherwise than they had expected with the naked men in front, and they found themselves in a very difficult and helpless predicament. For the Gaulish shield does not cover the whole body; so that their nakedness was a disadvantage, and the bigger they were the better chance had the missiles of going home. At length, unable to drive off the javelineers owing to the distance and the hail of javelins, and reduced to the utmost distress and perplexity, some of them, in their impotent rage, rushed wildly on the enemy and sacrificed their lives, while others, retreating step by step on the ranks of their comrades, threw them into disorder by their display of faint-heartedness.

Thus was the spirit of the Gaesatae broken down by the javelineers; but the main body of the Insubres, Boii, and Taurisci, once the javelineers had withdrawn into the ranks and the Roman maniples attacked them, met the enemy and kept up a stubborn hand-to-hand combat. For, though being almost cut to pieces, they held their ground, equal to their foes in courage, and inferior only, as a force and individually, in their arms. The Roman shields, it should be added, were far more serviceable for defence and their swords for attack, the Gaulish sword being only good for a cut and not for a thrust. But finally, attacked from higher ground and on their flank by the Roman cavalry, which rode down the hill and charged them vigorously, the Celtic infantry were cut to pieces where they stood, their cavalry taking to flight.

About forty thousand Celts were slain and at least ten thousand taken prisoners, among them the king Concolitanus. The other king, Aneroëstes, escaped with a few followers to a certain place where he put an end to his life and to those of his friends. The Roman Consul collected the spoils and sent them to Rome, returning the booty of the Gauls to the owners. With his legions he traversed Liguria and invaded the territory of the Boii, from whence, after letting his legions pillage to their heart's content, he returned at their head in a few days to Rome. He sent to ornament the Capitol the standards and necklaces (the gold necklets worn by the Gauls), but the rest of the spoil and the prisoners he used for his entry into Rome and the adornment of his triumph.

Thus were destroyed these Celts during whose invasion, the most serious that had ever occurred, all the Italians and especially the Romans had been exposed to great and terrible peril. This success encouraged the Romans to hope that they would be able entirely to expel the Celts from the plain of the Po; and both the Consuls of the next year, Quintus Fulvius and Titus Manlius, were sent against them with a formidable expeditionary force. They surprised and terrified the Boii, compelling them to submit to Rome, but the rest of the campaign had no practical results whatever, owing to the very heavy rains, and an epidemic which broke out among them.

Next year's [223 B.C.] Consuls, however, Publius Furius and Gaius Flaminius, again invaded the Celtic territory, through the country of the Anares who dwelt not far from Marseilles. Having admitted this tribe to their friendship, they crossed into the territory of the Insubres, near the junction of the Po and Adda. Both in crossing and in encamping on the other side, they suffered some loss, and at first remained on the spot, but later made a truce and evacuated the territory under its terms. After a circuitous march of some days, they crossed the river Clusius and reached the country of the Cenomani, who were their allies, and accompanied by them, again invaded from the district at the foot of the Alps the plains of the Insubres and began to lay the country waste and pillage their dwellings. The chieftains of the Insubres, seeing that the Romans adhered to their purpose of attacking them, decided to try their luck in a decisive battle. Collecting all their forces in one place, they took down the golden standards called "immovable" from the temple of Minerva, and having made all other necessary preparations, boldly took up a menacing position opposite the enemy. They were about fifty thousand strong.

The Romans, on the one hand, as they saw that the enemy were much more numerous than themselves, were desirous of employing also the forces of their Celtic allies, but on the other hand, taking into consideration Gaulish fickleness and the fact that they were going to fight against those of the same nation as these allies, they were shy of asking such men to participate in an action of such vital importance. Finally, remaining themselves on their side of the river, they sent the Celts who were with them across it, and demolished the bridges that crossed the stream, firstly as a precaution against their allies, and secondly to leave themselves no hope of safety except in victory, the river, which was impassable, lying in their rear. After taking these measures they prepared for battle.

The Romans are thought to have managed matters very skillfully in this battle, their tribunes having instructed them how they should fight, both as individuals and collectively. For they had observed from former battles that Gauls in general are most formidable and spirited in their fast onslaught, while still fresh, and that, from the way their swords are made, as has been already explained, only the first cut takes effect; after this they at once assume the shape of a strigil [a curved blade used for scraping skin in the baths], being so much bent both length-wise and side-wise that unless the men are given leisure to rest them on the ground and set them straight with the foot, the second blow is quite ineffectual. The tribunes therefore distributed amongst the front lines the spears of the triarii who were stationed behind them, ordering them to use their swords instead only after the spears were done with. They then drew up opposite the Celts in order of battle and engaged. Upon the Gauls slashing first at the spears and making their swords unserviceable the Romans came to close quarters, having rendered the enemy helpless by depriving them of the power of raising their hands and cutting, which is the peculiar and only stroke of the Gauls, as their swords have no points. The Romans, on the contrary, instead of slashing, continued to thrust with their swords which did not bend, the points being very effective. Thus, striking one blow after another on the breast or face, they slew the greater part of their adversaries. This was solely due to the foresight of the tribunes, the Consul Flaminius being thought to have mismanaged the battle by deploying his force at the very edge of the river-bank and thus rendering impossible a tactical movement peculiar to the Romans, as he left the lines no room to fall back gradually. For had the troops been even in the slightest degree pushed back from their ground during the battle, they would have had to throw themselves into the river, all owing to their general's blunder. However, as it was, they gained a decisive victory by their own skill and valour, as I said, and returned to Rome with a quantity of booty and many trophies.

Next year [222 B.C.] the Celts sent ambassadors begging for peace and engaging to accept any conditions, but the new Consuls Marcus Claudius and Gnaeus Cornelius strongly urged that no peace should be granted them. On meeting with a refusal, the Celts decided to resort to their last hope and again appealed to the Gaesatae on the Rhône, and hired a force of about thirty thousand men. When they had these troops they kept them in readiness and awaited the attack of the enemy. The Roman Consuls, when the season came, invaded the territory of the Insubres with their legions. Encamping round a city called Acerrae lying between the Po and the Alps, they laid siege to it. The Insubres could not come to the assistance of the besieged, as the Romans had occupied all the advantageous positions, but, with the object of making the latter raise the siege, they crossed the Po with part of their forces, and entering the territory of the Anares, laid siege to a town there called Clastidium. On the Consuls learning of this, Marcus Claudius set off in haste with the cavalry and a small body of infantry to relieve the besieged if possible. The Celts, as soon as they were aware of the enemy's arrival, raised the siege and, advancing to meet them, drew up in order of battle. When the Romans boldly charged them with their cavalry alone, they at first stood firm, but afterwards, being taken both in the rear and on the flank, they found themselves in difficulties and were finally put to rout by the cavalry unaided, many of them throwing themselves into the river and being swept away by the current, while the larger number were cut to pieces by the enemy.

The Romans now took Acerrae, which was well stocked with corn, the Gauls retiring to Mediolanum [Milan], the chief place in the territory of the Insubres. Gnaeus followed close on their heels, and suddenly appeared before Mediolanum. The Gauls at first did not stir, but, when he was on his way back to Acerrae, they sallied out, and made a bold attack on his rear, in which they killed a considerable number of the Romans and even forced a portion of them to take to flight, until Gnaeus, calling back the forces in advance, urged the fugitives to rally and withstand the enemy. After this the Romans, on their part obeying their Consul, continued to fight vigorously with their assailants, and the Celts after holding their ground for a time, encouraged as they were by their momentary success, were shortly put to flight and took refuge on the mountains. Gnaeus, following them, laid waste the country and took Mediolanum itself by assault, upon which the chieftains of the Insubres, despairing of safety, put themselves entirely at the mercy of the Romans.

Such was the end of the war against the Celts, a war which, if we look to the desperation and daring of the combatants and the numbers who took part and perished in the battles, is second to no war in history, but is quite contemptible as regards the plan of the campaigns, and the judgement shown in executing it, not most steps but every single step that the Gauls took being commended to them rather by the heat of passion than by cool calculation. As I have witnessed them not long afterwards entirely expelled from the plain of the Po, except a few regions close under the Alps, I did not think it right to make no mention either of their original invasion or of their subsequent conduct and their final expulsion; for I think it is the proper task of History to record and hand down to future generations such episodes of Fortune, that those who live after us may not, owing to entire ignorance of these incidents, be unduly terrified by sudden and unexpected invasions of barbarians, but that, having a fair comprehension of how short-lived and perishable is the might of such peoples, they may confront the invaders and put every hope of safety to the test, before yielding a jot of anything they value.

—IV—

GAUL

Gaul—bound by the Alps, the Rhine, the Atlantic Ocean, the Pyrenees, and the Mediterranean and pretty much the size and shape of present-day France—at first interested Rome simply because it lay between the Italian peninsula and Spain. But over the years, as local barbarians threatened Massilia (Marseille) in the south and tribes of Celts and Germans began to war more furiously against each other in the north, Rome's involvement became more active.

Julius Caesar (100–44 B.C.) invaded Gaul in 58 B.C. and over the next seven years completed his "conquest" and pacification with a surprisingly low number of Roman casualties. Then, always referring to himself in a majestic third person, he also got a book out of it to advance his political agenda back in Rome. This chapter begins and ends with selections from Caesar's *The Gallic War*, which English writer Anthony Trollope called "the beginning of modern history." The first section contains his observations on the customs and manners of the Gauls, with more attention paid to the Druids than one might expect from a general; the second is an account of a minor border dispute that demonstrates both the mobility of the barbarians and the Romans' rather prim notions about how people—except perhaps Romans—should stay where they belong.

Between the two excerpts by Caesar is an entry written at about the same time from the Greek historian Diodorus Siculus's *The Library of History*. His subject is the peculiarities of the Gauls, including whether or not their hair is naturally blond and how they can foretell the future by studying the death throes of victims they have knifed in the stomach.

Julius Caesar

"On the Gauls"

58 B.C.

Since we have come to this place, it does not appear to be foreign to our subject to lay before the reader an account of the manners of Gaul. . . . In Gaul there are factions not only in all the states, and in all the cantons and their divisions, but almost in each family, and of these factions those are the leaders who are considered according to their judgment to possess the greatest influence, upon whose will and determination the management of all affairs and measures depends. And that seems to have been instituted in ancient times with this view, that no one of the common people should be in want of support against one more powerful; for none of those leaders suffers his party to be oppressed and defrauded, and if he do otherwise, he has no influence among his party. This same policy exists throughout the whole of Gaul; for all the states are divided into two factions.

When Caesar arrived in Gaul, the Aedui were the leaders of one faction, the Sequani of the other. Since the latter were less powerful by themselves, inasmuch as the chief influence was from of old among the Radii, and their dependencies were great, they had united to themselves the Germans and Ariovistus, and had brought them over to their party by great sacrifices and promises. And having fought several successful battles and slain all the nobility of the Radii, they had so far surpassed them in power, that they brought over, from the Aedui to themselves, a large portion of their dependents and received from them the sons of their leading men as hostages, and compelled them to swear in their public character that they would enter into no design against them; and held a portion of the neighbouring land, seized on by force, and possessed the sovereignty of the whole of Gaul. Divitiacus, urged by this necessity, had proceeded to Rome to the senate, for the purpose of entreating assistance, and had returned without accomplishing his object. A change of affairs ensued on the arrival of Caesar, the hostages were returned to the Radii, their old dependencies restored, and new acquired through Caesar (because those who had attached themselves to their alliance saw that they enjoyed a better state and a milder government), their other interests, their influence, their reputation were likewise increased, and in consequence, the Sequani lost the sovereignty. The Remi succeeded to their place, and, as it was perceived that they equalled the Aedui in favour with Caesar, those, who on account of their old animosities could by no means coalesce with the Radii, consigned themselves in clientship to the Remi. The latter carefully protected them. Thus they possessed both a new and suddenly acquired influence. Affairs were then in that position, that the Aedui were considered by far the leading people, and the Remi held the second post of honour.

Throughout all Gaul there are two orders of those men who are of any rank and dignity: for the commonality is held almost in the condition of slaves, and dares to undertake nothing of itself and is admitted to no deliberation. The greater part, when they are pressed either by debt, or the large amount of their tributes, or the oppression of the more powerful, give themselves up in vassalage to the nobles, who possess over them the same rights without exception as masters over their slaves. But of these two orders, one is that of the Druids, the other that of the knights. The former are engaged in things sacred, conduct the public and the private sacrifices, and interpret all matters of religion. To these a large number of the young men resort for the purpose of instruction, and they [the Druids] are in great honour among them. For they determine respecting almost all controversies, public and private; and if any crime has been perpetrated, if murder has been committed, if there be any dispute about an inheritance, if any about boundaries, these same persons decide it; they decree rewards and punishments; if any one, either in a private or public capacity, has not submitted to their decision, they interdict him from the sacrifices. This among them is the most heavy punishment. Those who have been thus interdicted are esteemed in the number of the impious and the criminal: all shun them, and avoid their society and conversation, lest they receive some evil from their contact; nor is

Justice administered to them when seeking it, nor is any dignity bestowed on them. Over all these Druids one presides, who possesses supreme authority among them. Upon his death, if any individual among the rest is pre-eminent in dignity, he succeeds; but, if there are many equal, the election is made by the suffrages of the Druids; sometimes they even contend for the presidency with arms. These assemble at a fixed period of the year in a consecrated place in the territories of the Carnutes, which is reckoned the central region of the whole of Gaul. Hither all, who have disputes, assemble from every part, and submit to their decrees and determinations. This institution is supposed to have been devised in Britain, and to have been brought over from it into Gaul; and now those who desire to gain a more accurate knowledge of that system generally proceed thither for the purpose of studying it.

The Druids do not go to war, nor pay tribute together with the rest; they have an exemption from military service and a dispensation in all matters. Induced by such great advantages, many embrace this profession of their own accord, and many are sent to it by their parents and relations. They are said there to learn by heart a great number of verses; accordingly some remain in the course of training twenty years. Nor do they regard it lawful to commit these to writing, though in almost all other matters, in their public and private transactions, they use Greek characters. That practice they seem to me to have adopted for two reasons; because they neither desire their doctrines to be divulged among the mass of the people, nor those who learn, to devote themselves the less to the efforts of memory, relying on writing: since it generally occurs to most men, that, in their dependence on writing, they relax their diligence in learning thoroughly, and their employment of the memory. They wish to inculcate this as one of their leading tenets, that souls do not become extinct, but pass after death from one body to another, and they think that men by this tenet are in a great degree excited to valour, the fear of death being disregarded. They likewise discuss and impart to the youth many things respecting the stars and their motion, respecting the extent of the world and of our earth, respecting the nature of things, respecting the power and the majesty of the immortal gods.

The other order is that of the knights. These, when there is occasion and any war occurs (which before Caesar's arrival was for the most part wont to happen every year, as either they on their part were inflicting injuries or repelling those which others inflicted on them), are all engaged in war. And those of them most distinguished by birth and resources, have the greatest number of vassals and dependents about them. They acknowledge this sort of influence and power only.

The nation of all the Gauls is extremely devoted to superstitious rites; and on that account they who are troubled with unusually severe diseases and they who are engaged in battles and dangers, either sacrifice men as victims, or vow that they will sacrifice them, and employ the Druids as the performers of those sacrifices; because they think that unless the life of a man be offered for the life of a man, the mind of the immortal gods cannot be rendered propitious, and they have sacrifices of that kind ordained for national purposes. Others have figures of vast size, the limbs of which (formed of willow branches) they fill with living men, and, setting the figures on fire, cause the men to perish enveloped in the flames. They consider that the oblation of such as have been taken in theft, or in robbery, or any other offense, is more acceptable to the immortal gods; but when a supply of that class is wanting, they have recourse to the oblation of even the innocent.

They worship as their divinity, Mercury in particular, and have many images of him, and regard him as the inventor of all arts; they consider him the guide of their journeys and marches, and believe him to have very great influence over the acquisition of gain and mercantile transactions. Next to him they worship Apollo, and Mars, and Jupiter, and Minerva; respecting these deities they have for the most part the same belief as other nations: that Apollo averts diseases, that Minerva imparts the invention of manufactures, that Jupiter possesses the sovereignty of the heavenly powers, that Mars presides over wars. To him, when they have determined to engage in battle, they commonly vow those things which they shall take in war. When they have conquered, they sacrifice whatever captured animals may have survived the conflict, and collect the other things into one place. In many states you may see piles of these things heaped up in their consecrated spots; nor does it often happen that any one, disregarding the sanctity of the case, dares either to secrete in his house things captured, or take away those deposited; and the most severe punishment, with torture, has been established for such a deed.

All the Gauls assert that they are descended from the god Dis [god of the underworld], and say that this tradition has been handed down by the Druids. For that reason they compute the divisions of every season, not by the number of days, but of nights; they keep birth-days and the beginnings of months and years in such an order that the day follows the night. Among the other usages of their life, they differ in this from almost all other nations, that they do not permit their children to approach them openly until they are grown up so as to be able to bear the service of war; and they regard it as indecorous for a son of boyish age to stand in public in the presence of his father.

Whatever sums of money the husbands have received in the name of dowry from their wives, making an estimate of it, they add the same amount out of their own estates. An account is kept of all this money conjointly, and the profits are laid by; whichever of them shall have survived the other, to that one the portion of both reverts together with the profits of the previous time. Husbands have power of life and death over their wives as well as over their children: and when the father of a family, born in a more than commonly distinguished rank, has died, his relations assemble, and, if the circumstances of his death are suspicious, hold an investigation upon the wives in the manner adopted towards slaves; and, if proof be obtained, put them to severe torture, and kill them. Their funerals, considering the state of civilization among the Gauls, are magnificent and costly; and they cast into the fire all things, including living creatures, which they suppose to have been dear to them when alive; and a little before this period, slaves and dependents, who were ascertained to have been beloved by them, were, after the regular funeral rites were completed, burnt together with them.

Those states which are considered to conduct their commonwealth more judiciously, have it ordained by their laws that, if any person shall have heard by rumour and report from his neighbours anything concerning the commonwealth he shall convey it to the magistrate and not impart it to any other; because it has been discovered that inconsiderate and inexperienced men were often alarmed by false reports and driven to some rash act, or else took hasty measures in affairs of the highest importance. The magistrates conceal those things which require to be kept unknown; and they disclose to the people whatever they determine to be expedient. It is not lawful to speak of the commonwealth except in council.

Diodorus Siculus

"On the People and Customs of Gaul"

ca. 50 B.C.

A peculiar thing and unexpected takes place over the larger part of Gaul which we think we should not omit to mention. For from the direction of the sun's summer setting and from the north, winds are wont to blow with such violence and force that they pick up from the ground rocks as large as can be held in the hand together with a dust composed of coarse gravel; and, generally speaking, when these winds rage violently they tear the weapons out of men's hands and the clothing off their backs and dismount riders from their horses. Furthermore, since temperateness of climate is destroyed by the excessive cold, the land produces neither wine nor oil, and as a consequence those Gauls who are deprived of these fruits make a drink out of barley which they call Ethos or beer, and they also drink the water with which they cleanse their honeycombs. The Gauls are exceedingly addicted to the use of wine and fill themselves with the wine which is brought into their country by merchants, drinking it unmixed, and since they partake of this drink without moderation by reason of their craving for it, when they are drunken they fall into a stupor or a state of madness.

Consequently many of the Italian traders, induced by the love of money which characterizes them, believe that the love of wine of these Gauls is their own godsend. For these transport the wine on the navigable rivers by means of boats and through the level plain on wagons, and receive for it an incredible price; for in exchange for a jar of wine they receive a slave, getting a servant in return for the drink.

Throughout Gaul there is found practically no silver, but there is gold in great quantities, which Nature provides for the inhabitants without their having to mine for it or to undergo any hardship. For the rivers, as they course through the country, having as they do sharp bends which turn this way and that and dashing against the mountains which line their banks and bearing off great pieces of them, are full of gold-dust. This is collected by those who occupy themselves in this business, and these men grind or crush the lumps which hold the dust, and after washing out with water the earthy elements in it they give the gold-dust over to be melted in the furnaces. In this manner they amass a great amount of gold, which is used for ornament not only by the women but also by the men. For around their wrists and arms they wear bracelets, around their necks heavy necklaces of solid gold, and huge rings they wear as well, and even corselets of gold. And a peculiar and striking practice is found among the upper Celts, in connection with the sacred precincts of the gods; for in the temples and precincts made consecrate in their land, a great amount of gold has been deposited as a dedication to the gods, and not a native of the country ever touches it because of religious scruple, although the Celts are an exceedingly covetous people.

The Gauls are tall of body, with rippling muscles, and white of skin, and their hair is blond, and not only naturally so, but they also make it their practice by artificial means to increase the distinguishing colour which nature has given it. For they are always washing their hair in lime-water, and they pull it back from the forehead to the top of the head and back to the nape of the neck, with the result that their appearance is like that of Satyrs and Pans, since the treatment of their hair makes it so heavy and coarse that it differs in no respect from the mane of horses. Some of them shave the beard, but others let it grow a little; and the nobles shave their cheeks, but they let the moustache grow until it covers the mouth. Consequently, when they are eating, their moustaches become entangled in the food, and when they are drinking, the beverage passes, as it were, through a kind of a strainer. When they dine they all sit, not upon chairs, but upon the ground, using for cushions the skins of wolves or of dogs. The service at the meals is performed by the youngest children, both male and female, who are of suitable age; and near at hand are their fireplaces heaped with coals, and on them are caldrons and spits holding whole pieces of meat. Brave warriors they reward with the choicest portions of the meat. . . . They invite strangers to their feasts, and do not inquire until after the meal who they are and of what things they stand in need. And it is their custom, even during the course of the meal, to seize upon any trivial matter as an occasion for keen disputation and then to challenge one another to single combat, without any regard for their lives; for the belief of Pythagoras prevails among them, that the souls of men are immortal and that after a prescribed number of years they commence upon a new life, the soul entering into another body. Consequently, we are told, at the funerals of their dead some cast letters upon the pyre which they have written to their deceased kinsmen, as if the dead would be able to read these letters.

In their journeyings and when they go into battle the Gauls use chariots drawn by two horses, which carry the charioteer and the warrior; and when they encounter cavalry in the fighting they first hurl their javelins at the enemy and then step down from their chariots and join battle with their swords. Certain of them despise death to such a degree that they enter the perils of battle without protective armour and with no more than a girdle about their loins. They bring along to war also their free men to serve them, choosing them out from among the poor, and these attendants they use in battle as charioteers and as shield-bearers. It is also their custom, when they are formed for battle, to step out in front of the line and to challenge the most valiant men from among their opponents to single combat, brandishing their weapons in front of them to terrify their adversaries. And when any man accepts the challenge to battle, they then break forth into a song in praise of the valiant deeds of their ancestors and in boast of their own high achievements, reviling all the while and belittling their opponent, and trying, in a word, by such talk to strip him of his bold spirit before the combat.

When their enemies fall they cut off their heads and fasten them about the necks of their horses; and turning over to their attendants the arms of their opponents, all covered with blood, they carry them off as booty, singing a paean over them and striking up a song of victory, and these first-fruits of battle they fasten by nails upon their houses, just as men do, in certain kinds of hunting, with the heads of wild beasts they have mastered. The heads of their most distinguished enemies they embalm in cedar-oil and carefully preserve in a chest, and these they exhibit to strangers, gravely maintaining that in exchange for this head some one of their ancestors, or their father, or the man himself, refused the offer of a great sum of money. And some men among them, we are told, boast that they have not accepted an equal weight of gold for the head they show, displaying a barbarous sort of greatness of soul; for not to sell that which constitutes a witness and proof of one's valour is a noble thing, but to continue to fight against one of our own race, after he is dead, is to descend to the level of beasts.

The clothing they wear is striking—shirts which have been dyed and embroidered in varied colours, and breeches, which they call in their tongue *bracae*; and they wear striped coats, fastened by a buckle on the shoulder, heavy for winter wear and light for summer, in which are set checks, close together and of varied hues. For armour they use long shields, as high as a man, which are wrought in a manner peculiar to them, some of them even having the figures of animals embossed on them in bronze, and these are skillfully worked with an eye not only to beauty but also to protection. On their heads they put bronze helmets which have large embossed figures standing out from them and give an appearance of great size to those who wear them; for in some cases horns are attached to the helmet so as to form a single piece, in other cases images of the fore-parts of birds or four-footed animals. Their trumpets are of peculiar nature and such as barbarians use, for when they are blown upon they give forth a harsh sound, appropriate to the tumult of war. Some of them have iron cuirasses, chain-wrought, but others are satisfied with the armour which Nature has given them and go into battle naked. In place of the short sword they carry long broadswords which are hung on chains of iron or bronze and are worn along the right flank. And some of them gather up their shirts with belts plated with gold or silver. The spears they brandish, which they call *lanciae*, have iron heads a cubit in length and even more, and a little under two palms in breadth; for their swords are not shorter than the javelins of other peoples, and the heads of their javelins are larger than the swords of others. Some of these javelins come from the forge straight, others twist in and out in spiral shapes for their entire length, the purpose being that the thrust may not only cut the flesh, but mangle it as well, and that the withdrawal of the spear may lacerate the wound.

The Gauls are terrifying in aspect and their voices are deep and altogether harsh; when they meet together they converse with few words and in riddles, hinting darkly at things for the most part and using one word when they mean another; and they like to talk in superlatives, to the end that they may extol themselves and depreciate all other men. They are also boasters and threateners and are fond of pompous language, and yet they have sharp wits and are not without cleverness at learning. Among them are also to be found lyric poets whom they call Bards. These men sing to the accompaniment of instruments which are like lyres, and their songs may be either of praise or of obloquy. Philosophers, as we may call them, and men learned in religious affairs are unusually honoured among them and are called by them Druids. The Gauls likewise make use of diviners, accounting them worthy of high approbation, and these men foretell the future by means of the flight or cries of birds and of the slaughter of sacred animals, and they have all the multitude subservient to them.

They also observe a custom which is especially astonishing and incredible, in case they are taking thought with respect to matters of great concern; for in such cases they devote to death a human being and plunge a dagger into him in the region above the diaphragm and when the stricken victim has fallen they read the future from the manner of his fall and from the twitching of his limbs as well as from the gushing of the blood, having learned to place confidence in an ancient and long-continued practice of observing such matters. And it is a custom of theirs that no one should perform a sacrifice without a "philosopher"; for thank-offerings should be rendered to the gods, they say, by the hands of men who are experienced in the nature of the divine, and who speak, as it were, the language of the gods, and it is also through the mediation of such men, they think, that blessings likewise should be sought. Nor is it only in the exigencies of peace, but in their wars as well, that they obey, before all others, these men and their chanting poets, and such obedience is observed not only by their friends but also by their enemies; many times, for instance, when two armies approach each other in battle with swords drawn and spears thrust forward, these men step forth between them and cause them to cease, as though having cast a spell over certain kinds of wild beasts. In this way, even among the wildest barbarians, does passion give place before wisdom, and Ares stands in awe of the Muses. . . .

The women of the Gauls are not only like the men in their great stature but they are a match for them in courage as well. Their children are usually born with grayish hair, but as they grow older the colour of their hair changes to that of their parents. The most savage peoples among them are those who dwell beneath the Bears [in northern Europe, beneath Ursa Major and Ursa Minor] and on the borders of Scythia, and some of these, we are told, eat human beings, even as the Britains do who dwell on Iris [Ireland], as it is called. And since the valour of these peoples and their savage ways have been famed abroad, some men say that it was they who in ancient times overran all Asia. . . .

For it has been their ambition from old to plunder, invading for this purpose the lands of others, and to regard all men with contempt. For they are the people who captured Rome, who plundered the sanctuary at Delphi, who levied tribute upon a large part of Europe and no small part of Asia, and settled themselves upon the lands of the peoples they had subdued in war, being called in time Greco-Gauls, because they became mixed with the Greeks, and who, as their last accomplishment, have destroyed many large Roman armies. And in pursuance of their savage ways they manifest an outlandish impiety also with respect to their sacrifices; for their criminals they keep prisoner for five years and then impale in honour of the gods, dedicating them together with many other offerings of first-fruits and constructing pyres of great size. Captives also are used by them as victims for their sacrifices in honour of the gods. Certain of them likewise slay, together with the human beings, such animals as are taken in war, or burn them or do away with them in some other vengeful fashion.

Although their wives are comely, they have very little to do with them, but rage with lust, in outlandish fashion, for the embraces of males. It is their practice to sleep upon the ground on the skins of wild beasts and to tumble with a catamite on each side. And the most astonishing thing of all is that they feel no concern for their proper dignity, but prostitute to others without a qualm the flower of their bodies; nor do they consider this a disgraceful thing to do, but rather when any one of them is thus approached and refuses the favour offered him, this they consider an act of dishonour.

Julius Caesar

"Border Battles"

55 B.C.

In the following winter—the year in which Gnaeus Pompeius and Marcus Crassus were consuls [55 B.C.]—the Usipetes from Germany, and likewise the Tencteri, crossed the Rhine with a large host of men, not far from the sea into which it flows. The reason for their crossing was that for several years they had been much harassed by the Suebi, who pressed on them by force of arms and prevented them from husbandry. The Suebi are by far the largest and the most warlike nation among the Germans. It is said that they have a hundred cantons, from each of which they draw one thousand armed men yearly for the purpose of war outside their borders. The remainder, who have stayed at home, support themselves and the absent warriors; and again, in turn, are under arms the following year, while the others remain at home. By this means neither husbandry nor the theory and practice of war is interrupted. They have no private or separate holding of land, nor are they allowed to abide longer than a year in one place for their habitation. They make not much use of corn for food, but chiefly of milk and of cattle, and are much engaged in hunting; and this, owing to the nature of the food, the regular exercise, and the freedom of life—for from boyhood up they are not schooled in a sense of duty or discipline, and do nothing whatever against their wish—nurses their strength and makes men of immense bodily stature. Moreover, they have regularly trained themselves to wear nothing, even in the coldest localities, except skins, the scantiness of which leaves a great part of the body bare, and they bathe in the rivers.

They give access to traders rather to secure purchasers for what they have captured in war than to satisfy any craving for imports. And, in fact, the

Germans do not import for their use draught-horses, in which the Gauls take the keenest delight, procuring them at great expense; but they take their home-bred animals, inferior and ill-favoured, and by regular exercising they render them capable of the utmost exertion. In cavalry combats they often leap from their horses and fight on foot, having trained their horses to remain in the same spot, and retiring rapidly upon them at need; and their tradition regards nothing as more disgraceful or more indolent than the use of saddles. And so, however few in number, they dare approach any party, however large, of sad-dle-horsemen. They suffer no importation of wine whatever, believing that men are thereby rendered soft and womanish for the endurance of hardship.

As a nation, they count it the highest praise to have the land on their borders untenanted over as wide a tract as may be, for this signifies, they think, that a great number of states cannot withstand their force. Thus it is said that on one side for about six hundred miles from the territory of the Suebi the land is untenanted, On the other side the Ubii come nearest, a state which was once extensive and prosperous, according to German standards. Its inhabitants are somewhat more civilised than the other folk of the same race, because their borders touch the Rhine and traders visit them frequently, and, further, because the Ubii themselves by close neighbourhood have grown accustomed to Gallic fashions. Upon this people the Suebi had made frequent attempts in many wars, but had proved unable to drive them from their territory because the state was populous and powerful: however, they made the Ubii tributary to themselves, and greatly diminished their strength and importance.

The Usipetes and the Tencteri, mentioned above, were in the same case. For several years they withstood the force of the Suebi, but at last they were driven out of their lands, and after wandering for three years in many districts of Germany they reached the Rhine. The localities thereabout were inhabited by the Menapii, who possessed lands, buildings, and villages on both banks of the river; but, being alarmed by the approach of so great a host, they removed from the buildings which they had possessed beyond the river, and, setting garrisons at intervals on the near side of the Rhine, sought to prevent the Germans from crossing. The Germans tried every expedient, but when they found that they could neither force their way because of their lack of vessels nor cross privily because of the Menapian piquets, they pretended to retire to their own homes and districts. They proceeded for a three days' journey, and then returned; and their cavalry, having completed the whole of this distance in a single night, caught the Menapii uninformed and unawares, for, having learnt through their scouts of the departure of the Germans, they had moved back without fear over the Rhine into their own villages. So they were put to the sword and their vessels seized; then the Germans crossed the river before the section of the Menapii on the near side of the Rhine could learn of it, seized all their buildings, and for the remainder of the winter sustained themselves on the supplies of the Menapii.

Caesar was informed of these events; and fearing the fickleness of the Gauls, because they are capricious in forming designs and intent for the most part on change, he considered that no trust should be reposed in them. It is indeed a regular habit of the Gauls to compel travellers to halt, even against their will, and to ascertain what each of them may have heard or learnt upon every subject; and in the towns the common folk surround traders, compelling them to declare from what districts they come and what they have learnt there. Such stories and hearsay often induce them to form plans upon vital questions of which they must forthwith repent; for they are the slaves of uncertain rumours and most men reply to them in fictions made to their taste.

Caesar was aware of this their habit, and that otherwise he might have to face a more serious campaign, set out for the army earlier than was his wont. When he reached headquarters he learnt that his suspicions had been realised; deputations had been sent by some states to the Germans, inviting them to leave the Rhine, and promising to furnish all things demanded of them. The hope thus inspired encouraged the Germans to range more widely, and they had already reached the borders of the Eburones and the Condrusi, dependents of the Treveri. Thereupon Caesar summoned the chiefs of Gaul from their homes; but, thinking it best to conceal the information in his possession, he comforted and encouraged them, and, having made requisition of cavalry, determined to make war on the Germans.

Having secured his corn-supply and selected his cavalry, he began to march into the localities in which the Germans were reported to be. When he was a few days' march away deputies arrived from them, whose address was to the following effect: The Germans did not take the first step in making war on the Roman people, nor yet, if provoked, did they refuse the conflict of arms, for it was the ancestral custom of the Germans to resist anyone who made war upon them, and not to beg off. They declared, however, that they had come against their will, being driven out of their homes: if the Romans would have their goodwill, they might find their friendship useful. Let the Romans either grant them lands, or suffer them to hold the lands their arms had acquired. They yielded to the Suebi alone, to whom even the immortal gods could not be equal; on earth at any rate there was no one else whom they could not conquer.

To this Caesar replied as seemed good; but the conclusion of his speech was as follows: He could have no friendship with them, if they remained in Gaul. On the one hand, it was not just that men who had not been able to defend their own territories should seize those of others; on the other hand, there was no land in Gaul which could be granted without injustice, especially to so numerous a host. However, they had permission, if they pleased, to settle in the territories of the Ubii, whose deputies were in his camp, complaining of the outrages of the Suebi and seeking his assistance: he would give orders to the Ubii to this effect.

The envoys said that they would report this to their people and, after deliberation upon the matter, return to Caesar in three days: they asked him not to move his camp nearer in the meanwhile. Caesar replied that he could not even grant that request. He knew, in fact, that they had sent a large detachment of cavalry some days before to the country of the Ambivariti across the Meuse, to get booty and corn: he supposed that they were waiting for this cavalry, and for that reason sought to interpose delay.

The Meuse flows from the range of the Vosges, in the territory of the Lingones, and, receiving from the Rhine a certain tributary called the Waal, forms the island of the Batavi; then, no more than eighty miles from the Ocean, it flows into the Rhine. The Rhine rises in the land of the Lepontii, who inhabit the Alps; in a long, swift course it runs through the territories of the Nantuates, Helvetii, Sequani, Mediomatrices, Triboci, and Treveri, and on its approach to the Ocean divides into several streams, forming many large islands (a great number of which are inhabited by fierce barbaric tribes, believed in some instances to live on fish and birds' eggs); then by many mouths it flows into the Ocean.

When Caesar was no more than twelve miles away from the enemy, the deputies returned to him as agreed: they met him on the march, and besought him earnestly not to advance further. When their request was not granted, they asked him to send forward to the cavalry in advance of his column and to prevent them from engaging, and to grant themselves an opportunity of sending deputies into the land of the Ubii. They put forward the hope that, if the chiefs and the senate of the Ubii pledged their faith on oath, they (the Germans) would accept the terms which Caesar offered; and they asked him to give them an interval of three days to settle these affairs. Caesar supposed that all these pleas had the same object as before, to secure by a three days' interval the return of their absent cavalry; however, he said that on that day he would advance no further than four miles, in order to get water. He instructed them to meet him there next day with as large a number as they could, in order that he might take cognisance of their demands. Meanwhile he sent instructions to the commanders who had gone forward with all the cavalry not to provoke the enemy to an engagement, and, if provoked themselves, to hold their ground until he himself with the army had come up nearer.

The enemy had no more than eight hundred cavalry, for the party which was gone across the Meuse to get corn was not yet returned. Our own men, five thousand strong, had nothing to fear, for the deputies of the Germans had left Caesar but a short while before, having asked for a truce that day. However, directly they saw our cavalry, the enemy charged, and speedily threw our men into confusion. When our men turned to resist, the enemy, according to their custom, dismounted, and, by stabbing our horses and bringing down many of our troopers to the ground, they put the rest to rout, and indeed drove them in such panic that they did not desist from flight until they were come in sight of our column. In that engagement were slain seventy-four of our cavalry, and among them the gallant Piso of Aquitania, the scion of a most distinguished line, whose grandfather had held the sovereignty in his own state, and had been saluted as Friend by the Roman Senate. Piso went to the assistance of his brother, who had been cut off by the enemy, and rescued him from danger, but was thrown himself, his horse having been wounded. He resisted most gallantly as long as he could; then he was surrounded, and fell after receiving many wounds. His brother, who had escaped from the fight, saw him fall from a distance; then spurred his horse, flung himself upon the enemy, and was slain.

After this engagement was over, Caesar felt that he ought no longer to receive deputies nor to accept conditions from tribes which had sought for peace by guile and treachery, and then had actually begun war. Further, he judged it the height of madness to wait till the enemy's forces should be increased and their cavalry returned. Knowing as he did the fickleness of the Gauls, he apprehended how much influence the enemy had already acquired over them by a single engagement; and he considered that no time to form plans should be given them. Thus determined, he communicated to the lieutenant generals and the quartermaster-general his purpose not to lose a day in giving battle. Then, most fortunately, a certain thing occurred. The next morning, as treacherous and as hypocritical as ever, a large company of Germans, which included all the principal and senior men, came to his quarters, with a double object—to clear themselves (so they alleged) for engaging in a battle the day before, contrary to the agreement and to their own request therein, and also by deceit to get what they could in respect of the truce. Caesar rejoiced that they were delivered into his hand, and ordered them to be detained; then in person he led all his troops out of camp, commanding the cavalry, which he judged to be shaken by the recent engagement, to follow in the rear.

A triple line of columns was formed, and the eight-mile march was so speedily accomplished that Caesar reached the enemy's camp before the Germans could have any inkling of what was toward. They were struck with sudden panic by everything—by the rapidity of our approach, the absence of their own chiefs; and, as no time was given them to think, or to take up arms, they were too much taken aback to decide which was best—to lead their forces against the enemy, to defend the camp, or to seek safety by flight. When their alarm was betrayed by the uproar and bustle, our troops, stung by the treachery of the day before, burst into the camp. In the camp those who were able speedily to take up arms resisted the Romans for a while, and fought among the carts and baggage-wagons; the remainder, a crowd of women and children (for the Germans had left home and crossed the Rhine with all their belongings), began to flee in all directions, and Caesar dispatched the cavalry in pursuit.

Hearing the noise in rear, and seeing their own folk slain, the Germans threw away their arms, abandoned their war-standards, and burst out of the camp. When they reached the junction of the Meuse and the Rhine, they gave up hope of escaping further; a large number were already slain, and the rest hurled themselves into the river, there to perish overcome by terror, by exhaustion, by the force of the stream. The Romans, with not a man lost and but few wounded, freed from the fear of a stupendous war—with an enemy whose numbers had been 430,000 souls—returned to camp. Caesar gave to the Germans detained in camp permission to depart; but they, fearing punishments and tortures at the hand of the Gauls whose land they had harassed, said that they would stay in his company, and he gave them liberty so to do.

—V—

GERMANY

To call it anthropology may be stretching the point, but one of the first serious studies of a single group of barbarians was *Germania: On the Origin and Situation of the Germans*, written around A.D. 98 by Cornelius Tacitus (ca. 55–ca. 117). It is included here in its entirety. For a work by a Roman consul who was a son-in-law of Agricola, the great general who battled the Celts in Britain, it is surprisingly appreciative. Perhaps as a way of criticizing the corruption he found in the Romans at home, Tacitus tended to see the Germans as noble savages. Their habits might have been curious and untidy and their fondness for living in forests inexplicable, but in them he found heroic qualities sadly lacking in the languid decadence of the Romans.

Germania has had a long publishing history. It was the first of Tacitus's books to appear in print (Venice, 1470) and was translated into German only three years later. Historian Simon Schama has written in *Landscape and Memory* about the Nazis' fascination with it. To them, *Germania* was a polemic on Aryan supremacy and racial purity. Hitler went so far as to ask Mussolini to give him an ancient manuscript copy of it—the *Codex Aesinas*—that he claimed had once been kept in a German monastery. Il Duce agreed but later changed his mind, and the *Codex* remained in Italy.

Before getting to Tacitus, this chapter opens with a brief section from Julius Caesar's *The Gallic War* on the customs of the Germans. Written about 150 years before *Germania* by a man Tacitus refers to as "that highest authority," it depicts a sparsely set-tled, pastoral culture with no class structure—that Caesar could see—or private ownership. The dramatic cultural change between the two commentaries came about in part because for a century and a half the Roman army had been sitting along the Rhine. The strong military presence kept the previously nomadic Germanic tribes from moving on and, in effect, forced them to put down roots.

One reason for this heavily armed border was the memory of a bloody massacre that occurred in A.D. 9, during the reign of Caesar Augustus. Tacitus refers to it briefly in *Germania*. A German the Romans called Arminius (the latinized form of Hermann), who had served in the Roman army and become a Roman citizen, returned to his homeland and was appalled by the conditions he found there. He turned on his former comrades, organized the Germans, and led a revolt that resulted in an ambush in the Teutoburg Forest of three legions under the command of Quintilius Varus. Nearly 27,000 Romans were killed. The anniversary of the slaughter—which went on for three days—became a Roman day of mourning, and Augustus was said from then on to awake at night calling out, "Varus, Varus, bring back my legions!" The Romans never attempted to reoccupy the lands east of the Rhine.

Julius Caesar

"On the Germans"

55 B.C.

The Germans . . . have neither Druids to preside over sacred offices, nor do they pay great regard to sacrifices. They rank in the number of the gods those alone whom they behold, and by whose instrumentality they are obviously benefited, namely, the sun, fire, and the moon; they have not heard of the other deities even by report. Their whole life is occupied in hunting and in the pursuits of the military art; from childhood they devote themselves to fatigue and hardships. Those who have remained chaste for the longest time, receive the greatest commendation among their people: they think that by this the growth is promoted, by this the physical powers are increased and the sinews are strengthened. And to have had knowledge of a woman before the twentieth year they reckon among the most disgraceful acts; of which matter there is no concealment, because they bathe promiscuously in the rivers and only use skins or small cloaks of deers' hides, a large portion of the body being in consequence naked.

They do not pay much attention to agriculture, and a large portion of their food consists in milk, cheese, and flesh, nor has any one a fixed quantity of land or his own individual limits; but the magistrates and the leading men each year apportion to the tribes and families, who have united together, as much land as, and in the place in which, they think proper, and the year after compel them to move elsewhere. For this enactment they advance many reasons—lest seduced by long-continued custom, they may exchange their ardour in the waging of war for agriculture; lest they may be anxious to acquire extensive estates, and the more powerful drive the weaker from their possessions; lest they construct their houses with too great a desire to avoid cold and heat; lest the desire of wealth spring up, from which cause divisions and discords arise; and that they may keep the common people in a contented state of mind, when each sees his own means placed on an equality with those of the most powerful.

It is the greatest glory to the several states to have as wide deserts as possible around them, their frontiers having been laid waste. They consider this the real evidence of their prowess, that their neighbours shall be driven out of their lands and abandon them, and that no one dare settle near them; at the same time they think that they shall be on that account the more secure, because they have removed the apprehension of a sudden incursion. When a state either repels war waged against it, or wages it against another, magistrates are chosen to preside over that war with such authority, that they have power of life and death. In peace there is no common magistrate, but the chiefs of provinces and cantons administer justice and determine controversies among their own people. Robberies which are committed beyond the boundaries of each state bear no infamy, and they avow that these are committed for the purpose of disciplining their youth and of preventing sloth. And when any of their chiefs has said in an assembly "that he will be their leader, let those who are willing to follow, give in their names," they who approve of both the enterprise and the man arise and promise their assistance and are applauded by the people; such of them as have not followed him are accounted in the number of deserters and traitors, and confidence in all matters is afterwards refused them. To injure guests they regard as impious; they defend from wrong those who have come to them for any purpose whatever, and esteem them inviolable; to them the houses of all are open and maintenance is freely supplied.

And there was formerly a time when the Gauls excelled the Germans in prowess, and waged war on them offensively, and, on account of the great number of their people and the insufficiency of their land, sent colonies over the Rhine. Accordingly, the Volcae Tectosages seized on those parts of Germany which are the most fruitful and lie around the Hercynian forests (which, I perceive, was known by report to Eratosthenes and some other Greeks, and which they call Orcynia) and settled there. Which nation to this time retains its position in those settlements, and has a very high character for justice and military merit: now also they continue in the same scarcity, indulgence, hardihood, as the Germans, and use the same food and dress; but their proximity to the Province and knowledge of commodities from countries beyond the sea supplies to the Gauls many things tending to luxury as well as civilization. Accustomed by degrees to be overmatched and worsted in many engagements, they do not even compare themselves to the Germans in prowess.

The breadth of this Hercynian forest, which has been referred to above, is to a quick traveller, a journey of nine days. For it cannot be otherwise computed, nor are they acquainted with the measures of roads. It begins at the frontiers of the Helvetii, Nemetes, and Rauraci, and extends in a right line along the river Danube to the territories of the Daci and the Anartes: it bends thence to the left in a different direction from the river, and owing to its extent touches the confines of many nations; nor is there any person belonging to this part of Germany who says that he either has gone to the extremity of that forest, though he had advanced a journey of sixty days, or has heard in what place it begins. It is certain that many kinds of wild beasts are produced in it which have not been seen in other parts; of which the following are such as differ principally from other animals, and appear worthy of being committed to record.

There is an ox of the shape of a stag, between whose ears a horn rises from the middle of the forehead, higher and straighter than those horns which are known to us. From the top of this, branches, like palms, stretch out a considerable distance. The shape of the female and of the male is the same; the appearance and the size of the horns is the same.

There are also animals which are called elks. The shape of these, and the varied colour of their skins, is much like roes, but in size they surpass them a little and are destitute of horns, and have legs without joints and ligatures; nor do they lie down for the purpose of rest, nor, if they have been thrown down by any accident, can they raise or lift themselves up. Trees serve as beds to them; they lean themselves against them, and thus reclining only slightly, they take their rest; when the huntsmen have discovered from the footsteps of these animals whither they are accustomed to betake themselves, they either undermine all the trees at the roots, or cut into them so far that the upper part of the trees may appear to be left standing. When they have leant upon them, according to their habit, they knock down by their weight the unsupported trees, and fall down themselves along with them.

There is a third kind, consisting of those animals which are called uri. These are a little below the elephant in size, and of the appearance, colour, and shape of a bull. Their strength and speed are extraordinary; they spare neither man nor wild beast which they have espied. These the Germans take with much pains in pits and kill them. The young men harden themselves with this exercise, and practice themselves in this kind of hunting, and those who have slain the greatest number of them, having produced the horns in public, to serve as evidence, receive great praise. But not even when taken very young can they be rendered familiar to men and tamed. The size, shape, and appearance of their horns differ much from the horns of our oxen. These they anxiously seek after, and bind at the tips with silver, and use as cups at their most sumptuous entertainments.

TACITUS

GERMANIA

A.D. 98

Germany is separated from the Galli, the Rhaeti, and Pannonii, by the rivers Rhine and Danube; mountain ranges, or the fear which each feels for the other, divide it from the Sarmatae and Daci. Elsewhere ocean girds it, embracing broad peninsulas and islands of unexplored extent, where certain tribes and kingdoms are newly known to us, revealed by war. The Rhine springs from a precipitous and inaccessible height of the Rhaetian Alps, bends slightly westward, and mingles with the Northern Ocean. The Danube pours down from the gradual and gently rising slope of Mount Abnoba, and visits many nations, to force its way at last through six channels into the Pontus; a seventh mouth is lost in marshes.

The Germans themselves I should regard as aboriginal, and not mixed at all with other races through immigration or intercourse. For, in former times, it was not by land but on shipboard that those who sought to emigrate would arrive; and the boundless and, so to speak, hostile ocean beyond us, is seldom entered by a sail from our world. And, beside the perils of rough and unknown seas, who would leave Asia, or Africa, or Italy for Germany, with its wild country, its inclement skies, its sullen manners and aspect, unless indeed it were his home? In their ancient songs, their only way of remembering or recording the past, they celebrate an earth-born god, Tuisco, and his son Mannus, as the origin of their race, as their founders. To Mannus they assign three sons, from whose names, they say, the coast tribes are called Ingaevones; those of the interior, Herminones; all the rest, Istaevones. Some, with the freedom of conjecture permitted by antiquity, assert that the god had several descendants, and the nation several appellations, as Marsi, Gambrivii, Suevi, Vandilii, and that these are genuine old names. The name Germany, on the other hand, they say, is modern and newly introduced, from the fact that the tribes which first crossed the Rhine and drove out the Gauls, and are now called Tungrians, were then called Germans. Thus what was the name of a tribe, and not of a race, gradually prevailed, till all called themselves by this self-invented name of Germans, which the conquerors had first employed to inspire terror.

They say that Hercules, too, once visited them; and when going into battle, they sing of him first of all heroes. They have also those songs of theirs, by the recital of which ("baritus," they call it), they rouse their courage, while from the note they augur the result of the approaching conflict. For, as their line shouts, they inspire or feel alarm. It is not so much an articulate sound, as a general cry of valour. They aim chiefly at a harsh note and a confused roar, putting their shields to their mouth, so that, by reverberation, it may swell into a fuller and deeper sound. Ulysses, too, is believed by some, in his long legendary wanderings, to have found his way into this ocean, and, having visited German soil, to have founded and named the town of Asciburgium, which stands on the bank of the Rhine, and is to this day inhabited. They even say that an altar dedicated to Ulysses, with the addition of the name of his father, Laertes, was formerly discovered on this same spot, and that certain monuments and tombs, with Greek inscriptions, still exist on the borders of Germany and Rhaetia. These statements I have no intention of sustaining by proofs, or of refuting; every one may believe or disbelieve them as he feels inclined.

For my own part, I agree with those who think that the tribes of Germany are free from all taint of intermarriages with foreign nations, and that they appear as a distinct, unmixed race, like none but themselves. Hence, too, the same physical peculiarities throughout so vast a population. All have fierce blue eyes, red hair, huge frames, fit only for a sudden exertion. They are less able to bear laborious work. Heat and thirst they cannot in the least endure; to cold and hunger their climate and their soil inure them.

Their country, though somewhat various in appearance, yet generally either bristles with forests or reeks with swamps; it is more rainy on the side of Gaul, bleaker on that of Noricum and Pannonia. It is productive of grain, but unfavourable to fruit-bearing trees; it is rich in flocks and herds, but these are for the most part undersized, and even the cattle have not their usual beauty or noble head. It is number that is chiefly valued; they are in fact the most highly prized, indeed the only riches of the people. Silver and gold the gods have refused to them, whether in kindness or in anger I cannot say. I would not, however, affirm that no vein of German soil produces gold or silver, for who has ever made a search? They care but little to possess or use them. You may see among them vessels of silver, which have been presented to their envoys and chieftains, held as cheap as those of clay. The border population, however, value gold and silver for their commercial utility, and are familiar with, and show preference for, some of our coins. The tribes of the interior use the simpler and more ancient practice of the barter of commodities. They like the old and well-known money, coins milled, or showing a two-horse chariot. They likewise prefer silver to gold, not from any special liking, but because a large number of silver pieces is more convenient for use among dealers in cheap and common articles.

Even iron is not plentiful with them, as we infer from the character of their weapons. But few use swords or long lances. They carry a spear (*framea* is their name for it), with a narrow and short head, but so sharp and easy to wield that the same weapon serves, according to circumstances, for close or distant conflict. As for the horse-soldier, he is satisfied with a shield and spear; the foot-soldiers also scatter showers of missiles, each man having several and hurling them to an immense distance, and being naked or lightly clad with a little cloak. There is no display about their equipment: their shields alone are marked with very choice colours. A few only have corslets, and just one or two here and there a metal or leathern helmet. Their horses are remarkable neither for beauty nor for fleetness. Nor are they taught various evolutions after our fashion, but are driven straight forward, or so as to make one wheel to the right in such a compact body that none is left behind another. On the whole, one would say that their chief strength is in their infantry, which fights along with the cavalry; admirably adapted to the action of the latter is the swiftness of certain foot-soldiers, who are picked from the entire youth of their country, and stationed in front of the line. Their number is fixed—a hundred from each canton; and from this they take their name among their countrymen, so that what was originally a mere number has now become a title of distinction. Their line of battle is drawn up in a wedge-like formation. To give ground, provided you return to the attack, is considered prudence rather than cowardice. The bodies of their slain they carry off even in indecisive engagements. To abandon your shield is the basest of crimes; nor may a man thus disgraced be present at the sacred rites, or enter their council; many, indeed, after escaping from battle, have ended their infamy with the halter.

They choose their kings by birth, their generals for merit. These kings have not unlimited or arbitrary power, and the generals do more by example than by authority. If they are energetic, if they are conspicuous, if they fight in the front, they lead because they are admired. But to reprimand, to imprison, even to flog, is permitted to the priests alone, and that not as a punishment, or at the general's bidding, but, as it were, by the mandate of the god whom they believe to inspire the warrior. They also carry with them into battle certain figures and images taken from their sacred groves. And what most stimulates their courage is, that their squadrons or battalions, instead of being formed by chance or by a fortuitous gathering, are composed of families and clans. Close by them, too, are those dearest to them, so that they hear the shrieks of women, the cries of infants. They are to every man the most sacred witnesses of his bravery—they are his most generous applauders. The soldier brings his wounds to mother and wife, who shrink not from counting or even demanding them and who administer both food and encouragement to the combatants.

Tradition says that armies already wavering and giving way have been rallied by women who, with earnest entreaties and bosoms laid bare, have vividly represented the horrors of captivity, which the Germans fear with such extreme dread on behalf of their women, that the strongest tie by which a state can be bound is the being required to give, among the number of hostages, maidens of noble birth. They even believe that the sex has a certain sanctity and prescience, and they do not despise their counsels, or make light of their answers. In Vespasian's days we saw Veleda, long regarded by many as a divinity. In former times, too, they venerated Aurinia, and many other women, but not with servile flatteries, or with sham deification.

Mercury is the deity whom they chiefly worship, and on certain days they deem it right to sacrifice to him even with human victims. Hercules and Mars they appease with more lawful offerings. Some of the Suevi also sacrifice to Isis. Of the occasion and origin of this foreign rite I have discovered nothing, but that the image, which is fashioned like a light galley, indicates an imported worship. The Germans, however, do not consider it consistent with the grandeur of celestial beings to confine the gods within walls, or to liken them to the form of any human countenance. They consecrate woods and groves, and they apply the names of deities to the abstraction which they see only in spiritual worship.

Augury and divination by lot no people practice more diligently. The use of the lots is simple. A little bough is lopped off a fruit-bearing tree, and cut into small pieces; these are distinguished by certain marks, and thrown carelessly and at random over a white garment. In public questions the priest of the particular state, in private the father of the family, invokes the gods, and, with his eyes towards heaven, takes up each piece three times, and finds in them a meaning according to the mark previously impressed on them. If they prove unfavourable, there is no further consultation that day about the matter; if they sanction it, the confirmation of augury is still required. For they are also familiar with the practice of consulting the notes and the flight of birds. It is peculiar to this people to seek omens and monitions from horses. Kept at the public expense, in these same woods and groves, are white horses, pure from the taint of earthly labour; these are yoked to a sacred car, and accompanied by the priest and the king, or chief of the tribe, who note their neighings and snortings. No species of augury is more trusted, not only by the people and by the nobility, but also by the priests, who regard themselves as the ministers of the gods, and the horses as acquainted with their will. They have also another method of observing auspices, by which they seek to learn the result of an important war. Having taken, by whatever means, a prisoner from the tribe with whom they are at war, they pit him against a picked man of their own tribe, each combatant using the weapons of their country. The victory of the one or the other is accepted as an indication of the issue.

About minor matters the chiefs deliberate, about the more important the whole tribe. Yet even when the final decision rests with the people, the affair is always thoroughly discussed by the chiefs. They assemble, except in the case of a sudden emergency, on certain fixed days, either at new or at full moon; for this they consider the most auspicious season for the transaction of business. Instead of reckoning by days as we do, they reckon by nights, and in this manner fix both their ordinary and their legal appointments. Night they regard as bringing on day. Their freedom has this disadvantage, that they do not meet simultaneously or as they are bidden, but two or three days are wasted in the delays of assembling. When the multitude think proper, they sit down armed. Silence is proclaimed by the priests, who have on these occasions the right of keeping order. Then the king or the chief, according to age, birth, distinction in war, or eloquence, is heard, more because he has influence to persuade than because he has power to command. If his sentiments displease them, they reject them with murmurs; if they are satisfied, they brandish their spears. The most complimentary form of assent is to express approbation with their weapons.

In their councils an accusation may be preferred or a capital crime prosecuted. Penalties are distinguished according to the offense. Traitors and deserters are hanged on trees; the coward, the unwarlike, the man stained with abominable vices, is plunged into the mire of the morass, with a hurdle put over him. This distinction in punishment means that crime, they think, ought, in being punished, to be exposed, while infamy ought to be buried out of sight. Lighter offenses, too, have penalties proportioned to them; he who is convicted, is fined in a certain number of horses or of cattle. Half of the fine is paid to the king or to the state, half to the person whose wrongs are avenged and to his relatives. In these same councils they also elect the chief magistrates, who administer law in the cantons and the towns. Each of these has a hundred associates chosen from the people, who support him with their advice and influence.

They transact no public or private business without being armed. It is not, however, usual for anyone to wear arms till the state has recognised his power to use them. Then in the presence of the council one of the chiefs, or the young man's father, or some kinsman, equips him with a shield and a spear. These arms are what the "toga" is with us, the first honour with which youth is invested. Up to this time he is regarded as a member of a household, afterwards as a member of the commonwealth. Very noble birth or great services rendered by the father secure for lads the rank of a chief; such lads attach themselves to men of mature strength and of long-approved valour. It is no shame to be seen among a chief's followers. Even in his escort there are gradations of rank, dependent on the choice of the man to whom they are attached. These followers vie keenly with each other as to who shall rank first with his chief, the chiefs as to who shall have the most numerous and the bravest followers. It is an honour as well as a source of strength to be thus always surrounded by a large body of picked youths; it is an ornament in peace and a defence in war. And not only in his own tribe but also in the neighbouring states it is the renown and glory of a chief to be distinguished for the number and valour of his followers, for such a man is courted by embassies, is honoured with presents, and the very prestige of his name often settles a war.

When they go into battle, it is a disgrace for the chief to be surpassed in valour, a disgrace for his followers not to equal the valour of the chief. And it is an infamy and a reproach for life to have survived the chief, and returned from the field. To defend, to protect him, to ascribe one's own brave deeds to his renown, is the height of loyalty. The chief fights for victory; his vassals fight for their chief. If their native state sinks into the sloth of prolonged peace and repose, many of its noble youths voluntarily seek those tribes which are waging some war, both because inaction is odious to their race, and because they win renown more readily in the midst of peril, and cannot maintain a numerous following except by violence and war. Indeed, men look to the liberality of their chief for their war-horse and their bloodstained and victorious lance. Feasts and entertainments, which, though inelegant, are plentifully furnished, are their only pay. The means of this bounty come from war and rapine. Nor are they as easily persuaded to plough the earth and to wait for the year's produce as to challenge an enemy and earn the honour of wounds. Nay, they actually think it tame and stupid to acquire by the sweat of toil what they might win by their blood.

Whenever they are not fighting, they pass much of their time in the chase, and still more in idleness, giving themselves up to sleep and to feasting, the bravest and the most warlike doing nothing, and surrendering the management of the household, of the home, and of the land, to the women, the old men, and all the weakest members of the family. They themselves lie buried in sloth, a strange combination in their nature that the same men should be so fond of idleness, so averse to peace. It is the custom of the state to bestow by voluntary and individual contribution on the chiefs a present of cattle or of grain, which, while accepted as a compliment, supplies their wants. They are particularly delighted by gifts from neighbouring tribes, which are sent not only by individuals but also by the state, such as choice steeds, heavy armour, trappings, and neck-chains. We have now taught them to accept money also.

It is well known that the nations of Germany have no cities, and that they do not even tolerate closely contiguous dwellings. They live scattered and apart, just as a spring, a meadow, or a wood has attracted them. Their villages they do not arrange in our fashion, with the buildings connected and joined together, but every person surrounds his dwelling with an open space, either as a precaution against the disasters of fire, or because they do not know how to build. No use is made by them of stone or tile; they employ timber for all purposes, rude masses without ornament or attractiveness. Some parts of their buildings they stain more carefully with a clay so clear and bright that it resembles painting, or a coloured design. They are wont also to dig out subterranean caves, and pile on them great heaps of dung, as a shelter from winter and as a receptacle for the year's produce, for by such places they mitigate the rigour of the cold. And should an enemy approach, he lays waste the open country, while what is hidden and buried is either not known to exist, or else escapes him from the very fact that it has to be searched for.

They all wrap themselves in a cloak which is fastened with a clasp, or, if this is not forthcoming, with a thorn, leaving the rest of their persons bare. They pass whole days on the hearth by the fire. The wealthiest are distinguished by a dress which is not flowing, like that of the Sarmatae and Parthi, but is tight, and exhibits each limb. They also wear the skins of wild beasts; the tribes on the Rhine and Danube in a careless fashion, those of the interior with more elegance, as not obtaining other clothing by commerce. These select certain animals, the hides of which they strip off and vary them with the spotted skins of beasts, the produce of the outer ocean, and of seas unknown to us. The women have the same dress as the men, except that they generally wrap themselves in linen garments, which they embroider with purple, and do not lengthen out the upper part of their clothing into sleeves. The upper and lower arm is thus bare, and the nearest part of the bosom is also exposed.

Their marriage code, however, is strict, and indeed no part of their manners is more praiseworthy. Almost alone among barbarians they are content with one wife, except a very few among them, and these not from sensuality, but because their noble birth procures for them many offers of alliance. The wife does not bring a dowry to the husband, but the husband to the wife. The parents and relatives are present, and pass judgment on the marriage-gifts, gifts not meant to suit a woman's taste, nor such as a bride would deck herself with, but oxen, a caparisoned steed, a shield, a lance, and a sword. With these presents the wife is espoused, and she herself in her turn brings her husband a gift of arms. This they count their strongest bond of union, these their sacred mysteries, these their gods of marriage. Lest the woman should think herself to stand apart from aspirations after noble deeds and from the perils of war, she is reminded by the ceremony which inaugurates marriage that she is her husband's partner in toil and danger, destined to suffer and to dare with him alike both in peace and in war. The yoked oxen, the harnessed steed, the gift of arms, proclaim this fact. She must live and die with the feeling that she is receiving what she must hand down to her children neither tarnished nor depreciated, what future daughters-in-law may receive, and may be so passed on to her grand-children.

Thus with their virtue protected they live uncorrupted by the allurements of public shows or the stimulant of feastings. Clandestine correspondence is equally unknown to men and women. Very rare for so numerous a population is adultery, the punishment for which is prompt, and in the husband's power. Having cut off the hair of the adulteress and stripped her naked, he expels her from the house in the presence of her kinsfolk, and then flogs her through the whole village. The loss of chastity meets with no indulgence; neither beauty, youth, nor wealth will procure the culprit a husband. No one in Germany laughs at vice, nor do they call it the fashion to corrupt and to be corrupted. Still better is the condition of those states in which only maidens are given in marriage, and where the hopes and expectations of a bride are then finally ter-minated. They receive one husband, as having one body and one life, that they may have no thoughts beyond, no further-reaching desires, that they may love not so much the husband as the married state. To limit the number of their children or to destroy any of their subsequent offspring is accounted infamous, and good habits are here more effectual than good laws elsewhere.

In every household the children, naked and filthy, grow up with those stout frames and limbs which we so much admire. Every mother suckles her own offspring, and never entrusts it to servants and nurses. The master is not distinguished from the slave by being brought up with greater delicacy. Both live amid the same flocks and lie on the same ground till the freeborn are distinguished by age and recognised by merit. The young men marry late, and their vigour is thus unimpaired. Nor are the maidens hurried into marriage; the same age and a similar stature is required; well-matched and vigorous they wed, and the offspring reproduce the strength of the parents. Sister's sons are held in as much esteem by their uncles as by their fathers; indeed, some regard the relation as even more sacred and binding, and prefer it in receiving hostages, thinking thus to secure a stronger hold on the affections and a wider bond for the family. But every man's own children are his heirs and successors, and there are no wills.

Should there be no issue, the next in succession to the property are his brothers and his uncles on either side. The more relatives he has, the more numerous his connections, the more honoured is his old age; nor are there any advantages in childlessness.

It is a duty among them to adopt the feuds as well as the friendships of a father or a kinsman. These feuds are not implacable; even homicide is expiated by the payment of a certain number of cattle and of sheep, and the satisfaction is accepted by the entire family, greatly to the advantage of the state, since feuds are dangerous in proportion to a people's freedom.

No nation indulges more profusely in entertainments and hospitality. To exclude any human being from their roof is thought impious; every German, according to his means, receives his guest with a well-furnished table. When his supplies are exhausted, he who was but now the host becomes the guide and companion to further hospitality, and without invitation they go to the next house. It matters not; they are entertained with like cordiality. No one distinguishes between an acquaintance and a stranger, as regards the rights of hospitality. It is usual to give the departing guest whatever he may ask for, and a present in return is asked with as little hesitation. They are greatly charmed with gifts, but they expect no return for what they give, nor feel any obligation for what they receive.

On waking from sleep, which they generally prolong to a late hour of the day, they take a bath, oftenest of warm water, which suits a country where winter is the longest of the seasons. After their bath they take their meal, each having a separate seat and table of his own. Then they go armed to business, or no less often to their festal meetings. To pass an entire day and night in drinking disgraces no one. Their quarrels, as might be expected with intoxicated people, are seldom fought out with mere abuse, but commonly with wounds and bloodshed. Yet it is at their feasts that they generally consult on the reconciliation of enemies, on the forming of matrimonial alliances, on the choice of chiefs, finally even on peace and war, for they think that at no time is the mind more open to simplicity of purpose or more warmed to noble aspirations. A race without either natural or acquired cunning, they disclose their hidden thoughts in the freedom of the festivity. Thus the sentiments of all having been discovered and laid bare, the discussion is renewed on the following day, and from each occasion its own peculiar advantage is derived. They deliberate when they have no power to dissemble; they resolve when error is impossible.

A liquor for drinking is made out of barley or other grain, and fermented into a certain resemblance to wine. The dwellers on the river-bank also buy wine. Their food is of a simple kind, consisting of wild-fruit, fresh game, and curdled milk. They satisfy their hunger without elaborate preparation and without delicacies. In quenching their thirst they are not equally moderate. If you indulge their love of drinking by supplying them with as much as they desire, they will be overcome by their own vices as easily as by the arms of an enemy.

One and the same kind of spectacle is always exhibited at every gathering. Naked youths who practice the sport bound in the dance amid swords and lances that threaten their lives. Experience gives them skill, and skill again gives grace; profit or pay are out of the question; however reckless their pastime, its reward is the pleasure of the spectators. Strangely enough they make games of hazard a serious occupation even when sober, and so venturesome are they about gaining or losing, that, when every other resource has failed, on the last and final throw they stake the freedom of their own persons. The loser goes into voluntary slavery; though the younger and stronger, he suffers himself to be bound and sold. Such is their stubborn persistency in a bad practice; they themselves call it honour. Slaves of this kind the owners part with in the way of commerce, and also to relieve themselves from the scandal of such a victory.

The other slaves are not employed after our manner with distinct domestic duties assigned to them, but each one has the management of a house and home of his own. The master requires from the slave a certain quantity of grain, of cattle, and of clothing, as he would from a tenant, and this is the limit of subjection. All other household functions are discharged by the wife and children. To strike a slave or to punish him with bonds or with hard labour is a rare occurrence. They often kill them, not in enforcing strict discipline, but on the impulse of passion, as they would an enemy, only it is done with impunity. The freedmen do not rank much above slaves, and are seldom of any weight in the family, never in the state, with the exception of those tribes which are ruled by kings. There indeed they rise above the freeborn and the noble; elsewhere the inferiority of the freedman marks the freedom of the state.

Of lending money on interest and increasing it by compound interest they know nothing—a more effectual safeguard than if it were prohibited.

Land proportioned to the number of inhabitants is occupied by the whole community in turn, and afterwards divided among them according to rank. A wide expanse of plains makes the partition easy. They till fresh fields every year, and they have still more land than enough; with the richness and extent of their soil, they do not laboriously exert themselves in planting orchards, enclosing meadows, and watering gardens. Corn is the only produce required from the earth; hence even the year itself is not divided by them into as many seasons as with us. Winter, spring, and summer have both a meaning and a name; the name and blessings of autumn are alike unknown.

In their funerals there is no pomp; they simply observe the custom of burning the bodies of illustrious men with certain kinds of wood. They do not heap garments or spices on the funeral pile. The arms of the dead man and in some cases his horse are consigned to the fire. A turf mound forms the tomb. Monuments with their lofty elaborate splendour they reject as oppressive to the dead. Tears and lamentations they soon dismiss; grief and sorrow but slowly. It is thought becoming for women to bewail, for men to remember, the dead.

Such on the whole is the account which I have received of the origin and manners of the entire German people. I will now touch on the institutions and religious rites of the separate tribes, pointing out how far they differ, and also what nations have migrated from Germany into Gaul.

That highest authority, the great Julius [Caesar], informs us that Gaul was once more powerful than Germany. Consequently we may believe that Gauls even crossed over into Germany. For what a trifling obstacle would a river be to the various tribes, as they grew in strength and wished to possess in exchange settlements which were still open to all, and not partitioned among powerful monarchies! Accordingly the country between the Hercynian forest and the rivers Rhine and Moenus, and that which lies beyond, was occupied respectively by the Helvetii and Boii, both tribes of Gaul. The name Boiemum still survives, marking the old tradition of the place, though the population has been changed. Whether however the Aravisci migrated into Pannonia from the Osi, a German race, or whether the Osi came from the Aravisci into Germany, as both nations still retain the same language, institutions, and customs, is a doubtful matter; for as they were once equally poor and equally free, either bank had the same attractions, the same drawbacks. The Treveri and Nervii are even eager in their claims of a German origin, thinking that the glory of this descent distinguishes them from the uniform level of Gallic effeminacy. The Rhine bank itself is occupied by tribes unquestionably German—the Vangiones, the Triboci, and the Nemetes. Nor do even the Ubii, though they have earned the distinction of being a Roman colony, and prefer to be called Agrippinenses, from the name of their founder, blush to own their origin. Having crossed the sea in former days, and given proof of their allegiance, they were settled on the Rhine-bank itself, as those who might guard it but need not be watched.

Foremost among all these nations in valour, the Batavi occupy an island within the Rhine and but a small portion of the bank. Formerly a tribe of the Chatti, they were forced by internal dissension to migrate to their present settlements and there become a part of the Roman Empire. They yet retain the honourable badge of an ancient alliance; for they are not insulted by tribute, nor ground down by the tax-gatherer. Free from the usual burdens and contributions, and set apart for fighting purposes, like a magazine of arms, we reserve them for our wars. The subjection of the Mattiaci is of the same character. For the greatness of the Roman people has spread reverence for our empire beyond the Rhine and the old boundaries. Thus this nation, whose settlements and territories are on their own side of the river, are yet in sentiment and purpose one with us; in all other respects they resemble the Batavi, except that they still gain from the soil and climate of their native land a keener vigour. I should not reckon among the German tribes the cultivators of the tithe-lands, although they are settled on the further side of the Rhine and Danube. Reckless adventurers from Gaul, emboldened by want, occupied this land of questionable ownership. After a while, our frontier having been advanced, and our military positions pushed forward, it was regarded as a remote nook of our empire and a part of a Roman province.

Beyond them are the Chatti, whose settlements begin at the Hercynian forest, where the country is not so open and marshy as in the other cantons into which Germany stretches. They are found where there are hills, and with them grow less frequent, for the Hercynian forest keeps close till it has seen the last of its native Chatti. Hardy frames, close-knit limbs, fierce countenances, and a peculiarly vigorous courage, mark the tribe. For Germans, they have much intelligence and sagacity; they promote their picked men to power, and obey those whom they promote; they keep their ranks, note their opportunities, check their impulses, portion out the day, intrench themselves by night, regard fortune as a doubtful, valour as an unfailing, resource; and what is most unusual, and only given to systematic discipline, they rely more on the general than on the army. Their whole strength is in their infantry, which, in addition to its arms, is laden with iron tools and provisions. Other tribes you see going to battle, the Chatti to a campaign. Seldom do they engage in mere raids and casual encounters. It is indeed the peculiarity of a cavalry force quickly to win and as quickly to yield a victory. Fleetness and timidity go together; deliberateness is more akin to steady courage.

A practice, rare among the other German tribes, and simply characteristic of individual prowess, has become general among the Chatti, of letting the hair and beard grow as soon as they have attained manhood, and not till they have slain a foe laying aside that peculiar aspect which devotes and pledges them to valour. Over the spoiled and bleeding enemy they show their faces once more; then, and not till then, proclaiming that they have discharged the obligations of their birth, and proved themselves worthy of their country and of their parents. The coward and the unwarlike remain unshorn. The bravest of them also wear an iron ring (which otherwise is a mark of disgrace among the people) until they have released themselves by the slaughter of a foe. Most of the Chatti delight in these fashions. Even hoary-headed men are distinguished by them, and are thus conspicuous alike to enemies and to fellow-countrymen. To begin the battle always rests with them, they form the first line, an unusual spectacle. Nor even in peace do they assume a more civilised aspect. They have no home or land or occupation; they are supported by whomsoever they visit, as lavish of the property of others as they are regardless of their own, till at length the feebleness of age makes them unequal to so stern a valour.

Next to the Chatti on the Rhine, which has now a well-defined channel, and serves as a boundary, dwell the Usipii and Tencteri. The latter, besides the more usual military distinctions, particularly excel in the organization of cavalry, and the Chatti are not more famous for their foot-soldiers than are the Tencteri for their horsemen. What their forefathers originated, posterity maintains. This supplies sport to their children, rivalry to their youths: even the aged keep it up. Horses are bequeathed along with the slaves, the dwelling-house, and the usual rights of inheritance; they go to the son, not to the eldest, as does the other property, but to the most warlike and courageous.

After the Tencteri came, in former days, the Bructeri; but the general account now is, that the Chamavi and Angrivarii entered their settlements, drove them out and utterly exterminated them with the common help of the neighbouring tribes either from hatred of their tyranny, or from the attractions of plunder, or from heaven's favourable regard for us. It did not even grudge us the spectacle of the conflict. More than sixty thousand fell, not beneath the Roman arms and weapons, but, grander far, before our delighted eyes. May the tribes, I pray, ever retain if not love for us, at least hatred for each other: for while the destinies of empire hurry us on, fortune can give no greater boon than discord among our foes.

The Angrivarii and Chamavi are bounded in the rear by the Dulgubini and Chasuarii, and other tribes not equally famous. Towards the river are the Frisii, distinguished as the Greater and Lesser Frisii, according to their strength. Both these tribes, as far as the ocean, are skirted by the Rhine, and their territory also embraces vast lakes which Roman fleets have navigated. We have even ventured on the ocean itself in these parts. Pillars of Hercules, so rumour commonly says, still exist; whether Hercules really visited the country, or whether we have agreed to ascribe every work of grandeur, wherever met with, to his renown. Drusus Germanicus indeed did not lack daring; but the ocean barred the explorer's access to itself and to Hercules. Subsequently no one has made the attempt, and it has been thought more pious and reverential to believe in the actions of the gods than to inquire.

Thus far we have taken note of Western Germany. Northwards the country takes a vast sweep. First comes the tribe of the Chauci, which, beginning at the Frisian settlements, and occupying a part of the coast, stretches along the frontier of all the tribes which I have enumerated, till it reaches with a bend as far as the Chatti. This vast extent of country is not merely possessed, but densely peopled, by the Chauci, the noblest of the German races, a nation who would maintain their greatness by righteous dealing. Without ambition, without lawless violence, they live peaceful and secluded, never provoking a war or injuring others by rapine and robbery. Indeed, the crowning proof of their valour and their strength is that they keep up their superiority without harm to others. Yet all have their weapons in readiness, and an army if necessary, with a multitude of men and horses; and even while at peace they have the same renown of valour.

Dwelling on one side of the Chauci and Chatti, the Cherusci long cherished, unassailed, an excessive and enervating love of peace. This was more pleasant than safe, for to be peaceful is self-deception among lawless and powerful neighbours. Where the strong hand decides, moderation and justice are terms applied only to the more powerful; and so the Cherusci, ever reputed good and just, are now called cowards and fools, while in the case of the victorious Chatti success has been identified with prudence. The downfall of the Cherusci brought with it also that of the Fosi, a neighbouring tribe, which shared equally in their disasters, though they had been inferior to them in prosperous days.

In the same remote corner of Germany, bordering on the ocean, dwell the Cimbri, a now insignificant tribe, but of great renown. Of their ancient glory widespread traces yet remain; on both sides of the Rhine are encampments of vast extent, and by their circuit you may even now measure the warlike strength of the tribe, and find evidence of that mighty emigration. Rome was in her 640th year when we first heard of the Cimbrian invader in the consulship of Caecilius Metellus and Papirius Carbo, from which time to the second consulship of the Emperor Trajan we have to reckon about 210 years. So long have we been in conquering Germany. In the space of this long epoch many losses have been sustained on both sides. Neither Samnite nor Carthaginian, neither Spain nor Gaul, not even the Parthians, have given us more frequent warnings. German independence truly is fiercer than the despotism of an Arsaces. What else, indeed, can the East taunt us with but the slaughter of Crassus, when it has itself lost Pacorus, and been crushed under a Ventidius? But Germans, by routing or making prisoners of Carbo, Cassius, Scaurus Aurelius, Servilius Caepio, and Marcus Manlius, deprived the Roman people of five consular armies, and they robbed even a Caesar of Varus and his three legions. Not without loss to us were they discomfited by Marius in Italy, by the great Julius in Gaul, and by Drusus, Nero, and Germanicus, on their own ground. Soon after, the mighty menaces of Caius Caesar were turned into a jest. Then came a lull, until on the occasion of our discords and the civil war, they stormed the winter camp of our legions, and even designed the conquest of Gaul. Again were they driven back; and in recent times we have celebrated triumphs rather than won conquests over them.

I must now speak of the Suevi, who are not one nation as are the Chatti and Tencteri, for they occupy the greater part of Germany, and have hitherto been divided into separate tribes with names of their own, though they are called by the general designation of "Suevi." A national peculiarity with them is to twist their hair back, and fasten it in a knot. This distinguishes the Suevi from the other Germans, as it also does their own freeborn from their slaves. With other tribes, either from some connection with the Suevic race, or, as often happens, from imitation, the practice is an occasional one, and restricted to youth. The Suevi, till their heads are grey, affect the fashion of drawing back their unkempt locks, and often they are knotted on the very top of the head. The chiefs have a more elaborate style; so much do they study appearance, but in perfect innocence, not with any thoughts of love-making; but arranging their hair when they go to battle, to make themselves tall and terrible, they adorn themselves, so to speak, for the eyes of the foe.

The Semnones give themselves out to be the most ancient and renowned branch of the Suevi. Their antiquity is strongly attested by their religion. At a stated period, all the tribes of the same race assemble by their representatives in a grove consecrated by the auguries of their forefathers, and by immemorial associations of terror. Here, having publicly slaughtered a human victim, they celebrate the horrible beginning of their barbarous rite. Reverence also in other ways is paid to the grove. No one enters it except bound with a chain, as an inferior acknowledging the might of the local divinity. If he chance to fall, it is not lawful for him to be lifted up, or to rise to his feet; he must crawl out along the ground. All this superstition implies the belief that from this spot the nation took its origin, that here dwells the supreme and all-ruling deity, to whom all else is subject and obedient. The fortunate lot of the Semnones strengthens this belief; a hundred cantons are in their occupation, and the vastness of their community makes them regard themselves as the head of the Suevi race.

To the Langobardi, on the contrary, their scanty numbers are a distinction. Though surrounded by a host of most powerful tribes, they are safe, not by submitting, but by daring the perils of war. Next come the Reudigni, the Aviones, the Anglii, the Varini, the Eudoses, the Suardones, and Nuithones who are fenced in by rivers or forests. None of these tribes have any noteworthy feature, except their common worship of Ertha, or mother-Earth, and their belief that she interposes in human affairs, and visits the nations in her car [chariot]. In an island of the ocean there is a sacred grove, and within it a consecrated chariot, covered over with a garment. Only one priest is permitted to touch it. He can perceive the presence of the goddess in this sacred recess, and walks by her side with the utmost reverence as she is drawn along by heifers. It is a season of rejoicing, and festivity reigns wherever she deigns to go and be received. They do not go to battle or wear arms; every weapon is under lock; peace and quiet are known and welcomed only at these times, till the goddess, weary of human intercourse, is at length restored by the same priest to her temple. Afterwards the car, the vestments, and, if you like to believe it, the divinity herself, are purified in a secret lake. Slaves perform the rite, who are instantly swallowed up by its waters. Hence arises a mysterious terror and a pious ignorance concerning the nature of that which is seen only by men doomed to die. This branch of the Suevi stretches into the remoter regions of Germany.

Nearer to us is the state of the Hermunduri (I shall follow the course of the Danube as I did before that of the Rhine), a people loyal to Rome. Consequently they, alone of the Germans, trade not merely on the banks of the river, but far inland, and in the most flourishing colony of the province of Raetia. Everywhere they are allowed to pass without a guard; and while to the other tribes we display only our arms and our camps, to them we have thrown open our houses and country-seats, which they do not covet. It is in their lands that the Elbe takes its rise, a famous river known to us in past days; now we only hear of it. The Narisci border on the Hermunduri, and then follow the Marcomanni and Quadi. The Marcomanni stand first in strength and renown, and their very territory, from which the Boii were driven in a former age, was won by valour. Nor are the Narisci and Quadi inferior to them. This I may call the frontier of Germany, so far as it is completed by the Danube. The Marcomanni and Quadi have, up to our time, been ruled by kings of their own nation, descended from the noble stock of Maroboduus and Tudrus. They now submit even to foreigners; but the strength and power of the monarch depend on Roman influence. He is occasionally supported by our arms, more frequently by our money, and his authority is none the less.

Behind them the Marsigni, Gotini, Osi, and Buri, close in the rear of the Marcomanni and Quadi. Of these, the Marsigni and Buri, in their language and manner of life, resemble the Suevi. The Gotini and Osi are proved by their respective Gallic and Pannonian tongues, as well as by the fact of their enduring tribute, not to be Germans. Tribute is imposed on them as aliens, partly by the Sarmatae, partly by the Quadi. The Gotini, to complete their degradation, actually work iron mines. All these nations occupy but little of the plain country, dwelling in forests and on mountain-tops. For Suevia is divided and cut in half by a continuous mountain-range, beyond which live a multitude of tribes. The name of Ligii, spread as it is among many states, is the most widely extended. It will be enough to mention the most powerful, which are the Harii, the Helvecones, the Manimi, the Helisii, and the Nahanarvali. Among these last is shown a grove of immemorial sanctity. A priest in female attire has the charge of it. But the deities are described in Roman language as Castor and Pollux. Such, indeed, are the attributes of the divinity, the name being Alcis. They have no images, or, indeed, any vestige of foreign superstition, but it is as brothers and as youths that the deities are worshipped. The Harii, besides being superior in strength to the tribes just enumerated, savage as they are, make the most of their natural ferocity by the help of art and opportunity. Their shields are black, their bodies dyed. They choose dark nights for battle, and, by the dread and gloomy aspect of their death-like host, strike terror into the foe, who can never confront their strange and almost infernal appearance. For in all battles it is the eye which is first vanquished.

Beyond the Ligii are the Gothones, who are ruled by kings, a little more strictly than the other German tribes, but not as yet inconsistently with freedom. Immediately adjoining them, further from the coast, are the Rugii and Lemovii, the badge of all these tribes being the round shield, the short sword, and servile submission to their kings.

And now begin the states of the Suiones, situated on the Ocean itself, and these, besides men and arms, are powerful in ships. The form of their vessels is peculiar in this respect, that a prow at either extremity acts as a forepart, always ready for running into shore. They are not worked by sails, nor have they a row of oars attached to their sides; but, as on some rivers, the apparatus of rowing is unfixed, and shifted from side to side as circumstances require. And they likewise honour wealth, and so a single ruler holds sway with no restrictions, and with no uncertain claim to obedience. Arms are not with them, as with the other Germans, at the general disposal, but are in the charge of a keeper, who is actually a slave; for the ocean forbids the sudden inroad of enemies, and, besides, an idle multitude of armed men is easily demoralized. And indeed it is by no means the policy of a monarch to place either a nobleman, a freeborn citizen, or even a freedman, at the head of an armed force.

Beyond the Suiones is another sea, sluggish and almost motionless, which, we may certainly infer, girdles and surrounds the world, from the fact that the last radiance of the setting sun lingers on till sunrise, with a brightness sufficient to dim the light of the stars. Even the very sound of his rising, as popular belief adds, may be heard, and the forms of gods and the glory round his head may be seen. Only thus far (and here rumour seems truth) does the world extend.

At this point the Suevic sea, on its eastern shore, washes the tribes of the Aestii, whose rites and fashions and style of dress are those of the Suevi, while their language is more like the British. They worship the mother of the gods, and wear as a religious symbol the device of a wild boar. This serves as armour and as a universal defence, rendering the votary of the goddess safe even amidst enemies. They often use clubs, iron weapons but seldom. They are more patient in cultivating corn and other produce than might be expected from the general indolence of the Germans. But they also search the deep, and are the only people who gather amber (which they call *glesum*), in the shallows, and also on the shore itself. Barbarians as they are they have not investigated or discovered what natural cause or process produces it. Nay, it even lay amid the sea's other refuse, till our luxury gave it a name. To them it is utterly useless; they gather it in its raw state, bring it to us in shapeless lumps, and marvel at the price which they receive. It is however a juice from trees, as you may infer from the fact that there are often seen shining through it, reptiles, and even winged insects, which, having become entangled in the fluid, are gradually enclosed in the substance as it hardens. I am therefore inclined to think that the islands and countries of the West, like the remote recesses of the East, where frankincense and balsam exude, contain fruitful woods and groves; that these productions, acted on by the near rays of the sun, glide in a liquid state into the adjacent sea, and are thrown up by the force of storms on the opposite shores. If you test the composition of amber by applying fire, it burns like pinewood, and sends forth a rich and fragrant flame; it is soon softened into something like pitch or resin.

Closely bordering on the Suiones are the tribes of the Sitones, which, resembling them in all else, differ only in being ruled by a woman. So low have they fallen, not merely from freedom, but even from slavery itself. Here Suevia ends.

As to the tribes of the Peucini, Veneti, and Fenni, I am in doubt whether I should class them with the Germans or the Sarmatae, although indeed the

Peucini, called by some Bastarnae, are like Germans in their language, mode of life, and in the permanence of their settlements. They all live in filth and sloth, and by the intermarriages of the chiefs they are becoming in some degree debased into a resemblance to the Sarmatae. The Veneti have borrowed largely from the Sarmatian character; in their plundering expeditions they roam over the whole extent of forest and mountain between the Peucini and Fenni. They are however to be rather referred to as the German race, for they have fixed habitations, carry shields, and delight in strength and fleetness of foot, thus presenting a complete contrast to the Sarmatae, who live in waggons and on horseback. The Fenni are strangely beast-like and squalidly poor; neither arms nor homes have they; their food is herbs, their clothing skins, their bed the earth. They trust wholly to their arrows, which, for want of iron, are pointed with bone. The men and the women are alike supplied by the chase; for the latter are always present, and demand a share of the prey. The little children have no shelter from wild beasts and storms but a covering of interlaced boughs. Such are the homes of the young, such the resting place of the old. Yet they count this greater happiness than groaning over field-labour, toiling at building, and poising the fortunes of themselves and others between hope and fear. Heedless of men, heedless of gods, they have attained that hardest of results, the not needing so much as a wish. All else is fabulous, as that the Hellusii and Oxiones have the faces and expressions of men, with the bodies and limbs of wild beasts. All this is unauthenticated, and I shall leave it open.

—VI—

BRITAIN

Julius Caesar invaded Britain for the first time in 55 B.C. Suetonius says he did it because he had heard the island abounded in pearls there for the taking. The Roman historian Dio Cassius later wrote that the adventure was to the advantage neither of the general nor of Rome. Still, Caesar's description of the ancient Britons in *The Gallic War* has been called the first accredited account of the islanders.

Following Caesar in this chapter is his contemporary Diodorus Siculus's brief comments on the Britons, whose use of chariots in battle, he feels, is very much like the Greeks during the Trojan War. He is also interested in mineral wealth, but he is concerned with tin rather than pearls.

Then, after a jump of about a hundred and fifty years, the chapter concludes with a long passage from Tacitus's *Agricola,* the biography of his father-in-law, the great Roman general who pushed the native Britons back to the northern and western portions of their island. This brings the story of the conquest of Britain to its high-water mark: a confrontation—sometime around A.D. 80—between Romans and Celtic Caledonians in southern Scotland. The battle itself is a fine war story, but more interesting are the speeches Tacitus created for the opposing generals beforehand. Agricola's sounds like something he might have used before. Galgacus, the Caledonian chief, gives a rousing speech that brings up an issue that must have troubled many Romans: the Roman army, Galgacus points out, was made up of more barbarian mercenaries than Roman citizens, and he predicts that once the battle begins, the barbarians will turn against their masters. He proved to be wrong, but the threat was real and would continue for centuries.

Tacitus wrote that Caesar did not conquer Britain, he simply pointed the way. The true conqueror was Agricola, who built forts in Scotland, invaded Wales, and even circumnavigated the island.

Julius Caesar

"The First Invasion of Britain"

55 B.C.

During the short part of summer which remained, Caesar, although in these countries, as all Gaul lies towards the north, the winters are early, nevertheless resolved to proceed into Britain, because he discovered that in almost all the wars with the Gauls succours had been furnished to our enemy from that country; and even if the time of year should be insufficient for carrying on the war, yet he thought it would be of great service to him if he only entered the island, and saw into the character of the people, and got knowledge of their localities, harbours, and landing-places, all which were for the most part unknown to the Gauls. For neither does any one except merchants generally go thither, nor even to them was any portion of it known, except the sea-coast and those parts which are opposite to Gaul. Therefore, after having called up to him the merchants from all parts, he could learn neither what was the size of the island, nor what or how numerous were the nations which inhabited it, nor what system of war they followed, nor what customs they used, nor what harbours were convenient for a great number of large ships.

He sent before him Caius Volusenus with a ship of war, to acquire a knowledge of these particulars before he in person should make a descent into the island, as he was convinced that this was a judicious measure. He commissioned him to thoroughly examine into all matters, and then return to him as soon as possible. He himself proceeded to the Morini [in what is now Belgium] with all his forces. He ordered ships from all parts of the neighbouring countries, and the fleet which the preceding summer he had built for the war with the Veneti, to assemble in this place. In the meantime, his purpose having been discovered, and reported to the Britons by merchants, ambassadors came to him from several states of the island, to promise that they would give hostages, and submit to the government of the Roman people. Having given them an audience, he, after promising liberally, and exhorting them to continue in that purpose, sent them back to their own country, and despatched with them Commius, whom, upon subduing the Atrebates, he had created king there, a man whose courage and conduct he esteemed, and who he thought would be faithful to him, and whose influence ranked highly in those countries. He ordered him to visit as many states as he could, and persuade them to embrace the protection of the Roman people, and apprise them that he would shortly come thither. Volusenus, having viewed the localities as far as means could be afforded one who dared not leave his ship and trust himself to barbarians, returned to Caesar on the fifth day, and reported what he had there observed.

While Caesar remained in these parts for the purpose of procuring ships, ambassadors came to him from a great portion of the Morini, to plead their excuse respecting their conduct on the late occasion; alleging that it was as men uncivilized, and as those who were unacquainted with our custom, that they had made war upon the Roman people, and promising to perform what he should command. Caesar, thinking that this had happened fortunately enough for him, because he neither wished to leave an enemy behind him, nor had an opportunity for carrying on a war, by reason of the time of year, nor considered that employment in such trifling matters was to be preferred to his enterprise on Britain, imposed a large number of hostages; and when these were brought, he received them to his protection. Having collected together, and provided about eighty transport ships, as many as he thought necessary for conveying over two legions, he assigned such ships of war as he had besides to the quaestor, his lieutenants, and officers of cavalry. There were in addition to these eighteen ships of burden which were prevented, eight miles from that place, by winds, from being able to reach the same port. These he distributed amongst the cavalry; the rest of the army he delivered to Q. Titurius Sabinus and L. Aurunculeius Cotta, his lieutenants, to lead into the territories of the Menapli and those cantons of the Morini from which ambassadors had not come to him. He ordered P. Sulpicius Rufus, his lieutenant, to hold possession of the harbour, with such a garrison as he thought sufficient.

These matters being arranged, finding the weather favourable for his voyage, he set sail about the third watch, and ordered the horse to march forward to the farther port, and there embark and follow him. As this was performed rather tardily by them, he himself reached Britain with the first squadron of ships, about the fourth hour of the day, and there saw the forces of the enemy drawn up in arms on all the hills. The nature of the place was this: the sea was confined by mountains so close to it that a dart could be thrown from their summit upon the shore. Considering this by no means a fit place for disembarking, he remained at anchor till the ninth hour, for the other ships to arrive there. Having in the meantime assembled the lieutenants and military tribunes, he told them both what he had learnt from Volusenus, and what he wished to be done; and enjoined them (as the principle of military matters, and especially as maritime affairs, which have a precipitate and uncertain action, required) that all things should be performed by them at a nod and at the instant. Having dismissed them, meeting both with wind and tide favourable at the same time, the signal being given and the anchor weighed, he advanced about seven miles from that place, and stationed his fleet over against an open and level shore [near Deal in what is now Kent]. But the barbarians, upon perceiving the design of Romans, sent forward their cavalry and charioteers, a class of warriors of whom it is their practice to make great use in their battles, and following with the rest of their forces, endeavoured to prevent our men landing. In this was the greatest difficulty, for the following reasons, namely, because our ships, on account of their great size, could be stationed only in deep water; and our soldiers, in places unknown to them, with their hands embarrassed, oppressed with a large and heavy weight of armour, had at the same time to leap from the ships, stand amidst the waves, and encounter the enemy; whereas they, either on dry ground, or advancing a little way into the water, free in all their limbs, in places thoroughly known to them, could confidently throw their weapons and spur on their horses, which were accustomed to this kind of service. Dismayed by these circumstances and altogether untrained in this mode of battle, our men did not all exert the same vigour and eagerness which they had been wont to exert in engagements on dry ground.

When Caesar observed this, he ordered the ships of war, the appearance of which was somewhat strange to the barbarians and the motion more ready for service, to be withdrawn a little from the transport vessels, and to be propelled by their oars, and be stationed towards the open flank of the enemy, and the enemy to be beaten off and driven away, with slings, arrows, and engines: which plan was of great service to our men; for the barbarians being startled by the form of our ships and the motions of our oars and the nature of our engines, which was strange to them, stopped, and shortly after retreated a little. And while our men were hesitating whether they should advance to the shore, chiefly on account of the depth of the sea, he who carried the eagle of the tenth legion, after supplicating the gods that the matter might turn out favourably to the legion, exclaimed, "Leap, fellow soldiers, unless you wish to betray your eagle to the enemy. I, for my part, will perform my duty to the commonwealth and my general." When he had said this with a loud voice, he leaped from the ship and proceeded to bear the eagle toward the enemy. Then our men, exhorting one another that so great a disgrace should not be incurred, all leaped from the ship. When those in the nearest vessels saw them, they speedily followed and approached the enemy.

The battle was maintained vigorously on both sides. Our men, however, as they could neither keep their ranks, nor get firm footing, nor follow their standards, and as one from one ship and another from another assembled around whatever standards they met, were thrown into great confusion. But the enemy, who were acquainted with all the shallows, when from the shore they saw any coming from a ship one by one spurred on their horses, and attacked them while embarrassed, many surrounded a few, others threw their weapons upon our collected forces on their exposed flank. When Caesar observed this, he ordered the boats of the ships of war and the spy sloops to be filled with soldiers, and sent them up to the succour of those whom he had observed in distress. Our men, as soon as they made good their footing on dry ground, and all their comrades had joined them, made an attack upon the enemy, and put them to flight, but could not pursue them very far, because the horse had not been able to maintain their course at sea and reach the island. This alone was wanting to Caesar's accustomed success.

The enemy being thus vanquished in battle, as soon as they recovered after their flight, instantly sent ambassadors to Caesar to negotiate about peace. They promised to give hostages and perform what he should command. Together with these ambassadors came Commius the Atrebatian, who, as I have above said, had been sent by Caesar into Britain. Him they had seized upon when leaving his ship, although in the character of ambassador he bore the general's commission to them, and thrown into chains: then after the battle was fought, they sent him back, and in suing for peace cast the blame of that act upon the common people, and entreated that it might be pardoned on account of their indiscretion. Caesar, complaining, that after they had sued for peace, and had voluntarily sent ambassadors into the continent for that purpose, they had made war without a reason, said that he would pardon their indiscretion, and imposed hostages, a part of whom they gave immediately; the rest they said they would give in a few days, since they were sent for from remote places. In the meantime they ordered their people to return to the country parts, and the chiefs assembled from all quarters, and proceeded to surrender themselves and their states to Caesar.

A peace being established by these proceedings four days after we had come into Britain, the eighteen ships, to which reference has been made above, and which conveyed the cavalry, set sail from the upper port with a gentle gale, when, however, they were approaching Britain and were seen from the camp, so great a storm suddenly arose that none of them could maintain their course at sea; and some were taken back to the same port from which they had started—others, to their great danger, were driven to the lower part of the island, nearer to the west; which, however, after having cast anchor, as they were getting filled with water, put out to sea through necessity in a stormy night, and made for the continent.

It happened that night to be full moon, which usually occasions very high tides in that ocean; and that circumstance was unknown to our men. Thus, at the same time, the tide began to fill the ships of war which Caesar had provided to convey over his army, and which he had drawn up on the strand; and the storm began to dash the ships of burden which were riding at anchor against each other; nor was any means afforded our men of either managing them or of rendering any service. A great many ships having been wrecked, inasmuch as the rest, having lost their cables, anchors, and other tackling, were unfit for sailing, a great confusion, as would necessarily happen, arose throughout the army; for there were no other ships in which they could be conveyed back, and all things which are of service in repairing vessels were wanting, and corn for the winter had not been provided in those places, because it was understood by all that they would certainly winter in Gaul.

On discovering these things the chiefs of Britain, who had come up after the battle was fought to perform those conditions which Caesar had imposed, held a conference, when they perceived that cavalry, and ships, and corn were wanting to the Romans, and discovered the small number of our soldiers from the small extent of the camp (which, too, was on this account more limited than ordinary, because Caesar had conveyed over his legions without baggage), and thought that the best plan was to renew the war, and cut off our men from corn and provisions and protract the affair till winter; because they felt confident, that, if they were vanquished or cut off from a return, no one would afterwards pass over into Britain for the purpose of making war. Therefore, again entering into a conspiracy, they began to depart from the camp by degrees and secretly bring up their people from the country parts.

But Caesar, although he had not as yet discovered their measures, yet, both from what had occurred to his ships, and from the circumstance that they had neglected to give the promised hostages, suspected that the thing would come to pass which really did happen. He therefore provided remedies against all contingencies; for he daily conveyed corn from the country parts into the camp, used the timber and brass of such ships as were most seriously damaged for repairing the rest, and ordered whatever things besides were necessary for this object to be brought to him from the continent. And thus, since that business was executed by the soldiers with the greatest energy, he affected that, after the loss of twelve ships, a voyage could be made well enough in the rest.

While these things were being transacted one legion had been sent to forage, according to custom, and no suspicion of war had arisen as yet, and some of the people remained in the country parts, others went backwards and forwards to the camp; they who were on duty at the gates of the camp reported to Caesar that a greater dust than was usual was seen in that direction in which the legion had marched. Caesar, suspecting that which was really the case, that some new enterprise was undertaken by the barbarians, ordered the two cohorts which were on duty, to march into that quarter with him, and two other cohorts to relieve them on duty; the rest to be armed and follow him immediately. When he had advanced some little way from the camp, he saw that his men were overpowered by the enemy and scarcely able to stand their ground, and that, the legion being crowded together, weapons were being cast on them from all sides. For as all the corn was reaped in every part with the exception of one, the enemy, suspecting that our men would repair to that, had concealed themselves in the woods during the night. Then when our men had laid aside their arms, and were engaged in reaping, the enemy, attacking them suddenly, scattered as they were, killed a small number, threw the rest into confusion, and surrounded them with their cavalry and chariots.

Their mode of fighting with their chariots is this: firstly, they drive about in all directions and throw their weapons and generally break the ranks of the enemy with the very dread of their horses and the noise of their wheels; and when they have worked themselves in between the troops of horse, leap from their chariots and engage on foot. The charioteers in the meantime withdraw some little distance from the battle, and so place themselves with the chariots that, if their masters are overpowered by the number of the enemy, they may have a ready retreat to their own troops. Thus they display in battle the speed of horse, together with the firmness of infantry; and by daily practice and exercise attain to such expertness that they are accustomed, even on a declining and steep place, to check their horses at full speed, and manage and turn them in an instant and run along the pole, and stand on the yoke, and thence betake themselves with the greatest celerity to their chariots again.

Under these circumstances, our men being dismayed by the novelty of this mode of battle, Caesar most seasonably brought assistance; for upon his arrival the enemy paused, and our men recovered from their fear; upon which, thinking the time unfavourable for provoking the enemy and coming to an action, he kept himself in his own quarter, and, a short time having intervened, drew back the legions into the camp. While these things were going on, and all our men engaged, the rest of the Britons, who were in the fields, departed. Storms then set in for several successive days, which both confined our men to camp and hindered the enemy from attacking us. In the meantime the barbarians dispatched messengers to all parts, and reported to their people the small number of our soldiers, and how good an opportunity was given for obtaining spoil and for liberating themselves for ever, if they should only drive the Romans from their camp. Having by these means speedily got together a large force of infantry and of cavalry they came up to the camp.

Although Caesar anticipated that the same thing which had happened on former occasions would then occur—that if the enemy were routed, they would escape from danger by their speed; still, having got about thirty horses, which Commius the Atrebatian, of whom mention has been made, had brought over with him from Gaul, he drew up the legions in order of battle before the camp. When the action commenced, the enemy were unable to sustain the attack of our men long, and turned their backs; our men pursued them as far as their speed and strength permitted, and slew a great number of them; then, having destroyed and burnt everything far and wide, they retreated to their camp.

The same day, ambassadors sent by the enemy came to Caesar to negotiate peace. Caesar doubled the number of hostages which he had before demanded; and ordered that they should be brought over to the continent, because, since the time of the equinox was near, he did not consider that, with his ships out of repair, the voyage ought to be deferred till winter. Having met with favourable weather, he set sail a little after midnight, and all his fleet arrived safe at the continent, except two of the ships of burden which could not make the same port which the other ships did, and were carried a little lower down.

DIODORUS SICULUS

"THE PEOPLE AND CUSTOMS OF BRITAIN"

ca. 50 B.C.

I n ancient times this island remained unvisited by foreign armies; for neither Dionysus, tradition tells us, nor Heracles, nor any other hero or leader
made a campaign against it; in our day, however, Gaius Caesar, who has
been called a god because of his deeds, was the first man of whom we have
record to have conquered the island, and after subduing the Britains he compelled them to pay fixed tributes. But we shall give a detailed account of the
events of this conquest in connection with the appropriate period of time, and
at present we shall discuss the island and the tin which is found in it.

Britain is triangular in shape, very much as is Sicily, but its sides are not
equal. This island stretches obliquely along the coast of Europe, and the point
where it is least distant from the mainland, we are told, is the promontory which
men call Cantium [Kent], and this is about one hundred stades from the land,
at the place where the sea has its outlet, whereas the second promontory, known
as Belerium [Cornwall], is said to be a voyage of four days from the mainland,
and the last, writers tell us, extends out into the open sea and is named Orca. Of
the sides of Britain, the shortest, which extends along Europe, is seven thousand
five hundred stades, the second, from the Strait to the (northern) tip, is fifteen
thousand stades, and the last is twenty thousand stades, so that the entire circuit
of the island amounts to forty-two thousand five hundred stades.

And Britain, we are told, is inhabited by tribes which are autochthonous and
preserve in their ways of living the ancient manner of life. They use chariots, for
instance, in their wars, even as tradition tells us the old Greek heroes did in the
Trojan War, and their dwellings are humble, being built for the most part out of

reeds or logs. The method they employ of harvesting their grain crops is to cut off no more than the heads and store them away in roofed granges, and then each day they pick out the ripened heads and grind them, getting in this way their food. As for their habits, they are simple and far removed from the shrewdness and vice which characterize the men of our day. Their way of living is modest, since they are well clear of the luxury which is begotten of wealth. The island is also thickly populated, and its climate is extremely cold, as one would expect, since it actually lies under the Great Bear. It is held by many kings and potentates, who for the most part live at peace among themselves. . . .

The inhabitants of Britain who dwell about the promontory known as Belerium are especially hospitable to strangers and have adopted a civilized manner of life because of their intercourse with merchants of other peoples. They it is who work the tin, treating the bed which bears it in an ingenious manner. This bed, being like rock, contains earthy seams and in them the workers quarry the ore, which they then melt down and cleanse of its impurities. Then they work the tin into pieces the size of knuckle-bones and convey it to an island which lies off Britain and is called Ictis; for at the time of ebb-tide the space between this island and the mainland becomes dry and they can take the tin in large quantities over to the island on their wagons. (And a peculiar thing happens in the case of the neighbouring islands which lie between Europe and Britain, for at flood-tide the passages between them and the mainland run full and they have the appearance of islands, but at ebb-tide the sea recedes and leaves dry a large space, and at that time they look like peninsulas.)

On the island of Ictis the merchants purchase the tin of the natives and carry it from there across the Strait to Galatia or Gaul; and finally, making their way on foot through Gaul for some thirty days, they bring their wares on horseback to the mouth of the river Rhône.

TACITUS

"A Battle Between Romans and Caledonians in Southern Scotland"

ca. A.D. 84

SPEECH BEFORE BATTLE BY THE CALEDONIAN CHIEF, GALGACUS

"Whenever I consider the origin of this war and the necessities of our position, I have a sure confidence that this day, and this union of yours, will be the beginning of freedom to the whole of Britain. To all of us slavery is a thing unknown; there are no lands beyond us, and even the sea is not safe, menaced as we are by a Roman fleet. And thus in war and battle, in which the brave find glory, even the coward will find safety. Former contests, in which, with varying fortune, the Romans were resisted, still left in us a last hope of succour, inasmuch as being the most renowned nation of Britain, dwelling in the very heart of the country, and out of sight of the shores of the conquered, we could keep even our eyes unpolluted by the contagion of slavery. To us who dwell on the uttermost confines of the earth and of freedom, this remote sanctuary of Britain's glory has up to this time been a defence. Now, however, the furthest limits of Britain are thrown open, and the unknown always passes for the marvellous. But there are no tribes beyond us, nothing indeed but waves and rocks, and the yet more terrible Romans, from whose oppression escape is vainly sought by obedience and submission. Robbers of the world, having by their universal plunder exhausted the land, they rifle the deep. If the enemy be rich, they are rapacious; if he be poor, they lust for dominion; neither the east nor the west has been able to satisfy them. Alone among men they covet with equal eagerness poverty and riches. To robbery, slaughter, plunder, they give the lying name of empire; they make a solitude and call it peace.

"Nature has willed that every man's children and kindred should be his dearest objects. Yet these are torn from us by conscriptions to be slaves elsewhere. Our wives and our sisters, even though they may escape violation from the enemy, are dishonoured under the names of friendship and hospitality. Our goods and fortunes they collect for their tribute, our harvests for their granaries. Our very hands and bodies, under the lash and in the midst of insult, are worn down by the toil of clearing forests and morasses. Creatures born to slavery are sold once and for all, and are, moreover, fed by their masters, but Britain is daily purchasing, is daily feeding, her own enslaved people. And as in a household the last comer among the slaves is always the butt of his companions, so we in a world long used to slavery, as the newest and the most contemptible, are marked out for destruction.

"We have neither fruitful plains, nor mines, nor harbours, for the working of which we may be spared. Valour, too, and high spirit in subjects, are offensive to rulers; besides, remoteness and seclusion, while they give safety, provoke suspicion. Since then you cannot hope for quarter, take courage, I beseech you, whether it be safety or renown that you hold most precious. Under a woman's leadership the Brigantes were able to burn a colony, to storm a camp, and had not success ended in supineness, might have thrown off the yoke. Let us, then, a fresh and unconquered people, never likely to abuse our freedom, show forthwith at the very first onset what heroes Caledonia has in reserve.

"Do you suppose that the Romans will be as brave in war as they are licentious in peace? To our strifes and discords they owe their fame, and they turn the errors of an enemy to the renown of their own army, an army which, composed as it is of every variety of nations, is held together by success and will be broken up by disaster. These Gauls and Germans, I blush to say, these numerous Britons, who, though they lend their lives to support a stranger's rule, have been its enemies longer than its subjects, you cannot imagine to be bound by fidelity and affection. Fear and terror there certainly are, feeble bonds of attachment; remove them, and those who have ceased to fear will begin to hate. All the incentives to victory are on our side. The Romans have no wives to kindle their courage; no parents to taunt them with flight; many have either no country or one far away. Few in number, dismayed by their ignorance, looking around upon a sky, a sea, and forests which are all unfamiliar to them; hemmed in, as it were, and enmeshed, the Gods have delivered them into our hands.

"Be not frightened by idle display, by the glitter of gold and of silver, which can neither protect nor wound. In the very ranks of the enemy we shall find our own forces. Britons will acknowledge their own cause; Gauls will remember past freedom; the other Germans will abandon them, as but lately did the Usipii. Behind them there is nothing to dread. The forts are ungarrisoned; the colonies in the hands of aged men; what with disloyal subjects and oppressive rulers, the towns are ill-affected and rife with discord. On the one side you have a general and an army; on the other, tribute, the mines, and all the other penalties of an enslaved people. Whether you endure these for ever, or instantly avenge them, this field is to decide. Think, therefore, as you advance to battle, at once of your ancestors and of your posterity."

They received his speech with enthusiasm, and as is usual among barbarians, with songs, shouts, and discordant cries. And now was seen the assembling of troops and the gleam of arms, as the boldest warriors stepped to the front.

SPEECH BY THE ROMAN GENERAL AGRICOLA TO HIS MEN

As the line was forming, Agricola, who, though his troops were in high spirits and could scarcely be kept within the entrenchments, still thought it right to encourage them, spoke as follows:

"Comrades, this is the eighth year since, thanks to the greatness and good fortune of Rome and to your own loyalty and energy, you conquered Britain. In our many campaigns and battles, whether courage in meeting the foe, or toil and endurance in struggling, I may say, against nature herself, have been needed, I have ever been well satisfied with my soldiers, and you with your commander.

And so you and I have passed beyond the limits reached by former armies or by former governors, and we now occupy the last confines of Britain, not merely in rumour and report, but with an actual encampment and armed force. Britain has been both discovered and subdued. Often on the march, when morasses, mountains, and rivers were wearing out your strength, did I hear our bravest men exclaim, 'When shall we have the enemy before us? When shall we fight?' He is now here, driven from his lair, and your wishes and your valour have free scope, and everything favours the conqueror, everything is adverse to the vanquished. For as it is a great and glorious achievement, if we press on, to have accomplished so great a march, to have traversed forests and to have crossed estuaries, so, if we retire, our present most complete success will prove our greatest danger. We have not the same knowledge of the country or the same abundance of supplies, but we have arms in our hands, and in them we have everything. For myself I have long been convinced that neither for an army nor for a general is retreat safe. Better, too, is an honourable death than a life of shame, and safety and renown are for us to be found together. And it would be no inglorious end to perish on the extreme confines of earth and of nature.

"If unknown nations and an untried enemy confronted you, I should urge you on by the example of other armies. As it is, look back upon your former honours, question your own eyes. These are the men who last year under cover of darkness attacked a single legion, whom you routed by a shout. Of all the Britons these are the most confirmed runaways, and this is why they have survived so long. Just as when the huntsman penetrates the forest and the thicket, all the most courageous animals rush out upon him, while the timid and feeble are scared away by the very sound of his approach, so the bravest of the Britons have long since fallen; and the rest are a mere crowd of spiritless cowards. You have at last found them, not because they have stood their ground, but because they have been overtaken. Their desperate plight, and the extreme terror that paralyses them, have rivetted their line to this spot, that you might achieve in it a splendid and memorable victory. Put an end to campaigns; crown your fifty years' service with a glorious day; prove to your country that her armies could never have been fairly charged with protracting a war or with causing a rebellion."

THE BATTLE

While Agricola was yet speaking, the ardour of the soldiers was rising to its height, and the close of his speech was followed by a great outburst of enthusiasm. In a moment they flew to arms. He arrayed his eager and impetuous troops in such a manner that the auxiliary infantry, 8,000 in number, strengthened his centre, while 3,000 cavalry were posted on his wings. The legions were drawn up in front of the intrenched camp; his victory would be vastly more glorious if won without the loss of Roman blood, and he would have a reserve in case of repulse. The enemy, to make a formidable display, had posted himself on high ground; his van was on the plain, while the rest of his army rose in an arch-like form up the slope of a hill. The plain between resounded with the noise and with the rapid movements of chariots and cavalry. Agricola, fearing that from the enemy's superiority of force he would be simultaneously attacked in front and on the flanks, widened his ranks, and though his line was likely to be too extended, and several officers advised him to bring up the legions, yet, so sanguine was he, so resolute in meeting danger, he sent away his horse and took his stand on foot before the colours.

The action began with distant fighting. The Britons with equal steadiness and skill used their huge swords and small shields to avoid or to parry the missiles of our soldiers, while they themselves poured on us a dense shower of darts, till Agricola encouraged three Batavian and two Tungrian cohorts to bring matters to the decision of close fighting with swords. Such tactics were familiar to these veteran soldiers, but were embarrassing to an enemy armed with small bucklers and unwieldy weapons. The swords of the Britons are not pointed, and do not allow them to close with the foe, or to fight in the open field. No sooner did the Batavians begin to close with the enemy, to strike them with their shields, to disfigure their faces, and overthrowing the force on the plain to advance their line up the hill, than the other auxiliary cohorts joined with eager rivalry in cutting down all the nearest of the foe. Many were left behind half dead, some even unwounded, in the hurry of victory. Meantime the enemy's cavalry had fled, and the charioteers had mingled in the engagement of the infantry. But although these at first spread panic, they were soon impeded by the close array of our ranks and by the inequalities of the ground. The battle had anything but the appearance of a cavalry action, for men and horses were carried along in confusion together, while chariots, destitute of guidance, and terrified horses without drivers, dashed as panic urged them, sideways, or in direct collision against the ranks.

Those of the Britons who, having as yet taken no part in the engagement, occupied the hill-tops, and who without fear for themselves sat idly disdaining the smallness of our numbers, had begun to descend and to hem in the rear of the victorious army, when Agricola, who feared this very movement, opposed their advance with four squadrons of cavalry held in reserve by him for any sudden emergencies of battle. Their repulse and rout was as severe as their onset had been furious. Thus the enemy's design recoiled on himself, and the cavalry which by the general's order had wheeled round from the van of the contending armies, attacked his rear. Then, indeed, the open plain presented an awful and hideous spectacle. Our men pursued, wounded, made prisoners of the fugitives only to slaughter them when others fell in their way. And now the enemy, as prompted by their various dispositions, fled in whole battalions with arms in their hands before a few pursuers, while some, who were unarmed, actually rushed to the front and gave themselves up to death. Everywhere there lay scattered arms, corpses, and mangled limbs, and the earth reeked with blood. Even the conquered now and then felt a touch of fury and of courage. On approaching the woods, they rallied, and as they knew the ground, they were able to pounce on the foremost and least cautious of the pursuers. Had not Agricola, who was present everywhere, ordered a force of strong and lightly equipped cohorts, with some dismounted troopers for the denser parts of the forest, and a detachment of cavalry where it was not so thick, to scour the woods like a party of huntsmen, serious loss would have been sustained through the excessive confidence of our troops. When, however, the enemy saw that we again pursued them in firm and compact array, they fled no longer in masses as before, each looking for his comrade; but dispersing and avoiding one another, they sought the shelter of distant and pathless wilds. Night and weariness of bloodshed put an end to the pursuit. About 10,000 of the enemy were slain; on our side there fell 360 men, and among them Aulus Atticus, the commander of the cohort, whose youthful impetuosity and mettlesome steed had borne him into the midst of the enemy.

Elated by their victory and their booty, the conquerors passed a night of merriment. Meanwhile the Britons, wandering amidst the mingled wailings of men and women, were dragging off their wounded, calling to the unhurt, deserting their homes, and in their rage actually firing them, choosing places of concealment only instantly to abandon them. One moment they would take counsel together, the next part company, while the sight of those who were dearest to them sometimes melted their hearts, but oftener roused their fury. It was an undoubted fact that some of them vented their rage on their wives and children, as if in pity for their lot. The following day showed more fully the extent of the calamity for the silence of desolation reigned everywhere: the hills were forsaken, houses were smoking in the distance, and no one was seen by the scouts. . . .

—VII—

THE GOTHS TURN SOUTH TO ROME

Few events seem to better typify—and dramatize—the struggle between barbarian and Roman than the Battle of Hadrianople (A.D. 378) and the chaotic events that led up to it. After Hadrianople, the sack of Rome was all but inevitable.

As with so many events in the history of barbarians, it began with the movement of a vast number of people. In 375, the old Germanic tribes, now called Goths, pushed from behind by a terrible new menace from the east called the Huns, moved south across the Danube into Roman territory. They came with Rome's uneasy permission, but their welcome was not a happy one. The weakened Roman Empire—now divided into two parts, with the Eastern Empire ruled by Valens, the Western Empire by his brother Valentinian—probably saw the barbarian immigrants as potentially useful military conscripts. The Goths, however, arrived not as random refugees but as a nation with its leadership intact.

Then, as historian Ammianus Marcellinus (ca. 330–395) described it, "the barbarians, like beasts who had broken loose from their cages, poured unrestrainedly over the vast extent of the country." There was open, bloody warfare between the Goths and their hosts, and it all came to a head three years later with the death of the foolish emperor Valens outside the gates of Hadrianople on the Balkan Peninsula in a battle that would mark a shift forever in power between Romans and barbarians.

The story of what happened from the Goths' crossing of the Danube through the battle at Hadrianople is told here in a long—and gory—panoramic passage from Ammianus Marcellinus's history of the later Roman Empire. A Greek born in Antioch who served in the army under the emperor Julian in both Gaul and Persia, he wrote his history—which he began after 378—in Latin.

The sack of Rome by Alaric's Visigoths did not follow immediately after Hadrianople. But it eventually came, after several failed attempts, in 410. The account of it that follows is from *The History of the Wars* by Procopius (ca. 500–ca. 570), a Greek born in Caesarea in Palestine who served as a senator and a prefect of Constantinople and was on the staff of the general Belisarius during his Persian, African, and Italian campaigns.

The chapter ends on a macabre note with a brief coda by Edward Gibbon (1737–1794) on Alaric's death and burial from *The History of the Decline and Fall of the Roman Empire.*

Ammianus Marcellinus

"The Gothic Invasion and the Battle of Hadrianople"

A.D. 378

A.D. 375: HUNS THREATEN THE GOTHS

The following circumstances were the original cause of all the destruction and various calamities which the fury of Mars roused up, throwing everything into confusion by his usual ruinous violence.

The people called Huns, slightly mentioned in the ancient records, live beyond the Sea of Azov, on the border of the Frozen Ocean, and are a race savage beyond all parallel. At the very moment of their birth the cheeks of their infant children are deeply marked by an iron, in order that the usual vigour of their hair, instead of growing at the proper season, may be withered by the wrinkled scars; and accordingly they grow up without beards, and consequently without any beauty, like eunuchs, though they all have closely knit and strong limbs, and plump necks; they are of great size, and low legged, so that you might fancy them two-legged beasts, or the stout figures which are hewn out in a rude manner with an axe on the posts at the end of bridges.

They are certainly in the shape of men, however uncouth, but are so hardy that they neither require fire nor well-flavoured food, but live on the roots of such herbs as they get in the fields, or on the half-raw flesh of any animal, which they merely warm rapidly by placing it between their own thighs and the backs of their horses.

They never shelter themselves under roofed houses, but avoid them as people ordinarily avoid sepulchres as things not fitted for common use. Nor is there even to be found among them a cabin thatched with reed; but they wander about, roaming over the mountains and the woods, and accustom themselves to bear frost and hunger and thirst from their very cradles. And even when abroad they never enter a house unless under the compulsion of some extreme necessity; nor, indeed, do they think people under roofs as safe as others.

They wear linen clothes, or else garments made of the skins of field mice: nor do they wear a different dress out of doors from that which they wear at home; but after a tunic is once put round their necks, however it becomes worn, it is never taken off or changed till, from long decay, it becomes actually so ragged as to fall to pieces.

They cover their heads with round caps and their shaggy legs with the skins of kids; their shoes are not made on any lasts, but are so unshapely as to hinder them from walking with a free gait. And for this reason they are not well suited to infantry battles, but are nearly always on horseback, their horses being ill-shaped, but hardy, and sometimes they even sit upon them like women if they want to do anything more conveniently. There is not a person in the whole nation who cannot remain on his horse day and night. On horseback they buy and sell, they take their meat and drink, and there they recline on the narrow neck of their steed, and yield to sleep so deep as to indulge in every variety of dream.

And when any deliberation is to take place on any weighty matter, they all hold their common council on horseback. They are not under the authority of a king, but are contented with the irregular government of their nobles, and under their lead they force their way through all obstacles.

Sometimes when provoked, they fight; and when they go into battle, they form in a solid body, and utter all kinds of terrific yells. They are very quick in their operations, of exceeding speed, and fond of surprising their enemies. With a view to this, they suddenly disperse, then reunite, and again, after having inflicted vast loss upon the enemy, scatter themselves over the whole plain in irregular formations: always avoiding a fort or an entrenchment.

And in one respect you may pronounce them the most formidable of all warriors, for when at a distance they use missiles of various kinds tipped with sharpened bones instead of the usual points of javelins, and these bones are admirably fastened into the shaft of the javelin or arrow; but when they are at close quarters they fight with the sword, without any regard for their own safety; and often while their antagonists are warding off their blows they entangle them with twisted cords, so that, their hands being fettered, they lose all power of either riding or walking.

None of them plough or even touch a plough handle: for they have no settled abode, but are homeless and lawless, perpetually wandering with their waggons, which they make their homes; in fact they seem to be people always in flight. Their wives live in these waggons, and there weave their miserable garments; and here too they sleep with their husbands, and bring up their children till they reach the age of puberty; nor, if asked, can any one of them tell you where he was born, as he was conceived in one place, born in another at a great distance, and brought up in another still more remote.

In truces they are treacherous and inconstant, being able to change their minds at every breeze of fresh hope which presents itself, giving themselves up wholly to the impulse and inclination of the moment; and, like brute beasts, they are utterly ignorant of the distinction between right and wrong. They express themselves with great ambiguity and obscurity; have no respect for any religion or superstition whatever; are immoderately covetous of gold; and are so fickle and irascible, that they very often on the same day that they quarrel with their companions without any provocation, again become reconciled to them without any mediator.

This active and indomitable race, being excited by an unrestrainable desire of plundering the possessions of others, went on ravaging and slaughtering all the nations in their neighbourhood till they reached the Alani, who were formerly called the Massagetae. . . .

The Danube, which is greatly increased by other rivers falling into it, passes through the territory of the Sauromatae, which extends as far as the river Don, the boundary between Asia and Europe. On the other side of this river the Alani inhabit the enormous deserts of Scythia, deriving their own name from the mountains around; and they, like the Persians, having gradually subdued all the bordering nations by repeated victories, have united them to themselves, and comprehended them under their own name. . . .

Next to these are the Melanchlaenae and the Anthropophagi, who roam about upon different tracts of land and live on human flesh. And these men are so avoided on account of their horrid food, that all the tribes which were their neighbours have removed to a distance from them. And in this way the whole of that region to the northeast, till you come to the Chinese, is uninhabited.

Then the Alani, being thus divided among the two quarters of the globe (the various tribes which make up the whole nation it is not worth while to enumerate), although widely separated, wander, like the Nomades, over enormous districts. But in the progress of time all these tribes came to be united under one generic appellation, and are called Alani. . . .

They have no cottages, and never use the plough, but live solely on meat and plenty of milk, mounted on their waggons, which they cover with a curved awning made of the bark of trees, and then drive them through their boundless deserts. And when they come to any pasture land, they pitch their waggons in a circle, and live like a herd of beasts, eating up all the forage—carrying, as it were, their cities with them in their waggons. In them the husbands sleep with their wives—in them their children are born and brought up; these waggons, in short, are their perpetual habitation, and wherever they fix them, that place they look upon as their home.

They drive before them their flocks and herds to their pasturage; and, above all other cattle, they are especially careful of their horses. The fields in that country are always green, and are interspersed with patches of fruit trees, so that, wherever they go, there is no dearth either of food for themselves or fodder for their cattle. And this is caused by the moisture of the soil, and the number of the rivers which flow through these districts.

All their old people, and especially the weak, keep close to the waggons, and occupy themselves in the lighter employments. But the young men, who from their earliest childhood are trained to the use of horses, think it beneath them to walk. They are also all trained by careful discipline of various sorts to become skillful warriors. . . .

Nearly all the Alani men are of great stature and beauty; their hair is somewhat yellow, their eyes are terribly fierce; the lightness of their armour renders them rapid in their movements; and they are in every respect equal to the Huns, only more civilized in their food and their manner of life. They plunder and hunt as far as the Sea of Azov and the Cimmerian Bosphorus, ravaging also Armenia and Media.

And as ease is a delightful thing to men of a quiet and placid disposition, so danger and war are a pleasure to the Alani, and among them that man is called happy who has lost his life in battle. For those who grow old, or who go out of the world from accidental sicknesses, they pursue with bitter reproaches as degenerate and cowardly. Nor is there anything of which they boast with more pride than of having killed a man, and the most glorious spoils they esteem the scalps which they have torn from the heads of those whom they have slain, which they put as trappings and ornaments on their warhorses.

Nor is there any temple or shrine seen in their country, nor even any cabin thatched with straw, their only idea of religion being to plunge a naked sword into the ground with barbaric ceremonies, and then they worship that with great respect, as Mars, the presiding deity of the regions over which they wander. They presage the future in a most remarkable manner; for they collect a number of straight twigs of osier, then with certain secret incantations they separate them from one another on particular days; and from them they learn clearly what is about to happen. They have no idea of slavery, inasmuch as they themselves are all born of noble families; and those whom even now they appoint to be judges are always men of proved experience and skill in war. But now let us return to the subject which we proposed to ourselves. . . .

The Huns, after having traversed the territory of the Alani, and having slain many of them and acquired much plunder, they made a treaty of friendship and alliance with those who remained. And when they had united them to themselves, with increased boldness they made sudden incursion into the fertile districts of Ermenrichus, a very warlike prince, and one whom his numerous gallant actions of every kind had rendered formidable to all the neighbouring nations.

He was astonished at the violence of this sudden tempest, and although, like a prince whose power was well established, he long attempted to hold his ground, he was at last overpowered by a dread of the evils impending over his country, till he terminated his fear of great danger by a voluntary death. . . .

In the meantime a report spread extensively through the nations of the Goths, that a race of men, hitherto unknown, had suddenly descended like a whirlwind from the lofty mountains, as if they had risen from some secret recess of the earth, and were ravaging and destroying everything which came in their way. And then the greater part of the population which, because of their want of necessaries, had deserted Athanaric, resolved to flee and to seek a home remote from all knowledge of the barbarians; and after a long deliberation where to fix their abode, they resolved that a retreat into Thrace [within the Roman Empire] was the most suitable for these two reasons: first of all, because it is a district most fertile in grass; and also because, by the great breadth of the Danube, it is wholly separated from the barbarians, who were already exposed to the thunderbolts of foreign warfare. And the whole population of the tribe adopted this resolution unanimously.

A.D. 376: THE GOTHS CROSS THE DANUBE

Accordingly, under the command of their leader Alavivus, they occupied the banks of the Danube; and having sent ambassadors to [Roman Emperor] Valens, they humbly entreated to be received by him as his subjects, promising to live quietly, and to furnish a body of auxiliary troops if any necessity for such a force should arise.

While these events were passing, a terrible rumour arose that the tribes of the north were planning new and unprecedented attacks upon us [Romans]; and that over the whole region a barbarian host composed of different distant nations, which had suddenly been driven by force from their own country, was now, with all their families, wandering about in different directions on the banks of the river Danube.

At first this intelligence was lightly treated by our people, because they were not in the habit of hearing of any wars in those remote districts till they were terminated either by victory or by treaty. But presently, as the belief in these occurrences grew stronger, being confirmed, too, by the arrival of the foreign ambassadors, who, with prayers and earnest entreaties, begged that the people thus driven from their homes and now encamped on the other side of the river, might be kindly received by us, the affair seemed a cause of joy rather than of fear, according to the skillful flatterers who were always extolling and exaggerating the good fortune of the emperor; congratulating him that an embassy had come from the fartherest corners of the earth unexpectedly, offering him a large body of recruits; and that, by combining the strength of his own nation with these foreign forces, he would have an army absolutely invincible; observing further that, by the yearly payment for military reinforcements which came in every year from the provinces, a vast treasure of gold might be accumulated in his coffers.

Full of this hope he sent forth several officers to bring this ferocious people and their waggons into our territory. And such great pains were taken to gratify this nation which was destined to overthrow the empire of Rome, that not one was left behind, not even of those who were stricken with mortal disease. Moreover, having obtained permission of the emperor to cross the Danube and to cultivate some districts in Thrace, they crossed the stream day and night, without ceasing, embarking in troops on board ships and rafts, and canoes made of the hollow trunks of trees, in which enterprise, as the Danube is the most difficult of all rivers to navigate, and was at that time swollen with continual rains, a great many were drowned, who, because they were too numerous for the vessels, tried to swim across, and in spite of all their exertions were swept away by the stream.

In this way, through the turbulent zeal of violent people, the ruin of the Roman empire was brought on. This, at all events, is neither obscure nor uncertain, that the unhappy officers who were intrusted with the charge of conducting the multitude of the barbarians across the river, though they repeatedly endeavoured to calculate their numbers, at last abandoned the attempt as hopeless; and the man who would wish to ascertain the number might as well (as the most illustrious of poets [Virgil] says) attempt to count the waves in the African sea, or the grains of sand tossed about by the zephyr.

The innumerable multitudes of different nations, diffused over all our provinces, and spreading themselves over the vast expanse of our plains, filled all the champaign country and all the mountain ranges; and the emperor assigned them a temporary provision for their immediate support, and ordered lands to be assigned them to cultivate.

At that time the defences of our provinces were much exposed, and the armies of barbarians spread over them like the lava of Mount Etna. The imminence of our danger manifestly called for generals already illustrious for their past achievements in war; but nevertheless, as if some unpropitious deity had made the selection, the men who were sought out for the chief military appointments were of tainted character. The chief among them were Lupicinus and Maximus, the one being Count of Thrace, the other a leader notoriously wicked—and both men of great ignorance and rashness.

And their treacherous covetousness was the cause of all our disasters. For (to pass over other matters in which the officers aforesaid, or others with their unblushing connivance, displayed the greatest profligacy in their injurious treatment of the foreigners) this one melancholy and unprecedented piece of conduct (which, even if they were to choose their own judges, must appear wholly unpardonable) must be mentioned:

When the barbarians who had been conducted across the river were in great distress from want of provisions, those detested generals conceived the idea of a most disgraceful traffic; and having collected hounds from all quarters [to be used as food], they exchanged them for an equal number of slaves, among whom were several sons of noble birth. . . .

When this series of occurrences had been made generally known by frequent messengers, Sueridus and Colias, two nobles of the Goths, who had some time before been friendly received with their people, and had been sent to Hadrianople to pass the winter in that city, thinking their own safety the most important of all objects, looked on all the events which were taking place with great indifference.

But, on a sudden, letters having arrived from the emperor, in which they were ordered to cross over to the province of the Hellespont, they asked, in a very modest manner, to be provided with money to defray the expenses of their march, as well as provisions, and to be allowed a respite of two days. But the chief magistrate of the city was indignant at this request, being also out of humour with them on account of some injury which had been done to property of his own in the suburbs, and collected a great mob of the lowest of the people, with a body of armourers, of whom there is a great number in that place, and led them forth armed to hasten the departure of the Goths. And ordering the trumpeters to sound an alarm, he menaced them with destruction unless they at once departed with all speed, as they had been ordered.

The Goths, bewildered by this unexpected calamity, and alarmed at this outbreak of the citizens, which looked more as if caused by a sudden impulse than by an deliberate purpose, stood without moving. And being assailed beyond all endurance by reproaches and manifestations of ill will, and also by occasional missiles, they at last broke out into open revolt; having slain several of those who had at first attacked them with too much petulance, and having put the rest to flight, and wounded many with all kinds of weapons, they stripped their corpses and armed themselves with the spoils in the Roman fashion; and then, seeing Fritigern [a Gothic chieftain] near them, they united themselves to him as obedient allies, and blockaded the city. They remained some time, maintaining this difficult position and making promiscuous attacks, during which they lost some of their number by their own audacity, without being able to avenge them; while many were slain by arrows and large stones hurled from slings.

Then Fritigern, perceiving that his men, who were unaccustomed to sieges, were struggling in vain, and sustaining heavy losses, advised his army to leave a force sufficient to maintain the blockade, and to depart with the rest, acknowledging their failure, and saying that "He did not war with stone walls." Advising them also to lay waste all the fertile regions around without any distinction, and to plunder those places which were not defended by any garrisons.

His counsel was approved, as his troops knew that he was always a very able commander in bringing their plans to success; and then they dispersed over the whole district of Thrace, advancing cautiously; while those who came of their own accord to surrender, or those whom they had taken prisoners, pointed out to them the richest towns, and especially those where it was said that supplies of provisions could be found. And in addition to their natural confidence they were greatly encouraged by this circumstance, that a multitude of that nation came in daily to join them who had formerly been sold as slaves by the merchants, with many others whom, when at their first passage of the river they were suffering from severe want, they had bartered for a little bad wine or morsels of bread.

To those were added no inconsiderable number of men skilled in tracing out veins of gold, but who were unable to endure the heavy burden of their taxes; and who, having been received with the cheerful consent of all, they were of great use to them while traversing strange districts—showing them the secret stores of grain, the retreats of men, and other hiding places of divers kinds.

Nor while these men led them on as their guides did anything remain untouched by them, except what was inaccessible or wholly out of the way; for without any distinction of age or sex they went forward destroying everything in one vast slaughter and conflagration: tearing infants even from their mother's breast and slaying them; ravishing their mothers; slaughtering women's husbands before the eyes of those whom they thus made widows; while boys of tender and of adult age were dragged over the corpses of their parents.

Lastly, numbers of old men, crying out that they had lived long enough, having lost all their wealth, together with beautiful women, had their hands bound behind their back, and were driven into banishment, bewailing the ashes of their native homes.

A.D. 377: WAR BETWEEN GOTHS AND ROMANS

This news from Thrace was received with great sorrow, and caused the Emperor Valens much anxiety. He instantly sent Victor, the commander of the cavalry, into Persia, to make such arrangements in Armenia as were required by the impending danger. While he himself prepared at once to quit Antioch and go to Constantinople, sending before him Profuturus and Trajan, both officers of rank and ambition, but of no great skill in war.

When they arrived at the place where it seemed most expedient to combat this hostile multitude in detail and by ambuscades and surprises, they very injudiciously adopted the ill-considered plan of opposing the legions which had arrived from Armenia to barbarians who were still raging like madmen. Though the legions had repeatedly proved equal to the dangers of a pitched battle and regular warfare, they were not suited to encounter an innumerable host which occupied all the chains of the lofty hills, and also all the plains.

Our men had never yet experienced what can be effected by indomitable rage united with despair, and so having driven back the enemy beyond the abrupt precipices of the Balkan, they seized upon the rugged defiles in order to hem in the barbarians on ground from which they would be unable to find any exit, and where it seemed they might be overcome by famine. . . .

Profuturus and Trajan advanced towards the town of Salices—at no great distance from which was a countless host of barbarians, arranged in a circle, with a great multitude of waggons for a rampart around them, behind which, as if protected by a spacious wall, they enjoyed ease and an abundance of booty.

Filled with hopes of success, the Roman generals—resolved on some gallant enterprise should fortune afford them an opportunity—were carefully watching the movements of the Goths; having formed the design—if they moved their camp in any other direction, which they were very much in the habit of doing—to fall upon their rear, making no doubt that they should slay many of them, and recover a great portion of their spoil.

When the barbarians learnt this, probably through the information of some deserter, from whom they obtained a knowledge of our operations, they remained for some time in the same place; but at last, being influenced by fear of the opposing army, and of the reinforcements which might be expected to throng to them, they assembled, by a preconcerted signal, the predatory bands dispersed in different districts, and which, the moment they received the orders of their leaders, returned like firebrands, with the swiftness of birds, to their "encampment of chariots" (as they call it), and thus gave their countrymen confidence to attempt greater enterprises.

After this there was no cessation of hostilities between the two parties except what was afforded by a few short truces; for after those men had returned to the camp whom necessity had forced to quit it, the whole body which was crowded within the circuit of the encampment, being full of fierce discontent, excitement, and a most ferocious spirit, and now reduced to the greatest extremities, were eager for bloodshed: nor did their chiefs, who were present with them, resist their desire; and as the resolution to give battle was taken when the sun was sinking, and when the approach of night invited the sullen and discontented troops to rest, they took some food quietly, but remained all night sleepless.

On the other hand the Romans, knowing what was going on, kept themselves also awake, fearing the enemy and their insane leaders as so many furious wild beasts. Nevertheless, with fearless minds they awaited the result, which, though they acknowledged it to be doubtful in respect of their inferiority in number, they still trusted would be propitious because of the superior justice of their cause.

Therefore the next day, as soon as it was light, the signal for taking arms having been given by the trumpets on both sides, the barbarians, after having, in accordance with their usual custom, taken an oath to remain faithful to their standards, attempted to gain the higher ground, in order that from it they might descend down the steep like wheels, overwhelming their enemy by the vigour of their attack. When this was seen, our soldiers all flocked to their proper regiments, and then stood firm, neither turning aside nor in any instance even leaving their ranks to rush forward.

Therefore when the armies on both sides, advancing more cautiously, at last halted and stood immovable, the warriors, with mutual sternness, surveying each other with fierce looks. The Romans in every part of their line sang warlike songs, with a voice rising from a lower to a higher key, which they call *barritus* [the word used for the trumpeting of an elephant], and so encouraged themselves to gallant exertions. But the barbarians, with dissonant clamour, shouted out the praises of their ancestors, and amid their various discordant cries, tried occasional light skirmishes.

And now each army began to assail the other with javelins and other similar missiles; and then with threatening shouts rushed on to close combat, and packing their shields together like a testudo, they came foot to foot with their foes. The barbarians, active, and easily rallied, hurled huge bludgeons, burnt at one end, against our men, and vigorously thrust their swords against the opposing breasts of the Romans, till they broke our left wing; but as it recoiled, it fell back on a strong body of reserve which was vigorously brought up on their flank, and supported them just as they were on the very point of destruction.

Therefore, while the battle raged with vast slaughter, each individual soldier rushing fiercely on the dense ranks of the enemy, the arrows and javelins flew like hail; the blows of swords were equally rapid; while the cavalry, too pressed on, cutting down all who fled with terrible and mighty wounds on their backs; as also on both sides did the infantry, slaughtering and hamstringing those who had fallen down, and through fear were unable to fly.

And when the whole place was filled with corpses, some also lay among them still half alive, vainly cherishing a hope of life, some of them having been pierced with bullets hurled from slings, others with arrows barbed with iron. Some again had their heads cloven in half with blows of swords, so that one side of their heads hung down on each shoulder in a most horrible manner.

Meanwhile, stubborn as the conflict was, neither party was wearied, but they still fought on with equal valour and equal fortune, nor did any one relax in his sternness as long as his courage could give him strength for exertion. But at last the day yielded to the evening, and put an end to the deadly contest: the barbarians all withdrew, in no order, each taking his own path, and our men returned sorrowfully to their tents.

Then having paid the honours of burial to some among the dead, as well as the time and place permitted, the rest of the corpses were left as a banquet to the ill-omened birds, which at that time were accustomed to feed on carcasses—as is even now shown by the places which are still white with bones. It is quite certain that the Romans, who were comparatively few, and contending with vastly superior numbers, suffered serious losses, while at the same time the barbarians did not escape without much lamentable slaughter.

Upon the melancholy termination of this battle, our men sought a retreat in the neighbouring city of Marcianopolis. The Goths, of their own accord, fell back behind the ramparts formed by their waggons, and for seven days they never once ventured to come forth or show themselves. . . .

In the meantime Valens, having heard of the miserable result of these wars and devastions, gave Saturninus the command of the cavalry, and sent him Trajan and Profuturus. At that time, throughout the whole countries of Scythia and Moesia, everything which could be eaten had been consumed; and so, urged equally by their natural ferocity and by hunger, the barbarians made desperate efforts to force their way out of the position in which they were enclosed but though they made frequent attempts, they were constantly overwhelmed by the vigour of our men, who made an effectual resistance by the aid of the rugged ground which they occupied; and at last, being reduced to the extremity of distress, they allured some of the Huns and Alani to their alliance by the hope of extensive plunder.

When this was known, Saturninus gradually collected his men, and was preparing to retreat, in pursuance of a sufficiently well-devised plan, lest the multitude of barbarians by some sudden movement (like a river which had burst its barriers by the violence of a flood) should easily overthrow his whole force.

The moment that, by the seasonable retreat of our men, the passage of these defiles was opened, the barbarians, in no regular order, but wherever each individual could find a passage, rushed forth without hindrance to spread confusion among us; and raging with a desire for devastation and plunder, spread themselves with impunity over the whole region of Thrace, from the districts watered by the Danube, to the strait which separates the Aegean from the Black Sea, spreading ravage, slaughter, bloodshed, and conflagration, and throwing everything into the foulest disorder by all sorts of acts of violence committed even on the freeborn.

Then one might see, with grief, actions equally horrible to behold and to speak of; women panic-stricken, beaten with cracking scourges; some even in pregnancy, whose very offspring, before they were born, had to endure countless horrors; here were seen children twining round their mothers; there one might hear the lamentations of noble youths and maidens all seized and doomed to captivity.

Again, grown-up virgins and chaste matrons were dragged along with countenances disfigured by bitter weeping, wishing to avoid the violation of their modesty by any death however agonizing. Here some wealthy nobleman was dragged along like a wild beast, complaining of fortune as merciless and blind, who in a brief moment had stripped him of his riches, of his beloved relations, and his home; had made him see his house reduced to ashes, and had reduced him to expect either to be torn limb from limb himself, or else to be exposed to scourging and torture, as the slave of a ferocious conqueror.

But the barbarians, like beasts who had broken loose from their cages, poured unrestrainedly over the vast extent of country.

At this time, Valens was . . . eager for some glorious exploit. He was at the head of a numerous force, neither unwarlike nor contemptible, and had united with them many veteran bands, among whom were several officers of high rank, especially Trajan, who a little while before had been commander of the forces.

And as by means of spies and observation it was ascertained that the enemy were intending to blockade the different roads by which the necessary supplies must come, with strong divisions, he sent a sufficient force to prevent this, despatching a body of the archers of the infantry and a squadron of cavalry, with all speed, to occupy the narrow passes in the neighbourhood.

Three days afterwards, the barbarians, who were advancing slowly because they feared an attack in the unfavourable ground they were traversing, arrived fifteen miles from the post at Nike, which was the aim of their march. The emperor, with wanton impetuosity, resolved on attacking them instantly, because those who had been sent forward to reconnoitre (what led to such a mistake is unknown) affirmed that their entire body did not exceed ten thousand men.

AUGUST 9, 378: THE BATTLE OF HADRIANOPLE:

Marching on with his army in battle array, he came near the suburb of Hadrianople, where he pitched his camp, strengthening it with a rampart of palisades, and then impatiently waited for Gratian. While here, Richomeres, Count of the Domestici, arrived and imploring Valens to wait a little while that he might share his danger, and not rashly face the enemy before him single handed, he took counsel with his officers as to what was best to be done.

Some, following the advice of Sebastian [Valens's nephew] recommended with urgency that he should at once go forth to battle; while Victor, master-general of the cavalry, a Sarmatian by birth, but a man of slow and cautious temper, recommended him to wait for his imperial colleague, and this advice was supported by several other officers, who suggested that the reinforcement of [Gratian's] Gallic army would be likely to awe the fiery arrogance of the barbarians.

However, the fatal obstinacy of the emperor prevailed, fortified by the flattery of some of the princes, who advised him to hasten with all speed so that Gratian might have no share in a victory which, as they fancied, was already almost gained. And while all necessary preparations were being made for the battle, a presbyter of the Christian religion (as he called himself), having been sent by [the Goth] Fritigern as his ambassador, came with some colleagues of low rank to the emperor's camp; and having been received with courtesy, he presented a letter from that chieftain, openly requesting that the emperor would grant to him and to his followers—who were now exiles from their native homes, from which they had been driven by the rapid invasions of savage nations—Thrace, with all its flocks and all its crops, for a habitation. And if Valens would consent to this, Fritigern would agree to a perpetual peace.

In addition to this message, the same Christian, as one acquainted with his commander's secrets, and well trusted, produced other secret letters from his chieftain who, being full of craft and every resource of deceit, informed Valens, as one who was hereafter to be his friend and ally, that he had no other means to appease the ferocity of his countrymen, or to induce them to accept conditions advantageous to the Roman state, unless from time to time he showed them an army under arms and by frightening them with the name of the emperor. The ambassadors retired unsuccessful, having been looked on as suspicious characters by the emperor.

When the day broke which the annals mark as the fifth of the Ides of August, the Roman standards were advanced with haste, the baggage having been placed close to the walls of Hadrianople, under a sufficient guard of soldiers of the legions; the treasurers and the chief insignia of the emperor's rank were within the walls, with the prefect and the principal members of the council.

Then, having traversed the broken ground, which divided the two armies, as the burning day was progressing towards noon, at last, after marching eight miles, our men came in sight of the waggons of the enemy all arranged in a circle. According to their custom, the barbarian host raised a fierce and hideous yell, while the Roman generals marshalled their line of battle. The right wing of the cavalry was placed in front; the chief portion of the infantry was kept in reserve.

The left wing of the cavalry, of which a considerable number were still straggling on the road, were advancing with speed, but with great difficulty; and while this wing was deploying, not as yet meeting with any obstacle, the barbarians being alarmed at the terrible clang of their arms and the threatening crash of their shields (since a large portion of their own army was still at a distance, under Alatheus and Saphrax, and, though sent for, had not yet arrived), again sent ambassadors to ask for peace.

The emperor, offended at the lowness of their rank, replied, that if they wished to make a lasting treaty, they must send him nobles of sufficient dignity. They delayed in order to give time for their cavalry to return and for our soldiers, already suffering from the summer heat, to become parched and exhausted by the conflagration of the vast plain; as the enemy had set fire to the crops by means of burning faggots and fuel. To this evil another was added, both men and cattle were suffering from extreme hunger.

In the meantime Fritigern, being skillful in divining the future, and fearing a doubtful struggle, sent one of his men as a herald, requesting that some nobles and picked men should, at once be sent to him as hostages and he himself would fearlessly bring us both military aid and supplies.

The proposition of this formidable chief was received with praise and approbation, and the tribune Equitius, a relation of Valens, who was at that time high steward of the palace, was appointed to go with all speed to the barbarians as a hostage. But he refused, because he had once before been taken prisoner by the enemy, and had escaped so that he feared their vengeful anger. Upon this Richomeres voluntarily offered himself, and willingly undertook to go, thinking it a bold action, and one becoming a brave man, and so he set out, bearing vouchers of his rank and high birth.

And as he was on his way towards the enemy's camp, the accompanying archers and Scutarii, who on that occasion were under the command of Bacurius, a native of Iberia, and of Cassio, yielded to an indiscreet impetuosity, and on approaching the enemy, attacked them rashly, and then by a cowardly flight disgraced the beginning of the campaign.

This ill-timed attack frustrated the willing services of Richomeres, as he was not permitted to proceed; in the mean time the cavalry of the Goths had returned with Alatheus and Saphrax, and with them a battalion of Alani; these descending from the mountains like a thunderbolt, spread confusion and slaughter among all whom in their rapid charge they came across.

And while arms and missiles of all kinds were meeting in fierce conflict, and Bellona [the goddess of war], blowing her mournful trumpet, was raging more fiercely than usual to inflict disaster on the Romans, our men began to retreat; but roused by the reproaches of their officers, they made a fresh stand, and the battle increased like a conflagration, terrifying our soldiers, numbers of whom were pierced by strokes from the javelins hurled at them, and from arrows.

Then the two lines of battle dashed against each other, like the rams of warships, and thrusting with all their might, were tossed to and fro, like the waves of the sea. Our left wing had advanced actually up to the waggons, with the intent to push on still further if they were properly supported; but they were deserted by the rest of the cavalry, and so pressed upon by the superior numbers of the enemy, that they were overwhelmed and beaten down, like the ruin of a vast rampart. Presently our infantry also was left unsupported, while the different companies became so huddled together that a soldier could hardly draw his sword, or withdraw his hand after he had once stretched it out. And by this time such clouds of dust arose that it was scarcely possible to see the sky, which resounded with horrible cries; and in consequence, the darts, which were bearing death on every side, reached their mark, and fell with deadly effect because no one could see them beforehand so as to guard against them.

But when the barbarians, rushing on with their enormous host, beat down our horses and men, and left no spot to which our ranks could fall back to deploy, they were so closely packed that it was impossible to escape by forcing a way through them. Our men at last began to despise death, and again took to their swords, and slew all they encountered, while with mutual blows of battle-axes, helmets, and breastplates were dashed in pieces.

Then you might see the barbarian towering in his fierceness, hissing or shouting, fall with his legs pierced through, or his right hand cut off, sword and all, or his side transfixed, and still, in the last gasp of life, casting round him defiant glances. The plain was covered with carcasses, strewing the mutual ruin of the combatants, while the groans of the dying, or of men fearfully wounded, were intense and caused great dismay all around.

Amidst all this great tumult and confusion our infantry were exhausted by toil and danger, till at last they had neither strength left to fight, nor spirits to plan anything; their spears were broken by the frequent collisions, so that they were forced to content themselves with their drawn swords, which they thrust into the dense battalions of the enemy, disregarding their own safety, and seeing that every possibility of escape was cut off from them.

The ground, covered with streams of blood, made their feet slip, so that all that they endeavoured to do was to sell their lives as dearly as possible; and with such vehemence did they resist their enemies who pressed on them, that some were even killed by their own weapons. At last one black pool of blood disfigured everything, and wherever the eye turned, it could see nothing but piled-up heaps of dead, and lifeless corpses trampled on without mercy.

The sun being now high in the heavens, having traversed the sign of Leo, and reached the abode of the heavenly Virgo, scorched the Romans, who were emaciated by hunger, worn out with toil, and scarcely able to support even the weight of their armour. At last our columns were entirely beaten back by the overpowering weight of the barbarians, and so they took to disorderly flight, which is the only resource in extremity, each man trying to save himself as well as he could.

While they were all flying and scattering themselves over roads with which they were unacquainted, the emperor, bewildered with terrible fear, made his way over heap of dead, and fled to the battalions of the Lancearii and the Mattiarii, who, till the superior numbers of the enemy became wholly irresistible, stood firm and immovable. As soon as he saw him, Trajan exclaimed that all hope was lost, unless the emperor, thus deserted by his guards, could be protected by the aid of his foreign allies.

When this exclamation was heard, a count named Victor hastened to bring up with all speed the Batavians, who were placed in the reserve and who ought to have been near at hand, but as none of them could be found, he too retreated, and in a similar manner Richomeres and Saturninus saved themselves from danger.

So now, with rage flashing in their eyes, the barbarians pursued our men, who were in a state of torpor, the warmth of their veins having deserted them. Many were slain without knowing who smote them; some were overwhelmed by the mere weight of the crowd which pressed upon them; and some were slain by wounds—inflicted by their own comrades. The barbarians spared neither those who yielded nor those who resisted.

Besides these, many half-slain lay blocking up the roads, unable to endure the torture of their wounds; and heaps of dead horses were piled up and filled the plain with their carcasses. At last a dark moonless night put an end to the irremediable disaster which cost the Roman state so dear.

Just when it first became dark, the emperor being among a crowd of common soldiers, as it was believed—for no one said either that he had seen him, or been near him—was mortally wounded with an arrow, and, very shortly after, died, though his body was never found. For as some of the enemy loitered for a long time about the field in order to plunder the dead, none of the defeated army or of the inhabitants ventured to go to them. Others report that Valens did not die immediately, but that he was borne by a small body of picked soldiers and eunuchs to a cabin in the neighbourhood, which was strongly built, with two stories, and that while these unskillful hands were tending his wounds, the cottage was surrounded by the enemy, though they did not know who was in it; still, however, he was saved from the disgrace of being made a prisoner. For when his pursuers, while vainly attempting to force the barred doors, were assailed with arrows from the roof, they, not to lose by so inconvenient a delay the opportunity of collecting plunder, gathered some faggots and stubble, and setting fire to them, burnt down the building, with those who were in it.

But one of the soldiers dropped from the windows, and, being taken prisoner by the barbarians, revealed to them what had taken place, which caused them great concern because they looked upon themselves as defrauded of great glory in not having taken the ruler of the Roman state alive. This same young man afterwards secretly returned to our people, and gave this account of the affair.

When Spain had been recovered after a similar disaster, we are told that one of the Scipios was lost in a fire, the tower in which he had taken refuge having been burnt. At all events it is certain that neither Scipio nor Valens enjoyed that last honour of the dead—a regular funeral. Many illustrious men fell in this disastrous defeat, and among them one of the most remarkable was Trajan, and another was Sebastian. Scarcely one-third of the whole army escaped. Nor, except the battle of Cannae, is so destructive a slaughter recorded in our annals.

After this disastrous battle, when night had veiled the earth in darkness, those who survived fled, some to the right, some to the left, or wherever fear guided them, each man seeking refuge among his relations, as no one could think of anything but himself, while all fancied the lances of the enemy sticking in their backs. And far off were heard the miserable wailings of those who were left behind—the sobs of the dying, and the agonizing groans of the wounded.

But when daylight returned, the conquerors, like wild beasts rendered still more savage by the blood they had tasted and allured by the temptations of groundless hope, marched in a dense column upon Hadrianople.

Procopius of Caesarea

"Alaric Sacks Rome"

A.D. 410

N ow while Honorius [emperor: A.D. 395–423] was holding the imperial power in the West, barbarians took possession of his land; and I
shall tell who they were and in what manner they did so. There were
many Gothic nations in earlier times, just as also at the present, but the greatest and most important of all are the Goths, Vandals, Visigoths, and Gepaedes.
In ancient times, however, they were named Sauromatae and Melanchlaeni;
and there were some too who called these nations Getic. All these, while they
are distinguished from one another by their names, as has been said, do not differ in anything else at all. For they all have white bodies and fair hair, and are
tall and handsome to look upon, and they use the same laws and practice a
common religion. For they are all of the Arian [Christian] faith, and have one
language called Gothic; and, as it seems to me, they all came originally from one
tribe, and were distinguished later by the names of those who led each group. . . .

But the Visigoths, separating from the others, removed from there and at
first entered into an alliance with the Emperor Arcadius, but at a later time (for
faith with the Romans cannot dwell in barbarians), under the leadership of
Alaric, they became hostile to both emperors, and, beginning with Thrace,
treated all Europe as an enemy's land. Now the Emperor Honorius had before
this time been sitting in Rome, with never a thought of war in his mind, but
glad, I think, if men allowed him to remain quiet in his palace. But when word
was brought that the barbarians with a great army were not far off, but some-
where among the Taulantii, he abandoned the palace and fled in disorderly
fashion to Ravenna, a strong city lying just about at the end of the Ionian Gulf,

while some say that he brought in the barbarians himself, because an uprising had been started against him among his subjects; but this does not seem to me trustworthy, as far, at least, as one can judge of the character of the man. And the barbarians, finding that they had no hostile force to encounter them, became the most cruel of all men.

For they destroyed all the cities which they captured, especially those south of the Ionian Gulf, so completely that nothing has been left to my time to know them by, unless, indeed, it might be one tower or one gate or some such thing which chanced to remain. And they killed all the people, as many as came in their way, both old and young alike, sparing neither women nor children. Wherefore even up to the present time Italy is sparsely populated. They also gathered as plunder all the money out of all Europe, and, most important of all, they left in Rome nothing whatever of public or private wealth when they moved on to Gaul. But I shall now tell how Alaric captured Rome.

After much time had been spent by him in the siege, and he had not been able either by force or by any other device to capture the place, he formed the following plan. Among the youths in the army whose beards had not yet grown, but who had just come of age, he chose out three hundred whom he knew to be of good birth and possessed of valour beyond their years, and told them secretly that he was about to make a present of them to certain of the patricians in Rome, pretending that they were slaves. And he instructed them that, as soon as they got inside the houses of those men, they should display much gentleness and moderation and serve them eagerly in whatever tasks should be laid upon them by their owners; and he further directed them that not long afterwards, on an appointed day at about midday, when all those who were to be their masters would most likely be already asleep after their meal, they should all come to the gate called Salarian and with a sudden rush kill the guards, who would have no previous knowledge of the plot, and open the gates as quickly as possible.

After giving these orders to the youths, Alaric straightway sent ambassadors to the members of the senate, stating that he admired them for their loyalty toward their emperor, and that he would trouble them no longer, because of their valour and faithfulness, with which it was plain that they were endowed to a remarkable degree, and in order that tokens of himself might be preserved among men both noble and brave, he wished to present each one of them with some domestics. After making this declaration and sending the youths not long afterwards, he commanded the barbarians to make preparations for the departure, and he let this be known to the Romans. And they heard his words gladly, and, receiving the gift began to be exceedingly happy, since they were completely ignorant of the plot of the barbarian. For the youths, by being unusually obedient to their owners, averted suspicion, and in the camp some were already seen moving from their positions and raising the siege, while it seemed that the others were just on the point of doing the very same thing. But when the appointed day had come, Alaric armed his whole force for the attack and was holding them in readiness close by the Salarian Gate; for it happened that he had encamped there at the beginning of the siege. And all the youths at the time of the day agreed upon came to this gate, and, assailing the guards suddenly, put them to death; then they opened the gates and received Alaric and the army into the city at their leisure.

And they set fire to the houses which were next to the gate, among which was also the house of Sallust, who in ancient times wrote the history of the Romans, and the greater part of this house has stood half-burned up to my time; and after plundering the whole city and destroying the most of the Romans, they moved on. At that time they say that the Emperor Honorius in Ravenna received the message from one of the eunuchs, evidently a keeper of the poultry, that Rome had perished. And he cried out and said, "And yet it has just eaten from my hands!" For he had a very large cock, Rome by name; and the eunuch comprehending his words said that it was the city of Rome which had perished at the hands of Alaric, and the emperor with a sigh of relief answered quickly: "But I, my good fellow, thought that my fowl Rome had perished." So great, they say, was the folly with which this emperor was possessed.

But some say that Rome was not captured in this way by Alaric, but that Prolix, a woman of very unusual eminence in wealth and in fame among the Roman senatorial class, felt pity for the Romans who were being destroyed by hunger and the other suffering they endured; for they were already even tasting each other's flesh; and seeing that every good hope had left them, since both the river and the harbour were held by the enemy, she commanded her domestics, they say, to open the gates by night. Now when Alaric was almost to depart from Rome, he declared Attalus, one of their nobles, emperor of the Romans, investing him with the diadem and the purple and whatever else pertains to the imperial dignity. And he did this with the intention of removing Honorius from his throne and of giving over the whole power in the West to Attalus. With such a purpose, then, both Attalus and Alaric were going with a great army against Ravenna. But this Attalus was neither able to think wisely himself, nor to be persuaded by one who had wisdom to offer. So while Alaric did not by any means approve the plan, Attalus sent commanders to Libya without an army. Thus, then, were these things going on.

And the island of Britain revolted from the Romans, and the soldiers there chose as their king Constantinus, a man of no mean station. And he straightway gathered a fleet of ships and a formidable army and invaded both Spain and Gaul with a great force, thinking to enslave these countries. But Honorius was holding ships in readiness and waiting to see what would happen in Libya, in order that, if those sent by Attalus were repulsed, he might himself sail for Libya and keep some portion of his own kingdom, while if matters there should go against him, he might reach Theodosius and remain with him. For Arcadius had already died long before, and his son Theodosius, still a very young child, held the power of the East. But while Honorius was thus anxiously awaiting the outcome of these events and tossed amid the billows of uncertain fortune, it so chanced that some wonderful pieces of good fortune befell him. For God is accustomed to succour those who are neither clever nor able to devise anything of themselves, and to lend them assistance, if they be not wicked, when they are in the last extremity of despair; such a thing, indeed, befell this emperor. For it was suddenly reported from Libya that the commanders of Attalus had been destroyed, and that a host of ships was at hand from Byzantium with a very great number of soldiers who had come to assist him, though he had not expected them, and that Alaric, having quarrelled with Attalus, had stripped him of the emperor's garb and was now keeping him under guard in the position of a private citizen.

And afterwards Alaric died of disease, and the army of the Visigoths under the leadership of Adaulphus proceeded into Gaul, and Constantinus, defeated in battle, died with his sons. However the Romans never succeeded in recovering Britain, but it remained from that time on under tyrants. And the Goths, after making the crossing of the Ister, at first occupied Pannonia, but afterwards, since the emperor gave them the right, they inhabited the country of Thrace. And after spending no great time there they conquered the West.

Edward Gibbon

"The Death and Funeral of Alaric"

A.D. 410

Whether fame, or conquest, or riches were the object of Alaric, he pursued that object with an indefatigable ardour which could neither be quelled by adversity nor satisfied by success. No sooner had he reached the extreme land of Italy than he was attracted by the neighbouring prospect of a fertile and peaceful island. Yet even the possession of Sicily he considered only as an intermediate step to the important expedition which he already meditated against the continent of Africa. The streights of Rhegium and Messina are twelve miles in length, and, in the narrowest passage, about one mile and a half broad, and the fabulous monsters of the deep, the rocks of Scylla and the whirlpool of Charibdis, could terrify none but the most timid and unskilled mariners. Yet as soon as the first division of the Goths had embarked, a sudden tempest arose, which sunk, or scattered, many of the transports, their courage was daunted by the terrors of a new element, and the whole design was defeated by the premature death of Alaric, which fixed, after a short illness, the fatal term of his conquests.

The ferocious character of the barbarians was displayed in the funeral of a hero, whose valour and fortune they celebrated with mournful applause. By the labour of a captive multitude, they forcibly diverted the course of the Busentinus, a small river that washes the walls of Consentia. The royal sepulchre, adorned with the splendid spoils and trophies of Rome, was constructed in the vacant bed; the waters were then restored to their natural channel; and the secret spot, where the remains of Alaric had been deposited, was forever concealed by the inhuman massacre of the prisoners, who had been employed to execute the work.

—VIII—

THE HUNS

Ammianus Marcellinus introduced the Huns in the preceding chapter as the scourge from the east ("in the shape of men") who drove the Goths into the Roman Empire in A.D. 375. Their origins—perhaps from the northern borders of China—remain unknown, but they appeared seemingly out of nowhere, in 370, and soon cut their way across the Ukraine and into southeastern Europe. Their battle tactics were almost always the same: a fast cavalry charge, followed by a feigned retreat to set a trap, then an ambush.

By the fifth century, what is now Hungary had become their homeland. With Attila (ca. 406–453) as their leader they advanced to the gates of Constantinople and through central Europe all the way to Gaul, where they terrorized the countryside until 451, when they were turned back near Châlons by a mixed army of Romans and Visigoths.

A few more raids into northern Italy followed, and although Attila never sacked Rome, he does appear in a Vatican mural by Raphael (see figure 10). He is shown meeting Pope Leo I, and both men are on horseback, while overhead hover—rather heavily, as though they were not quite lighter than air—figures of St. Peter and St. Paul brandishing swords against the invader. After Attila's death on his wedding night in 453, his kingdom fell apart, having had—most historians seem to agree—little effect on Europe except for the myths surrounding his name.

The first entry here is a nineteenth-century translation of a short poem by the

Egyptian-born poet Claudian (Claudius Claudianus, ca. 370–ca. 404). He seems to be remembered best for having composed bad but fawning verses about the court of Emperor Honorius, but even with all its contrived classical allusions, "The Huns" gives some suggestion of imperial Rome's fascination with the mysterious barbarians.

This excerpt is followed by a long eyewitness report of dining and negotiating with Attila by Priscus, an eastern Roman politician and historian who was sent on a diplomatic mission to the king of the Huns by Emperor Theodosius II in the summer of 449. He wrote his account—in Greek—not long afterward. It contains not only a rare portrait of Attila, but also the story of an assassination plot and a glimpse or two of the western bureaucrats who were attached to his court.

Attila's story is completed—with an emphasis on his final years—by a selection from *The Origins and Deeds of the Goths*, written by Jordanes, the earliest surviving Gothic historian, probably written in 551. He was most likely born on the lower Danube and claimed that before his conversion to Christianity he had been a secretary to a Gothic chief.

Claudian

"The Huns"

ca. A.D. 400

There is a race on Scythia's verge extreme
Eastward, beyond the Tanais' chilly stream.
The Northern Bear looks on no uglier crew:
Base is their garb, their bodies foul to view;
Their souls are ne'er subdued to sturdy toil
Or Ceres' arts: their sustenance is spoil.
With horrid wounds they gash their brutal brows,
And o'er their murdered parents bind their vows
Not e'en the Centaur-offspring of the Cloud
Were horsed more firmly than this savage crowd.
Brisk, lithe, in loose array they first come on,
Fly, turn, attack the foe who deems them gone.

PRISCUS

"NEGOTIATING AND DINING WITH ATTILA"

A.D. 449

We set out with the barbarians, and arrived at Sardica [Sofia], which is thirteen days for a fast traveler from Constantinople. [The traveling party included Maximin (the Roman emperor Theodosius II's ambassador to Attila), Maximin's friend Priscus, Bigilas (an unusually outspoken intrepreter), and a large group of Huns returning from Constantinople, including Edecon (king of the Skirian tribe, who had been bribed by some Romans to murder Attila), Orestes (a Roman bureaucrat in the Hun court whose son would become Romulus Augustus, the last Roman Emperor of the West) and a number of deserters from Attila's army who were being sent home.]

Halting there we considered it advisable to invite Edecon and the barbarians with him to dinner. The inhabitants of the place sold us sheep and oxen, which we slaughtered, and we prepared a meal. In the course of the feast, as the barbarians lauded Attila and we lauded the Emperor, Bigilas remarked that it was not fair to compare a man and a god, meaning Attila by the man and Theodosius by the god. The Huns grew excited and hot at this remark. But we turned the conversation in another direction, and soothed their wounded feelings; and after dinner, when we separated, Maximin presented Edecon and Orestes with silk garments and Indian gems. . . .

When we arrived at Naissus we found the city deserted, as though it had been sacked; only a few sick persons lay in the churches. We halted at a short distance from the river, in an open space, for all the ground adjacent to the bank was full of the bones of men slain in war. On the morrow we came to the station of Agintheus, the commander-in-chief of the Illyrian armies (*magister militant per Illyricum*), who was posted not far from Naissus, to announce to him the Imperial commands, and to receive five of those seventeen deserters, about whom Attila had written to the Emperor. We had an interview with him, and having treated the deserters with kindness, he committed them to us. The next day we proceeded from the district of Naissus towards the Danube; we entered a covered valley with many bends and windings and circuitous paths. We thought we were traveling due west, but when the day dawned the sun rose in front; and some of us unacquainted with the topography cried out that the sun was going the wrong way, and portending unusual events. The fact was that that part of the road faced the east, owing to the irregularity of the ground. Having passed these rough places we arrived at a plain which was also well wooded.

At the river we were received by barbarian ferrymen, who rowed us across the river in boats made by themselves out of single trees hewn and hollowed. These preparations had not been made for our sake, but to convey across a company of Huns; for Attila pretended that he wished to hunt in Roman territory, but his intent was really hostile, because all the deserters had not been given up to him. Having crossed the Danube, and proceeded with the barbarians about seventy stadia, we were compelled to wait in a certain plain, that Edecon and his party might go on in front and inform Attila of our arrival. As we were dining in the evening we heard the sound of horses approaching, and two Scythians arrived with directions that we were to set out to Attila. We asked them first to partake of our meal, and they dismounted and made good cheer. On the next day, under their guidance, we arrived at the tents of Attila, which were numerous, about three o'clock, and when we wished to pitch our tent on a hill the barbarians who met us prevented us, because the tent of Attila was on low ground, so we halted where the Scythians desired.

Then a message was received from Attila, who was aware of the nature of their embassy, saying that if they had nothing further to communicate to him he would not receive them, so they reluctantly prepared to return. When the baggage had been packed on the beasts of burden, and we were perforce preparing to start in the night time, messengers came from Attila bidding us wait on account of the late hour. Then men arrived with an ox and river fish, sent to us by Attila, and when we had dined we retired to sleep. When it was day we expected a gentle and courteous message from the barbarian, but he again bade us depart if we had no further mandates beyond what he already knew. We made no reply, and prepared to set out, though Bigilas insisted that we should feign to have some other communication to make. When I saw that Maximin was very dejected, I went to Scottas (one of the Hun nobles, brother of Onegesius), taking with me Rusticius, who understood the Hun language. He had come with us to Scythia, not as a member of the embassy, but on business with Constantius, an Italian whom Aetius had sent to Attila to be that monarch's private secretary. I informed Scottas, Rusticius acting as interpreter, that Maximin would give him many presents if he would procure him an interview with Attila; and, moreover, that the embassy would not only conduce to the public interests of the two powers, but to the private interest of Onegesius, for the Emperor desired that he should be sent as an ambassador to Byzantium, to arrange the disputes of the Huns and Romans, and that there he would receive splendid gifts.

As Onegesius was not present it was for Scottas, I said, to help us, or rather help his brother, and at the same time prove that the report was true which ascribed to him an influence with Attila equal to that possessed by his brother. Scottas mounted his horse and rode to Attila's tent, while I returned to Maximin, and found him in a state of perplexity and anxiety, lying on the grass with Bigilas. I described my interview with Scottas, and bade him make preparations for an audience of Attila. They both jumped up, approving of what I had done, and recalled the men who had started with the beasts of burden. As we were considering what to say to Attila, and how to present the Emperor's gifts, Scottas came to fetch us, and we entered Attila's tent, which was surrounded by a multitude of barbarians. We found Attila sitting on a wooden chair. We stood at a little distance and Maximin advanced and saluted the barbarian, to whom he gave the Emperor's letter, saying that the Emperor prayed for the safety of him and his. The king replied, "It shall be unto the Romans as they wish it to be unto me," and immediately addressed Bigilas, calling him a shameless beast, and asking him why he ventured to come when all the deserters had not been given up.

After the departure of Bigilas, who returned to the Empire (nominally to find the deserters whose restoration Attila demanded, but really to get the money for his fellow-conspirator Edecon), we remained one day in that place, and then set out with Attila for the northern parts of the country. We accompanied the barbarian for a time, but when we reached a certain point took another route by the command of the Scythians who conducted us, as Attila was proceeding to a village where he intended to marry the daughter of Eskam, though he had many other wives, for the Scythians practice polygamy. We proceeded along a level road in a plain and met with navigable rivers—of which the greatest, next to the Danube, are the Drecon, Tigas, and Tiphesas—which we crossed in the monoxyles, boats made of one piece, used by the dwellers on the banks: the smaller rivers we traversed on rafts which the barbarians carry about with them on carts, for the purpose of crossing morasses. In the villages we were supplied with food—millet instead of corn, and mead, as the natives call it, instead of wine. The attendants who followed us received millet, and a drink made of barley, which the barbarians call *kam*. Late in the evening, having traveled a long distance, we pitched our tents on the banks of a fresh-water lake, used for water by the inhabitants of the neighbouring village. But a wind and storm, accompanied by thunder and lightning and heavy rain, arose, and almost threw down our tents; all our utensils were rolled into the waters of the lake.

Terrified by the mishap and the atmospherical disturbance, we left the place and lost one another in the dark and the rain, each following the road that seemed most easy. But we all reached the village by different ways, and raised an alarm to obtain what we lacked. The Scythians of the village sprang out of their huts at the noise, and, lighting the reeds which they use for kindling fires, asked what we wanted. Our conductors replied that the storm had alarmed us; so they invited us to their huts and provided warmth for us by lighting large fires of reeds. The lady who governed the village—she had been one of Bleda's wives—sent us provisions and good-looking girls to console us (this is a Scythian compliment). We treated the young women to a share in the eatables but declined to take any further advantage of their presence. We remained in the huts till day dawned and then went to look for our lost utensils, which we found partly in the place where we had pitched the tent, partly on the bank of the lake, and partly in the water. We spent that day in the village drying our things; for the storm had ceased and the sun was bright. Having looked after our horses and cattle, we directed our steps to the princess, to whom we paid our respects and presented gifts in return for her courtesy. The gifts consisted of things which are esteemed by the barbarians as not produced in their country- three silver *phialai*, red skins, Indian pepper, palm fruit, and other delicacies.

Having advanced a distance of seven days farther, we halted at a village; for as the rest of the route was the same for us and Attila, it behooved us to wait, so that he might go in front. Here we met with some of the "western Romans," who had also come on an embassy to Attila—the count Romulus, Promotus governor of Noricum, and Romanus, a military captain. With them was Constantius, whom Aetius had sent to Attila to be his secretary, and Tatulus, the father of Orestes; these two were not connected with the embassy, but were friends of the ambassadors. Constantius had known them of old in the Italies, and Orestes had married the daughter of Romulus.

The object of the embassy was to soften the soul of Attila, who demanded the surrender of one Silvanus, a dealer in silver plate in Rome, because he had received golden vessels from a certain Constantius. This Constantius, a native of Gaul, had preceded his namesake in the office of secretary to Attila. When Sirmium in Pannonia was besieged by the Scythians, the bishop of the place consigned the vessels to his (Constantius's) care, that if the city were taken and he survived they might be used to ransom him; and in case he were slain, to ransom the citizens who were led into captivity. But when the city was enslaved, Constantius violated his engagement, and, as he happened to be at Rome on business, pawned the vessels to Silvanus for a sum of money, on condition that if he gave back the money within a prescribed period the dishes should be returned, but otherwise should become the property of Silvanus. Constantius, suspected of treachery, was crucified by Attila and Bleda; and afterwards, when the affair of the vessels became known to Attila, he demanded the surrender of Silvanus on the ground that he had stolen his property. Accordingly Aetius and the Emperor of the Western Romans sent to explain that Silvanus was the cred- itor of Constantius, the vessels having been pawned and not stolen, and that he had sold them to priests and others for sacred purposes. If, however, Attila refused to desist from his demand, he, the Emperor, would send him the value of the vessels, but would not surrender the innocent Silvanus.

Having waited for some time until Attila advanced in front of us, we proceeded, and having crossed some rivers we arrived at a large village, where Attila's home was said to be more splendid than his residences in other places. It was made of polished boards, and surrounded with a wooden enclosure, designed, not for protection, but for appearance. The home of Onegesius was second to the king's in splendour, and was also encircled with a wooden enclosure, but it was not adorned with towers like that of the king. Not far from the enclosure was a large bath which Onegesius—who was the second in power among the Scythians—built, having transported the stones from Pannonia; for the barbarians in this district had no stones or trees, but used imported material. The builder of the bath was a captive from Sirmium, who expected to win his freedom as payment for making the bath. But he was disappointed, and greater trouble befell him than mere captivity among the Scythians, for Onegesius appointed him bathman, and he used to minister to him and his family when they bathed.

When Attila entered the village he was met by girls advancing in rows, under thin white canopies of linen, which were held up by the outside women who stood under them, and were so large that seven or more girls walked beneath each. There were many lines of damsels thus canopied, and they sang Scythian songs. When he came near the house of Onegesius, which lay on his way, the wife of Onegesius issued from the door, with a number of servants, bearing meat and wine, and saluted him and begged him to partake of her hospitality. This is the highest honour that can be shown among the Scythians. To gratify the wife of his friend, he ate, just as he sat on his horse, his attendants raising the tray to his saddlebow; and having tasted the wine, he went on to the palace, which was higher than the other houses and built on an elevated site. But we remained in the house of Onegesius, at his invitation, for he had returned from his expedition with Attila's son. His wife and kinsfolk entertained us to dinner, for he had no leisure himself, as he had to relate to Attila the result of his expedition, and explain the accident which had happened to the young prince, who had slipped and broken his right arm. After dinner we left the house of Onegesius, and took up our quarters nearer the palace, so that Maximin might be at a convenient distance for visiting Attila or holding intercourse with his court. The next morning, at dawn of day, Maximin sent me to Onegesius, with presents offered by himself as well as those which the Emperor had sent, and I was to find out whether he would have an interview with Maximin and at what time. When I arrived at the house, along with the attendants who carried the gifts, I found the doors closed, and had to wait until someone should come out and announce our arrival. As I waited and walked up and down in front of the enclosure which surrounded the house, a man, whom from his Scythian dress I took for a barbarian, came up and addressed me in Greek, with the word *Xaipe*, "Hail!"

I was surprised at a Scythian speaking Greek. For the subjects of the Huns, swept together from various lands, speak, besides their own barbarous tongues, either Hunnic or Gothic, or—as many as have commercial dealings with the western Romans—Latin; but none of them easily speak Greek, except captives from the Thracian or Illyrian seacoast; and these last are easily known to any stranger by their torn garments and the squalor of their heads, as men who have met with a reverse. This man, on the contrary, resembled a well-to-do Scythian, being well dressed, and having his hair cut in a circle after Scythian fashion. Having returned his salutation, I asked him who he was and whence he had come into a foreign land and adopted Scythian life. When he asked me why I wanted to know, I told him that his Hellenic speech had prompted my curiosity. Then he smiled and said that he was born a Greek and had gone as a merchant to Viminacium [Kostolas], on the Danube, where he had stayed a long time, and married a very rich wife. But the city fell prey to the barbarians, and he was stript of his prosperity, and on account of his riches was allotted to Onegesius in the division of the spoil, as it was the custom among the Scythians for the chiefs to reserve for themselves the rich prisoners. Having fought bravely against the Romans and the Acatiri, he had paid the spoils he won to his master, and so obtained freedom. He then married a barbarian wife and had children, and had the privilege of eating at the table of Onegesius.

He considered his new life among the Scythians better than his old life among the Romans, and the reasons he gave were as follows: "After war the Scythians live in inactivity, enjoying what they have got, and not at all, or very little, harassed. The Romans, on the other hand, are in the first place very liable to perish in war, as they have to rest their hopes of safety on others, and are not allowed, on account of their tyrants, to use arms. And those who use them are injured by the cowardice of their generals, who cannot support the conduct of war. But the condition of the subjects in time of peace is far more grievous than the evils of war, for the exaction of the taxes is very severe, and unprincipled men inflict injuries on others, because the laws are practically not valid against all classes. A transgressor who belongs to the wealthy classes is not punished for his injustice, while a poor man, who does not understand business, undergoes the legal penalty, that is if he does not depart this life before the trial, so long is the course of lawsuits protracted, and so much money is expended on them. The climax of the misery is to have to pay in order to obtain justice. For no one will give a court to the injured man unless he pays a sum of money to the judge and the judge's clerks."

In reply to this attack on the Empire, I asked him to be good enough to listen with patience to the other side of the question. "The creators of the Roman republic," I said, "who were wise and good men, in order to prevent things from being done at haphazard, made one class of men guardians of the laws, and appointed another class to the profession of arms, who were to have no other object than to be always ready for battle, and to go forth to war without dread, as though to their ordinary exercise, having by practice exhausted all their fear beforehand. Others again were assigned to attend to the cultivation of the ground, to support both themselves and those who fight in their defence, by contributing the military corn-supply. . . . To those who protect the interests of the litigants a sum of money is paid by the latter, just as a payment is made by the farmers to the soldiers. Is it not fair to support him who assists and requite him for his kindness? The support of the horse benefits the horseman. . . . Those who spend money on a suit and lose it in the end cannot fairly put it down to anything but the injustice of their case. And as to the long time spent on lawsuits, that is due to concern for justice, that judges may not fail in passing correct judgments, by having to give sentence offhand; it is better that they should reflect, and conclude the case more tardily, than that by judging in a hurry they should both injure man and transgress against the Deity, the institutor of justice. . . . The Romans treat their servants better than the king of the

Scythians treats his subjects. They deal with them as fathers or teachers, admonishing them to abstain from evil and follow the lines of conduct which they have esteemed honourable; they reprove them for their errors like their own children. They are not allowed, like the Scythians, to inflict death on them. They have numerous ways of conferring freedom; they can manumit not only during life, but also by their wills, and the testamentary wishes of a Roman in regard to his property are law."

My interlocutor shed tears, and confessed that the laws and constitution of the Romans were fair, but deplored that the governors, not possessing the spirit of former generations, were ruining the State.

As we were engaged in this discussion a servant came out and opened the door of the enclosure. I hurried up, and inquired how Onegesius was engaged, for I desired to give him a message from the Roman ambassador. He replied that I should meet him if I waited a little, as he was about to go forth. And after a short time I saw him coming out, and addressed him, saying, "The Roman ambassador salutes you, and I have come with gifts from him, and with the gold which the Emperor sent you. The ambassador is anxious to meet you, and begs you to appoint a time and place." Onegesius bade his servants receive the gold and the gifts, and told me to announce to Maximin that he would go to him immediately. I delivered the message, and Onegesius appeared in the tent without delay. He expressed his thanks to Maximin and the Emperor for the presents, and asked why he sent for him. Maximin said that the time had come for Onegesius to have greater renown among men, if he would go to the Emperor, and by his wisdom arrange the objects of dispute between the Romans and Huns, and establish concord between them; and thereby he will procure many advantages for his own family, as he and his children will always be friends of the Emperor and the Imperial family. Onegesius inquired what measures would gratify the Emperor and how he could arrange the disputes. Maximin replied: "If you cross into the lands of the Roman Empire you will lay the Emperor under an obligation, and you will arrange the matters at issue by investigating their causes and deciding them on the basis of the peace." Onegesius said he would inform the Emperor and his ministers of Attila's wishes, but the Romans need not think they could ever prevail with him to betray his master or neglect his Scythian training and his wives and children, or to prefer wealth among the Romans to bondage with Attila. He added that he would be of more service to the Romans by remaining in his own land and softening the anger of his master, if he were indignant for aught with the Romans, than by visiting them and subjecting himself to blame if he made arrangements that Attila did not approve of. He then retired, having consented that I should act as an intermediary in conveying messages from Maximin to himself, for it would not have been consistent with Maximin's dignity as ambassador to visit him constantly.

The next day I entered the enclosure of Attila's palace, bearing gifts to his wife, whose name was Kreka. She had three sons, of whom the eldest governed the Acatiri and the other nations who dwell in Pontic Scythia. Within the enclosure were numerous buildings, some of carved boards beautifully fitted together, others of straight, fastened on round wooden blocks which rose to a moderate height from the ground. Attila's wife lived here, and, having been admitted by the barbarians at the door, I found her reclining on a soft couch. The floor of the room was covered with woollen mats for walking on. A number of servants stood round her, and maids sitting on the floor in front of her embroidered with colours linen cloths intended to be placed over the Scythian dress for ornament. Having approached, saluted, and presented the gifts, I went out, and walked to another house, where Attila was, and waited for Onegesius, who, as I knew, was with Attila. I stood in the middle of a great crowd—the guards of Attila and his attendants knew me, and so no one hindered me. I saw a number of people advancing, and a great commotion and noise, Attila's egress being expected. And he came forth from the house with a dignified gait, looking round on this side and on that. He was accompanied by Onegesius, and stood in front of the house; and many persons who had lawsuits with one another came up and received his judgment. Then he returned into the house, and received ambassadors of barbarous peoples.

As I was waiting for Onegesius, I was accosted by Romulus and Promotus and Romanus, the ambassadors who had come from Italy about the golden vessels; they were accompanied by Rusticius and by Constantiolus, a man from the Pannonian territory, which was subject to Attila. They asked me whether we had been dismissed or were constrained to remain, and I replied that it was just

to learn this from Onegesius that I was waiting outside the palace. When I
inquired in my turn whether Attila had vouchsafed them a kind reply, they told
me that his decision could not be moved, and that he threatened war unless
either Silvanus or the drinking-vessels were given up. . . .

As we were talking about the state of the world, Onegesius came out; we
went up to him and asked him about our concerns. Having first spoken with
some barbarians, he bade me inquire of Maximin what consular the Romans
are sending as an ambassador to Attila. When I came to our tent I delivered the
message to Maximin, and deliberated with him what answer we should make
to the question of the barbarian. Returning to Onegesius, I said that the
Romans desired him to come to them and adjust the matters of dispute, otherwise the Emperor will send whatever ambassador he chooses. He then bade me
fetch Maximin, whom he conducted to the presence of Attila. Soon after
Maximin came out, and told me that the barbarian wished Nomus or Anatolius
or Senator to be the ambassador, and that he would not receive any other than
one of these three; when he (Maximin) replied that it was not meet to mention
men by name and so render them suspected in the eyes of the Emperor, Attila
said that if they do not choose to comply with his wishes the differences will be
adjusted by arms.

When we returned to our tent the father of Orestes came with an invitation
from Attila for both of us to a banquet at three o'clock. When the hour arrived
we went to the palace, along with the embassy from the western Romans, and
stood on the threshold of the hall in the presence of Attila. The cup-bearers gave
us a cup, according to the national custom, that we might pray before we sat
down. Having tasted the cup, we proceeded to take our seats; all the chairs were
ranged along the walls of the room on either side. Attila sat in the middle on a
couch; a second couch was set behind him, and from it steps led up to his bed,
which was covered with linen sheets and wrought coverlets for ornament, such
as Greeks and Romans use to deck bridal beds. The places on the right of Attila
were held chief in honour, those on the left, where we sat, were only second.
Berichus, a noble among the Scythians, sat on our side, but had the precedence
of us. Onegesius sat on a chair on the right of Attila's couch, and over against
Onegesius on a chair sat two of Attila's sons; his eldest son sat on his couch, not

near him, but at the extreme end, with his eyes fixed on the ground, in shy respect for his father. When all were arranged, a cup-bearer came and handed Attila a wooden cup of wine. He took it, and saluted the first in precedence, who, honoured by the salutation, stood up, and might not sit down until the king, having tasted or drained the wine, returned the cup to the attendant.

All the guests then honoured Attila in the same way, saluting him, and then tasting the cups; but he did not stand up. Each of us had a special cup-bearer, who would come forward in order to present the wine, when the cup-bearer of Attila retired. When the second in precedence and those next to him had been honoured in like manner, Attila toasted us in the same way according to the order of the seats. When this ceremony was over the cup-bearers retired, and tables, large enough for three or four, or even more, to sit at, were placed next the table of Attila, so that each could take of the food on the dishes without leaving his seat. The attendant of Attila first entered with a dish full of meat, and behind him came the other attendants with bread and viands, which they laid on the tables. A luxurious meal, served on silver plate, had been made ready for us and the barbarian guests, but Attila ate nothing but meat on a wooden trencher.

In everything else, too, he showed himself temperate; his cup was of wood, while to the guests were given goblets of gold and silver. His dress, too, was quite simple, affecting only to be clean. The sword he carried at his side, the ratchets of his Scythian shoes, the bridle of his horse were not adorned, like those of the other Scythians, with gold or gems or anything costly. When the viands of the first course had been consumed we all stood up, and did not resume our seats until each one, in the order before observed, drank to the health of Attila in the goblet of wine presented to him. We then sat down, and a second dish was placed on each table with eatables of another kind. After this course the same ceremony was observed as after the first. When evening fell torches were lit, and two barbarians coming forward in front of Attila sang songs they had composed, celebrating his victories and deeds of valour in war. And of the guests, as they looked at the singers, some were pleased with the verses, others reminded of wars were excited in their souls, while yet others, whose bodies were feeble with age and their spirits compelled to rest, shed tears. After the songs a Scythian, whose mind was deranged, appeared, and by uttering outlandish and senseless words forced the company to laugh.

After him Zerkon, the Moorish dwarf, entered. He had been sent by Attila as a gift to Aetius, and Edecon had persuaded him to come to Attila in order to recover his wife, whom he had left behind him in Scythia; the lady was a Scythian whom he had obtained in marriage through the influence of his patron Bleda. He did not succeed in recovering her, for Attila was angry with him for returning. On the occasion of the banquet he made his appearance, and threw all except Attila into fits of unquenchable laughter by his appearance, his dress, his voice, and his words, which were a confused jumble of Latin, Hunnic, and Gothic. Attila, however, remained immovable and of unchanging countenance, nor by word or act did he betray anything approaching to a smile of merriment except at the entry of Ernas, his youngest son, whom he pulled by the cheek, and gazed on with a calm look of satisfaction. I was surprised that he made so much of this son, and neglected his other children; but a barbarian who sat beside me and knew Latin, bidding me not reveal what he told, gave me to understand that prophets had forewarned Attila that his race would fall, but would be restored by this boy. When the night had advanced we retired from the banquet, not wishing to assist further at the potations.

JORDANES

"A GOTH'S BIOGRAPHY OF ATTILA"

A.D. 551

During this peace [ca. A.D. 439] Attila was lord over all the Huns and almost the sole earthly ruler of all tribes of Scythia; a man marvellous for his glorious fame among all nations.

. . . Now this Attila was the son of Mundiuch, and his brothers were Octar and Ruas who are said to have ruled before Attila, though not over quite so many tribes as he. After their death he succeeded to the throne of the Huns, together with his brother Bleda. In order that he might first be equal to the expedition he was preparing, he sought to increase his strength by murder.

Thus he proceeded from the destruction of his own kindred to the menace of all others. But though he increased his power by this shameful means, yet by the balance of justice he received the hideous consequences of his own cruelty. Now when his brother Bleda, who ruled over a great part of the Huns, had been slain by his treachery, Attila united all the people under his own rule. Gathering also a host of the other tribes which he then held under his sway, he sought to subdue the foremost nations of the world—the Romans and the Visigoths. His army is said to have numbered five hundred thousand men. He was a man born into the world to shake the nations, the scourge of all lands, who in some way terrified all mankind by the dreadful rumors noised abroad concerning him.

He was haughty in his walk, rolling his eyes hither and thither, so that the power of his proud spirit appeared in the movement of his body. He was indeed a lover of war, yet restrained in action, mighty in counsel, gracious to suppliants, and lenient to those who were once received into his protection. He was short of stature, with a broad chest and a large head; his eyes were small, his beard thin and sprinkled with gray; and he had a flat nose and a swarthy complexion, showing the evidences of his origin. And though his temper was such that he always had great self-confidence, yet his assurance was increased by finding the sword of Mars, always esteemed sacred among the kings of the Scythians. The historian Priscus says it was discovered under the following circumstances: "When a certain shepherd beheld one heifer of his flock limping and could find no cause for this wound, he anxiously followed the trail of blood and at length came to a sword it had unwittingly trampled while nibbling the grass. He dug it up and took it straight to Attila. He rejoiced at this gift and, being ambitious, thought he had been appointed ruler of the whole world, and that through the sword of Mars supremacy in all wars was assured to him."

Now when Gaiseric [Genseric], king of the Vandals, learned that his mind was bent on the devastation of the world, he incited Attila by many gifts to make war on the Visigoths, for he was afraid that Theodoric, king of the Visigoths [grandson of Alaric], would avenge the injury done to his daughter. She had been joined in wedlock with Hunneric the son of Gaiseric, and at first was happy in this union. But afterwards he was cruel even to his own children, and because of the mere suspicion that she was attempting to poison him, he cut off her nose and mutilated her ears. He sent her back to her father in Gaul thus despoiled of her natural charms. So the wretched girl presented a pitiable aspect ever after, and the cruelty which would stir even strangers still more surely incited her father to vengeance.

Attila, therefore, in his efforts to bring about the wars long ago instigated by the bribe of Gaiseric, sent ambassadors into Italy to the Emperor Valentinian to sow strife between the Goths and the Romans, thinking to shatter by civil discord those whom he could not crush in battle. He declared that he was in no way violating his friendly relations with the Empire, but that he had a quarrel with Theodoric, king of the Visigoths. As he wished to be kindly received, he filled the rest of the letter with the usual flattering salutations, striving to win credence for his falsehood. In like manner he despatched a message to Theodoric, king of the Visigoths, urging him to break his alliance with the Romans and reminding him of the battles to which they had recently provoked him. Beneath his great ferocity he was a subtle man, and fought with craft before he made war.

Then the Emperor Valentinian sent an embassy to the Visigoths and their king Theodoric, with this message:

"Bravest of nations, it is the part of prudence for us to unite against the lord of the earth who wishes to enslave the whole world; who requires no just cause for battle, but supposes whatever he does is right. He measures his ambition by his might. License satisfies his pride. Despising law and right, he shows himself an enemy to Nature herself. And thus he, who clearly is the common foe of each, deserves the hatred of all. Pray remember—what you surely cannot forget—that the Huns do not overthrow nations by means of war, where there is an equal chance, but assail them by treachery, which is a greater cause for anxiety. To say nothing about ourselves, can you suffer such insolence to go unpunished? Since you are mighty in arms, give heed to your own danger and join hands with us in common. Bear aid also to the Empire, of which you hold a part. If you would learn how such an alliance should be sought and welcomed by us, look into the plans of the foe."

By these and like arguments the ambassadors of Valentinian prevailed upon King Theodoric. He answered them, saying: "Romans, you have attained your desire; you have made Attila our foe also. We will pursue him wherever he summons us, and though he is puffed up by his victories over divers races, yet the Goths know how to fight this haughty foe. I call no war dangerous save one whose cause is weak; for he fears no ill on whom Majesty has smiled." The nobles shouted assent to the reply and the multitude gladly followed. All were fierce for battle and longed to meet the Huns, their foe. And so a countless host was led forth by Theodoric, king of the Visigoths, who sent home four of his sons, namely Friderich and Eurich, Retemer and Himnerith, taking with him only the two elder sons, Thorismud and Theodorid, as partners of his toil. O brave array, sure defense and sweet comradeship, having the aid of those who delight to share in the same dangers!

On the side of the Romans stood the Patrician Aetius, on whom at that time the whole Empire of the West depended; a man of such wisdom that he had assembled warriors from everywhere to meet them on equal terms. Now these were his auxiliaries: Franks, Sarmatians, Armoricians, Liticians, Burgundians, Saxons, Riparians, Olibriones (once Roman soldiers and now the flower of the allied forces), and some other Celtic or German tribes. And so they met in the Catalaunian Plains [in June 451, near Châlons, France], which are also called Mauriacian, extending in length one hundred leuva, as the Gauls express it, and seventy in width. Now a Gallic *leuva* measures a distance of fifteen hundred paces. That portion of the earth accordingly became the threshing-floor of countless races. The two hosts bravely joined battle. Nothing was done under cover, but they contended in open fight. What just cause can be found for the encounter of so many nations, or what hatred inspired them all to take arms against each other? It is proof that the human race lives for its kings, for it is at the mad impulse of one mind a slaughter of nations takes place; and at the whim of a haughty ruler that which nature has taken ages to produce perishes in a moment.

But before we set forth the order of the battle itself, it seems needful to relate what had already happened in the course of the campaign, for it was not only a famous struggle but one that was complicated and confused. Well then, Sangiban, king of the Alani, smitten with fear of what might come to pass, had promised to surrender to Attila, and to give into his keeping Aureliani [Orleans], a city of Gaul wherein he then dwelt. When Theodoric and Aetius learned of this, they cast up great earthworks around that city before Attila's arrival and kept watch over the suspected Sangiban, placing him with his tribe in the midst of their auxiliaries. Then Attila, king of the Huns, was taken aback by this event and lost confidence in his own troops, so that he feared to begin the conflict. While he was meditating on flight—a greater calamity than death itself—he decided to inquire into the future through soothsayers. So, as was their custom, they examined the entrails of cattle and certain streaks in bones that had been scraped, and foretold disaster to the Huns. Yet as a slight consolation they prophesied that the chief commander of the foe they were to meet should fall and mar by his death the rest of the victory and the triumph. Now Attila deemed the death of Aetius a thing to be desired even at the cost of his own life, for Aetius stood in the way of his plans. So although he was disturbed by this prophecy, yet inasmuch as he was a man who sought counsel of omens in all warfare, he began the battle with anxious heart at about the ninth hour of the day, in order that the impending darkness might come to his aid if the outcome should be disastrous.

The armies met, as we have said, in the Catalaunian Plains. The battlefield

Figure 1. Gold comb ornamented with a group of Scythians in combat. Sixth–fourth century B.C. Courtesy Werner Forman Archive/Art Resource.

Figure 2. Gold plaque in the form of a mounted Scythian. Fourth century B.C. Courtesy Werner Forman Archive/Art Resource.

Figure 3. Detail from Trajan's Column in Rome, commemorating Emperor Trajan's conquest of the region that is now Romania. Early second century B.C. Courtesy Scala/Art Resource.

Figure 4. Detail from the Sarcophagus Ludovisi (Roman) depicting a battle between Romans and barbarians. Second century B.C. Courtesy Scala/Art Resource.

Figure 5. Detail of a Celtic warrior with loot, from a terra-cotta temple frieze, Sassoferato, Italy. Early second century B.C. Courtesy Erich Lessing/Art Resource.

Figure 6. Detail of a Gaul on his chariot from a terra-cotta temple frieze, Sassoferato, Italy. Early second century B.C. Courtesy Erich Lessing/Art Resource.

Figure 7. Detail from a fifteenth-century illuminated manuscript, artist unknown, depicting Julius Caesar conquering the Bretons. From *Les Faits des Romains*, compiled after Lucian, Suetonius, and Sallust, A.D. 1480. Courtesy Giraudon/Art Resource.

Figure 8. Hadrian's Wall. Built under Emperor Hadrian and extended by Emperor Severus a century later, the wall demarcated the northern boundary and defense line of Roman Britain. It once spanned the narrow part of the island from Wallsend on the Tyne River to Bowness at the head of Solway Firth, and is one of the most significant remnants of the Roman occupation. Built mainly from A.D. 122–126. Courtesy Adam Woolfitt/Corbis.

Figure 9. *Entry of King Etzel (Attila) into Vienna: A Scene from the Epos of the Nibelungs* by Albin Egger-Lienz. Often called the Scourge of God, Attila the Hun appears in many legends, including the thirteenth-century German epic poem the *Nibelungenlied* (Song of the Nibelungen). Courtesy Erich Lessing/Art Resource.

Figure 10. *The Meeting of Pope Leo the Great and Attila* by Raphael. Although Attila never sacked Rome, he appears in this mural in the Vatican. The figures of St. Peter and St. Paul hover overhead, brandishing swords against the invader. Courtesy Scala/Art Resource.

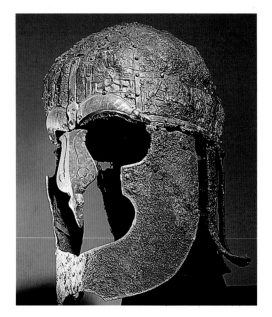

Figures 11 and 12. Viking warrior helmets from Viking boat graves numbers 1 and 14, respectively, in Uppland, Sweden. Seventh century A.D. Both courtesy Werner Forman Archive/Art Resource.

Figure 13. *The Last Voyage of a Dead Man,* a ninth-century Viking stone carving, depicts a Viking funeral pyre. Courtesy Giraudon/Art Resource.

Figure 14. This enamel figure from a bronze bowl is of Hiberno-Saxon origin, though found at the Oseberg ship burial in western Norway. Fine metalwork such as this was among the loot taken back to Scandinavia by Viking raiders. Ninth century A.D. Courtesy Werner Forman Archive/Art Resource.

Figure 15. Head of a woman who was a victim of human sacrifice, found in Jutland (Denmark). It was not uncommon for women to be sacrificed in Viking ceremonies, as Ibn Fadlan recounts in "A Viking Funeral" (see page 223). Courtesy Werner Forman Archive/Art Resource.

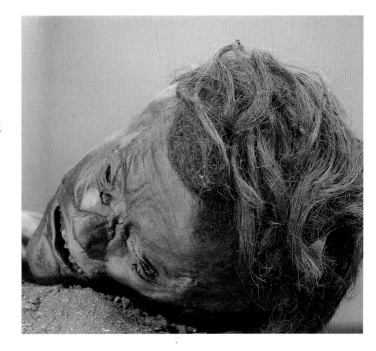

Figure 16. *Genghis Khan at Battle with the Khitai and Jurje Tribes*, artist unknown. Illustration from *The History of the Mongols*, a fourteenth-century Persian story. Courtesy Werner Forman Archive/Art Resource.

was a plain rising by a sharp slope to a ridge, which both armies sought to gain; for advantage of position is a great help. The Huns with their forces seized the right side, the Romans, the Visigoths and their allies the left, and then began a struggle for the yet untaken crest. Now Theodoric with the Visigoths held the right wing and Aetius with the Romans the left. They placed in the centre Sangiban (who, as said before, was in command of the Alani), thus contriving with military caution to surround by a host of faithful troops the man in whose loyalty they had little confidence. For one who has difficulties placed in the way of his flight readily submits to the necessity of fighting. On the other side, however, the battle line of the Huns was so arranged that Attila and his bravest followers were stationed in the centre. In arranging them thus the king had chiefly his own safety in view, since by his position in the very midst of his race he would be kept out of the way of threatening danger.

The innumerable peoples of divers tribes, which he had subjected to his sway, formed the wings. Amid them was conspicuous the army of the Ostrogoths under the leadership of the brothers Valamir, Thiudimer and Vidimer, nobler even than the king they served, for the might of the family of the Amali rendered them glorious. The renowned king of the Gepidae, Ardaric, was there also with a countless host, and because of his great loyalty to Attila, he shared his plans. For Attila, comparing them in his wisdom, prized him and Valamir, king of the Ostrogoths, above all the other chieftains. Valamir was a good keeper of secrets, bland of speech and skilled in wiles, and Ardaric, as we have said, was famed for his loyalty and wisdom. Attila might well feel sure that they would fight against the Visigoths, their kinsmen. Now the rest of the crowd of kings (if we may call them so) and the leaders of various nations hung upon Attila's nod like slaves, and when he gave a sign even by a glance, without a murmur each stood forth in fear and trembling, or at all events did as he was bid. Attila alone was king of all kings over all and concerned for all.

So then the struggle began for the advantage of position we have mentioned. Attila sent his men to take the summit of the mountain, but was outstripped by Thorismud and Aetius, who in their effort to gain the top of the hill reached higher ground and through this advantage of position easily routed the Huns as they came up.

Now when Attila saw his army was thrown into confusion by this event, he thought it best to encourage them by an extemporaneous address in this way: "Here you stand, after conquering mighty nations and subduing the world. I therefore think it foolish for me to goad you with words, as though you were men who had not been proved in action. Let a new leader or an untried army resort to that. It is not right for me to say anything common, nor ought you to listen. For what is war but your usual custom? Or what is sweeter for a brave man than to seek revenge with his own hand? It is a right of nature to glut the soul with vengeance. Let us then attack the foe eagerly; for they are ever the bolder who make the attack. Despise this union of discordant races! To defend oneself by alliance is proof of cowardice. See, even before our attack they are smitten with terror. They seek the heights, they seize the hills and, repenting too late, clamor for protection against battle in the open fields. You know how slight a matter the Roman attack is. While they are still gathering in order and forming in one line with locked shields, they are checked, I will not say by the first wound, but even by the dust of battle. Then on to the fray with stout hearts, as is your wont.

"Despise their battle line. Attack the Alani, smite the Visigoths! Seek swift victory in that spot where the battle rages. For when the sinews are cut the limbs soon relax, nor can a body stand when you have taken away the bones. Let your courage rise and your own fury burst forth! Now show your cunning, Huns, now your deeds of arms! Let the wounded exact in return the death of his foe; let the unwounded revel in slaughter of the enemy.

"No spear shall harm those who are sure to live; and those who are sure to die Fate overtakes even in peace. And finally, why should Fortune have made the Huns victorious over so many nations, unless it were to prepare them for the joy of this conflict. Who was it revealed to our sires the path through the Maeotian swamp, for so many ages a closed secret? Who, moreover, made armed men yield to you, when you were as yet unarmed? Even a mass of federated nations could not endure the sight of the Huns. I am not deceived in the issue; here is the field so many victories have promised us. I shall hurl the first spear at the foe. If any can stand at rest while Attila fights, he is a dead man." Inflamed by these words, they all dashed into battle.

And although the situation was itself fearful, yet the presence of their king dispelled anxiety and hesitation. Hand to hand they clashed in battle, and the fight grew fierce, confused, monstrous, unrelenting—a fight whose like no ancient time has ever recorded. There such deeds were done that a brave man who missed this marvellous spectacle could not hope to see anything so wonderful all his life long. For, if we may believe our elders, a brook flowing between low banks through the plain was greatly increased by blood from the wounds of the slain. It was not flooded by showers, as brooks usually rise, but was swollen by a strange stream and turned into a torrent by the increase of blood. Those whose wounds drove them to slake their parching thirst drank water mingled with gore. In their wretched plight they were forced to drink what they thought was the blood they had poured from their own wounds.

Here King Theodoric, while riding by to encourage his army, was thrown from his horse and trampled under foot by his own men, thus ending his days at a ripe old age. But others say he was slain by the spear of Andag of the host of the Ostrogoths, who were then under the sway of Attila. This was what the soothsayers had told to Attila in prophecy, though he understood it of Aetius.

Then the Visigoths, separating from the Alani, fell upon the horde of the Huns and nearly slew Attila. But he prudently took flight and straightway shut himself and his companions within the barriers of the camp, which he had fortified with wagons. A frail defense indeed; yet there they sought refuge for their lives, whom but a little while before no walls of earth could withstand. But Thorismud, the son of King Theodoric, who with Aetius had seized the hill and repulsed the enemy from the higher ground, came unwittingly to the wagons of the enemy in the darkness of night, thinking he had reached his own lines. As he was fighting bravely, someone wounded him in the head and dragged him from his horse. Then he was rescued by the watchful care of his followers and withdrew from the fierce conflict. Aetius also became separated from his men in the confusion of night and wandered about in the midst of the enemy. Fearing disaster had happened, he went about in search of the Goths. At last he reached the camp of his allies and passed the remainder of the night in the protection of their shields.

At dawn on the following day, when the Romans saw the fields were piled high with bodies and that the Huns did not venture forth, they thought the victory was theirs, but knew that Attila would not flee from the battle unless overwhelmed by a great disaster. Yet he did nothing cowardly, like one that is overcome, but with clash of arms sounded the trumpets and threatened an attack. He was like a lion pierced by hunting spears, who paces to and fro before the mouth of his den and dares not spring, but ceases not to terrify the neighborhood by his roaring. Even so this warlike king at bay terrified his conquerors. Therefore the Goths and Romans assembled and considered what to do with the vanquished Attila. They determined to wear him out by a siege, because he had no supply of provisions and was hindered from approaching by a shower of arrows from the bowmen placed within the confines of the Roman camp. But it was said that the king remained supremely brave even in this extremity and had heaped up a funeral pyre of horse saddles, so that if the enemy should attack him, he was determined to cast himself into the flames, that none might have the joy of wounding him and that the lord of so many races might not fall into the hands of his foes.

Now during these delays in the siege, the Visigoths sought their king and the king's sons their father, wondering at his absence when success had been attained. When, after a long search, they found him where the dead lay thickest, as happens with brave men, they honored him with songs and bore him away in the sight of the enemy. You might have seen bands of Goths shouting with dissonant cries and paying honor to the dead while the battle still raged. Tears were shed, but such as they were accustomed to devote to brave men. It was death indeed, but the Huns are witness that it was a glorious one. It was a death whereby one might well suppose the pride of the enemy would be lowered, when they beheld the body of so great a king borne forth with fitting honors. And so the Goths, still continuing the rites due to Theodoric, bore forth the royal majesty with sounding arms, and valiant Thorismud, as befitted a son, honored the glorious spirit of his dear father by following his remains.

When this was done, Thorismud was eager to take vengeance for his father's death on the remaining Huns, being moved to this both by the pain of bereavement and the impulse of that valor for which he was noted. Yet he consulted with the Patrician Aetius (for he was an older man and of more mature wisdom) with regard to what he ought to do next. But Aetius feared that if the Huns were totally destroyed by the Goths, the Roman Empire would be overwhelmed, and urgently advised him to return to his own dominions to take up the rule which his father had left. Otherwise his brothers might seize their father's possessions and obtain the power over the Visigoths. In this case Thorismud would have to fight fiercely and, what is worse, disastrously with his own countrymen. Thorismud accepted the advice without perceiving its double meaning, but followed it with an eye toward his own advantage. So he left the Huns and returned to Gaul. Thus while human frailty rushes into suspicion, it often loses an opportunity to do great things.

In this most famous war of the bravest tribes, one hundred and sixty-five thousand are said to have been slain on both sides, leaving out of account fifteen thousand of the Gepidae and Franks, who met each other the night before the general engagement and fell by wounds mutually received, the Franks fighting for the Romans and the Gepidae for the Huns.

Now when Attila learned of the retreat of the Goths, he thought it a ruse of the enemy—for so men are wont to believe when the unexpected happens—and remained for some time in his camp. But when a long silence followed the absence of the foe, the spirit of the mighty king was aroused to the thought of victory and the anticipation of pleasure, and his mind turned to the old oracles of his destiny. . . .

But Attila took occasion from the withdrawal of the Visigoths, observing what he had often desired—that his enemies were divided. At length feeling secured, he moved forward his array to attack the Romans [in northern Italy]. As his first move he besieged the city of Aquileia [west of Trieste], the metropolis of Venetia, which is situated on a point or tongue of land by the Adriatic Sea. On the eastern side its walls are washed by the river Natissa, flowing from Mount Piccis. The siege was long and fierce, but of no avail, since the bravest soldiers of the Romans withstood him from within. At last his army was discontented and eager to withdraw. Attila chanced to be walking around the walls, considering whether to break camp or delay longer, and noticed that the white birds, namely, the storks, who build their nests in the gables of houses, were bearing their young from the city and contrary to their custom, were car-

rying them out into the country. Being a shrewd observer of events, he understood this and said to his soldiers: "You see the birds foresee the future. They
are leaving the city sure to perish and are forsaking strongholds doomed to fall
by reason of imminent peril. Do not think this a meaningless or uncertain sign;
fear, arising from the things they foresee, has changed their custom." Why say
more? He inflamed the hearts of his soldiers to attack Aquileia again.
Constructing battering rams and bringing to bear all manner of engines of war,
they quickly forced their way into the city, laid it waste, divided the spoil, and
so cruelly devastated it as scarcely to leave a trace to be seen.

Then growing bolder and still thirsting for Roman blood, the Huns raged
madly through the remaining cities of the Veneti. They also laid waste
Mediolanum, the metropolis of Liguria, once an imperial city, and gave over
Ticinum to a like fate. Then they destroyed the neighboring country in their
frenzy and demolished almost the whole of Italy.

Attila's mind had been bent on going to Rome. But his followers, as the historian Priscus relates, took him away, not out of regard for the city to which
they were hostile, but because they remembered the case of Alaric, the former
king of the Visigoths. They distrusted the good fortune of their own king,
inasmuch as Alaric did not live long after the sack of Rome, but straightway
departed this life. Therefore while Attila's spirit was wavering in doubt between
going and not going, and he still lingered to ponder the matter, an embassy
came to him from Rome to seek peace.

Pope Leo himself came to meet him in the Ambuleian district of the Veneti
at the well-traveled ford of the river Mincius. Then Attila quickly put aside his
usual fury, turned back on the way he had advanced from beyond the Danube,
and departed with the promise of peace. But above all he declared and avowed
with threats that he would bring worse things upon Italy, unless they sent him
Honoria, the sister of the Emperor Valentinian and daughter of Augusta Placidia,
with her due share of the royal wealth. For it was said that Honoria, although
bound to chastity for the honor of the imperial court and kept in constraint by
command of her brother, had secretly despatched a eunuch to summon Attila
that she might have his protection against her brother's power; a shameful thing,
indeed, to get license for her passion at the cost of the public weal.

So Attila returned to his own country, seeming to regret the peace and to be vexed at the cessation of war. For he sent ambassadors to Marcian, Emperor of the East, threatening to devastate the provinces, because that which had been promised him by Theodosius, a former emperor, was in no wise performed, and saying that he would show himself more cruel to his foes than ever. But as he was shrewd and crafty, he threatened in one direction and moved his army in another; for in the midst of these preparations he turned his face towards the Visigoths who had yet to feel his vengeance.

But here he had not the same success as against the Romans. Hastening back by a different way than before, he decided to reduce to his sway that part of the Alani which was settled across the river Loire, in order that by attacking them, and thus changing the aspect of the war, he might become a more terrible menace to the Visigoths. Accordingly he started from the provinces of Dacia and Pannonia, where the Huns were then dwelling with various subject peoples, and moved his array against the Alani. But Thorismud, king of the Visigoths, with like quickness of thought perceived Attila's trick. By forced marches he came to the Alani before him, and was well prepared to check the advance of Attila when he came after him.

They joined battle in almost the same way as before at the Catalaunian Plains, and Thorismud dashed his hopes of victory, for he routed him and drove him from the land without a triumph, compelling him to flee to his own country. Thus while Attila, the famous leader and lord of many victories, sought to blot out the fame of his destroyer and in this way to annul what he had suffered at the hands of the Visigoths, he met a second defeat and retreated ingloriously. . . .

Shortly before he died, as the historian Priscus relates, he took in marriage a very beautiful girl named Ildico, after countless other wives, as was the custom of his race. He had given himself up to excessive joy at his wedding, and as he lay on his back, heavy with wine and sleep, a rush of superfluous blood, which would ordinarily have flowed from his nose, streamed in deadly course down his throat and killed him, since it was hindered in the usual passages. Thus did drunkenness put a disgraceful end to a king renowned in war. On the following day, when a great part of the morning was spent, the royal attendants suspected some ill and, after a great uproar, broke in the doors. There they found the death of Attila accomplished by an effusion of blood, without any wound, and the girl with downcast face weeping beneath her veil. Then, as is the custom of that race, they plucked out the hair of their heads and made their faces hideous with deep wounds, that the renowned warrior might be mourned, not by effeminate wailings and tears, but by the blood of men.

Moreover a wondrous thing took place in connection with Attila's death. For in a dream some god stood at the side of Marcian, Emperor of the East, while he was disquieted about his fierce foe, and showed him the bow of Attila broken in that same night, as if to intimate that the race of Huns owed much to that weapon. This account the historian Priscus says he accepts upon truthful evidence. For so terrible was Attila thought to be to great empires that the gods announced his death to rulers as a special boon.

We shall not omit to say a few words about the many ways in which his shade was honored by his race. His body was placed in the midst of a plain and lay in state in a silken tent as a sight for men's admiration. The best horsemen of the entire tribe of the Huns rode around in circles, after the manner of circus games, in the place to which he had been brought and told of his deeds in a funeral dirge in the following manner: "The chief of the Huns, King Attila, born of his sire Mundiuch, lord of bravest tribes, sole possessor of the Scythian and German realms—powers unknown before—captured cities and terrified both empires of the Roman world and, appeased by their prayers, took annual tribute to save the rest from plunder. And when he had accomplished all this by the favor of fortune, he fell not by wound of the foe, nor by treachery of friends, but in the midst of his nation at peace, happy in his joy and without sense of pain. Who can rate this as death, when none believes it calls for vengeance?"

When they had mourned him with such lamentations, a *strava*, as they call it, was celebrated over his tomb with great revelling. They gave way in turn to the extremes of feeling and displayed funereal grief alternating with joy. Then in the secrecy of night they buried his body in the earth. They bound his coffins, the first with gold, the second with silver, and the third with the strength of iron, showing by such means that these three things suited the mightiest of kings; iron because he subdued the nations, gold and silver because he received the honors of both empires. They also added the arms of foemen won in the fight, trappings of rare worth, sparkling with various gems, and ornaments of all sorts whereby princely state is maintained. And that so great riches might be kept from human curiosity, they slew those appointed to the work—a dreadful pay for their labor; and thus sudden death was the lot of those who buried him as well as of him who was buried.

After they had fulfilled these rites, a contest for the highest place arose among Attila's successors—for the minds of young men are wont to be inflamed by ambition for power—and in their rash eagerness to rule they all alike destroyed his empire. Thus kingdoms are often weighed down by a superfluity rather than by a lack of successors. For the sons of Attila, who through the license of his lust formed almost a people of themselves, were clamoring that the nations should be divided among them equally and that warlike kings with their peoples should be apportioned to them by lot like a family estate. When Ardaric, king of the Gepidae, learned this, he became enraged because so many nations were being treated like slaves of the basest condition, and was the first to rise against the sons of Attila. Good fortune attended him, and he effaced the disgrace of servitude that rested upon him. For by his revolt he freed not only his own tribe, but all the others who were equally oppressed; since all readily strive for that which is sought for the general advantage.

They took up arms against the destruction that menaced all and joined battle with the Huns in Pannonia, near a river called Nedao. There an encounter took place between the various nations Attila had held under his sway. Kingdoms with their peoples were divided, and out of one body were made many members not responding to a common impulse. Being deprived of their head, they madly strove against each other. They never found their equals ranged against them without harming each other by wounds mutually given. And so the bravest nations tore themselves to pieces. For then, I think, must have occurred a most remarkable spectacle, where one might see the Goths fighting with pikes, the Gepidae raging with the sword, the Rugi breaking off the spears in their own wounds, the Suevi fighting on foot, the Huns with bows, the Alani drawing up a battle-line of heavy-armed and the Heruli of light-armed warriors.

—IX—

THE VANDALS

Vandals. Vandalism. Since the eighteenth century, the name—with a lowercase "v"—has been a generic synonym for anyone who acts like a barbarian, and since the nineteenth century, "vandalism" has been the most common term for willful, pointless destruction. The Vandals' sack of Rome came fairly late in the game (A.D. 455) and was probably no more vicious or greedy than the Goths', but "Gothic" (like "Romanesque") has evolved into a comfortably respectable term, while "vandalism" has not. Perhaps it was because the Vandals stripped the metal roofs from temples in the Forum and tried to take them home. That is one thing almost everyone remembers about them. What is forgotten is the vast amount of territory in Europe and Africa the Vandals conquered during their relatively short history.

The Vandals were probably a Germanic Scandinavian tribe to begin with, one that settled for a time along the south coast of the Baltic Sea. Then, at the beginning of the fifth century, in an amazing burst of activity, they sped along a great wheeling curve across northern Europe, down through Gaul, and into Spain, where they paused before crossing the Strait of Gibraltar (at the Pillars of Hercules) into northern Africa.

The Vandals' story, from their arrival in Spain in A.D. 409 to the attacks on Rome from their North African capital 150 years later to their final defeat in 534 ("Africa had been their empire, it became their prison"), is told here in one voice, the great, majestic organ tone of Edward Gibbon (1737–1794), the man who perhaps more than any other historian created the modern world's perception of the fall of Rome and the rise of barbarianism. Gibbon once defined history as "little more than the crimes, follies, and misfortunes of mankind," but if Herodotus was the Father of History and Julius Caesar's *The Gallic War* was—as Trollope said—the beginning of modern historical writing, then it's fair to say Gibbon turned history into literature. His *History of the Decline and Fall of the Roman Empire* appeared in six massive volumes between 1776 and 1788.

EDWARD GIBBON

FROM *THE HISTORY OF THE DECLINE
AND FALL OF THE ROMAN EMPIRE*

FIFTH CENTURY

THE VANDALS IN SPAIN, A.D. 409

The situation of Spain, separated, on all sides, from the enemies of
Rome, by the sea, by the mountains, and by intermediate provinces,
had secured the long tranquillity of that remote and sequestered
country; and we may observe as a sure symptom of domestic happiness, that,
in a period of four hundred years, Spain furnished very few materials to the
history of the Roman empire. The footsteps of the Barbarians, who, in the
reign of Gallienus, had penetrated beyond the Pyrenees, were soon obliterated by the return of peace; and in the fourth century of the Christian era,
the cities of Emerita or Merida, of Cordoba, Seville, Bracara, and Tarragona,
were numbered with the most illustrious of the Roman world. The various
plenty of the animal, the vegetable, and the mineral kingdoms, was
improved and manufactured by the skill of an industrious people; and the
peculiar advantages of naval stores contributed to support an extensive and
profitable trade. The arts and sciences flourished under the protection of the
emperors; and if the character of the Spaniards was enfeebled by peace and
servitude, the hostile approach of the Germans, who had spread terror and
desolation from the Rhine to the Pyrenees, seemed to rekindle some sparks
of military ardour. As long as the defence of the mountains was entrusted to
the hardy and faithful militia of the country, they successfully repelled the

frequent attempts of the Barbarians.

But no sooner had the national troops been compelled to resign their post to the Honorian bands, in the service of Constantine; than the gates of Spain were treacherously betrayed to the public enemy, about ten months before the sack of Rome by the Goths. The consciousness of guilt, and the thirst of rapine, prompted the mercenary guards of the Pyrenees to desert their station; to invite the arms of the Suevi, the Vandals, and the Alani; and to swell the torrent which was poured with irresistible violence from the frontiers of Gaul to the sea of Africa. The misfortunes of Spain may be described in the language of its most eloquent historian, who has concisely expressed the passionate, and perhaps exaggerated, declamations of contemporary writers. "The irruption of these nations was followed by the most dreadful calamities: as the Barbarians exercised their indiscriminate cruelty on the fortunes of the Romans and the Spaniards; and ravaged with equal fury the cities and the open country.

"The progress of famine reduced the miserable inhabitants to feed on the flesh of their fellow-creatures; and even the wild beasts, who multiplied, without control, in the desert, were exasperated, by the taste of blood, and the impatience of hunger, boldly to attack and devour their human prey. Pestilence soon appeared, the inseparable companion of famine; a large proportion of the people was swept away; and the groans of the dying excited only the envy of their surviving friends. At length the Barbarians, satiated with carnage and rapine, and afflicted by the contagious evils which they themselves had introduced, fixed their permanent seats in the depopulated country. The ancient Gallicia, whose limits included the kingdom of Old Castille, was divided between the Suen and the Vandals; the Alani were scattered over the provinces of Carthagena and Lusitania, from the Mediterranean to the Atlantic Ocean; and the fruitful territory of Boetica was allotted to the Silingi, another branch of the Vandalic nation. After regulating this partition, the conquerors contracted with their new subjects some reciprocal engagements of protection and obedience: the lands were again cultivated; and the towns and villages were again occupied by a captive people. The greatest part of the Spaniards was even disposed to prefer this new condition of poverty and barbarism, to the severe oppressions of the Roman government: yet there were many who still asserted their native freedom; and who refused, more especially in the mountains of Gallicia, to submit to the Barbarian yoke.". . .

ADMINISTRATION OF THE ROMAN EMPIRE BY PLACIDIA, A.D. 425–450

Valentinian, when he received the title of Augustus, was no more than six years of age: and his long minority was entrusted to the guardian care of a mother, who might assert a female claim to the succession of the Western empire. Placidia, . . . the mother of Valentinian, was jealous of the power, which she was incapable of exercising: she reigned twenty-five years, in the name of her son; and the character of that unworthy emperor gradually countenanced the suspicion, that Placidia had enervated his youth by a dissolute education, and studiously diverted his attention from every manly and honourable pursuit. Amidst the decay of military spirit, her armies were commanded by two generals, Aetius and Boniface, who may be deservedly named as the last of the Romans. Their union might have supported a sinking empire; their discord was the fatal and immediate cause of the loss of Africa. The invasion and defeat of Attila has immortalized the fame of Aetius; and though time has thrown a shade over the exploits of his rival, the defence of Marscelles, and the deliverance of Africa, attest the military talents of Count Boniface. In the field of battle, in partial encounters, in single combats, he was still the terror of the Barbarians: the clergy, and particularly his friend Augustin, were edified by the Christian piety, which had once tempted him to retire from the world; the people applauded his spotless integrity; the army dreaded his equal and inexorable justice. . . .

The abilities of Aetius and Boniface might have been usefully employed against the public enemies, in separate and important commands; but the experience of their past conduct should have decided the real favour and confidence of the empress Placidia. In the melancholy season of her exile and distress, Boniface alone had maintained her cause with unshaken fidelity; and the troops and treasures of Africa had essentially contributed to extinguish the rebellion. The same rebellion had been supported by the zeal and activity of Reties, who brought an army of sixty thousand Huns from the Danube to the confines of Italy, for the service of the usurper [and] to entertain a secret, perhaps a treasonable, correspondence with his Barbarian allies, whose retreat had been purchased by liberal gifts, and more liberal promises.

But Aetius possessed an advantage of singular moment in a female reign: he was present: he besieged, with artful and assiduous flattery, the palace of Ravenna; disguised his dark designs with the mask of loyalty and friendship; and at length deceived both his mistress and his absent rival, by a subtle conspiracy, which a weak woman, and a brave man, could not easily suspect. He secretly persuaded Placidia to recall Boniface from the government of Africa; he secretly advised Boniface to disobey the Imperial summons: to the one, he represented the order as a sentence of death; to the other, he stated the refusal as a signal of revolt; and when the credulous and unsuspectful count had armed the province in his defence, Aetius applauded his sagacity in foreseeing the rebellion, which his own perfidy had excited. A temperate enquiry into the real motives of Boniface, would have restored a faithful servant to his duty and to the republic; but the arts of Aetius still continued to betray and to inflame, and the count was urged, by persecution, to embrace the most desperate counsels.

The success with which he eluded or repelled the first attacks, could not inspire a vain confidence, that, at the head of some loose, disorderly Africans, he should be able to withstand the regular forces of the West, commanded by a rival, whose military character it was impossible for him to despise. After some hesitation, the last struggles of prudence and loyalty, Boniface dispatched a trusty friend to the Court, or rather to the camp, of [the] king of the Vandals [in Spain], with the proposal of a strict alliance, and the offer of an advantageous and perpetual settlement. . . .

GENSERIC, KING OF THE VANDALS, A.D. 429

The terrible Genseric [is] a name, which, in the destruction of the Roman empire, has deserved an equal rank with the names of Alaric and Attila. The king of the Vandals is described to have been of a middle stature, with a lameness in one leg, which he had contracted by an accidental fall from his horse. His slow and cautious speech seldom declared the deep purposes of his soul: he disdained to imitate the luxury of the vanquished; but he indulged the sterner passions of anger and revenge. The ambition of Genseric was without bounds, and without scruples; and the warrior could dexterously employ the dark engines of policy to solicit the allies who might be useful to his success, or to scatter among his enemies the seeds of hatred and contention. . . . The vessels which transported the Vandals over the modern Streights of Gibraltar, a channel only twelve miles in breadth, were furnished by the Spaniards, who anxiously wished their departure; and by the African general, who had implored their formidable assistance.

Our fancy, so long accustomed to exaggerate and multiply the martial swarms of Barbarians that seemed to issue from the North, will perhaps be surprised by the account of the army which Genseric mustered on the coast of Mauritania. The Vandals, who in twenty years had penetrated from the Elbe to Mount Atlas, were united under the command of their warlike king; and he reigned with equal authority over the Alani, who had passed, within the term of human life, from the cold of Scythia to the excessive heat of an African climate. The hopes of the bold enterprise had excited many brave adventurers of the Gothic nation; and many desperate provincials were tempted to repair their fortunes by the same means which had occasioned their ruin. Yet this various multitude amounted only to fifty thousand effective men; and though Genseric artfully magnified his apparent strength, by appointing eighty chiliarchs, or commanders of thousands, the fallacious increase of old men, of children, and of slaves, would scarcely have swelled his army to the number of fourscore thousand persons. . . .

But his own dexterity, and the discontents of Africa, soon fortified the Vandal powers, by the accession of numerous and active allies. The parts of Mauritania, which border on the great desert and the Atlantic ocean, were filled with a fierce and untractable race of men, whose savage temper had been exasperated, rather than reclaimed, by their dread of the Roman arms. The wandering Moors, as they gradually ventured to approach the sea-shore, and the camp of the Vandals, must have viewed with terror and astonishment the dress, the armour, the martial pride and discipline of the unknown strangers, who had landed on their coast; and the fair complexions of the blue-eyed warriors of Germany, formed a very singular contrast with the swarthy or olive hue, which is derived from the neighbourhood of the torrid zone. After the first difficulties had in some measure been removed, which arose from the mutual ignorance of their respective language, the Moors, regardless of any future consequence, embraced the alliance of the enemies of Rome; and a crowd of naked savages rushed from the woods and vallies of Mount Atlas, to satiate their revenge on the polished tyrants, who had injuriously expelled them from the native sovereignty of the land. . . .

THE REPENTANCE OF BONIFACE, A.D. 430

The court and the people were astonished by the strange intelligence, that a virtuous hero, after so many favours, and so many services, had renounced his allegiance, and invited the Barbarians to destroy the province entrusted to his command. The friends of Boniface, who still believed that his criminal behaviour might be excused by some honourable motive, solicited, during the absence of Aetius, a free conference with the Count of Africa; and Darius, an officer of high distinction, was named for the important embassy. In their first interview at Carthage, the imaginary provocations were mutually explained; the opposite letters of Aetius were produced and compared; and the fraud was easily detected. Placidia and Boniface lamented their fatal error; and the Count had sufficient magnanimity to confide in the forgiveness of his sovereign, or to expose his head to her future resentment. His repentance was fervent and sincere; but he soon discovered that it was no longer in his power to restore the edifice which he had shaken to its foundations. Carthage, and the Roman garrisons, returned with their general to the allegiance of Valentinian; but the rest of Africa was still distracted with war and faction; and the inexorable king of the Vandals, disdaining all terms of accommodation, sternly refused to relinquish the possession of his prey.

The band of veterans, who marched under the standard of Boniface, and his hasty levies of provincial troops, were defeated with considerable loss: the victorious Barbarians insulted the open country; and Carthage, Cirta, and Hippo Regius, were the only cities that appeared to rise above the general inundation.

THE DESOLATION OF AFRICA, A.D. 430

The long and narrow tract of the African coast was filled with frequent monuments of Roman art and magnificence; and the respective degrees of improvement might be accurately measured by the distance from Carthage and the Mediterranean. A simple reflection will impress every thinking mind with the clearest idea of fertility and cultivation: the country was extremely populous; the inhabitants reserved a liberal subsistence for their own use; and the annual exportation, particularly of wheat, was so regular and plentiful, that Africa deserved the name of the common granary of Rome and of mankind. On a sudden, the seven fruitful provinces, from Tangier to Tripoli, were overwhelmed by the invasion of the Vandals; whose destructive rage has perhaps been exaggerated by popular animosity, religious zeal, and extravagant declamation.

War, in its fairest form, implies a perpetual violation of humanity and justice; and the hostilities of Barbarians are inflamed by the fierce and lawless spirit which incessantly disturbs their peaceful and domestic society. The Vandals, where they found resistance, seldom gave quarter; and the deaths of their valiant countrymen were expiated by the ruin of the cities under whose walls they had fallen. Careless of the distinctions of age, or sex, or rank, they employed every species of indignity and torture, to force from the captives a discovery of their hidden wealth. The stern policy of Genseric justified his frequent examples of military execution: he was not always the master of his own passions, or of those of his followers; and the calamities of war were aggravated by the licentiousness of the Moors, and the fanaticism of the Donatists.

Yet I shall not easily be persuaded, that it was the common practice of the Vandals to extirpate the olives, and other fruit-trees, of a country where they intended to settle: nor can I believe that it was a usual stratagem to slaughter great numbers of their prisoners before the walls of a besieged city, for the sole purpose of infecting the air, and producing a pestilence, of which they themselves must have been the first victims.

SIEGE OF HIPPO, A.D. 430

The generous mind of Count Boniface was tortured by the exquisite distress of beholding the ruin, which he had occasioned, and whose rapid progress he was unable to check. After the loss of a battle, he retired into Hippo Regius, where he was immediately besieged by an enemy, who considered him as the real bulwark of Africa. The maritime colony of Hippo, about two hundred miles westward of Carthage, had formerly acquired the distinguishing epithet of Regius, from the residence of Numidian kings; and some remains of trade and populousness still adhere to the modern city, which is known in Europe by the corrupted name of Bona. The military labours, and anxious reflections, of Count Boniface, were alleviated by the edifying conversation of his friend St. Augustine till that bishop, the light and pillar of the Catholic church, was gently released, in the third month of the siege, and in the seventy-sixth year of his age, from the actual and the impending calamities of his country. . . . When the city, some months after his death, was burnt by the Vandals, the library was fortunately saved, which contained his voluminous writings; two hundred and thirty-two separate books or treatises on theological subjects, besides a complete exposition of the Psalter and the Gospel, and a copious magazine of epistles and homilies.

According to the judgment of the most impartial critics, the superficial learning of Augustin was confined to the Latin language; and his style, though sometimes animated by the eloquence of passion, is usually clouded by false and affected rhetoric. But he possessed a strong, capacious, argumentative mind; he boldly sounded the dark abyss of grace, predestination, free-will, and original sin; and the rigid system of Christianity which he flamed or restored, has been entertained, with public applause, and secret reluctance, by the Latin church.

THE DEFEAT OF BONIFACE, A.D. 431

By the skill of Boniface, and perhaps by the ignorance of the Vandals, the siege of Hippo was protracted above fourteen months: the sea was continually open, and when the adjacent country had been exhausted by irregular rapine, the besiegers themselves were compelled by famine to relinquish their enterprise. The importance and danger of Africa were deeply felt by the regent of the West. Placidia implored the assistance of her eastern ally; and the Italian fleet and army were reinforced by Aspar, who sailed from Constantinople with a powerful armament. As soon as the force of the two empires was united under the command of Boniface, he boldly marched against the Vandals; and the loss of a second battle irretrievably decided the fate of Africa. He embarked with the precipitation of despair; and the people of Hippo were permitted, with their families and effects, to occupy the vacant place of the soldiers, the greatest part of whom were either slain or made prisoners by the Vandals. The Count, whose fatal credulity had wounded the vitals of the republic, might enter the palace of Ravenna with some anxiety, which was soon removed by the smiles of Placidia.

Boniface accepted with gratitude the rank of patrician, and the dignity of master-general of the Roman armies; but he must have blushed at the sight of those medals, in which he was represented with the name and attributes of victory. The discovery of his fraud, the displeasure of the empress, and the distinguished favour of his rival, exasperated the haughty and perfidious soul of

Aetius. He hastily returned from Gaul to Italy, with a retinue, or rather with an army, of Barbarian followers; and such was the weakness of the government, that the two generals decided their private quarrel in a bloody battle. Boniface was successful; but he received in the conflict a mortal wound from the spear of his adversary, of which he expired within a few days [in 432], in such Christian and charitable sentiments, that he exhorted his wife, a rich heiress of Spain, to accept Aetius for her second husband. But Aetius could not derive any immediate advantage from the generosity of his dying enemy: he was proclaimed a rebel by the justice of Placidia; and though he attempted to defend some strong fortresses erected on his patrimonial estate, the Imperial power soon compelled him to retire into Pannonia, to the tents of his faithful Huns. The republic was deprived, by their mutual discord, of the service of her two most illustrious champions.

PROGRESS OF THE VANDALS, A.D. 431–439

It might naturally be expected, after the retreat of Boniface, that the Vandals would achieve, without resistance or delay, the conquest of Africa. Eight years however elapsed, from the evacuation of Hippo to the reduction of Carthage. In the midst of that interval, the ambitious Genseric, in the full tide of apparent prosperity, negociated a treaty of peace, by which he gave his son Hunneric for an hostage; and consented to leave the Western emperor in the undisturbed possession of the three Mauritanias. This moderation, which cannot be imputed to the justice, must be ascribed to the policy of the conqueror. His throne was encompassed with domestic enemies, who accused the baseness of his birth, and asserted the legitimate claims of his nephews, the sons of Gonderic. Those nephews, indeed, he sacrificed to his safety; and their mother, the widow of the deceased king, was precipitated, by his order, into the river Ampsaga. But the public discontent burst forth in dangerous and frequent conspiracies; and the warlike tyrant is supposed to have shed more Vandal blood by the hand of the executioner than in the field of battle. The convulsions of Africa, which had favoured his attack, opposed the firm establishment of his power; and the various seditions of the Moors and Germans, the Donatists and Catholics, continually disturbed, or threatened, the unsettled reign of the conqueror.

As he advanced towards Carthage, he was forced to withdraw his troops from the Western provinces; the sea-coast was exposed to the naval enterprises of the Romans of Spain and Italy; and, in the heart of Numidia, the strong inland city of Corta still persisted in obstinate independence. These difficulties were gradually subdued by the spirit, the perseverance, and the cruelty of Genseric; who alternately applied the arts of peace and war to the establishment of his African kingdom. He subscribed a solemn treaty, with the hope of deriving some advantage from the term of its continuance, and the moment of its violation. The vigilance of his enemies was relaxed by the protestations of friendship, which concealed his hostile approach; and Carthage was at length surprised by the Vandals, five hundred and eighty-five years after the destruction of the city and republic by the younger Scipio.

VANDALS SURPRISE CARTHAGE, A.D. 439

A new city had arisen from its ruins, with the title of a colony; and although Carthage might yield to the royal prerogatives of Constantinople, and perhaps to the trade of Alexandria, or the splendour of Antioch, she still maintained the second rank in the West; as the Rome (if we may use the style of contemporaries) of the African world. That wealthy and opulent metropolis displayed, in a dependent condition, the image of a flourishing republic. Carthage contained the manufactures, the arms, and the treasures of the six provinces. A regular subordination of civil honours, gradually ascended from the procurators of the streets and quarters of the city, to the tribunal of the supreme magistrate, who, with the title of proconsul, represented the state and dignity of a

consul of ancient Rome. Schools and gymnasia were instituted for the education of the African youth; and the liberal arts and manners, grammar, rhetoric,
and philosophy, were publicly taught in the Greek and Latin languages. The
buildings of Carthage were uniform and magnificent: a shady grove was planted
in the midst of the capital; the new port, a secure and capacious harbour, was
subservient to the commercial industry of citizens and strangers; and the splendid games of the Circus and theatre were exhibited almost in the presence of
the Barbarians.

The reputation of the Carthaginians was not equal to that of their country,
and the reproach of Punic faith still adhered to their subtle and faithless character. The habits of trade, and the abuse of luxury, had corrupted their manners, but
their impious contempt of monks, and the shameless practice of unnatural lusts,
are the two abominations which excite the pious vehemence of Salvian, the
preacher of the age. . . . The king of the Vandals severely reformed the vices of a
voluptuous people; and the ancient, noble, ingenuous, freedom of Carthage . . .
was reduced by Genseric into a state of ignominious servitude. After he had permitted his licentious troops to satiate their rage and avarice, he instituted a more
regular system of rapine and oppression. An edict was promulgated, which
enjoined all persons, without fraud or delay, to deliver their gold, silver, jewels,
and valuable furniture or apparel, to the royal officers; and the attempt to secrete
any part of their patrimony, was inexorably punished with death and torture, as
an act of treason against the state. The lands of the proconsular province, which
formed the immediate district of Carthage, were accurately measured, and divided among the Barbarians; and the conqueror reserved for his peculiar domain, the
fertile territory of Byzacium, and the adjacent parts of Numidia and Getulia.

It was natural enough that Genseric should hate those whom he had injured:
the nobility and senators of Carthage were exposed to his jealousy and resentment; and all those who refused the ignominious terms, which their honour and
religion forbade them to accept, were compelled by the Arian tyrant to embrace
the condition of perpetual banishment. Rome, Italy, and the provinces of the East,
were filled with a crowd of exiles, of fugitives, and of ingenuous captives, who
solicited the public compassion. . . .

THE VANDAL NAVY, A.D. 439–455

The loss or desolation of the provinces, from the ocean to the Alps, impaired the glory and greatness of Rome: her internal prosperity was irretrievably destroyed by the separation of Africa. The rapacious Vandals confiscated the patrimonial estates of the senators, and intercepted the regular subsidies, which relieved the poverty, and encouraged the idleness, of the plebeians. The distress of the Romans was soon aggravated by an unexpected attack; and the province, so long cultivated for their use by industrious and obedient subjects, was armed against them by an ambitious Barbarian. The Vandals and Alani, who followed the successful standard of Genseric, had acquired a rich and fertile territory, which stretched along the coast above ninety days journey from Tangier to Tripoli; but their narrow limits were pressed and confined, on either side, by the sandy desert and the Mediterranean.

The discovery and conquest of the Black nations, that might dwell beneath the torrid zone, could not tempt the rational ambition of Genseric: but he cast his eyes towards the sea; he resolved to create a naval power, and his bold resolution was executed with steady and active perseverance. The woods of Mount Atlas afforded an inexhaustible nursery of timber; his new subjects were skilled in the arts of navigation and ship-building; he animated his daring Vandals to embrace a mode of warfare which would render every maritime country accessible to their arms; the Moors and Africans were allured by the hopes of plunder; and, after an interval of six centuries, the fleets that issued from the port of Carthage again claimed the empire of the Mediterranean. The success of the Vandals, the conquest of Sicily, the sack of Palermo, and the frequent descents on the coast of Lucania, awakened and alarmed the mother of Valentinian [Placidia].

Alliances were formed; and armaments, expensive and ineffectual, were prepared, for the destruction of the common enemy; who reserved his courage to encounter those dangers which his policy could not prevent or elude. The designs of the Roman government were repeatedly baffled by his artful delays, ambiguous promises, and apparent concessions; and the interposition of his formidable confederate the king of the Huns, recalled the emperors from the conquest of Africa to the care of their domestic safety. The revolutions of the palace, which left the Western empire without a defender, and without a lawful prince, dispelled the apprehensions, and stimulated the avarice, of Genseric. He immediately equipped a numerous fleet of Vandals and Moors, and cast anchor at the mouth of the Tyber, about three months after the death of Valentinian, and the elevation of Maximus to the Imperial throne. . . .

Whatever abilities Maximus might have shewn in a subordinate station, he was found incapable of administering an empire; and though he might easily have been informed of the naval preparations, which were made on the opposite shores of Africa, he expected with supine indifference the approach of the enemy, without adopting any measures of defence, of negociation, or of a timely retreat. When the Vandals disembarked at the mouth of the Tyber, the emperor was suddenly roused from his lethargy by the clamours of a trembling and exasperated multitude. The only hope which presented itself to his astonished mind was that of a precipitate flight, and he exhorted the senators to imitate the example of their prince. But no sooner did Maximus appear in the streets, than he was assaulted by a shower of stones: a Roman, or a Burgundian, soldier claimed the honour of the first wound; his mangled body was ignominiously cast into the Tyber; the Roman people rejoiced in the punishment which they had inflicted on the author of the public calamities. . . .

VANDALS SACK ROME, A.D. 455, JUNE 15–29

On the third day after the tumult, Genseric boldly advanced from the port of Ostia to the gates of the defenceless city. Instead of a sally of the Roman youth, there issued from the gates an unarmed and venerable procession of the bishop at the head of his clergy. The fearless spirit of [Pope] Leo, his authority and eloquence, again mitigated the fierceness of a Barbarian conqueror: the king of the Vandals promised to spare the unresisting multitude, to protect the buildings from fire, and to exempt the captives from torture; and although such orders were neither seriously given, nor strictly obeyed, the mediation of Leo was glorious to himself, and in some degree beneficial to his country. But Rome, and its inhabitants, were delivered to the licentiousness of the Vandals and Moors, whose blind passions revenged the injuries of Carthage.

The pillage lasted fourteen days and nights; and all that yet remained of public or private wealth, of sacred or profane treasure, was diligently transported to the vessels of Genseric. Among the spoils, the splendid relics of two temples, or rather of two religions, exhibited a memorable example of the vicissitude of human and divine things. Since the abolition of Paganism, the Capitol had been violated and abandoned; yet the statues of the gods and heroes were still respected, and the curious roof of gilt bronze was reserved for the rapacious hands of Genseric. The holy instruments of the Jewish worship, the gold table, and the gold candlestick with seven branches, originally framed according to the particular instructions of God himself, and which were placed in the sanctuary of his temple, had been ostentatiously displayed to the Roman people in the triumph of Titus.

They were afterwards deposited in the temple of Peace; and at the end of four hundred years, the spoils of Jerusalem were transferred from Rome to Carthage, by a Barbarian who derived his origin from the shores of the Baltic. These ancient monuments might attract the notice of curiosity, as well as of avarice. But the Christian churches, enriched and adorned by the prevailing superstition of the times, afforded more plentiful materials for sacrilege; and the pious liberality of Pope Leo, who melted six silver vases, the gift of Constantine, each of an hundred pounds weight, is an evidence of the damage which he attempted to repair. In the forty-five years, that had elapsed since the Gothic invasion, the pomp and luxury of Rome were in some measure restored; and it was difficult either to escape, or to satisfy, the avarice of a conqueror, who possessed leisure to collect, and ships to transport, the wealth of the capital. The Imperial ornaments of the palace, the magnificent furniture and wardrobe, the sideboards of massy plate, were accumulated with disorderly rapine: the gold and silver amounted to several thousand talents; yet even the brass and copper were laboriously removed. Eudoxia [widow of Emperor Valentinian, who may have encouraged Genseric to invade Rome] herself, who advanced to meet her friend and deliverer, soon bewailed the imprudence of her own conduct. She was rudely stripped of her jewels; and the unfortunate empress, with her two daughters, the only surviving remains of the great Theodosius, was compelled, as a captive, to follow the haughty Vandal; who immediately hoisted sail, and returned with a prosperous navigation to the port of Carthage.

Many thousand Romans of both sexes, chosen for some useful or agreeable qualifications, reluctantly embarked on board the fleet of Genseric; and their distress was aggravated by the unfeeling Barbarians, who, in the division of the booty, separated the wives from their husbands, and the children from their parents. The charity of Deogratias, bishop of Carthage, was their only consolation and support. He generously sold the gold and silver plate of the church to purchase the freedom of some, to alleviate the slavery of others, and to assist the wants and infirmities of a captive multitude, whose health was impaired by the hardships which they had suffered in the passage from Italy to Africa. By his order, two spacious churches were converted into hospitals: the sick were distributed in convenient beds, and liberally supplied with food and medicines; and the aged prelate repeated his visits both in the day and night, with an assiduity that surpassed his strength, and a tender sympathy which enhanced the value of his services. . . .

ROME PREPARES TO INVADE AFRICA, A.D. 457

While the emperor Majorian assiduously laboured to restore the happiness and virtue of the Romans, he encountered the arms of Genseric, from his character and situation, their most formidable enemy. A fleet of Vandals and Moors landed at the mouth of the Liris, or Garigliano: but the Imperial troops surprised and attacked the disorderly Barbarians, who were encumbered with the spoils of Campania; they were chased with slaughter to their ships, and their leader, the king's brother-in-law, was found in the number of the slain. Such vigilance might announce the character of the new reign; but the strictest vigilance, and the most numerous forces, were insufficient to protect the long-extended coast of Italy from the depredations of a naval war. The public opinion had imposed a nobler and more arduous task on the genius of Majorian. Rome expected from him alone the restitution of Africa; and the design, which he formed, of attacking the Vandals in their new settlements, was the result of bold and judicious policy.

If the intrepid emperor could have infused his own spirit into the youth of Italy; if he could have revived, in the field of Mars, the manly exercises in which he had always surpassed his equals; he might have marched against Genseric, at the head of a Roman army. Such a reformation of national manners might be embraced by the rising generation; but it is the misfortune of those princes who laboriously sustain a declining monarchy, that, to obtain some immediate advantage, or to avert some impending danger, they are forced to countenance, and even to multiply, the most pernicious abuses. Majorian, like the weakest of his predecessors, was reduced to the disgraceful expedient of substituting Barbarian auxiliaries in the place of his unwarlike subjects: and his superior abilities could only be displayed in the vigour and dexterity with which he wielded a dangerous instrument, so apt to recoil on the hand that used it. . . . His camp was fined with Barbarian allies; his throne was supported by the zeal of an affectionate people; but the emperor had foreseen, that it was impossible, without a maritime power, to achieve the conquest of Africa.

In the first Punic war [264–241 B.C.], the republic had exerted such incredible diligence, that, within sixty days after the first stroke of the axe had been given in the forest, a fleet of one hundred and sixty gallies proudly rode at anchor in the sea. Under circumstances much less favourable, Majorian equalled the spirit and perseverance of the ancient Romans. The woods of the Apennine were felled; the arsenals and manufactures of Ravenna and Misenum were restored; Italy and Gaul vied with each other in liberal contributions to the public service; and the Imperial navy of three hundred large gallies, with an adequate proportion of transports and smaller vessels, was collected in the secure and capacious harbour of Carthagena in Spain. The intrepid countenance of Majorian animated his troops with a confidence of victory; and if we might credit the historian Procopius, his courage sometimes hurried him beyond the bounds of prudence.

Anxious to explore, with his own eyes, the state of the Vandals, he ventured, after disguising the colour of his hair, to visit Carthage, in the character of his own ambassador: and Genseric was afterwards mortified by the discovery, that he had entertained and dismissed the emperor of the Romans. Such an anecdote may be rejected as an improbable fiction; but it is a fiction which would not have been imagined, unless in the life of a hero.

Without the help of a personal interview, Genseric was sufficiently acquainted with the genius and designs of his adversary. He practiced his customary arts of fraud and delay, but he practiced them without success. His applications for peace became each hour more submissive, and perhaps more sincere, but the inflexible Majorian had adopted the ancient maxim, that Rome could not be safe, as long as Carthage existed in a hostile state. The king of the Vandals distrusted the valour of his native subjects, who were enervated by the luxury of the South; he suspected the fidelity of the vanquished people, who abhorred him as an Arian tyrant; and the desperate measure, which he executed, of reducing Mauritania into a desert, could not defeat the operations of the Roman emperor, who was at liberty to land his troops on any part of the African coast. But Genseric was saved from impending and inevitable ruin, by the treachery of some powerful subjects; envious, or apprehensive, of their master's success. Guided by their secret intelligence, he surprised the unguarded fleet in the bay of Carthagena: many of the ships were sunk, or taken, or burnt; and the preparations of three years were destroyed in a single day. . . .

NAVAL WAR OF THE VANDALS, A.D. 361–467

In the spring of each year, they equipped a formidable navy in the port of Carthage; and Genseric himself, though in a very advanced age, still commanded in person the most important expeditions. His designs were concealed with impenetrable secrecy, till the moment that he hoisted sail. When he was asked by his pilot, what course he should steer; "Leave the determination to the winds (replied the Barbarian, with pious arrogance); they will transport us to the guilty coast, whose inhabitants have provoked the divine justice," but if

Genseric himself deigned to issue more precise orders, he judged the most wealthy to be the most criminal. The Vandals repeatedly visited the coasts of Spain, Liguria, Tuscany, Campania, Lucania, Bruttium, Apulia, Calabria, Venetia, Dalmatia, Epirus, Greece, and Sicily: they were tempted to subdue the island of Sardinia, so advantageously placed in the centre of the Mediterranean; and their arms spread desolation, or terror, from the columns of Hercules to the mouth of the Nile.

As they were more ambitious of spoil than of glory, they seldom attacked any fortified cities, or engaged any regular troops in the open field.

But the celerity of their motions enabled them, almost at the same time, to threaten and to attack the most distant objects, which attracted the desires; and as they always embarked a sufficient number of horses, they had no sooner landed, than they swept the dismayed country with a body of light cavalry. Yet, notwithstanding the example of their king, the native Vandals and Alani insensibly declined this toilsome and perilous warfare; the hardy generation of the first conquerors was almost extinguished, and their sons, who were born in Africa, enjoyed the delicious baths and gardens which had been acquired by the valour of their fathers. Their place was readily supplied by a various multitude of Moors and Romans, of captives and outlaws; and those desperate wretches, who had already violated the laws of their country, were the most eager to promote the atrocious acts which disgrace the victories of Genseric. In the treatment of his unhappy prisoners, he sometimes consulted his avarice, and sometimes indulged his cruelty; and the massacre of five hundred noble citizens of Cant or Zacynthus, whose mangled bodies he cast into the Ionian sea, was imputed, by the public indignation, to his latest posterity. . . .

CONVERSION OF THE BARBARIANS

The progress of Christianity has been marked by two glorious and decisive victories: over the learned and luxurious citizens of the Roman empire; and over the warlike Barbarians of Scythia and Germany, who subverted the empire, and embraced the religion, of the Romans. The Goths were the foremost of these savage proselytes; and the nation was indebted for its conversion to a country-man, or, at least, to a subject, worthy to be ranked among the inventors of use-ful arts, who have deserved the remembrance and gratitude of posterity. . . .

Their fiercer brethren, the formidable Visigoths, universally adopted the religion of the Romans, with whom they maintained a perpetual intercourse, of war, of friendship, or of conquest. In their long and victorious march from the Danube to the Atlantic ocean, they converted their allies; they educated the rising generation and the devotion which reigned in the camp of Alaric, or the court of Thoulouse, might edify, or disgrace, the palaces of Rome and Constantinople. During the same period, Christianity was embraced by almost all the Barbarians, who established their kingdoms on the ruins of the Western empire; the Burgundians in Gaul, the Suevi in Spain, the Vandals in Africa, the Ostrogoths in Pannonia, and the various bands of mercenaries, that raised Odoacer to the throne of Italy. The Franks and the Saxons still perse-vered in the errors of Paganism; but the Franks obtained the monarchy of Gaul by their submission to the example of Clovis; and the Saxon conquerors of Britain were reclaimed from their savage superstition by the missionaries of Rome. These Barbarian proselytes displayed an ardent and successful zeal in the propagation of the faith. . . .

The peace of the church was sometimes interrupted. The Catholics were indiscreet, the Barbarians were impatient; and the partial acts of severity or injustice which had been recommended by the Arian clergy, were exaggerated by the orthodox writers. The guilt of persecution may be imputed to Euric, king of the Visigoths; who suspended the exercise of ecclesiastical, or at least, of episcopal, functions; and punished the popular bishops of Aquitaine with imprisonment, exile, and confiscation. But the cruel and absurd enterprise of subduing the minds of a whole people, was undertaken by the Vandals alone. Genseric himself [429–477], in his early youth, had renounced the orthodox communion; and the apostate could neither grant, nor expect, a sincere for-giveness. He was exasperated to find, that the Africans, who had fled before him in the field, still presumed to dispute his will in synods and churches; and his ferocious mind was incapable of fear, or of compassion. His Catholic subjects were oppressed by intolerant laws, and arbitrary punishments. The language of Genseric was furious, and formidable; the knowledge of his intentions might justify the most unfavourable interpretation of his actions; and the Arians were reproached with the frequent executions, which stained the palace, and the dominions, of the tyrant. Arms and ambition were, however, the ruling passions of the monarch of the sea.

But Hunneric, his inglorious son, who seemed to inherit only his vices, tormented the Catholics with the same unrelenting fury, which had been fatal to his brother, his nephews, and the friends and favourites of his father: and, even to the Arian patriarch, who was inhumanly burnt alive in the midst of Carthage. The religious war was preceded and prepared by an insidious truce; persecution was made the serious and important business of the Vandal court; and the loathsome disease, which hastened the death of Hunneric, revenged the injuries, without contributing to the deliverance, of the church. The throne of Africa was successively filled by the two nephews of Hunneric; by Gundamund, who reigned about twelve, and by Thrasirnund, who governed the nation above twenty-seven years. . . .

NEW WAR AGAINST THE VANDALS, A.D. 533

In the seventh year of the reign of Justinian, and about the time of the summer solstice, the whole fleet of six hundred ships was ranged in martial pomp before the gardens of the palace [in Constantinople]. The patriarch pronounced his benediction, the emperor signified his last commands, the general's trumpet gave the signal of departure, and every heart, according to its fears or wishes, explored with anxious curiosity the omens of misfortune and success. The first halt was made at Perinthus or Heraclea, where Belisarius waited five days to receive some Thracian horses, a military gift of his sovereign. From thence the fleet pursued their course through the midst of the Propontis; but as they struggled to pass the streights of the Hellespont, an unfavourable wind detained them four days at Abydus, where the general exhibited a memorable lesson of firmness and severity. Two of the Huns, who in a drunken quarrel had slain one of their fellow-soldiers, were instantly shown to the army suspended on a lofty gibbet. The national indignity was resented by their countrymen, who disclaimed the servile laws of the empire, and asserted the free privilege of Scythia, where a small fine was allowed to expiate the hasty sallies of intemperance and anger. Their complaints were specious, their clamours were loud, and the Romans were not averse to the example of disorder and impunity. But the rising sedition was appeased by the authority and eloquence of the general: and he represented to the assembled troops the obligation of justice, the importance of discipline, the rewards of piety and virtue, and the unpardonable guilt of murder, which, in his apprehension, was aggravated rather than excused by the vice of intoxication. . . .

If Gelimer [king of the Vandals] had been informed of the approach of the enemy, he must have delayed the conquest of Sardinia, for the immediate defence of his person and kingdom. A detachment of five thousand soldiers, and one hundred and twenty gallies, would have joined the remaining forces of the Vandals; and the descendant of Genseric might have surprised and oppressed a fleet of deep-laden transports incapable of action, and of light brigantines that seem only qualified for flight. Belisarius had secretly trembled when he overheard his soldiers, in the passage, emboldening each other to confess their apprehensions: if they were once on shore, they hoped to maintain the honour of their arms; but if they should be attacked at sea, they did not blush to acknowledge that they wanted courage to contend at the same time with the winds, the waves, and the Barbarians. The knowledge of their sentiments decided Belisarius to seize the first opportunity of landing them on the coast of Africa; and he prudently rejected, in a council of war, the proposal of sailing with the fleet and army into the port of Carthage. Three months after their departure from Constantinople, the men and horses, the arms and military stores, were safely disembarked, and five soldiers were left as a guard on board each of the ships, which were disposed in the form of a semicircle. The remainder of the troops occupied a camp on the sea-shore, which they fortified, according to ancient discipline, with a ditch and rampart; and the discovery of a source of fresh water, while it allayed the thirst, excited the superstitious confidence, of the Romans. . . .

The inhabitants, instead of deserting their houses, or hiding their corn, supplied the Romans with a fair and liberal market: the civil officers of the province continued to exercise their functions in the name of Justinian; and the clergy, from motives of conscience and interest, assiduously laboured to promote the cause of a Catholic emperor. The small town of Sullecte, one day's journey from the camp, had the honour of being foremost to open her gates, and to resume her ancient allegiance: the larger cities of Leptis and Adrumetum imitated the example of loyalty as soon as Belisarius appeared; and he advanced without opposition as far as Grasse, a palace of the Vandal kings, at the distance of fifty miles from Carthage. The weary Romans indulged themselves in the refreshment of shady groves, cool fountains, and delicious fruits; and the preference which Procopius allows to these gardens over any that he had seen, either in the East or West, may be ascribed either to the taste or the fatigue of the historian.

In three generations, prosperity and a warm climate had dissolved the hardy virtue of the Vandals, who insensibly became the most luxurious of mankind. In their villas and gardens, which might deserve the Persian name of paradise, they enjoyed a cool and elegant repose; and, after the daily use of the bath, the Barbarians were seated at a table profusely spread with the delicacies of the land and sea. Their silken robes, loosely flowing after the fashion of the Medes, were embroidered with gold: love and hunting were the labours of their life, and their vacant hours were amused by pantomimes, chariot races, and the music and dances of the theatre.

In a march of ten or twelve days, the vigilance of Belisarius was constantly awake and active against his unseen enemies, by whom in every place, and at every hour, he might be suddenly attacked. An officer of confidence and merit, John the Armenian, led the vanguard of three hundred horse; six hundred Massagetae covered at a certain distance the left flank; and the whole fleet, steering along the coast, seldom lost sight of the army, which moved each day about twelve miles, and lodged in the evening in strong camps, or in friendly towns. The near approach of the Romans to Carthage filled the mind of Gelimer with anxiety and terror. He prudently wished to protract the war till his brother, with his veteran troops, should return from the conquest of Sardinia; and he now lamented the rash policy of his ancestors, who, by destroying the fortifications of Africa, had left him only the dangerous resource of risking a battle in the neighbourhood of his capital.

The Vandal conquerors, from their original number of fifty thousand, were multiplied, without including their women and children, to one hundred and sixty thousand fighting men: and such forces, animated with valour and union, might have crushed, at their first landing, the feeble and exhausted bands of the Roman general. But the friends of the captive king were more inclined to accept the invitations, than to resist the progress, of Belisarius; and many a proud Barbarian disguised his aversion to war under the more specious name of his hatred to the usurper. Yet the authority and promises of Gelimer collected a formidable army, and his plans were concerted with some degree of military skill. An order was dispatched to his brother Ammatas, to collect all the forces of Carthage, and to encounter the van of the Roman army at the distance of ten miles from the city: his nephew Gibamund, with two thousand horses, was destined to attack their left, when the monarch himself, who silently followed, should charge their rear, in a situation which excluded them from the aid or even the view of their fleet. But the rashness of Ammatas was fatal to himself and his country. He anticipated the hour of the attack, outstripped his tardy followers, and was pierced with a mortal wound, after he had slain with his own hand twelve of his boldest antagonists.

His Vandals fled to Carthage; the highway, almost ten miles, was strewed with dead bodies; and it seemed incredible that such multitudes could be slaughtered by the swords of three hundred Romans. . . . As soon as the tumult had subsided, the several parts of the army informed each other of the accidents of the day; and Belisarius pitched his camp on the field of victory, to which the tenth milestone from Carthage had applied the Latin appellation of decimus. From a wise suspicion of the stratagems and resources of the Vandals, he marched the next day in order of battle, halted in the evening before the gates of Carthage, and allowed a night of repose, that he might not, in darkness and disorder, expose the city to the licence of the soldiers, or the soldiers themselves to the secret ambush of the city. But as the fears of Belisarius were the result of calm and intrepid reason, he was soon satisfied that he might confide, without danger, in the peaceful and friendly aspect of the capital. Carthage blazed with innumerable torches, the signals of the public joy; the chain was removed that guarded the entrance of the port; the gates were thrown open, and the people, with acclamations of gratitude, hailed and invited their Roman deliverers. The defeat of the Vandals, and the freedom of Africa, were announced to the city on the eve of St. Cyprian, when the churches were already adorned and illuminated for the festival of the martyr, whom three centuries of superstition had almost raised to a local deity. . . .

The Romans marched through the streets in close ranks, prepared for battle if an enemy had appeared; the strict order maintained by the general imprinted on their minds the duty of obedience; and in an age in which custom and impunity almost sanctified the abuse of conquest, the genius of one man repressed the passions of a victorious army. The voice of menace and complaint was silent; the trade of Carthage was not interrupted; while Africa changed her master and her government, the shops continued open and busy; and the soldiers, after sufficient guards had been posted, modestly departed to the houses which were allotted for their reception. Belisarius fixed his residence in the palace; seated himself on the throne of Genseric; accepted and distributed the Barbaric spoil; granted their lives to the suppliant Vandals; and laboured to repair the damage which the suburb of Mandracium had sustained in the preceding night.

At supper he entertained his principal officers with the form and magnificence of a royal banquet. The victor was respectfully served by the captive officers of the household; and in the moments of festivity, when the impartial spectators applauded the fortune and merit of Belisarius, his envious flatterers secretly shed their venom on every word and gesture which might alarm the suspicions of a jealous monarch. . . .

FINAL DEFEAT OF THE VANDALS, A.D. 534

But the purest reward of Belisarius was in the faithful execution of a treaty for which his honour had been pledged to the king of the Vandals. The religious scruples of Gelimer, who adhered to the Arian heresy, were incompatible with the dignity of senator or patrician: but he received from the emperor an ample estate in the province of Galatia, where the abdicated monarch retired with his family and friends, to a life of peace, of affluence, and perhaps of content. . . .

The bravest of the Vandal youth were distributed into five squadrons of cavalry, which adopted the name of their benefactor, and supported in the Persian wars the glory of their ancestors. But these rare exceptions, the reward of birth or valour, are insufficient to explain the fate of a nation, whose numbers, before a short and bloodless war, amounted to more than six hundred thousand persons. After the exile of their king and nobles, the servile crowd might purchase their safety, by abjuring their character, religion, and language; and their degenerate posterity would be insensibly mingled with the common herd of African subjects. Yet even in the present age, and in the heart of the Moorish tribes, a curious traveller has discovered the white complexion and long flaxen hair of a northern race; and it was formerly believed that the boldest of the Vandals fled beyond the power, or even the knowledge, of the Romans, to enjoy their solitary freedom on the shores of the Atlantic Ocean. Africa had been their empire; it became their prison.

— X —

THE VIKINGS

As with so many other barbarians, the Vikings seemed to come from nowhere. Suddenly, in the ninth century, raiding parties of Scandinavians in longboats with crews of ninety men or more began attacking seacoast settlements in the British Isles, Russia, western Europe, and even as far away as Pisa and Sicily in the Mediterranean Sea. Often called Northmen or Norsemen or Danes, they sometimes established camps (or *wic*s in Old English, which may have been the origin of the word "viking"), but more often they plundered—or accepted a tribute not to plunder—and moved on to return again another day.

The anonymous Anglo-Saxon poem "The Battle of Maldon," published here in a prose translation, was probably composed—as opposed to written down—soon after a Viking raid in 991 at Maldon on the Blackwater River in Sussex, England, and is an unusually vivid depiction of what hand-to-hand combat must have been like. The Vikings, led by Anlaf, offer to take a ransom and leave, but Byrhtnoth, leader of the English defenders, declines, and when the tide goes out, fighting begins. Unfortunately, the manuscript breaks off before there is a victor, but the situation does not look good for the English. The poet was probably a scop, or minstrel, who used the technique of heroic verse to record what was in fact the news of the day.

The religious chroniclers kept a careful record of Viking attacks. In *The Annals of St. Bertin*, named for the French monastery where the manuscript was found, Prudence, bishop of Troyes, kept count of local raids from 843 to 859; and, in the following excerpt from *The Anglo-Saxon-Chronicle* for the years 994 to 1016, different groups of monks in

Winchester, Canterbury, and Peterborough kept track of similar outrages in England.

A more immediate—and considerably more racy—description of Viking life comes from Ibn Fadlan, who in 921 and 922 served as secretary of an embassy sent by the khalif of Baghdad to the Bulgars on the middle Volga River in Russia. There, he encountered a Viking tribe he called the Rus and had the remarkable good luck of witnessing a ship funeral that has reminded some scholars of Beowulf's pyre.

But not all Scandinavians put to sea as Vikings. One tribe, the Eruli, which Procopius called "beastly," chose early on to align itself with Rome and for centuries provided warriors for its mercenary army. Procopius, writing in the sixth century, tells their story in *The History of the Wars*, which is typical of the mutually distrustful professional relationship many barbarians had with the Romans.

"THE BATTLE OF MALDON"

ESSEX, ENGLAND

991

Then [Byrhtnoth, ealdorman or leader of the English] commanded each of the warriors to leave his horse, to drive it away and to go forth, to think of his hands and of good courage. Then the kinsman of Offa first found out that the earl was not minded to suffer cowardice. Then he let the loved hawk fly from his hands to the wood, and went forward to the battle. Thereby one might know that the youth would not weaken in the fight when he grasped the weapons. Eadric also wished to attend his leader, his prince, to battle. Then he began to bear his spear to the fight. He had a good heart while with his hands he could hold shield and broad sword. He achieved his boast, that he should fight before his prince.

Then Byrhtnoth began there to exhort his warriors. He rode and instructed; he directed the warriors how they should stand and keep their station, and bade them hold their shields upright firmly with their hands and be not afraid. When he had fairly exhorted those people, then he alighted with his men where he best wished, where he knew his most trusty household troops were. Then the messenger of the Vikings stood on the shore, called out fiercely, spoke with words; he boastfully announced to the earl where he stood on the bank the message of the seafarers:

"Bold seamen have sent me to thee, bade me say to thee that thou mayest quickly send rings as a defence; and it is better for you that ye should avert with tribute this rush of spears than that we, so hardy, should deal out battle. We need not destroy each other, if ye will consent to that. We will establish a truce with that gold. If thou who art mightiest here wilt agree to disband thy men, wilt give to the seamen at their own judgment money for peace and accept a truce from us, we are willing to embark with that tribute, to go to sea, and keep peace with you." Byrhtnoth spoke; he grasped the shield; he brandished the slender spear of ash. He uttered words; angry and resolute, he gave him answer: "Dost thou hear, seafarer, what this people say? They will give you darts for tribute, poisonous spears and ancient swords, gear which will profit you naught in the fight. Messenger of the seamen, take word back again, say to thy people far more hateful tidings, that here stands a noble earl with his troop who will defend this land, the home of Æthelred, my prince, the people, and the ground. The heathen shall fall in the battle. It seems to me too shameful that ye should embark with our tribute with impunity, now that ye have come thus far hither to our land. Nor shall ye win treasure so lightly; point and edge shall reconcile us first, grim battle-play, ere we yield tribute."

Then he commanded shields to be borne, the warriors to go, so that they all stood on the river bank. One troop could not come at the other there by reason of the water; there the flood came flowing after the ebb-tide; the streams ran together; they were impatient to clash their spears. There they stood in array beside the stream of Panta, the battle-line of the East Saxons and the ship-army. Nor could one of them injure the other, unless anyone received death from the arrow's flight. The tide went out; the pirates stood ready, many Vikings eager for battle. Then the protector of heroes commanded a warrior, stern in fight, to hold the bridge; he was called Wulfstan, bold among his race—he was the son of Ceola—who with his spear struck the first man who there most boldly stepped upon the bridge. There stood with Wulfstan warriors unafraid, Ælfare and Maccus, two brave men. They would not take to flight at the ford, but they firmly kept guard against the foe as long as they could wield weapons. When they beheld that and clearly saw that they found the guardians of the bridge fierce there, the hostile strangers began then to practice deceit. They asked to be allowed to approach, to go over the ford, to lead their soldiers. Then the earl began in his pride to yield the hateful people too much land. Then the son of Byrhtelm began to call over the cold water; the warriors listened:

"Now is space granted to you; come hither to us quickly, warriors to the battle. God alone can tell who will hold the place of battle."

Then the slaughterous wolves, the horde of Vikings, passed west over Panta. They cared not for the water; they bore shields over the gleaming water; the seamen carried targes to land. There Byrhtnoth stood ready with his warriors to oppose the enemy; he commanded the war hedge to be made with shields and that troop to hold out stoutly against the foes. Then was the fight near, glory in battle; the time had come when doomed men must needs fall there. Then clamour arose; ravens wheeled, the eagle greedy for carrion; there was shouting on earth. Then they let the spears, hard as a file, go from their hands; let the darts, ground sharp, fly; bows were busy; shield received point; bitter was the rush of battle. Warriors fell on either hand; young men lay low. Wulfmer was wounded; he, the kinsman of Byrhtnoth, his sister's son, chose a bed of slaughter; he was sorely stricken with swords. There requital was given to the Vikings. I heard that Eadweard slew one with his sword stoutly; he withheld not the stroke, so that the fated warrior fell at his feet. For that his prince gave thanks to him, to the chamberlain, when he had opportunity. Thus the brave warriors stood firm in battle; eagerly they considered who there could first mortally wound a fated man with spear, a warrior with weapons; the slain fell to the earth. They stood steadfast; Byrhtnoth incited them; he bade each warrior give thought to war who would win glory against the Danes. Then he who was hardy in battle advanced; he raised up the weapon, the shield for a defence, and stepped towards the man. Thus the earl went resolute to the churl; each of them planned evil to the other. Then the seafarer sent a spear from the south, so that the lord of warriors was wounded. He thrust then with the shield, so that the shaft burst; and that spear broke, and sprang back again. The warrior was enraged; with a spear he pierced the proud Viking who gave him the wound. The warrior was skilful; he let his lance go through the man's neck. His hand guided it, so that he reached the life of his sudden enemy. Then hastily he darted another, so that the corslet burst; he was wounded in the breast through the coat of ring-mail, the poisonous spear stood at his heart. The earl was the gladder; then the brave man laughed, gave thanks to God for that day's work which the Lord had granted him. Then one of the warriors let fly a javelin from his hand, from his fist, so that it went forth through the noble thane of Æthelred. By his side stood a youthful warrior, a stripling in the fight; full boldly he,

Wulfstan's son, the young Wulfmær, plucked the bloody spear from the warrior. He let the exceeding hard spear go forth again; the point went in, so that he who erstwhile had sorely smitten his prince lay on the ground. Then a warrior went armed to the earl; he was minded to seize the bracelets of the man, the armour and rings and ornamented sword. Then Byrhtnoth drew the sword from the sheath, broad and gleaming edged, and struck at the corslet. One of the seafarers hindered him too quickly and destroyed the earl's arm. Then the sword with golden hilt fell to the ground, nor could he hold the hard brand, wield the weapon.

Then the old warrior yet spoke these words, encouraged the fighters, bade the valiant comrades go forth; nor could he then longer stand firm on his feet; he looked to heaven: "I thank Thee, O Lord of the peoples, for all those joys which I have known in the world. Now, gracious Lord, I have most need that Thou shouldst grant good to my spirit, that my soul may journey to Thee, may pass in peace into Thy keeping, Prince of angels. I entreat Thee that devils may not do it despite." Then the heathen men hewed him, and both the men who stood by him, Ælfnoth and Wulfmær, were laid low; then they gave up their lives by the side of their prince.

Then they who were not minded to be there retired from the battle. There the sons of Odda were the first in flight; Godric fled from the battle and left the valiant one who had often given him many a steed; he leaped on the horse which his lord had owned, on the trappings, as was not right, and both his brothers, Godric and Godwig, galloped with him; they cared not for war, but they turned from the fight and sought the wood; they fled to that fastness and saved their lives, and more men than was at all fitting, if they had all remembered the rewards which he had given them for their benefit. Thus erstwhile Offa once said to him in the meeting-place, when he held assembly, that many spoke bravely there who would not endure in stress.

Then the people's prince had fallen, Æthelred's earl; all the hearth companions saw that their lord was laid low. Then proud thanes, brave men, went forth there, eagerly hastened. Then they all wished for one of two things—to depart from life or to avenge the loved one. Thus the son of Ælfric urged them on, a warrior young in years. He uttered words; Ælfwine spoke then; boldly he said:

"Remember the times when often we spoke at the mead-drinking, when on the bench we uttered boasting, heroes in hall, about hard strife. Now he who is brave may show it in the test. I will make known my lineage to all, that I was of a mighty race among the Mercians. My old father was called Ealhelm, a wise alderman, prosperous in the world. Thanes shall not reproach me among the people, that I wish to leave this army, to seek my home, now my prince lies low, hewn down in battle. That is the greatest of griefs to me; he was both my kinsman and my lord." Then he went forth; he forgot not the feud; he smote one pirate in the host with spear, so that he lay on the earth, slain by his weapon. Then he began to admonish his friends, companions, and comrades, that they should go forth.

Offa spoke; he shook his spear-shaft: "Lo! thou, Ælfwine, hast admonished all the thanes as is needed. Now that our prince lies low, the earl on the earth, it is the task of all of us, that each should exhort the other warrior to fight whilst he can grasp and hold a weapon, a hard brand, a spear, and good sword. Godric, the cowardly son of Odda, has betrayed us all. Very many men believed when he rode on a horse, on the proud steed, that it was our lord. Wherefore here on the field the army was divided, the shield array broken. May his enterprise fail for putting so many men to flight here."

Leofsunu spoke and raised his shield, his large in defence; he spoke to the man: "I promise that I will not flee hence a footstep, but will go forward, avenge in fight my friendly lord. The steadfast heroes about Sturmere I shall have no cause to taunt me with words, now that my friend has fallen, that I journey home lacking a lord, turn from the fight; but the weapon, spear and brand, shall take me." He went very wrathful, fought staunchly; he scorned flight.

Dunnere spoke then, shook his spear, a humble churl; he cried out over all, bade each man avenge Byrhtnoth: "He in the host who thinks to avenge the prince cannot waver nor mourn for life."

Then they went forth; they recked not of life. Then the retainers began to fight stoutly, fierce bearers of spears, and prayed God that they might avenge their friendly lord and work slaughter on their foes. The hostage began to help them eagerly; he was of a stout race among the Northumbrians, the son of Ecglaf; his name was Æscferth. He wavered not at the war-play, but often he urged forth the dart; at times he shot on to the shield) at times he wounded a man. Ever and again he dealt out wounds whilst he could wield weapons.

Then Eadweard the Tall still stood in the line of battle, ready and eager. With words of boasting he said that he would not flee a foot's length of land or move back, now that his leader lay low. He broke the wall of shields and fought with the men until he worthily avenged on the seamen his giver of treasure ere he lay among the slain. Likewise did Ætheric, the brother of Sibyrht, a noble companion, eager and impetuous; he fought earnestly, and many others also split the hollow shields; the bold men made defence. The border of the shield broke and the corslet sang a terrible song. Then in the fight Offa smote the seaman, so that he fell to the earth, and there the kinsman of Gadd sought the ground. Quickly was Offa hewn down in the battle; yet he had accomplished what he promised his prince, as erstwhile he boasted with his giver of rings, that they should both ride to the stronghold, unscathed to their home, or fall amid the host, perish of wounds on the field of battle. Near the prince he lay low, as befits a thane.

Then there was breaking of shields; the seamen advanced, enraged by war. Often the spear pierced the body of a fated man. Then Wistan went forth, the son of Thurstan; he fought with the men; he slew three of them in the press ere Wigelin's son was laid low among the slain. There was a stern meeting; the warriors stood firm in the struggle; fighters fell, wearied with wounds; the slaughtered dropped to the earth. Oswold and Ealdwold, both the brothers, exhorted the men all the while; they bade their kinsmen with words to bear up there in the stress, use their weapons resolutely. Byrhtwold spoke; he grasped his shield; he was an old companion; he shook his ash spear; full boldly he exhorted the warriors: "Thought shall be the harder, heart the keener, courage the greater, as our might lessens. Here lies our leader all hewn down, the valiant man in the dust; may he lament for ever who thinks now to turn from this war-play. I am old in age; I will not hence, but I purpose to lie by the side of my lord, by the man so dearly loved." Godric, the son of Æthelgar, likewise exhorted them all to fight. Often he let fly the spear, the deadly dart, against the Vikings, as he went foremost in the host. He hewed and struck down until he fell in the battle; that was not the Godric who fled from the fight.

"Viking Raids"

from *The Annals of St. Bertin: The Northmen in Frankland*

843–859

A.D. 843: Pirates of the Northmen's race came to Nantes, killed the bishop and many of the clergy and laymen, both men and women, and pillaged the city. Thence they set out to plunder the lands of lower Aquitaine. At length they arrived at a certain island [near the mouth of the Garonne River] and carried materials thither from the mainland to build themselves houses; and they settled there for the winter, as if that were to be their permanent dwelling-place.

A.D. 844: The Northmen ascended the Garonne as far as Toulouse and pillaged the lands along both banks with impunity. Some, after leaving this region went into Gallicia [in Spain] and perished, part of them by the attacks of the crossbowmen who had come to resist them, part by being overwhelmed by a storm at sea. But others of them went farther into Spain and engaged in long and desperate combats with the Saracens; defeated in the end, they withdrew.

A.D. 845: The Northmen with a hundred ships entered the Seine on the twentieth of March and, after ravaging first one bank and then the other, came without meeting any resistance to Paris. Charles the Bold resolved to hold out against them; but seeing the impossibility of gaining a victory, he made with them a certain agreement and by a gift of 7,000 livres he bought them off from advancing farther and persuaded them to return.

Euric, king of the Northmen, advanced, with six hundred vessels, along the course of the River Elbe to attack Louis of Germany. The Saxons prepared to meet him, gave battle, and with the aid of our Lord Jesus Christ won the victory.

The Northmen returned [from Paris] down the Seine and coming to the ocean pillaged, destroyed, and burned all the regions along the coast.

A.D. 846: The Danish pirates landed in Frisia. They were able to force from the people whatever contributions they wished and, being victors in battle, they remained masters of almost the entire province.

A.D. 847: The Northmen made their appearance in the part of Gaul inhabited by the Britons [Brittany] and won three victories. Noménoé, chief of the Britons, although defeated, at length succeeded in buying them off with presents and getting them out of his country.

A.D. 853–854: The Danish pirates, making their way into the country eastward from the city of Nantes, arrived without opposition, November eighth, before Tours. This they burned, together with the church of St. Martin and the neighboring places. But that incursion had been foreseen with certainty and the body of St. Martin had been removed to Cormery, a monastery of that church, and from there to the city of Orléans. The pirates went on to the chateau of Blois and burned it, proposing then to proceed to Orléans and destroy that city in the same fashion. But Agius, bishop of Orléans, and Burchard, bishop of Chartres, had gathered soldiers and ships to meet them; so they abandoned their design and returned to the lower Loire, though the following year [855] they ascended it anew to the city of Angers.

A.D. 855: They left their ships behind and undertook to go overland to the city of Poitiers; but the Aquitanians came to meet them and defeated them, so that not more than 300 escaped.

A.D. 856: On the eighteenth of April, the Danish pirates came to the city of Orleans, pillaged it, and went away without meeting opposition. Other Danish pirates came into the Seine about the middle of August and, after plundering and ruining the towns on the two banks of the river, and even the monasteries and villages farther back, came to a well located place near the Seine called Jeufosse, and there quietly passed the winter.

A.D. 859: The Danish pirates having made a long sea-voyage (for they had sailed between Spain and Africa) entered the Rhône, where they pillaged many cities and monasteries and established themselves on the island called Camargue. . . . They devastated everything before them as far as the city of Valence [150 miles from the coast]. Then after ravaging all these regions they returned to the island where they had fixed their habitation. Thence they went on toward Italy, capturing and plundering Pisa and other cities.

"VIKING RAIDS"

FROM *THE ANGLO-SAXON CHRONICLE*

994–1016

A.D. 994

This year Anlaf and Swegen came to London with ninety-four ships on the Feast of the Nativity of St Mary, and they set about attacking the city vigorously and tried to set fire to it as well. But there they suffered greater casualties and injury than they ever thought any garrison could do to them. . . . Then they went off and did the greatest damage any invading force could do, burning, ravaging and killing both along the coast and in Essex, Kent, Sussex and Hampshire. In the end they seized horses, rode as widely as they wanted and kept on doing indescribable damage.

Then the king and his councillors determined to send to them and offer them blackmail money and supplies on condition they gave up the devastation. That they accepted, and all the Viking army came to Southampton and took up winter quarters there, and they were victualled from the whole of Wessex. And they were paid 16,000 pounds in cash.

Then the king [Æthelred the Unready] sent Bishop Ælfhere and Ealdorman Æthelweard to fetch Anlaf, and meanwhile hostages were handed over to the Viking ships. And then with great formality they conducted Anlaf to the king at Andover. And King Æthelred stood sponsor for him before the bishop and endowed him royally with gifts. And Anlaf promised him that he would never return to England in hostility—and he kept his word too.

A.D. 1010

After Easter this year the Viking army we spoke of before came to East Anglia. They landed at Ipswich and marched straight to where they had heard Ulfcytel was with his local forces. That was on Ascension Day. And the East Anglians ran off at once but the men of Cambridgeshire stood firm. And Athelstan the king's son-in-law was killed, and Oswig and his son, and Wulfric Leofwine's son, and Eadwig Ælfic's brother, and many other good men of rank, and a mass of the people. Thurcytel Mare's Head it was who started the flight. The Danes held the battlefield. Then they got horses and afterwards took control of East Anglia, and plundered and burned the countryside for four months—they even went as far as the wild fens and killed men and beasts and set fires throughout the fens, and burned down Thetford and Cambridge and then turned south to the Thames.

Then their cavalry rode towards the ships and then suddenly turned west into Oxfordshire, from there to Buckinghamshire and then along the Ouse until they reached Bedford and so on to Tempsford, burning everything as they went along. Then they turned back towards their ships with their plunder. And as they were going to their ships, the English army should have come back into the field to prevent them turning inland again. And that's when the English army went home. And when the Vikings were in the east, the English army was kept to the west. And when the Vikings were in the south, our army was in the north. Then all the council was summoned to the king to determine how to defend the realm. But whatever was decided on did not last even a month. In the end there was no leading man who was prepared to call up his forces. Everyone ran off as best he could. And at last no shire was willing to help another.

Then before St Andrew's day the Vikings came to Northampton and straightway burned that market town down and grabbed as much as they wanted in the neighbourhood, and then crossed the Thames to Wessex, and so by Cannings marsh. And they destroyed everything by fire. And when they had overrun as far as they pleased, they got back to their ships by mid-winter.

A.D. 1011

In this year the king and his council sent to the Viking army asking for truce. And they promised payment of tribute and provisions on condition that they gave up their plundering. By this time the Vikings had overrun i) East Anglia, and ii) Essex, and iii) Middlesex, and iv) Oxfordshire, and v) Cambridgeshire, and vi) Hertfordshire, and vii) Buckinghamshire, and viii) Bedfordshire, and ix) half Huntingdonshire, and x) a good deal of Northamptonshire; and south of the Thames all Kent and Sussex and the region round Hastings, and Surrey, and Berkshire, and Hampshire, and a good deal of Wiltshire.

All these disasters came upon us through indecisive policy. Tribute was not offered them in time, and only when they had done their worst were they offered truce and terms of peace. Yet for all this truce and peace and tribute gangs of them went everywhere, plundering and robbing and killing our wretched folk.

And in this year, between the Nativity of the Holy Mary and Michaelmas they beseiged Canterbury, and by treachery were able to get inside because Ælmaer (whose life Archbishop Ælfeah had once saved) gave Canterbury over to them. And there they took captive Archbishop Ælfeah and the king's steward Ælfweard and Abbot Leofwine and Bishop Godwine. And Abbot Ælmaer [a different man from the traitor Ælmaer mentioned above] they let go. And in the town they took prisoner all the clergy, both men and women—it is impossible for anyone to tell how large a proportion of the people that was—and they stayed within the town for as long as they wished. And when the Vikings had worked their way through the town they went to their ships, taking the archbishop with them.

A.D. 1014

When Swegen (Svein) was dead, Cnut stayed with his army at Gainsborough until Easter. And he and the men of Lindsey came to an agreement that they should supply him with horses, and then they should all go out together and plunder. Then King Æthelred and his whole army came there to Lindsey before they were ready, and attacked and burned and killed every man they could get at. At this Cnut put out with all his ships, and so the miserable people were let down by him. And he turned south till he reached Sandwich, and put ashore there all the hostages his father had been given, and cut off their hands, ears and noses. . . .

THE BATTLES OF SHERSTON AND BRENTFORD

And he [King Edmund] fought a second battle after Midsummer at Sherston and there was great slaughter on both sides, and the armies went their own ways from the fight of their own accord . . . And then for the third time he gathered his army and went to London and relieved the garrison and dispersed the Viking army to its ships. Then two days afterwards the king crossed over at Brentford, and fought against the army and put it to flight. And there a large number of the English drowned through their own lack of care—they had gone ahead of the main army to gather in plunder. After that the king turned back to Wessex and collected his levies. At that the Viking army went straightway to London and beseiged the city, and attacked it in force by sea and by land, but Almighty God saved it.

THE BATTLE OF ASHINGDON

When the king heard that the Viking army had come inland, he collected all the English forces for the fifth time and pursued them. And he overtook them in Essex, at the hill called Assandun and there they clashed together fiercely. Then Ealdorman Eadric [a notorious English turncoat] did as he had so often done before, he started to run off along with the Magonsaete [the men of

Herefordshire] and so abandoned his king and lord and all the people. And there Cnut had the victory, and with it he gained control of all Anglia. And there was killed Bishop Eadnoth and Abbot Wulfsige and Ealdorman Ælfric and Ealdorman Godwine, and Ulfcytel of East Anglia, and Æthelward, son of Ealdorman Æthelsige, and all the best men of England. . . .

After this battle Cnut turned inland to Gloucester with his army since he had learned that King Edmund was there. Then Ealdorman Eadric and the members of the council who were assembled there advised the kings to come to terms. Hostages were exchanged. And the kings met at Alney, and there formalised their friendship with pledges and oaths. They arranged a payment to the Danish army, and then separated on these terms. And King Edmund took Wessex and Cnut Mercia.

Ibn Fadlan

"A Viking Funeral"

922

I have seen the Rus as they came on their merchant journeys and encamped by the Atil [Volga]. I have never seen more perfect physical specimens, tall as date palms, blond and ruddy; they wear neither qurtaqs [tunics] nor caftans, but the men wear a garment which covers one side of the body and leaves a hand free.

Each man has an axe, a sword, and a knife and keeps each by him at all times. The swords are broad and grooved, of Frankish sort. Every man is tattooed from finger nails to neck with dark green (or green or blue-black) trees, figures, etc.

Each woman wears on either breast a box of iron, silver, copper, or gold; the value of the box indicates the wealth of the husband. Each box has a ring from which depends a knife. The women wear neck rings of gold and silver, one for each 10,000 dirhems, which her husband is worth; some women have many. Their most prized ornaments are green glass beads (corals) of clay, which are found on the ships. They string them as necklaces for their women.

When they have come from their land and anchored on, or tied up at the shore of, the Atil, which is a great river, they build big houses of wood on the shore, each holding ten to twenty persons more or less. Each man has a couch on which he sits. With them are pretty slave girls destined for sale to merchants; a man will have sexual intercourse with his slave girl while his companion looks on. Sometimes whole groups will come together in this fashion, each in the presence of the others. A merchant who arrives to buy a slave girl from them may have to wait and look on while a Rus completes the act of intercourse with a slave girl.

Every day they must wash their faces and heads and this they do in the dirtiest and filthiest fashion possible: to wit, every morning a girl servant brings a great basin of water; she offers this to her master and he washes his hands and face and his hair—he washes it and combs it out with a comb in the water; then he blows his nose and spits into the basin. When he has finished, the servant carries the basin to the next person, who does likewise. She carries the basin thus to all the household in turn, and each blows his nose, spits, and washes his face and hair in it.

When the ships come to this mooring place, everybody goes ashore with bread, meat, onions, milk and nabid [an intoxicating drink, perhaps beer] and betakes himself to a long upright piece of wood that has a face like a man's and is surrounded by little figures [idols], behind which are long stakes in the ground. The Rus prostrates himself before the big carving and says, "O my Lord, I have come from a far land and have with me such and such a number of girls and such and such a number of sables," and he proceeds to enumerate all his other wares. Then he says, "I have brought you these gifts," and lays down what he has brought with him, and continues, "I wish that you would send me a merchant with many diners and dirhems, who will buy from me whatever I wish and will not dispute anything I say." Then he goes away.

If he has difficulty selling his wares and his stay is prolonged, he will return with a gift a second or third time. If he has still further difficulty, he will bring a gift to all of the little idols and ask their intercession, saying, "These are the wives of our Lord and his daughters and sons." And he addresses each idol in turn, asking intercession and praying humbly. Often the selling goes more easily and after selling out he says, "My Lord has satisfied my desires; I must repay him," and he takes a certain number of sheep or cattle and slaughters them, gives part of the meat as alms, brings the rest and deposits it before the great idol and the little idols around it, and suspends the heads of the cattle or sheep on the stakes. In the night, dogs come and eat all, but the one who has made the offering says, "Truly, my Lord is content with me and has consumed the present I brought him."

An ill person is put in a tent apart with some bread and water and people do not come to speak to him; they do not come even to see him every day, especially if he is a poor man or a slave. If he recovers, he returns to them, and if he dies, they cremate him. If he is a slave, he is left to be eaten by dogs and birds of prey. If the Rus catch a thief or robber, they hang him on a tall tree and leave him hanging until his body falls in pieces.

I had heard that at the deaths of their chief personages they did many things, of which the least was cremation, and I was interested to learn more. At last I was told of the death of one of their outstanding men. They placed him in a grave and put a roof over it for ten days while they cut and sewed garments for him.

If the deceased is a poor man they make a little boat, which they lay him in and burn. If he is rich, they collect his goods and divide them into three parts, one for his family, another to pay for his clothing, and a third for making nabid, which they drink until the day when his female slave will kill herself and be burned with her master. They stupify themselves by drinking this nabid night and day; sometimes one of them dies cup in hand.

When a great personage dies, the people of his family ask his young women and men slaves, "Who among you will die with him?" One answers, "I." Once he or she has said that, the thing is obligatory; there is no backing out of it. Usually it is the girl slaves who do this [volunteer].

When the man of whom I have spoken died, his girl slaves were asked, "Who will die with him?" One answered, "I." She was then put in the care of two young women, who watched over her and accompanied her everywhere, to the point that they occasionally washed her feet with their own hands. Garments were being made for the deceased and all else was being readied of which he had need. Meanwhile the slave drinks every day and sings, giving herself over to pleasure.

When the day arrived on which the man was to be cremated and the girl with him, I went to the river on which was his ship. I saw that they had drawn the ship onto the shore, that they had erected four posts of birch wood and other wood, and that around it [the ship] was made a structure like great ships'-tents out of wood. Then they pulled the ship up until it was on this wooden construction. Then they began to come and go and to speak words which I did not understand, while the man was still in his grave and had not yet been brought out. Then they brought a couch and put it on the ship and covered it with a mattress of Greek brocade. Then came an old woman whom they call the Angel of Death, and she spread upon the couch the furnishings mentioned. It is she who has charge of the clothes-making and arranging all things, and it is she who kills the girl slave. I saw that she was a strapping old woman, fat and louring.

When they came to the grave they removed the earth from above the wood, then the wood, and took out the dead man clad in the garments in which he had died. I saw that he had grown black from the cold of the country. They had put nabid, fruit, and a pandora in the grave with him. They removed all that. The dead man did not smell bad and only his color had changed. They dressed him in trousers, stockings, boots, a tunic, and caftan of brocade with gold buttons. They put a hat of brocade and fur on him. Then they carried him into the pavilion on the ship. They seated him on the mattress and propped him up with cushions. They brought nabid, fruits, and fragrant plants, which they put with him, then bread, meat, and onions, which they placed before him. Then they brought a dog, which they cut in two and put in the ship. Then they brought his weapons and placed them by his side. Then they took two horses, ran them until they sweated, then cut them to pieces with a sword and put them into the ship. They took two cows, which they likewise cut to pieces and put in the ship. Next they killed a rooster and a hen and threw them in. The girl slave who wished to be killed went here and there and into each of their tents, and the master of each tent had sexual intercourse with her and said, "Tell your lord I have done this out of love for him."

Friday afternoon they led the slave girl to a thing that they had made which resembled a door frame. She placed her feet on the palms of the men and they raised her up to overlook this frame. She spoke some words and they lowered her again. A second time they raised her up and she did again what she had done; then they lowered her. They raised her a third time and she did as she had done the two times before. Then they brought her a hen; she cut off the head, which she threw away, and then they took the hen and put it in the ship. I asked the interpreter what she had done. He answered, "The first time they raised her she said, 'Behold, I see my father and mother.' The second time she said, 'I see all my dead relatives seated.' The third time she said, 'I see my master seated in Paradise and Paradise is beautiful and green; with him are men and boy servants.

He calls me. Take me to him.'" Now they took her to the ship. She took off the two bracelets which she was wearing and gave them both to the old woman called the Angel of Death, who was to kill her; then she took off the two finger rings which she was wearing and gave them to the two girls who served her and were the daughters of the woman called the Angel of Death. Then they raised her onto the ship but they did not make her enter into the pavilion.

Then men came with shields and sticks. She was given a cup of nabid; she sang at taking it and drank. The interpreter told me that she in this fashion bade farewell to all her girl companions. Then she was given another cup; she took it and sang for a long time while the old woman incited her to drink up and go into the pavilion where her master lay. I saw that she was distracted; she wanted to enter the pavilion but put her head between it and the boat. Then the old woman seized her head and made her enter the pavilion and entered with her. Thereupon the men began to strike with the sticks on the shields so that her cries could not be heard and the other slave girls would not be frightened and seek to escape death with their masters. Then six men went into the pavilion and each had intercourse with the girl. Then they laid her at the side of her master, two held her feet and two her hands; the old woman known as the Angel of Death re-entered and looped a cord around her neck and gave the crossed ends to the two men for them to pull. Then she approached her with a broad-bladed dagger, which she plunged between her ribs repeatedly, and the men strangled her with the cord until she was dead.

Then the closest relative of the dead man, after they had placed the girl whom they have killed beside her master, came, took a piece of wood which he lighted at a fire, and walked backwards with the back of his head toward the boat and his face turned (toward the people), with one hand holding the kindled stick and the other covering his anus, being completely naked, for the purpose of setting fire to the wood that had been made ready beneath the ship. Then the people came up with tinder and other fire wood, each holding a piece of wood of which he had set fire to an end and which he put into the pile of wood beneath the ship. Thereupon the flames engulfed the wood, then the ship, the pavilion, the man, the girl, and everything in the ship. A powerful, fearful wind began to blow so that the flames became fiercer and more intense.

One of the Rus was at my side and I heard him speak to the interpreter, who was present. I asked the interpreter what he said. He answered, "He said, 'You Arabs are fools.'" "Why?" I asked him. He said, "You take the people who are most dear to you and whom you honor most and you put them in the ground where insects and worms devour them. We burn him in a moment, so that he enters Paradise at once." Then he began to laugh uproariously. When I asked why he laughed, he said, "His lord, for love of him, has sent the wind to bring him away in an hour." And actually an hour had not passed before the ship, the wood, the girl, and her master were nothing but cinders and ashes.

Then they constructed in the place where had been the ship which they had drawn up out of the river something like a small round hill, in the middle of which they erected a great post of birch wood, on which they wrote the name of the man and the name of the Rus king and they departed.

It is a custom of the king of the Rus to have with him in his palace four hundred men, the bravest of his companions and those on whom he can rely. These are the men who die with him and let themselves be killed for him. Each has a female slave who serves him, washes his head, and prepares all that he eats and drinks, and he also has another female slave with whom he sleeps. These four hundred men sit about the king's throne, which is immense and encrusted with fine precious stones. With him on the throne sit forty female slaves destined for his bed. Occasionally he has intercourse with one of them in the presence of the companions of whom we have spoken, without coming down from the throne. When he needs to answer the call of nature he uses a basin. When he wants to ride out, his horse is brought up to the throne and he mounts. If he wishes to dismount, he rides up so that he can dismount on to the throne. He has a lieutenant who commands his troops, makes war upon his enemies, and plays his role vis-à-vis his subjects.

PROCOPIUS OF CAESAREA

"THE BEASTLY ERULI"

ca. 560

Now as to who in the world the Eruli are, and how they entered into alliance with the Romans, I shall forthwith explain. They used to dwell beyond the Ister [Danube] River from of old, worshipping a great host of gods, whom it seemed to them holy to appease even by human sacrifices. And they observed many customs which were not in accord with those of other men. For they were not permitted to live either when they grew old or when they fell sick, but as soon as one of them was overtaken by old age or by sickness, it became necessary for him to ask his relatives to remove him from the world as quickly as possible. And these relatives would pile up a quantity of wood to a great height and lay the man on top of the wood, and then they would send one of the Eruli, but not a relative of the man, to his side with a dagger; for it was not lawful for a kinsman to be his slayer. And when the slayer of their relative had returned, they would straightway burn the whole pile of wood, beginning at the edges. And after the fire had ceased, they would immediately collect the bones and bury them in the earth. And when a man of the Eruli died, it was necessary for his wife, if she laid claim to virtue and wished to leave a fair name behind her, to die not long afterward beside the tomb of her husband by hanging herself with a rope. And if she did not do this, the result was that she was in ill repute thereafter and an offense to the relatives of her husband. Such were the customs observed by the Eruli in ancient times.

But as time went on they became superior to all the barbarians who dwelt about them both in power and in numbers, and, as was natural, they attacked and vanquished them severally and kept plundering their possessions by force.

And finally they made the Lombards, who were Christians, together with several other nations, subject and tributary to themselves, though the barbarians of that region were not accustomed to that sort of thing; but the Eruli were led to take this course by love of money and a lawless spirit. When [in 491], however, [Emperor] Anastasius took over the Roman empire, the Eruli, having no longer anyone in the world whom they could assail, laid down their arms and remained quiet, and they observed peace in this way for a space of three years. But the people themselves, being exceedingly vexed, began to abuse their leader Rodolphus without restraint, and going to him constantly they called him cowardly and effeminate, and railed at him in a most unruly manner, taunting him with certain other names besides. And Rodolphus, being quite unable to bear the insult, marched against the Lombards, who were doing no wrong, without charging against them any fault or alleging any violation of their agreement, but bringing upon them a war which had no real cause.

And when the Lombards got word of this, they sent to Rodolphus and made enquiry and demanded that he should state the charge on account of which the Eruli were coming against them in arms, agreeing that if they had deprived the Eruli of any of the tribute, then they would instantly pay it with large interest; and if their grievance was that only a moderate tribute had been imposed upon them, then the Lombards would never be reluctant to make it greater. Such were the offers which the envoys made, but Rodolphus with a threat sent them away and marched forward. And they again sent other envoys to him on the same mission and supplicated him with many entreaties. And when the second envoys had fared in the same way, a third embassy came to him and forbade the Eruli on any account to bring upon them a war without excuse. For if they should come against them with such a purpose, they too, not willingly, but under the direst necessity, would array themselves against their assailants, calling upon God as their witness, the slightest breath of whose favour, turning the scales, would be a match for all the strength of men; and He, in all likelihood, would be moved by the causes of the war and would determine the issue of the fight for both sides accordingly. So they spoke, thinking in this way to terrify their assailants, but the Eruli, shrinking from nothing whatever, decided to meet the Lombards in battle. And when the two armies came close to one another, it so happened that the sky above the Lombards was obscured by a sort of cloud, black and very thick, but above the Eruli it was exceedingly clear. And judging by this one would have supposed that the Eruli were entering the conflict to their own harm; for there can be no more forbidding portent than this for barbarians as they go into battle. However, the Eruli gave no heed even to this, but in absolute disregard of it they advanced against their enemy with utter contempt, estimating the outcome of war by mere superiority of numbers. But when the battle came to close quarters, many of the Eruli perished and Rodolphus himself also perished, and the rest fled at full speed, forgetting all their courage. And since their enemy followed them up, the most of them fell on the field of battle and only a few succeeded in saving themselves.

For this reason the Eruli were no longer able to tarry in their ancestral homes, but departing from there as quickly as possible they kept moving forward, traversing the whole country which is beyond the Ister River, together with their wives and children. But when they reached a land where the Rogi dwelt of old, a people who had joined the Gothic host and gone to Italy, they settled in that place. But since they were pressed by famine, because they were in a barren land, they removed from there not long afterward, and came to a place close to the country of the Gepaedes. And at first the Gepaedes permitted them to dwell there and be neighbours to them, since they came as suppliants. But afterwards for no good reason the Gepaedes began to practice unholy deeds upon them. For they violated their women and seized their cattle and other property, and abstained from no wickedness whatever, and finally began an unjust attack upon them. And the Eruli, unable to bear all this any longer, crossed the Ister River and decided to live as neighbours to the Romans in that region; this was during the reign of the Emperor Anastasius, who received them with great friendliness and allowed them to settle where they were. But a short time afterwards these barbarians gave him offense by their lawless treatment of the Romans there, and for this reason he sent an army against them. And the Romans, after defeating them in battle, slew most of their number, and had ample opportunity to destroy them all. But the remainder of them threw themselves upon the mercy of the generals and begged them to spare their lives and to have them as allies and servants of the emperor thereafter. And when Anastasius learned this, he was pleased, and consequently a number of the Eruli were left; however, they neither became allies of the Romans, nor did they do them any good.

But when Justinian took over the empire, he bestowed upon them good lands and other possessions, and thus completely succeeded in winning their friendship and persuaded them all to become Christians. As a result of this they adopted a gentler manner of life and decided to submit themselves wholly to the laws of the Christians, and in keeping with the terms of their alliance they are generally arrayed with the Romans against their enemies. They are still, however, faithless toward them, and since they are given to avarice, they are eager to do violence to their neighbours, feeling no shame at such conduct. And they mate in an unholy manner, especially men with asses, and they are the basest of all men and utterly abandoned rascals.

Afterwards, although some few of them remained at peace with the Romans, all the rest revolted for the following reason. The Eruli, displaying their beastly and fanatical character against their own "rex," one Ochus by name, suddenly killed the man for no good reason at all, laying against him no other charge than that they wished to be without a king thereafter. And yet even before this, while their king did have the title, he had practically no advantage over any private citizen whomsoever. But all claimed the right to sit with him and eat with him, and whoever wished insulted him without restraint; for no men in the world are less bound by convention or more unstable than the Eruli.

—XI—

IRELAND

The Roman legions never reached Ireland, but the Romans certainly knew it was there. Strabo had noted that the people who lived on the island—which many early geographers placed south of England—were even more savage than the Britons. They were said to be cannibals who devoured their dead fathers and slept with their (living) mothers and sisters, although he did add that he did not know for a fact that that was true.

After the Normans conquered England in 1066, they later sent troops—and castle builders—into Ireland and saw these fearful barbarians for themselves. One of the leaders of the Norman invasion of Ireland was Maurice fitzGerald, whose nephew Gerald (ca. 1146–ca. 1223), a clergyman in Wales, crossed the Irish Sea for a visit first in 1183 and then came again three more times. He stayed in Ireland for as long as two years at a time, which is surprising since—except for its music—he didn't seem to have liked the place at all.

Gerald of Wales (Geraldus Cambrensis) wrote his observations "on the nature of the island and the primitive origins of its race" in *The Typography of Ireland* and made something of a name for himself giving public readings from it in London. Unfortunately, the lectures never did help him become Bishop of St. David's in Wales as he had hoped.

To balance Geraldus's portrait of the "primitive origins" of the Irish is a mock-heroic tale from the Ulster Cycle of legends about the epic hero Cuchulain. "Bricriu's Feast and the War of Words of the Women of Ulster," from twelfth-century manuscripts, tells of an ancient dinner party that became a battle in which the weapons were at first swords and then words. Since Ireland is one of the few supposed barbaric societies that produced a sizable written literature, this is a rare opportunity to hear what Gerald of Wales would no doubt have thought to be the voice of a true barbarian.

The translation by Lady Gregory (1852–1932)—a good friend of William Butler Yeats's—is in a style she called "Kiltartarnese," English in a Gaelic syntax.

GERALDUS CAMBRENSIS

"THE CUSTOMS OF THE IRISH"

1185

I have considered it not superfluous to give a short account of the condition of this nation, both bodily and mentally; I mean their state of cultivation, both interior and exterior. This people are not tenderly nursed from their birth, as others are; for besides the rude fare they receive from their parents, which is only just sufficient for their sustenance, as to the rest, almost all is left to nature. They are not placed in cradles, or swathed, nor are their tender limbs either fomented by constant bathings, or adjusted with art. For the midwives make no use of warm water, nor raise their noses, nor depress the face, nor stretch the legs; but nature alone, with very slight aids from art, disposes and adjusts the limbs to which she has given birth, just as she pleases. As if to prove that what she is able to form she does not cease to shape also, she gives growth and proportions to these people, until they arrive at perfect vigour, tall and handsome in person, and with agreeable and ruddy countenances. But although they are richly endowed with the gifts of nature, their want of civilization, shown both in their dress and mental culture, makes them a barbarous people. For they wear but little woollen, and nearly all they use is black, that being the colour of the sheep in this country. Their clothes are also made after a barbarous fashion.

Their custom is to wear small, close-fitting hoods, hanging below the shoulders a cubit's length, and generally made of parti-coloured strips sewn together. Under these, they use woollen rugs instead of cloaks, with breeches and hose of one piece, or hose and breeches joined together, which are usually dyed of some colour. Likewise, in riding, they neither use saddles, nor boots, nor spurs, but only carry a rod in their hand, having a crook at the upper end, with which they both urge forward and guide their horses. They use reins which serve the purpose both of a bridle and a bit, and do not prevent the horses from feeding, as they always live on grass. Moreover, they go to battle without armour, considering it a burthen and esteeming it brave and honourable to fight without it.

The Irish are a rude people, subsisting on the produce of their cattle only, and living themselves like beasts—a people that has not yet departed from the primitive habits of pastoral life. In the common course of things, mankind progresses from the forest to the field, from the field to the town, and to the social condition of citizens; but this nation, holding agricultural labour in contempt, and little coveting the wealth of towns, as well as being exceedingly averse to civil institutions, lead the same life their fathers did in the woods and open pastures, neither willing to abandon their old habits nor learn anything new. They, therefore, only make patches of tillage; their pastures are short of herbage; cultivation is very rare, and there is scarcely any land sown. This want of tilled fields arises from the neglect of those who should cultivate them; for there are large tracts which are naturally fertile and productive. The whole habits of the people are contrary to agricultural pursuits, so that the rich glebe is barren for want of husbandmen, the fields demanding labour which is not forthcoming.

Very few sorts of fruit trees are found in this country, a defect arising not from the nature of the soil, but from want of industry in planting them; for the lazy husbandman does not take the trouble to plant the foreign sorts which would grow very well here. . . .

There are also veins of various kinds of metals ramifying in the bowels of the earth, which, from the same idle habits, are not worked and turned to account. Even gold, which the people require in large quantities, and still covet in a way that speaks their Spanish origin, is brought here by the merchants who traverse the ocean for the purposes of commerce. They neither employ themselves in the manufacture of flax or wool, nor in any kind of trade or mechanical art; but abandoning themselves to idleness, and immersed in sloth, their greatest delight is to be exempt from toil, their richest possession the enjoyment of liberty.

This people, then, is truly barbarous, being not only barbarous in their dress, but suffering their hair and beards (barbis) to grow enormously in an uncouth manner, just like the modern fashion recently introduced; indeed, all their habits are barbarisms. But habits are formed by mutual intercourse; and as this people inhabit a country so remote from the rest of the world, and lying at its farthest extremity, forming, as it were, another world, and are thus secluded from civilized nations, they learn nothing, and practice nothing but the barbarism in which they are born and bred, and which sticks to them like a second nature. Whatever natural gifts they possess are excellent, in whatever requires industry they are worthless. . . .

The faith having been planted in the island from the time of St. Patrick, so many ages ago, and propagated almost ever since, it is wonderful that this nation should remain to this day so very ignorant of the rudiments of Christianity. It is indeed a most filthy race, a race sunk in vice, a race more ignorant than all other nations of the first principles of the faith. Hitherto they neither pay tithes nor first fruits; they do not contract marriages, nor shun incestuous connections; they frequent not the church of God with proper reverence. Nay, what is most detestable, and not only contrary to the gospel, but to everything that is right, in many parts of Ireland brothers (I will not say marry) seduce and debauch the wives of their brothers deceased, and have incestuous intercourse with them; adhering in this to the letter, and not to the spirit, of the Old Testament; and following the example of men of old in their vices more willingly than in their virtues.

They are given to treachery more than any other nation, and never keep the faith they have pledged, neither shame nor fear withholding them from constantly violating the most solemn obligations, which, when entered into with themselves, they are above all things anxious to have observed. So that, when you have used the utmost precaution, when you have been most vigilant, for your own security and safety, by requiring oaths and hostages, by treaties of alliance firmly made, and by benefits of all kinds conferred, then begins your time to fear; for then especially their treachery is awake, when they suppose that, relying on the fulness of your security, you are off your guard. That is the moment for them to fly to their citadel of wickedness, turn against you their weapons of deceit, and endeavour to do you injury, by taking the opportunity of catching you unawares. . . .

It must be observed also, that the men who enjoy ecclesiastical immunity, and are called ecclesiastical men, although they be laics, and have wives, and wear long hair hanging down below their shoulders, but only do not bear arms, wear for their protection, by authority of the pope, fillets on the crown of their heads, as a mark of distinction. Moreover, these people, who have customs so very different from others, and so opposite to them, on making signs either with the hands or the head, beckon when they mean that you should go away, and nod backward as often as they wish to be rid of you. Likewise, in this nation, the men pass their water sitting, the women standing. They are also prone to the failing of jealousy beyond any other nation. The women, also, as well as the men, ride astride, with their legs stuck out on each side of the horse.

We come now to the clerical order. The clergy, then, of this country are commendable enough for their piety; and among many other virtues in which they excel, are especially eminent for that of continence. They also perform with great regularity the services of the psalms, hours, lessons, and prayers, and, confining themselves to the precincts of the churches, employ their whole time in the offices to which they are appointed. They also pay due attention to the rules of abstinence and a spare diet, the greatest part of them fasting almost every day till dusk, when by singing complines they have finished the offices of the several hours for the day. Would that after these long fasts, they were as sober as they are serious, as true as they are severe, as pure as they are enduring, such in reality as they are in appearance. But among so many thousands you will scarcely find one who, after his devotion to long fastings and prayers, does not make up by night for his privations during the day by the enormous quantities of wine and other liquors in which he indulges more than is becoming.

Dividing the day of twenty-four hours into two equal parts, they devote the hours of light to spiritual offices, and those of night to the flesh; so that in the light they apply themselves to the works of the light, and in the dark they turn to the works of darkness. Hence it may be considered almost a miracle, that where wine has the dominion lust does not reign also. This appears to have been thought difficult by St. Jerome; still more so by the apostle; one of whom forbids men to be drunken with wine, wherein there is excess: the other teaches that the belly, when it is inflamed by drink, easily vents itself in lust.

There are, however, some among the clergy who are most excellent men, and have no leaven of impurity. Indeed, this people are intemperate in all their actions, and most vehement in all their feelings. Thus the bad are bad indeed— there are nowhere worse; and than the good you cannot find better. But there is not much wheat among the oats and the tares. Many, you find, are called, but few chosen: there is very little grain, but much chaff. . . .

The only thing to which I find that this people apply a commendable industry is playing upon musical instruments; in which they are incomparably more skilful than any other nation I have ever seen. For their modulation on these instruments, unlike that of the Britons to which I am accustomed, is not slow and harsh, but lively and rapid, while the harmony is both sweet and gay. . . .

It must be remarked, however, that both Scotland and Wales strive to rival Ireland in the art of music; the former from its community of race, the latter from its contiguity and facility of communication. Ireland only uses and delights in two instruments, the harp and the tabor [drum]. Scotland has three, the harp, the tabor, and the crowth or crowd [fiddle]; and Wales, the harp, the pipes, and the crowd. The Irish also use strings of brass instead of leather. Scotland at the present day, in the opinion of many persons, is not only equal to Ireland, her teacher, in musical skill, but excels her; so that they now look to that country as the fountain head of this science.

The sweet harmony of music not only affords us pleasures, but renders us important services. It greatly cheers the drooping spirit, clears the face from clouds, smooths the wrinkled brow, checks moroseness, promotes hilarity; of all the most pleasant things in the world, nothing more delights and enlivens the human heart.

It appears, then, that music acts in contrary ways; when employed to give intensity to the feelings, it inflames, when to abate them, it lulls. Hence the Irish and Spaniards, and some other nations, mix plaintive music with their funeral wailings, giving poignancy to their present grief, as well as, perhaps, tranquillizing the mind when the worst is past.

"Bricriu's Feast and the War of Words of the Women of Ulster"

Twelfth Century

Bricriu of the Bitter Tongue made a great feast one time for Conchubar, son of Ness, and for all the chief men of Ulster. He was the length of a year getting the feast ready, and he built a great house to hold it in at Dun-Rudraige [Dundrum, County Down]. He built it in the likeness of the House of the Red Branch in Emain, but it was entirely beyond all the buildings of that time in shape and in substance, in plan and in ornament, in pillars and in facings, in doors and in carvings so that it was spoken of in all parts. It was on the plan of the drinking hall at Emain it was made inside, and it having nine divisions from hearth to wall, and every division faced with bronze that was overlaid with gold, thirty feet high. In the front part of the hall there was a royal seat made for Conchubar, high above all the other seats of the house. It was set with carbuncles and other precious stones of all colours, that shone like gold and silver, so that they made the night the same as the day; and round about it were the twelve seats of the twelve heroes of Ulster.

Good as the material was, the work done on it was as good. It took six horses to bring home every beam, and the strength of six men to fix every pole, and thirty of the best skilled men in Ireland were ordering it and directing it.

Then Bricriu made a sunny parlour for himself, on a level with Conchubar's seat and the seats of the heroes of valour, and it had every sort of ornament, and windows of glass were put on every side of it, the way he could see the hall from his seat, for he knew the men of Ulster would not let him stop inside.

When he had finished building the hall and the sunny parlour, and had furnished them with quilts and coverings, beds and pillows, and with a full supply of meat and drink, so that nothing was wanting, he set out for Emain Macha to see Conchubar and the chief men of Ulster.

It happened that day they were all gathered together at Emain Macha [near Armagh], and they made him welcome, and they put him to sit beside Conchubar, and he said to Conchubar and to them all, "Come with me to a feast I have made ready." "I am willing to go," said Conchubar, "if the men of Ulster are willing."

But Fergus, son of Rogh, and the others, said: "We will not go, for if we do, our dead will be more than our living, after Bricriu has set us to quarrel with one another."

"It will be worse for you if you do not come," said Bricriu. "What will you do if they do not go with you?" said Conchubar.

"I will stir up strife," said Bricriu, "between the kings and the leaders, and the heroes of valour, and the swordsmen, till every one makes an end of the other, if they will not come with me to use my feast."

"We will not go for the sake of pleasing you," said Conchubar.

"I will stir up anger between father and son, so that they will be the death of one another," said Bricriu; "if I fail in doing that, I will make a quarrel between mother and daughter; if that fails, I will put the two breasts of every woman of Ulster striking one against the other, and destroying one another."

"It is better for us to go," said Fergus.

"Let us consult with the chief men of Ulster," said Sencha, son of Ailell.

"Some harm will come of it," said Conchubar, "if we do not consult together against this man."

On that, all the chief men met together in council, and this is what Sencha advised: "It is best for you to get securities from Bricriu, as you have to go along with him; and put eight swordsmen around him, to make him leave the house as soon as he has laid out the feast for you." So Ferbenn Ferbeson, son of Conchubar, brought the answer to Bricriu. "I am satisfied to do that," said Bricriu. With that the men of Ulster set out from Emain, host, troop, and company under king, chief, and leader, and it was a good march they all made together to Dun-Rudraige.

Then Bricriu set himself to think how with the securities that were given for him, he could best manage to set the men of Ulster one against the other.

After he had been thinking a while, he went over to Laegaire Buadach, son of Connad, son of Iliath. "All good be with you, Laegaire, Winner of Battles, you mighty mallet of Bregia, you hot hammer of Meath, you flame-red thunderbolt, what hinders you from getting the championship of Ireland for ever?"

"If I want it I can get it," said Laegaire.

"You will be head of all the champions of Ireland," said Bricriu, "if you do as I advise."

"I will do that, indeed," said Laegaire.

"Well," said Bricriu, "if you can get the Champion's Portion at the feast in my house, the championship of Ireland will be yours forever. And the Champion's Portion of my house is worth fighting for," he said, "for it is not the portion of a fool's house. There goes with it a vat of good wine, with room enough in it to hold three of the brave men of Ulster; with that a seven-year-old boar, that has been fed since it was born on no other thing but fresh milk, and fine meal in spring-time, curds and sweet milk in summer, the kernel of nuts and wheat in harvest, beef and broth in the winter; with that a seven-year-old bullock that never had in its mouth, since it was a sucking calf, either heather or twig tops, but only sweet milk and herbs, meadow hay and corn; along with that, five-score wheaten cakes made with honey. That is the Champion's Portion of my house. And since you are yourself the best hero among the men of Ulster," he said, "it is but right to give it to you; and that is my wish, you to get it. And at the end of the day, when the feast is spread out, let your chariot-driver rise up, and it is to him the Champion's Portion will be given."

"There will be dead men if that is not done," said Laegaire. Then Bricriu laughed, for he liked to hear that.

When he had done stirring up Laegaire Buadach, he went on till he met with Conall Cearnach. "May good be with you, Conall," he said. "It is you are the hero of fights and of battles, it is many victories you have won up to this over the heroes of Ulster. By the time the men of Ulster cross the boundary of a strange country, it is three days and three nights in advance of them you are, over many a ford and river; it is you who protect their rear coming back again so that no enemy can get past you or through you, or over you. What would hinder you from being given the Champion's Portion of Emain to hold forever?"

Great as was his treachery with Laegaire, he showed twice as much in what he said to Conall Cearnach.

When he had satisfied himself that Conall was stirred up to a quarrel, he went on to Cuchulain. "May all good be with you Cuchulain, conqueror of Bregia, bright banner of the Lifé, darling of Emain, beloved by wives and by maidens. Cuchulain is no nickname for you to-day, for you are the champion of the men of Ulster; it is you keep off their great quarrels and disputes; it is you get justice for every man of them; it is you have what all the men of Ulster are wanting in; all the men of Ulster acknowledge that your bravery, your valour, and your deeds are beyond their own. Why, then, would you leave the Champion's Portion for some other one of the men of Ulster, when not one of them would be able to keep it from you?"

"By the god of my people," said Cuchulain, "whoever comes to try and keep it from me will lose his head." With that Bricriu left them and followed after the army, as if he had done nothing to stir up a quarrel at all.

After that they came to the feasting-houses and went in, and every one took his place, king, prince, landowner, swordsman, and young fighting man. One half of the house was set apart for Conchubar and his following, and the other half was kept for the wives of the heroes of Ulster.

And here were attending on Conchubar in the front part of the house Fergus, son of Rogh; Celthair, son of Uthecar; Eoghan, son of Durthact; the two sons of the king, Fiacha and Fiachaig; Fergus, son of Leti; Cuscraid, the Stutterer of Macha; Sencha, son of Ailell; the three sons of Fiachach, that is Rus and Dare and Imchad; Muinremar, son of Geirgind; Errge Echbel; Amergin, son of Ecit; Mend, son of Salchah; Dubthach Doel Uladh, the Beetle of Ulster; Feredach Find Fectnach; Fedelmid, son of Ilair Cheting; Furbaide Ferbend; Rochad, son of Fathemon; Laegaire Buadach; Conall Cearnach; Cuchulain; Conrad, son of Mornai; Erc, son of Fedelmid; Iollan, son of Fergus; Fintan, son of Nial; Cethern, son of Fintan; Factna, son of Sencad; Conla the False; Ailell the Honey-Tongued; the chief men of Ulster, with the young men and the song-makers.

While the feast was being spread out, the musicians and players made music for them. As soon as Bricriu had spread the feast with its well-tasting, savoury meats, he was ordered by his sureties to leave the hall on the moment; and they rose up with their drawn swords in their hands to put him out. So he and his followers went out, and when he was on the threshold of the house he turned and called out: "The Champion's Portion of my house is not the portion of a fool's house; let it be given to whoever you think the best hero of Ulster." And with that he left them. Then the distributers rose up to divide the food, and the chariot-driver of Laegaire Buadach, Sedlang, son of Riangabra, rose up and said to them, "Let you give the Champion's Portion to Laegaire, for he has the best right to it of all the young heroes of Ulster."

Then Id, son of Riangabra, chariot-driver to Conall Cearnach, rose up, and bade them to give it to his master. But Laeg, son of Riangabra, said, "It is to Cuchulain it must be brought; and it is no disgrace for all the men of Ulster to give it to him, for it is he is the bravest of you all." "That is not true," said Conall, and Laegaire said the same.

With that they got up upon the floor, and put on their shields and took hold of their swords, and they attacked and struck at one another till the one half of the hall was as if on fire with the clashing of swords and spears, and the other half was white as chalk with the whiteness of the shields. There was fear on the whole gathering; all the men were put from their places, and there was great anger on Conchubar himself and on Fergus, son of Rogh, to see the injustice and the hardship of two men fighting against one, Conall and Laegaire both together attacking Cuchulain; but there was no one among the men of Ulster dared part them till Sencha spoke to Conchubar. "It is time for you to part these men," he said.

With that, Conchubar and Fergus came between them, and the fighters let their hands drop to their sides. "Will you do as I advise?" said Sencha. "We will do it," they said. "Then my advice is," said Sencha, "for this night to divide the Champion's Portion among the whole gathering, and after that to let it be settled according to the judgment of Ailell, king of Connaught, for it will be better for the men of Ulster, this business to be settled in Cruachan [in County Roscommon]."

So with that they sat down to the feast again, and gathered round the fire and drank and made merry.

All this time Bricriu and his wife were in their upper room, and from there he had seen how things were going on in the great hall. And he began to search his mind how he could best stir up the women to quarrel with one another as he had stirred up the men. When he had done searching his mind, it just chanced as he could have wished, that Fedelm of the Fresh Heart came from the hall with fifty women after her, laughing and merry. Bricriu went to meet her. "All good be with you to-night, wife of Laegaire Buadach. Fedelm of the Fresh Heart is no nickname for you, with respect to your appearance and your wisdom and your family. Conchubar, king of Ulster, is of your kindred; Laegaire Buadach is your husband. I would not think well of it that any of the women of Ulster should go before you into the hall, for it is at your heel that all the other women of Ulster should walk. If you go first into the hall tonight, you will be queen over them all for ever and ever."

Fedelm went on after that, the length of three ridges from the hall.

After that there came out Lendabair, the Favourite, daughter of Eoghan, son of Durthact, wife of Conall Cearnach.

Bricriu came over to her, and he said, "Good be with you, Lendabair; and that is no nickname, for you are the favourite and the darling of the men of the whole world, because of the brightness of your beauty. As far as your husband is beyond the whole world in bravery and in comeliness, so far are you before the women of Ulster." Great as his deceit was in what he said to Fedelm, it was twice as great in what he said to Lendabair.

Then Emer came out and fifty women after her. "Health be with you, Emer, daughter of Forgall Manach, wife of the best man in Ireland! Emer of the Beautiful Hair is no nickname for you, the kings and princes of Ireland are quarrelling with one another about you. So far as the sun outshines the stars of heaven, so far do you outshine the women of the whole world in form, and shape, and birth, in youth, and beauty, and nicety, in good name, and wisdom, and speech." However great his deceit was towards the other women, it was twice as much towards Emer.

The three women went on then till they met at one spot, three ridges from the house, but none of them knew that Bricriu had been speaking to the other. They set out then to go back to the house. Their walk was even and quiet and easy on the first ridge; hardly did one of them put her foot before the other. But on the next ridge their steps were closer and quicker; and when they came to the ridge next the house, it was hardly one of them could keep up with the other, so that they took up their skirts nearly to their knees, each one trying to get first into the hall, because of what Bricriu had said to them, that whoever would be first to enter the house, would be queen of the whole province. And such was the noise they made in their race, that it was like the noise of forty chariots coming. The whole palace shook, and all the men started up for their arms, striking against one another.

"Stop," said Sencha, "it is not enemies that are coming, it is Bricriu has set the women quarrelling. By the god of my people!" he said, "unless the hall is shut against them, those that are dead among us will be more than those that are living." With that the doorkeepers shut the doors. But Emer was quicker than the other women, and outran them, and put her back against the door, and called to the doorkeepers before the other women came up, so that the men rose up, each of them to open the door before his own wife, so that she might be the first to come within.

"It is a bad night this will be," said Conchubar; and he struck the silver rod he had in his hand against the bronze post of the hall, and they all sat down. "Quiet yourselves," said Sencha; "it is not a war of arms we are going to have here, it is a war of words." Each woman then put herself under the protection of her husband outside, and then there followed the war of words of the women of Ulster.

Fedelm of the Fresh Heart was the first to speak, and this is what she said:

"The mother who bore me was free, noble, equal to my father in rank and in race; the blood that is in me is royal; I was brought up like one of royal blood. I am counted beautiful in form and in shape and in appearance; I was brought up to good behaviour, to courage, to mannerly ways. Look at Laegaire, my husband, and what his red hand does for Ulster. It was by himself alone its boundaries were kept from the enemies that were as strong as all Ulster put together; he is a defence and a protection against wounds; he is beyond all the heroes; his victories are greater than their victories. Why should not I, Fedelm, the beautiful, the lovely, the joyful, be the first to step into the drinking-hall to-night?"

Then Lendabair spoke, and this is what she said:

"I myself have beauty too, and good sense and good carriage; it is I should walk into the hall with free, even steps before all the women of Ulster.

"For my husband is pleasant Conall of the great shield, the Victorious; he is proud, going with brave steps up to the spears of the fight; he is proud coming back to me after it, with the heads of his enemies in his hands.

"He brings his hard sword into the battle for Ulster; he defends every ford or he destroys it to keep out the enemy; he is a hero will have a stone raised over him.

"The son of noble Amergin, who can speak against his courage or his deeds? It is Conall who leads the heroes.

"All eyes look on the glory of Lendabair; why would she not go first into the hall of the king?"

Then Emer spoke, and this is what she said:

"There is no woman comes up to me in appearance, in shape, in wisdom; there is no one comes up to me for goodness of form, or brightness of eye, or good sense, or kindness, or good behaviour.

"No one has the joy of loving or the strength of loving that I have; all Ulster desires me; surely I am a nut of the heart. If I were a light woman, there would not be a husband left to any of you to-morrow.

"And my husband is Cuchulain. It is he is not a hound that is weak; there is blood on his spear, there is blood on his sword, his white body is black with blood, his soft skin is furrowed with sword cuts, there are many wounds on his thigh.

"But the flame of his eyes is turned westward; he is the strong protector; his chariot is red, its cushions are red; he fights from over the ears of horses, from over the breath of men; he leaps in the air like a salmon when he makes his hero leap; he does strange feats, the dark feat, the blind feat, the feat of nine; he breaks down armies in the hard fight; he saves the life of proud armies; he finds joy in the terror of the ignorant.

"Your fine heroes of Ulster are not worth a stalk of grass compared with my husband, Cuchulain, letting on to have a woman's sickness on them; he is like the clear red blood, they are like the scum and the leavings, worth no more than a stalk of grass.

"Your fine women of Ulster, they are shaped like cows and led like cows, when they are put beside the wife of Cuchulain."

When the men in the hall heard what the women said, Laegaire and Conall made a rush at the wall, and broke a plank out of it at their own height, to let their own wives in. But Cuchulain raised up that part of the house that was opposite to his place, so that the stars and the sky could be seen through the wall. By that opening Emer came in with the fifty women that waited on her, and with them the women that waited on the other two. None of the other women could be compared at all with Emer, and no one at all could be compared with her husband. And then Cuchulain let the wall he had lifted fall suddenly again, so that seven feet of it went into the ground, and the whole house shook, and Bricriu's upper room was laid flat in such a way that Bricriu himself and his wife were thrown into the dirt among the dogs. "My grief," cried Bricriu, "enemies are come in!" And he got up quickly and took a turn round, and he saw that the hall was now crooked and leaning entirely to one side. He clapped his hands together and went inside, but he was so covered with dirt that none of the Ulster people could know him, it was only by his way of speaking they made out who he was.

Then he said, from the middle of the floor, "It is a pity I ever made a feast for you, men of Ulster. My house is more to me than everything else I have. I put geasa, that is, bonds, on you, not to drink or eat or to sleep till you leave my house the same way as you found it." At that, all the men of Ulster went out and tried to pull the house straight, but they did not raise it by so much as a hand's breadth.

"What are we to do?" they said. "There is nothing for you to do," said Sencha, "but to ask the man that pulled it crooked to set it straight again."

Upon that they bid Cuchulain to put the wall up straight again, and Bricriu said, "O king of the heroes of Ireland, unless you can set it up straight, there is no man in the world can do it."

And all the men of Ulster begged and prayed of Cuchulain to settle the matter. And that they might not have to go without food or drink, Cuchulain rose up and tried to lift the house with a tug, and he failed. Anger came on him then, and the hero light shone about him, and he put out all his strength, and strained himself till a man's foot could find place between each of his ribs, and he lifted the house up till it was as straight as it was before. After that they enjoyed the feast, with the chief men on the one side round about Conchubar, High King of Ulster, and their wives on the other side—Fedelm of the Nine Shapes (nine shapes she could take on, and each shape more beautiful than the other), and Findchoem, daughter of Cathbad, wife of Amergin of the Iron Jaw, and Devorgill, wife of Lugaid of the Red Stripes, besides Emer, and Fedelm of the Fresh Heart, and Lendabair; and it would be too long to count and to tell of all the other noble women besides.

There was soon a buzzing of words in the hall again, with the women praising their men, as if to stir up another quarrel between them. Then Sencha, son of Ailell, got up and shook his bell branch, and they all stopped to listen to him, and then to quiet the women he said:

"Have done with this word-fighting, lest you drive the men of Ulster to grow white-faced in the anger and the pride of battle with one another.

"It is through the fault of women the shields of men are broken, heroes go out to fight and struggle with one another in their anger.

"It is the folly of women brings men to do these things, to bruise what they cannot bind up again, to strike down what they cannot raise up again. Wives of heroes, keep yourself from this."

But Emer answered him, and it is what she said:

"It is right for me to speak, Sencha, and I the wife of the comely, pleasant hero, who is beyond all others in beauty, in wisdom, in speaking, since the learning that was easy to him is done with.

"No one can do his feats, the over-breath feat, the apple feat, the ghost feat, the screw feat, the cat feat, the red-whirling feat, the barbed-spear feat, the quick stroke, the fire of the mouth, the hero's cry, the wheel feat, the sword-edge feat; no one can throw himself against hard-spiked places the way he does.

"There is no one is his equal in youth, in form, in brightness, in birth, in mind, in voice, in bravery, in boldness, in fire, in skill; no one in his equal in hunting, in running, in strength, in victories, in greatness. There is no man to be found who can be put beside Cuchulain."

"If it is truth you are speaking, Emer," said Conall Cearnach, "let this lad of feats stand up, that we may see them."

"I will not," said Cuchulain. "I am tired and broken to-day, I will do no more till after I have had food and sleep." It was true what he said, for it was on that morning he had met with the Grey of Macha [his horse] by the side of the grey lake at Slieve Fuad. When it came out of the lake, Cuchulain slipped his hands round the neck of the horse, and the two of them struggled and wrestled with one another, and in that way they went all round Ireland, till late in the day he brought the horse home to Emain. It was in the same way he got the Black Sainglain from the black lake of Sainglen.

And Cuchulain said: "To-day myself and the Grey of Macha have gone through the great plains of Ireland, Bregia of Meath, the seashore marsh of Muirthemne Macha, through Moy Medba, Currech Cleitech Cerna, Lia of Linn Locharn, Fer Femen Fergna, Curros Domnand, Ros Roigne, and Eo. And now I would sooner eat and sleep than do any other thing. But I swear by the gods my people swear by," he said, "I would be ready to fight with any man of you if I had but my fill of food and of sleep."

"Well," said Bricriu, "this has gone on long enough. Let food and drink be brought, and let the women's war be put a stop to till the feast is done."

They did so, and it was a pleasant time they had till the end of three days and three nights.

—XII—

GENGHIS KHAN

Genghis Khan (the name means "Strong Ruler") did not call himself that until 1206. By that time he was indeed the strong ruler of most of the Turko-Mongolian world. Born in the 1160s as Temujin, the son of a Mongolian tribal chief who died when his boy was nine, he began making alliances with some neighboring tribes and leading raiding parties against others while still a teenager. As Genghis Khan, he led his mounted army (which was said to be able to move a hundred miles in a day) into China in 1211 and Muslim Central Asia in 1218, conquering—and often destroying—such great cities as Bukhara, Samarkand, and Herat. In China, an ailing Genghis all but obliterated the Tangut kingdom of Xi-Xia and finally died in the midst of his assault on Ningxia, its capital, in August, 1227.

In western Europe, the Mongols were often called Tartars, perhaps out of confusion with the Tatars, an eastern tribe Genghis conquered early in his career and made part of his kingdom. Or perhaps it was because the Asians were feared as inhuman denizens of Tartarus, the hellish underworld in Greek mythology.

The story that follows of the rise of Temujin and some of his conquests, including the taking of Bukhara, is from *The History of the World Conqueror*, by Ala-ad-Din Ata-Malik Juvaini (1226–1283), a Persian civil servant under the Mongols, who was governor of Baghdad at the time of his death. A devout Muslim (a relative of his was said to have accompanied Muhammed on his flight from Balkh), he does not hide his religious beliefs or his suspicion that Genghis Khan was an instrument of God's punishment. Genghis's life, as Juvaini tells it, contains some startling parallels with incidents in the stories of David and King Saul, John the Baptist, and even Macbeth. The book was probably completed in 1260.

The anecdotes about some incidents in and around Genghis Khan's tent during his battles with the Tatars come from a most curious book, *The Secret History of the Mongols*. The only known history by a Mongol, most of whom were illiterate, it probably survived because it was translated into Chinese in the fourteenth century. The account is sometimes difficult to read, even in its current academic English translation, but it does contain some rather intimate moments, such as the observation that young Temujin was afraid of dogs (not included in this excerpt) or what happened after one of Genghis's wives told him her sister was prettier than she was. Since *The Secret History* says it was written in the year of the Rat (the Mongolian calendar, like the Chinese, uses a twelve-year animal cycle), it was probably completed in either 1228 or 1240.

JUVAINI

FROM *THE HISTORY OF THE WORLD CONQUEROR*

1260

CHINGIZ-KHAN'S RISE TO POWER AND THE BEGINNING OF THE PASSING TO HIM OF THE EMPIRES AND KINGDOMS OF THE KINGS OF THE WORLD: A BRIEF ACCOUNT THEREOF

The tribes and clans of the Mongols are many; but that which to-day is most renowned for its nobility and greatness and has precedence over the others is the tribe of the Qiyat, of which the forefathers and ancestors of Chingiz-Khan [Genghis Khan] were the chieftains and from which they traced their descent.

Chingiz-Khan bore the name of Temujin until the time when in accordance with the decree of "'Be,' and it is," [Allah] he became master of all the kingdoms of the habitable world. In those days Ong-Khan, the ruler of the Kereit and the Saqiyat, surpassed the other tribes in strength and dignity and was stronger than they in gear and equipment and the number of his men. And in those days the Mongol tribes were not united and did not obey one another. When Chingiz-Khan rose from the grade of childhood to the degree of manhood, he became in the onslaught like a roaring lion and in the mêlée like a trenchant sword; in the subjugation of his foes his rigour and severity had the taste of poison, and in the humbling of the pride of each lord of fortune his harshness and ferocity did the work of Fate. Upon every occasion, by reason of the nearness of their confines and the proximity of their territories, he used to visit Ong-Khan, and there was a feeling of friendship between them. When Ong-Khan beheld his counsel and discernment, his valour, splendour and majesty, he marvelled at his courage and energy and did all that lay in his power to advance and honour him. Day by day he raised his station and position, until all affairs of state were dependent upon him and all Ong-Khan's troops and followers controlled by his discipline and justice. The sons and brothers of Ong-Khan and his courtiers and favourites became envious of the rank and favour he enjoyed: they accordingly cast the nets of guile across the passage provided by opportunity and set the traps of treachery to effect the blackening of his name; in the ambushes of private audiences they put out the story of his power and pre-eminence and repeated the tale of the inclination of all hearts towards obedience and allegiance to him.

In the guise of well-wishers they kept these stories fresh until Ong-Khan too became suspicious of him and was doubtful as to what he should do; and fear and dread of his courage and intrepidity became implanted in his heart. Since it was impossible to attack him and break with him openly, he thought to remove him by craft and guile and to hinder by fraud and treachery God's secret design in fortifying him. It was agreed, therefore, that at dawn, while eyes were anointed with the collyrium of sleep and mankind was rendered negligent by repose, Ong-Khan's men should make a night attack upon Chingiz-Khan and his followers and thus free themselves from their fears. They made every preparation for the deed and were about to put their intention into action; but since his luck was vigilant and his fortune kind, two youths in Ong-Khan's service, one of them named Kishlik and the other Bada, fled to Chingiz-Khan and informed him of the badness of their faith and the uncleanness of their treachery.

He at once sent off his family and followers and had the tents moved away. When at the appointed time, in the dawn, the enemy charged down upon the tents they found them empty. Though the accounts differ here as to whether they then returned or whether they at once took up the pursuit, the upshot of the matter was that Ong-Khan set off in search of him with a large force of men, while Chingiz-Khan had but a small force with him. There is a spring [in that region] which they call Baljuna: here they joined battle and fierce fighting ensued. In the end, Chingiz-Khan with his small army routed Ong-Khan with his great host and won much booty.

This event occurred in the year 599/1202–3, and the names of all who took part therein are recorded, whether base or noble, from princes down to slaves, tent-pitchers, grooms, Turks, Taziks, and Indians. As for those two youths, he made them tarkhan. Tarkhan are those who are exempt from compulsory contributions, and to whom the booty taken on every campaign is surrendered: whenever they so wish they may enter the royal presence without leave or permission. He also gave them troops and slaves and of cattle, horses and accoutrement more than could be counted or computed; and commanded that whatever offence they might commit they should not be called to account therefor; and that this order should be observed with their posterity also down to the ninth generation. To-day there are many people descended from these two persons, and they are honoured and respected in every country, and held in high esteem at the courts of kings. As for the rest of those that took part in this battle, they all obtained high rank, and the very tent-pitchers and camel-drivers attained to great dignity; some became kings of the age, while others rose to great offices of state and became famous throughout the world.

When Chingiz-Khan's army had been reinforced, in order to prevent Ong-Khan from rallying, he dispatched troops to pursue him. Several times they joined battle, and on each occasion he was victorious and Ong-Khan defeated. Finally all the latter's family and retainers, even his wives and daughters, fell into Chingiz-Khan's hand; and he himself was slain.

And when Chingiz-Khan's cause prospered and the stars of his fortune were in the ascendant, he dispatched envoys to the other tribes also; and all that came to tender submission, such as the Oirat and the Qonqurat, admitted to the number of his commanders and followers and were regarded with the eye of indulgence and favour; while as for the refractory and rebellious, he struck the breath from their bodies with the whip of calamity and the sword of annihilation; until all the tribes were of one colour and obedient to his command. Then he established new laws and laid the foundation of justice; and whichever of their customs were abominable, such as theft and adultery, he abolished. . . .

At this time there arose a man of whom I have heard from trustworthy Mongols that during the severe cold that prevails in those regions he used to walk naked through the desert and the mountains and then to return and say: "God has spoken with me and has said: 'I have given all the face of the earth to Temujin and his children and named him Chingiz-Khan. Bid him administer justice in such and such a fashion.'" They called this person Teb-Tengri [Most Heavenly], and whatever he said Chingiz-Khan used implicitly to follow. Thus he too grew strong; and many followers having gathered around him, there arose in him the desire for sovereignty. One day in the course of a banquet, he engaged in altercation with one of the princes [Chingiz's youngest brother]; and that prince, in the midst of the assembly, threw him so heavily upon the ground that he never rose again.

In short, when these regions had been purged of rebels and all the tribes had become as his army, he dispatched ambassadors to Khitai [China], and afterwards went there in person, and slew Altun-Khan, the Emperor of Khitai, and subjugated the country. And gradually he conquered other kingdoms also. . . .

. . . Beyond lieth a city which is called Samarqand, wherein is a fountain of the fountains of Paradise, and a tomb of the tombs of the prophets, and a garden of the gardens of Paradise; its dead, upon the Resurrection Day, shall be assembled with the martyrs. And beyond this city there lieth holy ground, which is called Qatavan, wherefrom there shall be sent seventy thousand martyrs, each of whom shall intercede for seventy of his family and kinsfolk. We shall give a particular account of the fate of these two cities; and as for the authenticity of this tradition, it is confirmed by the fact that the affairs of this world are relative and that "some evil is lighter than other"; or, as has been said: "Under all circumstances gratitude best befitteth the slave [of God], for much evil is worse than [simple] evil."

Chingiz-Khan came to these countries in person. The tide of calamity was surging up from the Tartar army, but he had not yet soothed his breast with vengeance nor caused a river of blood to flow, as had been inscribed by the pen of Destiny in the roll of Fate. When, therefore, he took Bokhara and Samarqand, he contented himself with slaughtering and looting once only, and did not go to the extreme of a general massacre. As for the adjoining territories that were subject to these towns or bordered on them, since for the most part they tendered submission, the hand of molestation was to some extent withheld from them. And afterwards, the Mongols pacified the survivors and proceeded with work of reconstruction, so that at the present time, i.e. in 658/1259–60, the prosperity and well-being of these districts have in some cases attained their original level and in others have closely approached it. It is otherwise with Khorasan and Iraq, which countries are afflicted with a hectic fever and a chronic ague: every town and every village has been several times subjected to pillage and massacre and has suffered this confusion for years, so that even though there be generation and increase until the Resurrection the population will not attain to a tenth part of what it was before. The history thereof may be ascertained from the records of ruins and midden-heaps declaring how Fate has painted her deeds upon palace walls.

In accordance with the general expectation the reins of those countries were placed in the competent hands of the Great Minister Yalavach and his dutiful son the Emir Mas'ud Beg. By their unerring judgement they repaired the ravages thereof and struck the face of opponents with the saying, "The druggist may not repair what time hath ravaged"; and Yalavach abolished compulsory service in the levies and the *cherig* [army] as also the burdens and superfluities of occasional imposts (avarizat). And the truth of this statement is to be seen in the records of freshness and prosperity (the glittering East of their justice and mercy), which are plainly written on the pages of those countries and are clearly visible in the affairs of the inhabitants thereof.

OF THE CAPTURE OF BOKHARA

In the Eastern countries it is the cupola of Islam and is in those regions like unto the City of Peace [Baghdad]. Its environs are adored with the brightness of the light of doctors and jurists and its surroundings embellished with the rarest of high attainments. Since ancient times it has in every age been the place of assembly of the great savants of every religion. Now the derivation of Bokhara is from *bukhar*, which in the language of the Magians signifies center of learning. This word closely resembles a word in the language of the Uighur and Khitayan idolaters, who call their places of worship, which are idol-temples, *bukhar*. But at the time of its foundation the name of the town was Bumijkath.

Chingiz-Khan, having completed the organization and equipment of his armies, arrived in the countries of the Sultan; and dispatching his elder sons and the noyans in every direction at the head of large forces, he himself advanced first upon Bokhara, being accompanied by Toli alone of his elder sons and by a host of fearless Turks that knew not clean from unclean, and considered the bowl of war to be a basin of rich soup and held a mouthful of the sword to be a beaker of wine.

He proceeded along the road to Zarnuq, and in the morning when the king of the planets raised his banner on the eastern horizon, he arrived unexpectedly before the town. When the inhabitants thereof, who were unaware of the fraudulent designs of Destiny, beheld the surrounding countryside choked with horsemen and the air black as night with the dust of cavalry, fright and panic overcame them, and fear and dread prevailed. They betook themselves to the citadel and closed the gates, thinking, "This is perhaps a single detachment of a great army and a single wave from a raging sea." It was their intention to resist and to approach calamity on their own feet, but they were aided by divine grace so that they stood firm and breathed not opposition. At this juncture, the World-Emperor, in accordance with his constant practice, dispatched Danishmand Hajib upon an embassy to them, to announce the arrival of his forces and to advise them to stand out of the way of a dreadful deluge. Some of the inhabitants, who were in the category of "Satan hath gotten mastery over them" were minded to do him harm and mischief; whereupon he raised a shout, saying: "I am such-and-such a person, a Moslem and the son of a Moslem. Seeking God's pleasure I am come on an embassy to you, at the inflexible command of Chingiz-Khan, to draw you out of the whirlpool of destruction and the trough of blood. It is Chingiz-Khan himself who has come with many thousands of warriors. The battle has reached thus far. If you are incited to resist in any way, in an hour's time your citadel will be level ground and the plain a sea of blood. But if you will listen to advice and exhortation with the ear of intelligence and consideration and become submissive and obedient to his command, your lives and property will remain in the stronghold of security."

When the people, both nobles and commoners, had heard his words, which bore the brand of veracity, they did not refuse to accept his advice, knowing for certain that the flood might not be stemmed by their obstructing his passage nor might the quaking of the mountains and the earth be quietened and allayed by the pressure of their feet. And so they held it proper to choose peace and advantageous to accept advice. But by way of caution and security they obtained from him a covenant that if, after the people had gone forth to meet the Khan and obeyed his command, any harm should befall any one of them, the retribution thereof should be on his head.

Thus were the people's minds set at ease, and they withdrew their feet from the thought of transgression and turned their faces towards the path of advantage. The chief men of Zarnuq sent forward a delegation bearing presents. When these came to the place where the Emperor's cavalry had halted, he asked about their leaders and notables and was wroth with them for their dilatoriness in remaining behind. He dispatched a messenger to summon them to his presence. Because of the great awe in which the Emperor was held a tremor of horror appeared on the limbs of these people like the quaking of the members of a mountain. They at once proceeded to his presence; and when they arrived he treated them with mercy and clemency and spared their lives, so that they were once more of good heart. An order was then issued that everyone in Zarnuq—be he who he might— both such as donned kalah and turban and such as wore kerchief and veil, should go out of the town on to the plain. The citadel was turned into level ground; and after a counting of heads they made a levy of the youths and young men for the attack on Bokhara, while the rest of the people were suffered to return home. They gave the place the name of Qutlugh-Baligh [Fortunate Town].

A guide, one of the Turkomans of that region, who had a perfect knowledge of the roads and highways, led them on by a little frequented road; which road has ever since been called the Khan's Road. (In the year 649/1251–2, when journeying to the Court of Mengu Qa'an in the company of the Emir Arghun we passed along this very road.)

Tayir Bahadur was proceeding in advance of the main forces. When he and his men drew near to the town of Nur [in Uzbekistan], they passed through some gardens. During the night they felled the trees and fashioned ladders out of them. Then holding the ladders in front of their horses they advanced very slowly; and the watcher on the walls thought that they were a caravan of merchants, until in this manner they arrived at the gates of the citadel of Nur; when the day of that people was darkened and their eyes dimmed.

It is the story of Zarqa [the Blue-Eyed Woman] of Yamama. She had built a lofty castle, and her keenness of sight was such that if an enemy attempted to attack her she would descry his army at a distance of several stages and would prepare and make ready to repel him and drive him off. And so her enemies achieved nought but frustration and there remained no stratagem which they had not tried. [Finally one of them] commanded that trees should be cut down with their branches and that each horseman should hold a tree in front of him. Thereupon Zarqa exclaimed: "I see a strange sight: the likeness of a forest is moving towards us." Her people said: "The keenness of thy sight hath suffered some hurt, else how should trees move?" They neglected to watch or take precautions; and on the third day their foes arrived, and overcame them, and took Zarqa prisoner, and slew her.

To be brief, the people of Nur closed their gates; and Tayir Bahadur sent an envoy to announce the arrival of the World-Conquering Emperor and to induce them to submit and cease resistance. The feelings of the inhabitants were conflicting, because they did not believe that the World-Conquering Emperor Chingiz-Khan had arrived in person, and on the other hand they were apprehensive about the Sultan. They were therefore uncertain what course to take, some being in favour of submission and surrender while others were for resistance or were afraid [to take any action]. Finally, after much coming and going of ambassadors it was agreed that the people of Nur should prepare an offering of food and send it to the Lord of the Age together with an envoy, and so declare their submission and seek refuge in servitude and obedience.

Tayir Bahadur gave his consent and was satisfied with only a small offering. He then went his own way; and the people of Nur dispatched an envoy in the manner that had been agreed upon. After the envoys had been honoured with the Emperor's acceptance of their offering, he commanded that they should surrender the town to Subetei [a Mongol general], who was approaching Nur with the vanguard. When Subetei arrived they complied with this command and delivered up the town. Hereupon an agreement was reached that the people of Nur should be content with the deliverance of the community from danger and the retention of what was absolutely necessary for their livelihood and the pursuit of husbandry and agriculture, such as sheep and cows; and that they should go out on to the plain leaving their houses exactly as they were so that they might be looted by the army. They executed this order, and the army entered the town and bore off whatever they found there. The Mongols abided by this agreement and did no harm to any of them. The people of Nur then selected sixty men and dispatched them, together with Il-Khoja, the son of the Emir of Nur, to Dabus [between Bokhara and Samarqand] to render assistance to the Mongols. When Chingiz-Khan arrived, they went forth to meet him bearing suitable [presents] and offerings of food. Chingiz-Khan distinguished them with royal favour and asked them what fixed taxes the Sultan drew from Nur. They replied that these amounted to 1500 dinars; and he commanded them to pay this sum in cash and they should suffer no further inconvenience. Half of this amount was produced from the women's ear-rings, and they gave security for the rest and [finally] paid it to the Mongols. And so were the people of Nur delivered from the humiliation of Tartar bondage and slavery, and Nur regained its splendour and prosperity.

And from thence Chingiz-Khan proceeded to Bokhara, and in the beginning of Muharram, 617 [March 1220], encamped before the gates of the citadel.

And then they pitched the king's pavilion on the plain in front of the stronghold.

And his troops were more numerous than ants or locusts, being in their multitude beyond estimation or computation. Detachment after detachment arrived, each like a billowing sea, and encamped round about the town. At sunrise twenty thousand men from the Sultan's auxiliary army issued forth from the citadel together with most of the inhabitants; being commanded by Kok-Khan and other officers such as Khamid-Bur, Sevinch-Khan and Keshli-Khan. Kok-Khan was said to be a Mongol and to have fled from Chingiz-Khan and joined the Sultan; as a consequence of which his affairs had greatly prospered. When these forces reached the banks of the Oxus, the patrols and advance parties of the Mongol army fell upon them and left no trace of them.

When it is impossible to flee from destruction in any manner, then patience is the best and wisest course.

On the following day when from the reflection of the sun the plain seemed to be a tray filled with blood, the people of Bokhara opened their gates and closed the door of strife and battle. The imams and notables came on a deputation to Chingiz-Khan, who entered to inspect the town and the citadel. He rode into the Friday mosque and pulled up before the maqsura, whereupon his son Toli dismounted and ascended the pulpit. Chingiz-Khan asked those present whether this was the palace of the Sultan; they replied that it was the house of God. Then he too got down from his horse, and mounting two or three steps of the pulpit he exclaimed: "The countryside is empty of fodder; fill our horses' bellies." Whereupon they opened all the magazines in the town and began carrying off the grain. And they brought the cases in which the Korans were kept out into the courtyard of the mosque, where they cast the Korans right and left and turned the cases into mangers for their horses. After which they circulated cups of wine and sent for the singing-girls of the town to sing and dance for them; while the Mongols raised their voices to the tunes of their own songs. Meanwhile, the imams, shaiks, sayyids, doctors and scholars of the age kept watch over their horses in the stable under the supervision of the equerries, and executed their commands. After an hour or two Chingiz-Khan arose to return to his camp, and as the multitude that had been gathered there moved away the leaves of the Koran were trampled in the dirt beneath their own feet and their horses' hoofs. In that moment, the Emir Imam Jalal-ad-Din 'Ali b. al-Hasan Zaidi, who was the chief and leader of the sayyids of Transoxiana and was famous for his piety and asceticism, turned to the learned imam Rukn-ad-Din Imamzada, who was one of the most excellent savants in the world—may God render pleasant the resting-places of them both—and said: "Maulana, what state is this?"

Maulana Imamzada answered: "Be silent: it is the wind of God's omnipotence that bloweth, and we have no power to speak."

When Chingiz-Khan left the town he went to the festival *musalla* and mounted the pulpit; and, the people having been assembled, he asked which were the wealthy amongst them. Two hundred and eighty persons were designated (a hundred and ninety of them being natives of the town and the rest strangers, viz. ninety merchants from various places) and were led before him. He then began a speech, in which, after describing the resistance and treachery of the Sultan (of which more than enough has been said already) he addressed them as follows: "O people, know that you have committed great sins, and that the great ones among you have committed these sins. If you ask me what proof I have for these words, I say it is because I am the punishment of God. If you had not committed great sins, God would not have sent a punishment like me upon you." When he had finished speaking in this strain, he continued his discourse with words of admonition, saying, "There is no need to declare your property that is on the face of the earth; tell me of that which is in the belly of the earth."

Then he asked them who were their men of authority; and each man indicated his own people. To each of them he assigned a Mongol or Turk in order that the soldiers might not molest them, and, although not subjecting them to disgrace or humiliation, they began to exact money from these men; and when they delivered it up they did not torment them by excessive punishment or demanding what was beyond their power to pay. And every day, at the rising of the greater luminary, the guards would bring a party of notables to the audience-hall of the World-Emperor.

Chingiz-Khan had given orders for the Sultan's troops to be driven out of the interior of the town and the citadel. As it was impossible to accomplish this purpose by employing the townspeople and as these troops, being in fear of their lives, were fighting, and doing battle, and making night attacks as much as was possible, he now gave orders for all the quarters of the town to be set on fire; and since the houses were built entirely of wood, within several days the greater part of the town had been consumed, with the exception of the Friday mosque and some of the palaces, which were built with baked bricks. Then the people of Bokhara were driven against the citadel. And on either side the furnace of battle was heated. On the outside, mangonels [catapults] were erected, bows bent and stones and arrows discharged; and on the inside, ballistas and pots of naphtha were set in motion. It was like a red-hot furnace fed from without by hard sticks thrust into the recesses, while from the belly of the furnace sparks shoot into the air. For days they fought in this manner; the garrison made sallies against the besiegers, and Kok-Khan in particular, who in bravery would have borne the palm from male lions, engaged in many battles: in each attack he overthrew several persons and alone repelled a great army. But finally they were reduced to the last extremity; resistance was no longer in their power; and they stood excused before God and man. The moat had been filled with animate and inanimate and raised up with levies and Bokharians; the outworks had been captured and fire hurled into the citadel; and their khans, leaders and notables, who were the chief men of the age and the favourites of the Sultan and who in their glory would set their feet on the head of Heaven, now became the captives of abasement and were drowned in the sea of annihilation.

> *Fate playeth with mankind the game of the sticks with the ball,*
> *Or the game of the wind blowing (know thou!) a handful of millet.*
> *Fate is a hunter, and man is naught but a lark.*

Of the Qanqli no male was spared who stood higher than the butt of a whip and more than thirty thousand were counted amongst the slain; whilst their small children, the children of their nobles and their womenfolk, slender as the cypress, were reduced to slavery.

When the town and the citadel had been purged of rebels and the walls and outworks levelled with the dust, all the inhabitants of the town, men and women, ugly and beautiful, were driven out on to the field of the musalla. Chingiz-Khan spared their lives; but the youths and full-grown men that were fit for such service were pressed into a levy for the attack on Samarqand and Dabusiya. Chingiz-Khan then proceeded against Samarqand; and the people of Bokhara, because of the desolation, were scattered like the constellation of the Bear and departed into the villages, while the site of the town became like "a level plain."

Now one man had escaped from Bokhara after its capture and had come to Khorasan. He was questioned about the fate of that city and replied: "They came, they sapped, they burnt, they slew, they plundered and they departed." Men of understanding who heard this description were all agreed that in the Persian language there could be nothing more concise than this speech. And indeed all that has been written in this chapter is summed up and epitomized in these two or three words.

"SOME INCIDENTS DURING GENGHIS'S WAR WITH THE TATARS"

FROM *THE SECRET HISTORY OF THE MONGOLS*

THIRTEENTH CENTURY

Wintering that winter, [in] the autumn of the year of the dog [1202], Cinggis Qahan [Genghis Khan] set himself at Dalan Nemürges against the Ca'a'an Tatar, Alci Tatar, Duta'ud Tatar and Aluqai Tatar—and, before joining battle, Cinggis Qahan spake with his soldiers saying, "If we overcome the enemy, let us not tarry for spoil. When we shall have made an end of overcoming, that spoil shall be ours. We shall divide it with one another. If we be made to withdraw by an enemy, let us return unto our place from whence we first rushed forward. We shall behead the man which shall not have returned unto the place of the first rushing forward." Joining battle at Dalan Nemürges, he made the Tatar retreat. Overcoming them, making them to join themselves unto their nation, he spoiled them. Then destroying the weighty peoples. . . . Altan, Qucar, and Daritai—all three—not keeping to their words, halted for spoil. Saying, "You have not kept to your words," sending both Jebe and Qubilai, he made them take from the three the herds and things which they had spoiled, the things which they had taken—everything.

Making an end of destroying and spoiling the Tatar, saying, "How shall we deal with their nation and people?", Cinggis Qahan entered into a solitary tent with his kinsmen, counseled great counsel with them. When they were counseling one another, saying, "From days of old the Tatar people have been making an end of our grandfathers and fathers. . . .

"Let us," comparing their height unto that of a linchpin, "destroy and slay them [i.e., kill all those whose height exceeds the linchpin on the axel of a cart.

In other words, kill everyone but the children]. Let us slay until we destroy them. Let us make slaves of those that shall have been left. Let us part them with one another severally."

As, together, making an end of their counsel, they went out from the tent, Yeke Ceren, a Tatar hostage, asked of Belgutei, saying, "What counsel have ye counseled one another?" When Belgutei spake, he said, "We have said unto one another that, comparing your height unto that of a linchpin, we would slay you all." At this word of Belgutei, Yeke Ceren [sent that message] to the Tatar fortress. When our troops assayed to attack the Tatar fortress, they suffered great loss. Destroying the Tatar, comparing their height unto that of a linchpin, the Tatar spake unto one another, saying, "Each person put a knife in his sleeve. Let us die 'taking a pillow with us'" [i.e., at the moment of death, killing an enemy to serve as a pillow].

Our soldiers suffered great loss. And so making an end of slaying the Tatar, Cinggis Qahan made a decree, saying, "Because of the fact that Belgutei had revealed the great counsel with our kinsmen, he made our soldiers to suffer great loss. After this, let Belgutei not enter into great counsel. Let him remain outside. When we shall have made an end of counsel, after we shall have drunk the ötög [wine], let Belgutei then enter."

Then Cinggis Qahan took to wife Yesugen Qatun, daughter of Yeke Ceren of the Tatar. When she was loved by Cinggis Qahan, when Yesugen Qadun spake, "If the Qahan favour me, he will take care of me, considering me a person and a thing worthy to keep. She who is named Yesui, a sister older than I, is better than I. At this word, when Cinggis Qahan spake, he said, "If thine elder sister have been better than thou, I shall make one to seek her. If thine elder sister come, wilt thou withdraw thyself for her?" When Yesugen Qatun spake, she said, "If I but see mine elder sister, I shall withdraw myself for mine elder sister." At this word, when Cinggis Qahan, proclaiming a decree, made one to seek her, our soldiers encountered her going in the woods. Her husband fled away. Then one brought Yesui Qatun. Yesugen Qatun, having seen her elder sister, keeping to the words which she had spoken before, arising, making her to sit on her seat on which she had sat, she herself sat below. As [Yesui Qatun] was like unto that which had been said of her by Yesugen Qatun, Cinggis Qahan, suffering her to enter into his thoughts, took Yesui Qatun to wife and suffered her to sit in the row of imperial wives.

Making an end of spoiling the Tatar people, one day, when Cinggis Qahan, sitting outside, was drinking together with Yesui Qatun and Yesugen Qatun, Yesui Qatun sighed deeply. Then when Cinggis Qahan, thinking within him, called and made the chiefs Bo'orcu, Muqali, and others to come, spake, he made a decree, saying "You—these people which have assembled themselves stand ye all tribe by tribe—set apart the persons of a tribe other than your own." And so, as they all stood, each with his tribe, a young, good, elegant person stood apart from the tribes. As one said, "What manner of person art thou?" when that person spake, he said, "I am the one unto whom was given the daughter named Yesui of Yeke Ceren of the Tatar. When we were spoiled by the enemy, being afraid, I fled away, but saying, 'It is now peaceable,' I have come back. Why should I be recognized among the many people?" [Hearing this] Cinggis Qahan said, "The same, thinking as an enemy, was gone, becoming a robber. Now he is come for what? We have compared the height of those that are like him unto that of a linchpin. Why should ye hesitate? Cast him away from the sight of mine eyes." And so he was beheaded.

— X I I I —

MONGOLS AND TARTARS

For nearly one hundred years after Genghis Khan's death, his descendents terrorized Europe both as a real and as an imagined threat. During the reign of Ögödei, Genghis's son and successor, Mongol troops led by Genghis's grandson Batu had swept through Hungary to the outskirts of Vienna, when Ogodei—rather conveniently for the Viennese—died in 1241. Sparing Vienna, Batu returned to Karakorum for the election of the new grand khan, but not before his Golden Horde had ravaged eastern Europe and Russia, demanding and receiving tribute as it went. ("horde" came from the Mongolian word *ordu* or "camp"; "golden" from the color of Batu's tent.) Grandson Hulagu battled Muslims in Persia and destroyed the Assassin sect there. Grandson Kublai replaced the Sung Dynasty in China but failed in two attempts to invade Japan. His death in 1294, and the internecine squabbles that followed, pretty much ended the Mongol Empire.

But in western Europe fear of the barbarous Mongols, or Tartars as they were usually called, far outweighed their actual threat. In 1245, Pope Innocent IV sent an expedition of Franciscan friars from Lyon, led by John de Plano Carpini, to report on the Tartars and perhaps convert a few. Two years later, someone who called himself C. de Bridia (nothing is known of him, not even his first name) wrote *Historia Tartarorum*—usually called *The Tartar Relation*—based on the friars' accounts. The excerpt reprinted here covers the last days of Genghis, some exploits of other Mongol leaders (including an encounter with a fierce tribe in which all the females were humans and all the males shaggy dogs), and then a general discussion of Tartar customs.

A more violent, less quizzical account was kept by monks in Novgorod, the fortified city that was capital of Russia when Moscow, to the south, was still a village. Their *Chronicle of Novogorod* records the constant menace of Batu Khan's Golden Horde and reports of atrocities elsewhere. In their piety, the monks—like the Muslim Juvaini in Persia—saw the Tartars as heathen avengers unwittingly doing God's work by punishing their victims' sins.

Another monk, Matthew Paris (ca. 1200–1259) of far-off St. Albans in England, also kept a worried eye on the Tartars. A witty illustrator as well as a colorful writer, his *Chronicles* include letters from kings and popes (which he may well have invented or embellished) and demonstrate an amazing level of paranoia. His hatred of Tartars blends into a loathing of both Arabs and Jews (in this he was a truly nonpartisan anti-Semite) that probably reflects the Crusader spirit of his time. Although only a monk, he seemed to have lofty connections. In 1236, he attended the wedding of Henry III and Eleanor of Provence at Westminster, and eleven years later he was sent by Pope Innocent IV to Norway to whip a wayward monastery into shape.

C. DE BRIDIA

FROM *THE TARTAR RELATION*

1247

After Chingis had taken the title of Khan and had remained quiet for a year without making war, he prepared three armies, one for each of the three quarters of the globe, intending them to conquer all men who dwell on earth. He sent one with his son Jochi, whom like himself they called Khan, to the west against the Comans, who dwell above the Az, and another with another son against greater India to the northeast. He himself marched with the third against the Caspian Mountains. After crossing the country called Solangia which he refrained from conquering at that time, he traveled persistently onward for three months through an uninhabited desert. When he drew near the Caspian Mountains, where the Jews called Gog and Magog by their fellow-countrymen are said to have been shut in by Alexander, lo and behold, everything made of iron, arrows from quivers, knives and swords from sheaths, stirrups from saddles, bits from bridles, horseshoes from horses' hooves, breastplates from bodies and helmets from heads, flew violently and with a tremendous clatter toward the mountain; and as the Tartars jestingly informed our Friar Benedict when they told this story, the heavier iron objects such as breastplates and helmets scurried along the ground to the mountain, raising a great cloud of dust and clanking, so that they were seized with blind horror. These mountains are believed to be magnetic.

Chingis fled in terror with his army, and leaving the mountains on the right marched northeast. At last after toiling continuously on his journey for three more months through the desert, he ordered them, as food was running short, to eat one man in every ten. After these three months he came to great mountains in a country called Narayrgen, that is, Men of the Sun, for *nara* is Tartar for sun, and *irgen* means men. Finding trodden trackways but no inhabitants, he and his men began to marvel exceedingly. Soon after he found a single native with his wife, and proceeded to ask him through numerous interpreters where the men of the country were. He learned that they dwelt in underground homes beneath the mountains, and sent the captured man, keeping the woman still prisoner, to ask if they were willing to come out and fight. While the man was on his way back day broke, and the Tartars threw themselves face downward on the ground at the noise of the rising sun, and many of them died on the spot! The natives of the country saw the enemy and made a night attack on them, killing a number of the Tartars, and seeing this Chingis Khan fled with the survivors, but took the captive wife with him nevertheless.

As the Tartars themselves told the friars, she stayed with them for a long time after, and asserted without a shadow of doubt that the aforesaid country is situated at the very end of the world, and beyond it no land is found, but only the ocean sea. Wherefore, owing to the excessive proximity of the sun when it rises over the sea at the point of summer sunrise, a crashing and roaring of such a nature and magnitude is heard there, due to the opposition of the sun and firmament, that no one dares to live in the open air on the surface until the sun proceeds through its zodiac to the south, for fear of dying instantly or being wounded as if struck by lightning. For this reason the natives beat huge drums and other instruments in their mountain caves, in order to shut out the noise of the sun with the sound of their drumming. This country is flat and fertile after the mountains are crossed, but not large.

While Chingis Khan was hurrying home from this country with his men after his defeat, he saw the Caspian mountains on the way, but did not go near them owing to his previous alarm. He noticed, however, that men had come out from the mountains owing to the noise made previously when the Tartars' iron-ware hurtled against them and wished to try his strength against them. As the two sides drew near to one another, lo and behold, a cloud came between them and divided them one from the other, like the Egyptians and the children of Israel long ago. This makes it credible enough that these people were the Jews whom the Lord protected and warned by signs given to their fathers. Whenever the Tartars advanced toward the cloud they were struck blind, and some were even smitten dead, though they could see one another more or less through the cloud. However, finding it impossible after two days' journeys to cross to either side of the cloud without having it still in their way, they began to proceed on their journey.

Traveling on foot and succumbing to starvation, they found in a state of semi-putrefaction the belly or entire entrails of an animal, which as the Tartars believe they had left behind after eating there on their outward journey. These entrails were brought to Chingis Khan, who ordered them to be cooked, after merely pressing out the gross excrement by hand without any rupture or injury to the guts. This was done, and Chingis Khan and the rest of his men ate them, now nearly dying of hunger. Chingis Khan announced that in future nothing must be thrown away from entrails excepting the gross inner part of the excrement contained in them. After this he returned home and by God's judgment was struck by lightning!

The second army which had been sent with the second son of Chingis Khan against the Indians conquered Lesser India [the area between the Indus and Ganges Rivers], the inhabitants of which are black-skinned and heathen. When they reached Greater India, which the Apostle Thomas converted, the king of the country, who is always called Prester John, although he was not well prepared, immediately sent an army against them which used a new and unheard-of device against the Tartars. They organized a special force of three thousand warriors carrying on the front of their saddles statues of iron or bronze containing live fire in their hollow interior, and before the Tartars' arrows could reach them they began to shoot fire against them, by blowing it with bellows which they carried on either side of the saddle under both thighs! After the fire they began to shoot arrows, and in this way the Tartar army was put in disorder. Some burned, others wounded, they took to flight, and the pursuing Indians felled many and ejected the others from their country, so that the Tartars never returned to India. All this the Tartars told our friars, saying that the Indians as they attacked lifted themselves on their stirrups above their horses' bodies in a regular line; "and as we wondered what this might be," they said, "they suddenly sat down on their saddles again, and instantly fire shot forth against us, followed by their arrows as well, and so our army was routed." Recently, when the Tartars had returned to their own country and the Indians had seen nothing of them for eighteen years or rather longer, they sent messengers to the Tartars, saying: "You invaded our country like thieves, not like fighting soldiers; but now take warning that we are daily preparing our own invasion. Therefore, although you will not come to us, you may expect us soon to come to you."

The Tartars, however, not daring to return to their own land before the appointed time, lest Chingis Khan should condemn them to death, proceeded to the southeast, and marching for more than a month through the desert reached the Land of Dogs, which in Tartar is called Nochoy Kadzar; for *nochoy* means dog in Tartar, and *kadzar* means land. They found only women there without men, and taking two of these prisoner they waited by the river which flows through the middle of the country. They asked the women where and of what kind the men were, and they replied that they were dogs by nature, and had crossed over the river on hearing of the enemy's approach. On the third day all the dogs in the country were seen to be gathering; and when the Tartars made mock of them, they crossed the river and rolled themselves in the sand, which owing to the coldness of the weather then froze. For a second and third time they did the same, and as the dogs were shaggy the mixture of ice and sand froze a hand's-breadth thick. This done, they charged upon the Tartars, who laughed and began to shoot them with their arrows, but succeeded in killing very few, as it was impossible to wound them except in the mouth or eyes. But the dogs ran swiftly up, throwing a horse to the ground with one bite and throttling it with the next. The Tartars, seeing that neither arrow nor sword could hurt the dogs, took to flight; and the dogs pursued them for three days, killed very many, dismissed them from their country, and so had peace from them ever after! One of the Tartars even told Friar Benedict that his father was killed by the dogs at that time; and Friar Benedict believes beyond doubt that he saw one of the dogs' women with the Tartars, and says she had even borne male children from them, but the boys were monsters. The aforesaid dogs are exceptionally shaggy, and understand every word the women say, while the women understand the dogs' sign language. If a woman bears a female child, it has a human form like the mother, while if the child is a male it takes the shape of a dog like the father.

On their way home from this country the Tartars conquered the country known as Burithebet. *Burith* means wolf, and this name suits the natives well, since it is their custom when their father dies to collect the whole family and eat his body, like ravening wolves. They have no hairs in their beard, but if hairs grow they pull them out with iron tweezers made for this purpose! Furthermore, they are exceedingly ugly.

The third army, however, which marched west with Chingis Khan's son Jochi Khan, conquered first the country called Terkemen, secondly the Bisermins, next the Kangits, and lastly invaded the country of Cuspeas or Comania. The Comanians, however, joined forces with the whole nation of the Russians and fought the Tartars near two small rivers, one called Kalka and the other called Coniuzzu (that is; Sheep's Water, for *coni* means sheep in Tartar and *uzzu* means water), and were beaten by the Tartars. Blood ran on both sides up to the horses' bridles, according to those who took part in this war. After this victory the Tartars began the return journey to their own country, and on the way conquered several countries to the north, for example the Bashkirs, or Greater Hungary, which borders on the Arctic Ocean.

After leaving this country they came to the Parossits [in the Urals], who are tall in stature but thin and frail, with a tiny round belly like a little cup. These people eat nothing at all but live on steam, for instead of a mouth they have a minute orifice, and obtain nourishment by inhaling the steam of meat stewed in a pot through a small opening; and as they have no regard for the flesh they throw it to their dogs! The Tartars took no heed of these people, as they thoroughly despise all monstrous things. Next they came to the people called Samoyeds, but took no notice of them either, because they are poverty-stricken men who dwell in forests and sustain life only from hunting! Lastly they came to the people called Ucorcolon, that is, Ox-feet, because *ucor* is Tartar for ox and *colon* for foot, or otherwise Nochoyterim, that is Dog-heads, *nochoy* being Tartar for dog and *terim* for head. They have feet like oxen from the ankles down, and a human head from the back of the head to the ears, but with a face in every respect like a dog's; and for that reason they take their name from the part of them which is monstrous in form. They speak two words and bark the third, and so can be called dogs for this reason also. They, too, live in forests and are nimble enough when they run, and the Tartars despised them like the others! Accordingly they returned home, where they found Chingis Khan had been struck by lightning.

Tartars also told our friars that they had been in the country of men with only one foot and one hand, but could do them no harm owing to their swiftness and their strength in shooting; for one holds the bow and another shoots the arrow more powerfully than any other nation, while they are said to excel in swiftness not only the men of other lands, but all four-footed animals in the world. Before the arrival of our friars among the Tartars two of the aforesaid men, a father and son, came to the court of the Tartar Emperor and said as follows: "For what reason have you tried to trouble us with wars? Do we not excel you in shooting of arrows and speed of running?" A horse of exceptional swiftness was appointed to race against them, and the Tartars released the horse at full speed. The two men began to revolve swiftly like a wheel in an extraordinary manner, and suddenly set out in pursuit of the horse. Finally they turned their backs on both horse and Tartars and ran to their own country, seeing which the Tartars decided not to invade them again. These people are called Unipeds.

Tartars are generally of low stature and rather thin, owing to their diet of mare's milk, which makes a man slim, and their strenuous life. They are broad of face with prominent cheekbones, and have a tonsure on their head like our clerics from which they shave a strip three fingers wide from ear to ear. On the forehead, however, they wear their hair in a crescent-shaped fringe reaching to the eyebrows, but gather up the remaining hair, and arrange and braid it like the Saracens.

As to their clothing, one needs to know that men and women wear the same kind of garments and are therefore not easy to tell apart; and as these matters seem more curious than useful I have not troubled to write further about their clothing and adornment.

Their houses are called stations and are of round shape, made of withies and stakes. At the top they have a round window to let out the smoke and let in the daylight. The roof and door are of felt. They differ in size and are movable insofar as the size permits them to be carried. The "stations" of the Khan and princes are called hordes. They have no towns but are organized in stations in various places. They have one city called Karakorum, from which our friars were a half a day's journey when they were at the Emperor's Sira Ordu or superior court. Owing to shortage of wood neither nobles nor commoners have any fuel but cattle dung and horse dung. According to the tradition of some, Chingis Khan was the founder of the Tartars, but the friars, although they stayed with them a long time, were unable to discover more about their origin.

They believe in one God, creator of things visible and invisible and giver in this world of good and evil alike. But for all that they do not worship Him as is right, for they have various idols. They have certain images of men made of felt which they place on either side of the door of their station above udders of felt likewise, and they assert that these are the guardians of their herds, and offer them milk and meat. But their chiefs give greater honor to certain silken idols which they keep on the wagon, or on the roof or door of their station, and if anyone steals anything therein he is immediately slain. But the captains of thousands and hundreds keep a goatskin stuffed with hay or straw in the middle of their stations and offer it milk of all kinds. When they begin to eat or drink, they offer to the idol on the wagon the heart of the animal on a platter, and take it away and eat it next morning. They place before the station of every Khan an idol which they first made in the image of Chingis Khan, and offer it gifts. The horses which are offered to it are never ridden again. They offer first to it the animals which they slaughter for food, and they do not break their bones. They bow southward to the same idol as to a god and compel many of their captives to the same act, especially noblemen.

Hence it happened recently [in September 1246] that when Michael, one of the grand dukes of Russia, submitted to their rule but refused to bow down to the aforesaid idol, saying that this was forbidden to Christians, and persisted in his constancy to the faith of Christ, he was ordered [by Batu Khan] to be kicked with the heel of the foot to the right of the heart; and when his attendant knight urged him to endure even to martyrdom, his throat was cut with a knife and the knight who exhorted him was beheaded. They make offerings also to the sun, the moon, water, and earth, usually in the morning.

They keep certain traditional laws made by Chingis Khan, who laid down (as has been stated above) that the filth contained in an animal's belly must not be extracted by opening up the entrails, but be squeezed out by hand, and the bowels be prepared for eating after cleansing in this manner. Again, should any man attempt out of pride to become Khan by his own personal influence, he must instantly be slain. Accordingly before the election of Kuyuk Khan, a nephew of Chingis Khan was killed because he aspired to be emperor! He also ordained that the Tartars should conquer every country in the world and make peace with none unless they surrendered unconditionally and without treaty, and even then he ordered that all of nobler rank should be slain and only plebeians be spared. It has been prophesied to them that in the end they must all be killed in the land of the Christians, except that the few survivors will adopt the law of the country in which their fathers are destined to be slain by various deaths. He ordered, moreover, that the army should be commanded by leaders of ten, a hundred, a thousand, and ten thousand—that is, one man to command ten thousand, which the Russians call tumbas.

Moreover, owing to dread handed down from their ancestors, they assert that certain things are great sins. One of these is to poke a fire or touch it in any way with a knife, or to take meat from a pot with a knife, or to chop wood with an axe near a fire, because they affirm that this causes the fire to be beheaded, or to lean on the whips with which they lash their horses (for they do not use spurs), or to touch arrows with a whip, or take young birds from a nest, or to strike a horse with a bridle, or to urinate in a hut. If this last is done intentionally, the culprit is slain; if unintentionally, he must pay a sorcerer who performs a rite of purification by making them carry their huts and property between two fires, and until this is done no one dares to touch anything in the hut. If anyone spits out a morsel of food (or a mouthful, which comes to the same thing) once it is put in his mouth, being unable to swallow it, a hole is dug under his hut through which he is dragged out and instantly put to death. If anyone treads on the threshold of a chief's hut, he is slain without mercy, and our friars were therefore instructed not to do so. They also consider it a sin to pour mare's milk on the ground intentionally, and when the friars told them it was a sin to shed human blood, or to get drunk, or to steal the property of others, they laughed at this and paid no attention whatever. They do not believe in the eternal life of the blessed or in perpetual damnation, but only that they live again after death and increase their herds and eat. They practice drug-potions and spells, but believe the demon's replies come from a god whom they call Iuga. They do not force anyone to abandon his faith provided he obeys their orders in every way, otherwise they compel him by force or kill him, as they compelled the younger brother of Duke Andrew in Russia, whom they wrongfully condemned and slew, to take his brother's widow to wife, and even laid them publicly together in the same bed in the sight of the rest.

They are accustomed to begin any undertaking at the new moon or full moon. They say the moon is a great emperor, and worship it on bended knees, and that the sun is the moon's mother, because the moon takes its light from thence and because of its fiery nature, which they revere above all things, for they believe everything is purified by fire. For this reason all messengers and the gifts they bring must be brought to their masters between two fires, so that any poison or spell they have brought may be purged. Accordingly, even our friars passed between fires.

When one of them is gravely ill, a spear nine cubits long bound in black felt is erected near his dwelling, and henceforth no one outside his family dares to enter the bounds of that hut. When his death-agony begins, it is unusual for anyone to stay by him, because no one who was present at his death could enter the horde of any chief or of the emperor until the ninth moon began.

When a rich man dies, he is buried secretly in the open country, sitting in his dwelling with a basket full of meat and a jar of mare's milk, and with him is buried a mare and foal, a horse with bridle and saddle, and a loom with quiver and arrows. His friends eat the flesh of a horse and its hide is stuffed with hay and raised on a wooden scaffold. They believe he needs all these things in the future life, the mare for milking, the horse for riding, and so on, and gold and silver is in like manner laid with him. Certain more important persons are buried as follows. They make a secret pit in open country with a small square opening but widened both ways inside, and another near his hut openly and publicly in which they pretend to bury the dead man; and they put the slave who was his favorite in life under the dead man's body in the still open grave. If the slave survives after lying in torment for three days beneath the corpse, he is freed and is honored and powerful in the whole family of the deceased. After this they cover up the grave and drive mares or cattle over the place all night, so that when it is flattened out the treasure buried with him may not be discovered by strangers, and sometimes they even replace the turf taken from the site.

They have two cemeteries in their own land, one for ordinary people and one for emperors, chiefs, and noblemen, and if at all possible dead noblemen are brought back there from every land where they are slain, as was done with those who were killed in Hungary. If anyone but the guardians enters this cemetery, he is ill-treated in many ways. Our friars who entered it unknowingly would have given grave offense if they had not been messengers of the great Pope, whom the Tartars call Yul Boba, which means Great Pope.

When anyone dies, everything appertaining to his dwelling has to be purified. Two fires are accordingly prepared, near which two spears are set upright and bound together at the top with a thong to which shreds of buckram are tied. Under this thong between the spears and fires must pass all the men, the animals, and the hut itself, and two witches stand on either side throwing on water and reciting spells. If a wagon is touched by the spears when passing or anything falls from it, it becomes the lawful perquisite of the witches. Similarly if anyone dies from being struck by lightning, all his possessions are shunned by everyone until purified in the aforesaid manner.

They have as many wives as they can afford, and generally buy them, so that except for women of noble birth they are mere chattels. They marry anyone they please, except their mother, daughter, and sister from the same mother. When their father dies, they marry their stepmother, and a younger brother or cousin marries his brother's widow. The wives do all the work, and make shoes, leather garments, and so on, while the men make nothing but arrows, and practice shooting with bows. They compel even boys three or four years old to the same exercise, and even some of the women, especially the maidens, practice archery and ride as a rule like men. If people are taken in adultery and fornication, man and woman alike are slain.

They are more obedient to their lords than other nations, more even than priests are to bishops, the more so as no mercy is shown to transgressors, and the emperor therefore holds them in his power in every way; for whether they are sent to their death or to live they must do their task with all speed. The emperor can take to himself the daughters, wives, or sisters of anyone he wishes, and after he has enjoyed them, if he does not want to keep them for himself, he gives them to whomsoever he pleases.

Envoys sent by him or to him are given their keep free of charge together with post-horses, but foreign envoys are given only meager keep, for two or three could eat what is doled out to five men. I shudder therefore to describe or enumerate the hardships undergone by our friars, since they themselves who endured them marvel how the grace of Jesus Christ sustained them in opposition to human nature. Oh, how often they rode more than thirty Bohemian miles [130 modern miles] in a single day on the Tartar's post-horses, tasting neither bread nor water, but obtaining with difficulty at noon or in the night only a little thin broth of boiled millet. That they rode so far is not surprising, for as soon as their horses grew weary, even before they could begin to rest, the Tartars brought up fresh strong mounts.

All homesteads are subject to the Khan in their settlings and movements, for he fixes the stations of the chiefs, who in turn assign their posts to the leaders of a thousand, these to the leaders of a hundred, and these to the leaders of ten. All are exceedingly covetous, both nobles and poor, and unrivalled in the extortion of gifts. If they do not receive immediate gifts, they torment envoys with starvation and pettifogging, in order that those who have neglected to give of their own free will may be compelled to do so later against their will. For this reason our friars spent for the most part on gifts the alms of good men which they had received on the way (with the exception of the spiritual envoy of the Apostolic See), for otherwise they would have been greatly hindered and indeed despised in the business of the Universal Church.

Of all men they are the most given to despising other nations. Hence Tartar interpreters, even when of lowly station, take precedence in walking and sitting over the envoys entrusted to their care, whether these are envoys or legates of the Apostolic See or of kings. Moreover, they are devoid of honesty in their dealings with foreigners; for it is their inhuman way to promise many good things at the beginning, but to practice endless cruelties at the end. Their promise is like a scorpion, which although it pretends to flatter with its face, strikes suddenly with the poisonous sting in its tail.

They are more given to drunkenness than any other nation on earth, and however much excessive drink they unload from their bellies, they at once begin again to drink on the spot, and it is their habit to do so several times in the same day. They also are accustomed to drink every kind of milk. They eat immoderately all forms of unclean food, wolves, foxes, dogs, carrion, afterbirths of animals, mice, and, when necessary, human flesh. Similarly, they reject no species of bird, but eat clean and unclean alike. They do not use napkins or tablecloths at dinner and so eat in excessive filth. They wash their platters rarely and very badly, and the same applies to their spoons.

Among themselves, however, they are peaceable, fornication and adultery are very rare, and their women excel those of other nations in chastity, except that they often use shameless words when jesting. Theft is unusual among them, and therefore their dwellings and all their property are not put under lock and key. If horses or oxen or other animal stock are found straying, they are either allowed to go free or are led back to their own masters. They are richer in horses and mares, oxen, cows and sheep than any other men on earth. They are kind enough among themselves, and share their property willingly by reciprocal concession. They are very hardy, for even when they fast for a day or two they sing and jest as if they had eaten excellently well. They willingly help one another to positions of honor. Rebellion is rarely raised among them, and it is no wonder if such is their way, for, as I have said above, transgressors are punished without mercy.

Now I must briefly discuss their warfare and the methods by which they can be opposed. Whenever the Tartars plan to attack any countries, the army directed to conquer them marches speedily but with great caution in wagons and on horseback, taking with it whole families, including wives, boy children, and servant-maids, with their tents and all their chattels, herds, and sheep, and a vast stock of arms, bows, quivers, and arrows. When the Tartars begin to draw near, they send ahead their swiftest skirmishers to spread terror unexpectedly and kill, and to prevent an army from being quickly mobilized against them. If they meet with no obstacle, however, they continue to advance, and the multitude follows with all their families without concealment.

If they see their opponents are too numerous to defeat, they immediately withdraw to the main body and draw up their forces in the following manner. They dispose the main strength of the army in abundant numbers round the triumphal standard in the middle, and on the wings place two smaller forces, one on each side, at a small distance but projecting a long way forward. They leave a few to guard the women, sick, boys, and the chattels brought with them.

When they are on the point of joining battle with the enemy, a number of them, each supplied with several quivers complete with arrows, begin to shoot before their opponents' arrows can reach them, sometimes even ahead of time when they are not in range. As soon as their arrows can reach the mark unhindered they are said owing to the density of their fire to rain arrows rather than to shoot them. If they find their enemies unprepared, they surround them suddenly in a ring leaving only a single way of escape, and attack them fiercely with a hail of javelins, so that anyone who does not resist in the middle perishes in flight. I consider therefore that it is better to die bravely fighting than to take refuge in cowardly flight.

It must be further noticed that if they meet with success, they press ever onward and leave in their rear stations of a thousand or a hundred men, according to their resources in men and livestock, the nearer ones being the stronger and larger.

If any cities or fortified places remain in the countries they have conquered, these cities can hold out very well against them, where the position is such that arrows can be aimed or missiles from war engines be shot against them; and where supplies of food, drink, or wood give out, the courage or daring of the opposing forces can compensate for the deficiencies of the position. So it happened in the country of the Old Saxons [on the Volga River], who made repeated sorties in small numbers from their city and killed many of the Tartars, and while the women extinguished the fires in the burning town the men defended the walls against the Tartars; and when the Tartars emerged through an underground passage in the middle of the town, they slew many and put the rest to flight. It is impossible for men to hide away from them in any forests which are accessible in summer and winter, since they lie in wait for men as they would for wild animals. However, safety from them can be had on the sea or in the places mentioned above.

The proper method of resisting the Tartars can be understood easily enough from the various accounts of the Maccabee kings, where the tactics of sending out archers ahead of the main army and laying different kinds of ambushes against the enemy are described. In my opinion, however, peace between our rulers is absolutely necessary, with a view to their massing together and drawing up three or more armies against the enemy as demanded by the quality of their soldiers, not omitting to post ambushes on the wings fitted with the best horses. Crossbow-men must be posted in front of the armies in three ranks at least, and these must shoot their arrows even before they can reach the Tartars' front line, in the right manner and in good time, to prevent our own front rank from being put to flight or disordered. But if the enemy take to flight, the crossbow-men with the archers and the ambushers must pursue them, and the army must follow a little way behind. If, however, there are no crossbow-men to spare, then cavalry with armored horses must be placed in the van, and these must take cover behind a wall of strong shields on the horses' heads and immediately baffle the Tartars' arrows. I leave other details concerning warfare to those who are instructed in its practice more by experience than by book-learning.

I beseech your fatherly authority therefore to attribute any disorder in the matters I have set down in writing to my ignorance rather than to my intention. Completed on 30th July in the year 1247 after the Incarnation of Our Lord. So ends the Life and History of the Tartars.

FROM *THE CHRONICLE OF NOVGOROD*

1224–1259

A.D. 1224

The same year, for our sins, unknown tribes came, whom no one exactly knows, who they are, nor whence they came out, nor what their language is, nor of what race they are, nor what their faith is, but they call them Tartars, and others say Taurmen, and others Pecheneg people, and others say that they are those of whom Bishop Mefodi of Patmos bore witness, that they came out from the Etrian desert which is between East and North. For thus Mefodi says, that, at the end of time, those are to appear whom Gideon scattered, and they shall subdue the whole land from the East to the Efrant, and from the Tigris to the Pontus sea except Ethiopia. God alone knows who they are and whence they came out. Very wise men know them exactly, who understand books; but we do not know who they are but have written of them here for the sake of the memory of the Russian Knyazes [princes] and of the misfortune which came to them from them. For we have heard that they have captured many countries, slaughtered a quantity of the godless Yas, Obez, Kasog, and Polovets peoples, and scattered others, who all died, killed thus by the wrath of God and of His immaculate Mother, for those cursed Polovets people had wrought much evil to the Russian Land. Therefore the all-merciful God wished to destroy the Kuman people, godless sons of Ishmael, that they [might] atone for the blood of Christians which was upon them, lawless ones. . . .

And Mstislav, Knyaz of Kiev, seeing this evil, never moved at all from his position; for he had taken stand on a hill above the river Kalka, and the place was stony, and there he set up a stockade of posts about him and fought with them from out of this stockade for three days. And other Tartars went after the Russian Knyazes fighting them up to the Dnieper, but two Voyevodas [generals],

- 285 -

Tsigirkan and Teshukan, stopped at that stockade [fighting] against Mstislav and his sons-in-law, Andrei and Olexander of Dubrovits, for these two Knyazes were with Mstislav. And there were there men in armour with the Tartars and Voyevoda Ploskyna; and this accursed Voyevoda, having kissed the honourable Cross to Mstislav and to both the Knyazes not to kill them, but to let them go on ransom, lied, accursed one; he delivered them bound to the Tartars, and they took the stockade and slaughtered the people, and there they fell dead. And having taken the Knyazes they suffocated them having put them under boards, and themselves took seat on the top to have dinner. And thus they ended their lives. And pursuing the other Knyazes to the Dnieper they killed six: Svyatoslav of Yanev, Izyaslav Ingvorovits, Svyatoslav Shumski, Mstislav of Chernigov with his son, and Gyurgi of Nesvezh. And then Mstislav Mstislavits having previously escaped across the Dnieper, cut loose the boats from the bank so the Tartars should not go after them, and himself barely escaped.

And of the rest of the troops every tenth returned to his home; some the Polovets men killed for their horses, and others for their clothes. And thus, for our sins God put misunderstanding into us, and a countless number of people perished, and there was lamentation and weeping and grief throughout towns and villages. This evil happened on May 31, on Saint Eremei's Day. And the Tartars turned back from the river Dnieper, and we know not whence they came, nor where they hid themselves again. . . .

A.D. 1238

But let us return to what lies before us. The pagan and godless Tartars, then, having taken Ryazan, went to Volodimir, a host of shedders of Christian blood. And Knyaz Yuri went out from Volodimir and fled to Yaroslavl, while his son Vsevolod with his mother and the Vladyka [archbishop] and the whole of the province shut themselves in Volodimir. And the lawless Ishmaelites approached the town and surrounded the town in force, and fenced it all round with a fence. And it was in the morning Knyaz Vsevolod and Vladyha Mitrofan saw that the town must be taken, and entered the Church of the Holy Mother of

God and were all shorn into the monastic order and into the schema, the Knyaz and the Knyaginya [princess], their daughter and daughter-in-law, and good men and women, by Vladyka Mitrofan. And when the lawless ones had already come near and set up battering rams, and took the town and fired it on Friday before Sexagesima Sunday, the Knyaz and Knyaginya and Vladyka, seeing that the town was on fire and that the people were already perishing, some by fire and others by the sword, took refuge in the Church of the Holy Mother of God and shut themselves in the Sacristy. The pagans breaking down the doors, piled up wood and set fire to the sacred church; and slew all, thus they perished, giving up their souls to God. Others went in pursuit of Knyaz Yuri to Yaroslavl. And Knyaz Yuri sent out Dorozh to scout with three thousand men; and Dorozh came running, and said: "They have already surrounded us, Knyaz."

And the Knyaz began to muster his forces about him, and behold, the Tartars came up suddenly, and the Knyaz, without having been able to do anything, fled. And it happened when he reached the river Sit they overtook him and there he ended his life. And God knows how he died; for some say much about him. And Rostov and Suzhdal went each its own way. And the accursed ones having come thence took Moscow, Perevaslavl, Yurev, Dmitrov, Volok, and Tver; there also they killed the son of Yaroslav. And thence the lawless ones came and invested Torzhok on the festival of the first Sunday in Lent. They fenced it all round with a fence as they had taken other towns, and here the accursed ones fought with battering rams for two weeks. And the people in the town were exhausted and from Novgorod there was no help for them; but already every man began to be in perplexity and terror. And so the pagans took the town, and slew all from the male sex even to the female, all the priests and the monks, and all stripped and reviled gave up their souls to the Lord in a bitter and a wretched death, on March 5, the day of the commemoration of the holy Martyr Nikon. . . . And the accursed godless ones then pushed on from Torzhok by the road of Seregeri right up to Ignati's cross, cutting down everybody like grass, to within 100 versts [66 miles] of Novgorod. God, however, and the great and sacred apostolic cathedral Church of St. Sophia, and St. Kyuril, and the prayers of the holy and orthodox Vladyka, of the faithful Knyazes, and of the very reverend monks of the hierarchical Veche, protected Novgorod.

A.D. 1257

Evil news came from Russia, that the Tartars desired the tamga [tax] and tithe on Novgorod and the people were agitated the whole year.

A.D. 1258

. . . The same winter the Tartars took the whole Lithuanian land, and killed the people.

A.D. 1259

There was a sign in the moon; such as no sign had ever been. . . . The same winter the accursed raw meat-eating Tartars . . . came with their wives, and many others, and there was a great tumult in Novgorod, and they did much evil in the province, taking contribution for the accursed Tartars. And the accursed ones began to fear death; they said to Olexander [Alexander Nevsky]: "Give us guards, lest they kill us." And the Knyaz ordered the son of the Posadnik [burgomaster] and all the sons of the Boyars [nobles] to protect them by night. The Tartars said: "Give us your numbers for tribute or we will return in greater strength." And the common people would not give their numbers for tribute but said: "Let us die honourably for St. Sophia and for the angelic houses." Then the people were divided: . . . the greater men bade the lesser be counted for tribute. And . . . the Knyaz rode down from the Gorodishche [fort] and the accursed Tartars with him, and by the counsel of the evil they numbered themselves for tribute; for the Boyars thought it would be easy for themselves, but fell hard on the lesser men. And the accursed ones began to ride through the streets, writing down the Christian houses; because for our sins God has brought wild beasts out of the desert to eat the flesh of the strong, and to drink the blood of Boyars. And having numbered them for tribute and taken it, the accursed ones went away, and Knyaz Olexander followed them, having set his son Dmitri on the throne. . . .

A.D. 1380

. . . In the month of August, news came to the Veliki Knyaz [grand prince] and to his brother Knyaz Volodimir from the Horde that the pagan race of Ishmaelites was rising against the Christians; . . . And having heard this, that a great Tartar force was coming against him, the Veliki Knyaz Dmitri Ivanovich gathered many soldiers and went against the godless Tartars, trusting in the mercy of God and in His Immaculate Mother, the Mother of God, the eternal Virgin Mary, calling to his aid the honourable Cross. For he entered their country beyond the Don, and there was there a clean field at the mouth of the river Nepryadva, and there the pagan Ishmaelites had ranged themselves against the Christians. And the Moscovites, of whom many were inexperienced, were frightened and in despair of their lives at sight of the great numbers of Tartars, others turned to flight, forgetful of the Prophet's saying that one shall reap one thousand and two shall move ten thousand if God does not abandon them.

And the Veliki Knyaz Dmitri with his brother Volodimir ranged their troops against the pagan people, and raising their eyes humbly to heaven, and sighing from the depth of their hearts, said, in the words of the psalm: "Brothers, God is our refuge and our strength." And both forces immediately met, and there was a fierce battle for a long time, and God terrified the sons of Hagar with an invisible might, and they turned their shoulders to wounds, and they were routed by the Christians, and some were struck down with weapons, and others were drowned in the river, a countless number of them.

And in the encounter Knyaz Fedor Belozerski was killed, also his son Knyaz Ivan; and other Knyazes and captains went in pursuit of the aliens. The godless Tartars fell from dread of God and by the arms of the Christians, and God raised the right hand of the Veliki Knyaz Dmitri Ivanovich and of his brother Knyaz Volodimir Andreyevich for the defeat of the aliens.

Matthew Paris

FROM *CHRONICLES*

1240–1253

1240: AN IRRUPTION OF THE TARTARS

In this year, that human joys might not long continue, and that the delights of this world might not last long unmixed with lamentation, an immense horde of that detestable race of Satan, the Tartars, burst forth from their mountain-bound regions, and making their way through rocks apparently impenetrable, rushed forth, like demons loosed from Tartarus (so that they are well called Tartars, as it were inhabitants of Tartarus [Hell]); and overrunning the country, covering the face of the earth like locusts, they ravaged the eastern countries with lamentable destruction, spreading fire and slaughter wherever they went. Roving through the Saracen territories, they razed cities to the ground, burnt woods, pulled down castles, tore up the vine-trees, destroyed gardens, and massacred the citizens and husbandmen; if by chance they did spare any who begged their lives, they compelled them, as slaves of the lowest condition, to fight in front of them against their own kindred. And if they only pretended to fight, or perhaps warned their countrymen to fly, the Tartars following in their rear, slew them; and if they fought bravely and conquered, they gained no thanks by way of recompense, and thus these savages ill-treated their captives as though they were horses. The men are inhuman and of the nature of beasts, rather to be called monsters than men, thirsting after and drinking blood, and tearing and devouring the flesh of dogs and human beings; they clothe themselves in the skins of bulls, and are armed with iron lances; they are short in stature and thickset, compact in their bodies, and of great strength; invincible in battle, indefatigable in labour; they wear no armour on the back part of their bodies, but are protected by it in front; they drink the blood which flows from their flocks, and consider it a delicacy; they have large and powerful horses, which eat leaves and even the trees themselves, and which, owing to the shortness of their legs, they mount by three steps instead of stirrups.

They have no human laws, know no mercy, and are more cruel than lions or bears; they have boats made of the hides of oxen, ten or twelve having one amongst them; they are skillful in sailing or swimming, hence they cross the largest and most rapid rivers without any delay or trouble; and when they have no blood, they greedily drink disturbed and even muddy water. They have swords and daggers with one edge, they are excellent archers, and they spare neither sex, age, or rank; they know no other country's language except that of their own, and of this all other nations are ignorant. For never till this time has there been any mode of access to them, nor have they themselves come forth, so as to allow any knowledge of their customs or persons to be gained through common intercourse with other men; they take their herds with them, as also their wives, who are brought up to war, the same as the men; and they came with the force of lightning into the territories of the Christians, laying waste the country, committing great slaughter, and striking inexpressible terror and alarm into every one. . . .

1241: OF THE DREADFUL RAVAGES COMMITTED BY THE TARTARS

During all this time that inhuman and brutal, outlawed, barbarous, and untameable people, the Tartars, in their rash and cruel violence visited the northern provinces of the Christians with dreadful devastation and destruction, and struck great fear and terror into all Christendom. Already had they, with unheard-of tyranny, in a great measure reduced to a desert the countries of Friesland, Gothland, Poland, Bohemia, and both divisions of Hungary, slaying or putting to flight princes, prelates, citizens, and rustics. This occurrence is evidently testified by the following letter, which was sent into these parts:

A Letter Written to the Duke of Brabant Concerning the Same People

Henry, by the grace of God, count of Lorraine, palatine of Saxony, to his well-beloved and always to be beloved lord and father-in-law the illustrious dolce of Brabant, good-will in his service whenever he shall demand it.

The dangers foretold in the Scriptures in times of old, are now, owing to our sins, springing up and breaking out; for a cruel and countless order of people, outlawed and wild, is now invading and taking possession of the territories adjoining ours, and has now, after roving through many other countries, and exterminating the inhabitants, extended their incursions as far as the Polish territory. Of these matters we have been fully informed, as well by our own messengers as by the letters of our beloved cousin the king of Bohemia, and have been called on to prepare ourselves with all haste to proceed to his assistance, and to the defence of the Christians. For we are truly and plainly informed by him that this said race of people, the Tartars, will, about the octaves of Easter, quell and impetuously invade the Bohemian territory, and if seasonable assistance be not given to the Bohemians, an unheard-of slaughter will take place. And as the house adjoining our own is already on fire, and as the neighbouring country is open to devastation, whilst some countries are even now being ravaged, we, on behalf of the Church universal, anxiously invoke and beg assistance and advice from God and our neighbouring brother princes. And as delay is pregnant with danger, we beg of you, with all possible diligence, to take arms and to hasten to our succour, as well for the sake of our freedom as for that of your own. . . .

The emperor then, on hearing of these things, wrote to the Christian princes, and especially to the king of England, as follows:

Frederic emperor, etc., to the king of England, greeting.

We cannot be silent on a matter which concerns not only the Roman empire, whose office it is to propagate the Gospel, but also all the kingdoms of the world. . . . A barbarous race and mode of life called (from what place or organ I know not) Tartars, has lately emerged from the regions of the south where it had long lain hid, burnt up by the sun of the torrid zone, and, thence marching towards the northern parts, took forcible possession of the country there, and remaining for a time, multiplied like locusts, and has now come forth, not without the premeditated judgment of God, but not, I hope, reserved to these latter times for the ruin of the whole of Christianity. Their arrival was followed by a general slaughter, a universal desolation of kingdoms, and by utter ruin to the fertile territory, which this impious horde of people roved through, sparing neither sex, age, nor rank, whilst they confidently hope to destroy the rest of the human race. . . .

By the sudden attacks and assaults of that savage race, which descends like the anger of God, or like lightning, Kiew, the chief city of that kingdom, was attacked and taken, and the whole of that noble kingdom, which ought to have united itself with that of Hungary, for its defence and protection, but which it carelessly neglected to do, was, after its inhabitants were slain, reduced to a state of utter destruction and desolation. Their king, an idle and careless man, was ordered by messengers and letters from these Tartars, if he wished to save his life and that of his subjects, by a surrender of himself and his kingdom, at once to anticipate their favour; but he was not frightened or warned by this, and thus gave a proof to his people and to others, that he and his ought sooner to have provided for their own protection and defence against their incursions. But, whilst these elated or ignorant people, despising their enemies, were idly sleeping with the enemy in their immediate neighbourhood, and trusting to the natural strength of the place, the Tartars made their way into the kingdom like a whirlwind, and suddenly surrounded them on all sides.

The Hungarians being thus surrounded before they expected an attack, and surprised when unprepared as it were, tried to defend their camp against them. When the two rival armies of the Tartars and Hungarians were distant about five miles from each other, the advanced portion of the Tartars suddenly rushed forwards at the dawn of the morning, and suddenly surrounding the camp of the Hungarians, slew the prelates and nobles of the kingdom who opposed them, and massacred such a host of the Hungarians, that a similar slaughter was never remembered to have taken place in one battle, from the most remote period. . . . And we have heard all this with great perturbation of mind. As we have been informed, and as the rumour of their proceedings, going in advance of them, declares, their innumerable army is divided into three ill-omened portions, and, owing to the Lord's indulging them in their damnable plans, has proceeded thus divided. One of these has entered Poland, where the prince and duke of that country have fallen victims to their exterminating pursuers, and afterwards the whole of that country has been devastated by them.

A second portion has entered the Bohemian territory, where it is brought to a stand, having been attacked by the king of that country, who has bravely met it with all the forces at his command; and the third portion of it is overrunning Hungary, adjoining to the Austrian territories. Hence fear and trembling have arisen amongst us, owing to the fury of these impetuous invaders, which arouses and calls upon us to arm . . . for this race of people is wild, outlawed, and ignorant of the laws of humanity; they follow and have for their lord one, whom they worship and reverence with all obedience, and whom they call the god of earth. The men themselves are small and of short stature, as far as regards height, but compact, stout, and bulky, resolute, strong, and courageous, and ready at the nod of their leader to rush into any undertaking of difficulty; they have large faces, scowling looks, and utter horrible shouts, suited to their hearts; they wear raw hides of bullocks, asses, and horses; and for armour, they are protected by pieces of iron stitched to them, which they have made use of till now.

But, and we cannot say it without sorrow, they are now, from the spoils of the conquered Christians, providing themselves with more suitable weapons, that we may, through God's anger, be the more basely slain with our own arms. Besides, they are supplied with better horses, they live on richer food, and adorn themselves with more handsome clothes, than formerly. They are incomparable archers, and carry skins artificially made, in which they cross lakes and the most rapid rivers without danger. When fodder fails them, their horses are said to be satisfied with the bark and leaves of trees, and the roots of herbs, which the men bring to them; and yet, they always find them to be very swift and strong in a case of necessity. . . .

1241: THE ENORMOUS WICKEDNESS OF THE JEWS

During all this time, numbers of the Jews on the continent, and especially those belonging to the empire, thinking that these Tartars were a portion of their race, whom God had, at the prayers of Alexander the Great, shut up in the Caspian mountains, assembled on a general summons in a secret place, where one of their number, who seemed to be the wisest and most influential amongst them, thus addressed them: "My brothers, seed of the illustrious Abraham, vineyard of the Lord of Sabaoth, whom our God Adonai has permitted to be so long oppressed under Christian rule, now the time has arrived for us to liberate our-selves, and by the judgment of God to oppress them in our turn, that the rem-nant of Israel may be saved. For our brethren of the tribes of Israel, who were formerly shut up, have gone forth to bring the whole world to subjection to them and to us. And the more severe and more lasting that our former suffer-ing has been, the greater will be the glory that will ensue to us. Let us therefore go to meet them with valuable gifts, and receive them with the highest honour: they are in need of corn, wine, and arms."

The whole assembly heard this speech with pleasure, and at once bought all the daggers, and armour, they could find for sale anywhere, and, in order to conceal their treachery, securely stowed them away in casks. They then openly told the Christian chiefs, under whose dominion they were, that these people, commonly called Tartars, were Jews, and would not drink wine unless made by Jews, and of this they have informed us, and with great earnestness have begged to be supplied with some wine made by us, their brethren. We, however, desir-ing to remove from amongst us these our inhuman public enemies, and to release you Christians from their impending tyrannical devastation, have pre-pared about thirty casks full of deadly intoxicating wine, to be carried to them as soon as possible.

The Christians therefore permitted these wicked Jews to make this wicked present to their wicked enemies. When, however, these said Jews had reached a distant part of Germany, and were about to cross a certain bridge with their casks, the master of the bridge, according to custom, demanded payment of the toll for their passage: the Jews, however, replied insolently, refusing to satisfy his demands, saying that they were employed in this business for the advantage of the empire, indeed of all Christendom, having been sent to the Tartars, secretly to poison them with their wine. The keeper of the bridge, however, doubting the assertion of these Jews, bored a hole through one of the casks; but no liquor flowed therefrom; and becoming certain of their treachery, he took off the hoops of the cask, and, breaking it open, discovered that it was full of arms. At this sight he cried out, "Oh, unheard-of treachery, why do we allow such people to live amongst us?"

And at once he and others, whom his astonishment had collected round him, broke open all the other casks, which, as soon as they had done, they found them also filled with Cologne swords and daggers, without hilts, closely and compactly stowed away; they then at once openly showed forth the hidden treachery and extraordinary deceit of the Jews, who chose rather to assist these open enemies of the world in general, who, they said, were very much in need of arms, than to aid the Christians, who allowed them to live amongst them and communicate with them in the way of traffic. They were therefore at once handed over to the executioners, to be either consigned to perpetual imprisonment, or to be slain with their own swords. . . .

1243: A SHOCKING LETTER ABOUT THE CRUELTY OF THE TARTARS

At the same time, the following letter, sent to the archbishop of Bordeaux, very greatly alarmed even the most undaunted men:

> To Gerald, by the grace of God, archbishop of Bordeaux, Yvo, named from Narbonnes, formerly the lowliest of his clerks, Health and strength to render account of the talents intrusted to his care.
>
> . . . Experience alone shows what great danger threatens the Christians through the invasion of the Tartars. For, touching the cruelty and cunning of that people, calumny itself could not lie; and, in briefly informing you of their

Figure 17. *Genghis Khan and His Sons* by Rashid al-Din, from a fourteenth-century Persian manuscript. Courtesy Art Resource.

Figure 18. Illustration from Matthew Paris's *Chronicles* featuring cannibalistic Mongols. Courtesy The Parker Library and The Master and Fellows of Corpus Christi College, Cambridge.

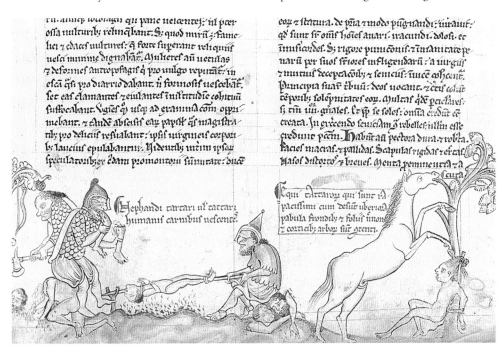

Figure 19. *Mongol Archer on Horseback* (Anonymous), Ming Dynasty. Courtesy Art Resource.

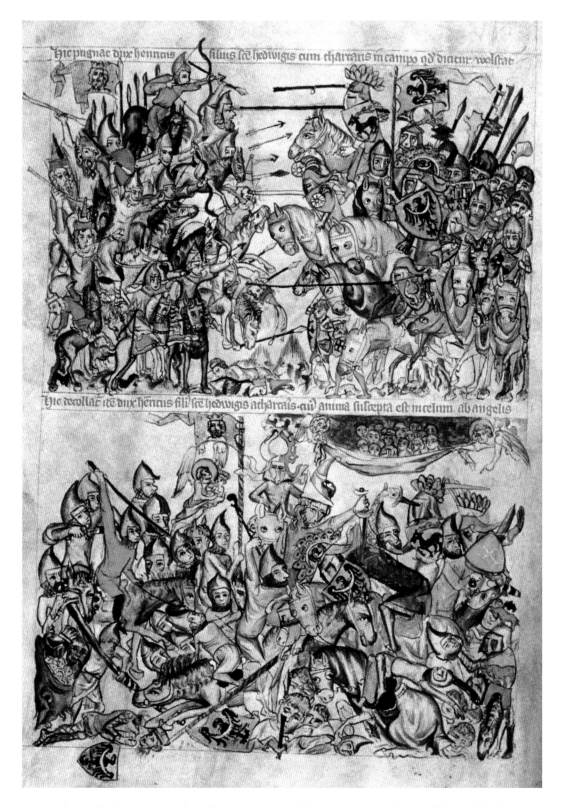

Figure 20. *Battle of Duke Henry, Son of Hedwig, Against the Tartars.* Courtesy Francis G. Mayer/Corbis.

Figure 21. *At the Gates of Tamerlane* by Vereshciaghin Vasilij. This nineteenth-century painting recreates the daunting entry into Tamerlane's palace in Samarkand, in modern Uzbekistan. The fourteenth-century Mongol conqueror was known to slaughter thousands upon capturing cities and build pyramids of their skulls. Courtesy Scala/Art Resource.

Figure 22. Tamerlane's Mausoleum, where the ruthless conqueror is entombed, in Samarkand, Uzbekistan. Courtesy Christine Osborne/Corbis.

Figure 23. Portrait of Tamerlane, artist unknown. Courtesy SEF/Art Resource.

Figure 24. *The Taking of Jerusalem*, artist unknown. Courtesy Scala/Art Resource.

Figure 25. Portrait of Saladin, Sultan of Egypt, artist unknown. Courtesy SEF/Art Resource.

Figure 26. *William of Clermont Defending Ptolemais* [Akko] by D. Papety. The Crusaders first took Akko in 1104 and held it until 1187 when it was re-taken by Saladin. Courtesy Art Resource.

Figure 27. *Conquest of Constantinople in 1204 by the Crusaders* by Tintoretto, from the Palazzo Ducale in Venice, Italy. Courtesy Erich Lessing/Art Resource.

wicked habits, I will recount nothing of which I hold either a doubt or mere opinion, but what I have with certainty proved, and what I know. . . .

A fierce race of inhuman beings, whose law is lawlessness, whose wrath is fury, the rod of God's anger, is passing through and dreadfully ravaging a wide tract of country, horribly exterminating with fire and sword everything that comes in their way. In the course of this very summer; these people, who are named Tartars, left Pannonia, which they had got by surrender, and with numberless thousands fiercely besieged the town above named [Vienna] in which I perchance was then residing. There were no soldiers on our side in the town, to oppose them, except fifty knights and twenty cross-bowmen, whom the duke had left in garrison. These, mounting on some neighbouring eminences, saw the immense army that lay round them, and shuddered at the fierceness of those satellites of Antichrist. Miserable groans were now heard ascending to the Lord of the Christians, from those who had been surprised in the neighbouring province, and, without distinction of rank, fortune, sex, or age, all perished alike, by different kinds of death.

"The Tartar chiefs, with the houndish cannibals their followers, fed upon the flesh of their carcasses, as if they had been bread, and left nothing but bones for the vultures. But, wonderful to tell, the vultures, hungry and ravenous, would not condescend to eat the remnants of flesh, if any by chance were left. The old and ugly women were given to their dog-headed cannibals—anthropophagi, as they are called, to be their daily food; but those who were beautiful, were saved alive, to be stifled and overwhelmed by the number of their ravishers, in spite of all their cries and lamentations. Virgins were deflowered until they died of exhaustion. Then their breasts were cut off to be kept as dainties for their chiefs, and their bodies furnished a jovial banquet to the savages. Meanwhile, those who were looking out from the top of a promontory, saw approaching the duke of Austria, the king of Bohemia, the patriarch of Aquileia, the duke of Carinthia, and, as was said, the marquis of Bade, with many princes of the neighbouring states, drawn up for battle. In a moment all that execrable race vanished, all those riders returned into wretched Hungary. As suddenly as they had come, so suddenly did they disappear; a circumstance which creates the greater fear in the minds of those who witnessed it. . . .

Concerning their manners and their superstitions, the disposition and dimensions of their persons, their country, and mode of fighting, [the Tartars] are greedy, passionate, deceitful, and merciless beyond all other men. The vigour and ferocity of the punishments which were inflicted on them by their chiefs, is that which restrains them from quarrels, or from mutually cheating and injuring one another. The founders of their tribes are called gods, and they celebrate their solemnities at certain seasons; they have many especial celebrations, but only four regular ones. They think that everything was made for them alone, and they think that there is no cruelty in practicing every kind of severity on those who rebel against them. They have hard and robust breasts, lean and pale faces, stiff high shoulders, and short distorted noses; their chins are sharp and prominent, the upper jaw low and deep, the teeth long and few, their eyebrows stretch from the hair to the nose, their eyes are black and restless, their countenances long and grim, their extremities bony and nervous, their legs thick but short below the knee. In stature they are equal to us, for what they lose below the knee is made up for in the greater length of their upper parts.

Their native country is that great waste, formerly a desert, lying beyond the Chaldees, from which they expelled the lions, bears, and other beasts, with their bows and other warlike weapons. Out of the tanned hides of these animals, they made for themselves armour of a light description, but impenetrable. They have horses, not large, but very strong, and that require little food, and they bind themselves firmly on their backs. They use darts, clubs, battle-axes, and swords in battle, and fight bravely and unyieldingly. But their chief prerogative is their use of the bow, and their great skill in fighting. Their back armour is thin, that they may not be tempted to run away; and they never retreat from battle until they see the chief standard of their leader retreating. When vanquished, they never ask for mercy, and themselves never spare the vanquished. In the intention and fixed purpose of reducing all the world under their dominion, they all persist, as one man.

—XIV—

TAMERLANE

Tamerlane (ca. 1336–1405) set out to conquer the world and for more than thirty years battled his way out of Mongolia (he was born near Samarkand) through Russia and Georgia to Persia and the Mediterranean. He conquered all the lands between the Caspian and Black Seas, defeated the Grand Duchy of Moscow, invaded India and took Delhi, fought the Ottoman Turks, and was planning an invasion of China when he died.

Although at times in his life he claimed to be a descendant of Genghis Khan, he was also described as simply "a lame robber chief" (his name means "Timur the Lame"). With all his inflated dreams of glory, Tamerlane was also a realist. He abandoned Delhi because he knew he could not hold it, and before he died he divided his kingdom among his sons because he knew that without him it could not remain intact.

Robber chief or not, the West's fascination with Tamerlane has been long-lasting. Perhaps it was a combination of the exotic lands he conquered and his flair for brutal showmanship (such as the pyramids of skulls he was known to leave at the ruined gates of cities he had looted), but he was a barbarian who left a unique mark on the supposedly civilized world. The Elizabethan playwright Christopher Marlowe, for example, wrote a bloodcurdling melodrama about him: "All Asia is in the arms of Tamburlaine . . . the scourge of God and terror of the world." In the eighteenth century, Handel composed an opera about him, and in early nineteenth-century America Edgar Allan Poe's first book was entitled *Tamerlane and Other Poems*.

In the fifteenth century, Ahmed ibn Mohammed Ibn' Arabshah, secretary to the sultan of Baghdad, wrote *The Life of Timur*, a near-contemporary biography of Tamerlane that begins on a mystical note: "They say that on the night he was born something like a helmet appeared, seemed to flutter in the air, then fell." Gibbon, who referred to the book, wrote that it was "much esteemed for the florid elegance of style," but added, "This Syrian author is ever a malicious, and often ignorant, enemy." Extracted here is Ibn' Arabshah's account of the capture of Haleb in Syria, which includes a lengthy eyewitness report by one of the city's residents and some general comments on Tamerlane's character.

Another firsthand account comes from Johann Schiltberger's *Travels and Bondage*. Schiltberger (1380–ca.1440), a Bavarian, left home at fourteen to join a Crusade. He was captured first by the Turks during the Battle of Nicopolis (1396) and then—in 1402—by Tamerlane at what he calls the Battle of Angora (usually written Ankara). For three years (although he claimed it was six), he traveled as a prisoner in Tamerlane's army of Turks and Mongols; then, through a series of sometimes bizarre escapes, captures, and recaptures, he says he traveled through Siberia, Egypt, and Palestine before returning home in 1427, after which he wrote his memoirs. In his chapters on Tamerlane, he wrote—almost always inflating troop numbers and casualties wildly—of battles and atrocities in Armenia, India, and Kurdistan, as well as of his captor's death and his howling ghost.

Ahmed ibn Mohammed Ibn' Arabshah

FROM *THE LIFE OF TIMUR*

FIFTEENTH CENTURY

HOW THE GOVERNORS IN HALEB PLOTTED AGAINST TIMUR, WHO WAS AT AINTAB

Then [ca. 1401] the Governors and Amirs and the heads of the army and chief men took counsel among themselves, how they should meet him [Tamerlane] and on what plain they should attack him, and one of them said: "It seems to me best that we should fortify the city and keep watch on its walls, guarding the towers of its orbs, as the heaven is guarded by its angels; but if round about it we see one of the demons of the enemy, we will send against him falling stars of arrows and stars of catapults, a well-directed flame."

And another said: "This is sheer distress and a sign of weakness and defeat; rather let us surround the city and drive off the enemy as he approaches it; thus we shall have a wider field of battle and freer space for the struggle."

Then each of them unfolded what he thought of the matter and they mingled feeble speech with weighty and noble counsel with base; and Al Malik Al Muid Sheikh Al Khaski, a man of sound judgment, who was then Governor of Turabulus [Tripoli], said: "O Council of Allies, lions of war and warlike knights! You should know that your business is arduous, since your enemy is an intractable villain, a prodigy of disaster and a dangerous man, his army strong; his plans forceful and his ravages spread far and wide; therefore beware of him and use your prudence to repel him skilfully, for prudent counsel can effect more than the sharpest sword. The consultation of wise men is the kindler of prudence and the disputation of learned men leads to clear vision. This sea cannot carry a continent.

"His army is numerous like rain and atoms; and though it is like a cloud that has burst, yet it is hidden, being a foreign army in our country.

"I therefore think it best to fortify the city on all sides and assembling outside on one flank, we should all watch him from an ambush and digging trenches round us, make walls of standards and flashing weapons and send letters flying to the Arabs, Kurds, Turkomans and peoples of countries, that they may attack him from all sides and that all the infantry and cavalry may rush upon him, slaying, destroying, plundering and spoiling; but if he holds out (but how could that happen?) he will certainly be in a sad state; if he comes to us, we will receive him with the arms of spears and the hands of shields and fingers of arrows; but if he goes back, which is most to be dared, he will go back with his purpose defeated, and we shall have honour and respect from our Sultan; but if his might presses us, truly (praise to Allah) we also have might and in our might deliverance. And at all events we ought to delay him and beware of his army; perchance Allah will give victory or some command from Himself."

This plan, which in truth was the best, was formerly used by that lion, Shah Mansur.

But Tamardash, the Governor of the city, said: "These opinions are weak and these plans feeble; nay, it is better to fight than to delay and to descend into this battlefield before the chance be lost; and the engagement should be in a place, where it is impossible to leave the battle and there is room everywhere for fighting; this is a bird in a cage and a spoil taken in hunting; therefore seize the opportunity, join battle with him and anticipate him with blow of lance and sword, lest he take us for cowards and smell from our idleness the odour of victory. Therefore collect your goods and hasten and do not dispute among yourselves or behave like cowards but be alert, constant and patient; for you are (praise to Allah) men of courage, vigorous and brave; and each of you is expert in the art of war and excels therein and is a tower in knowledge of shedding the blood of the enemy and has in it sufficiency and method and completion, of which others know only the elements and each of you is a full treasury and a perfect collection and a defence of all Islam; the law of your swords tends to the wounding of heads and is in expression sound and perfect and your spears fix their teeth in the breastplates of all that do violence with perfect and sound inflection.

"But if we rout him we shall achieve our aim and Allah will protect the faithful from slaughter and by the favour of Allah we shall have defended the armies of Egypt from harm; that will be our highest honour and add strength to our valour in victory and will heat and refine the air of our victory; and to his weeping eye bring tears and harm.

"But if the affair happens otherwise—which Allah forbid!—the fault will not be ours, since we shall have exerted every effort and furnished ourselves a just excuse and the Lord will exact our revenge and keep alive our fame.

"Therefore commit yourselves to Allah the Great and Mighty and prepare to meet these wicked men and when you meet their attack, do not turn your backs."

And Tamardash ceased not to press on them this futile counsel, until they agreed to it and planned to advance, since he was the lord of the city, and in his words was confidence; but Tamardash had spoken against all, since secretly he was working with Timur, which was his habit, his nature being disposed to cunning: and he was like a blind sheep or a woman confounded and jealous, when the two armies met, and he could scarce stand firm in either of them because of fear and cunning; but crossed now this way, now that, though he was a figure without meaning and a voice without sense; but Timur relied on him and entrusted business to him, as did the armies of Syria and the hosts of Islam.

Then they fortified the city and shut its gates, blocked up its highways and large open spaces and placed soldiers on guard in all the wards and cross-roads, but they opened the gates on the side of his attack, that is the gates called Bab Al Nasar, Bab Al Farj and Bab Al Qanat.

HOW HE POURED THUNDERS OR SWORDS AND BREASTPLATES UPON THE ARMIES OF SYRIA WHEN HE REACHED HALEB

Then Timur moved his troops and arrived on the seventh day at Haleb from Aintab and halted with that army on the ninth day of the first month Rabia, the fifth day of the week; and from that army a band of about two thousand advanced to battle, whom about three hundred of the lions of Syria encountered, who broke them with broad swords and scattered them with spears and dispersed and repelled and split them and put them to flight.

Then in the morning of the day of prayer about five thousand of the army of Timur advanced to the field of battle and were met by another band in squadrons and in scattered order, and when their wings engaged, between the two hosts the fingers of spears were mingled and they pressed each against the other and charged and raged and the spears ceased not like pens, to draw lines on the tablets of men's breasts and the edges of swords to cut the points of the pens and the arrows like lancets, to cut off foul sores and the earth to groan under the weight of mountains of slain, until the depth of night had drawn a great fog of darkness and dust, and they withdrew and Allah granted victory to whom He wished, and made two rivers of the blood of the enemy flow into the river Ooiq, only two men being lost of the armies of Islam.

Then on the morning of the Sabbath day, the eleventh, the hosts of Syria and the armies of Islam and of the Sultan drew up in perfect order, with complete equipment, excellent horses, straight spears and splendid banners. And nothing was wanting to those stalwart soldiers but a particle of divine help and aid, and they advanced against him to force him back and drive him off; and his army went forward to meet them, under the auspices of favourable fortune, with fate his minister and destiny aiding him, with renowned troops and armies loyal and victorious, and in front the lords and the elephants of war.

And now he hid the disaster which he was planning for them, and when night had come on, drew up his armies, which he stretched around them and sent skirmishers against them and opposed the vanguard to them and kept them engaged with his front ranks, while the rest went round them and so came upon them from the rear and the right and the left.

Then he went over them like a razor over hair and ran like locusts over a green crop.

This engagement occurred near the village of Hylan. And when matters were confused and disturbed and the tumult and violence of battle was raging, lions charging against each other and rams butting each the other, the right wing, which Tamardash was leading, took to flight, whereby the army was broken and stunned and because of the shock fear seized brave men and consternation and anguish conquered them and they scarcely held firm for one hour of the day, then turned their backs, which were scored with his spears and they attacked them from the front continuously, while from the rear his army harassed them, as I have said: "We made their backs in the battle like faces, on which we carved mouths, eyes and brows."

Therefore they made for the city towards the open gate, torn and wounded, while they were being cleft by swords and pierced by spears, so that swamps flowed with their blood and all the eagles and beasts of prey fed freely on their remaining flesh. But as soon as in their rout they reached the gate of the city, they hurled themselves into it with one rush and crowded together and without ceasing one trod down another, until the upper threshold of the gate was levelled with the ground and the gates were so blocked with dead men, that nothing at all could enter through them; therefore they scattered through the countries and dispersed in the deserts and mountains.

And the foreign slaves breaking the Antioch gate, went out thereby, making for Syria, and some of them reached Damascus in wretched state and their foul semblance told the manner of this battle.

But the governors climbed to the fort of Haleb, and there fortified themselves and the earth though wide became narrow for them. Therefore seeking security, they committed themselves to him, using Tamardash as mediator and now all despaired of their lives.

Then he advanced at his own ease, in keeping with his dignity, majesty and tranquillity, and entered Haleb, and took therein what he wished and seized men and plunder.

And when the Governors had surrendered to him, he laid hands on Saidi Sudun and Shaikh Ali Al Khaski; but clad Tamardash with a mantle; he also laid hands on Tunbagha Othrnani, the Governor of Safad, and Umar, son of Tahan, Governor of Gaza, all of whom he put in chains and strove to seize wealth and collect goods and booty; and men's hearts were filled with thoughts of terror of him and the sparks of his tyranny were scattered through the world and he was not content to have destroyed men but even built towers of skulls. The reason of this was that Timur was reminded of the fate of his kinsman Baridi, whom he had sent as envoy to Haleb, but whom the Governor of Syria had beheaded and plundered; he therefore wished to avenge his kinsman at the cost of the people of Haleb and they granted his desire and let him choose from themselves those with whom he would do as he wished; therefore slaying many of them, he built several towers of their skulls.

THIS DISASTER IS MORE FULLY SET FORTH FROM THOSE THINGS WHICH I HAVE TAKEN FROM THE CHRONICLE OF IBN AL SHAHANA

[Ibn Al Shahana, a citizen of the city,] said: "Al Hafiz Al Khwarizmi related to me that in the roll of Timur's armies were written 800,000 names; and that Timur attacked the fort of the Muslims, whose Governor was Al Nasari Mahomed son of Musa son of Shahari, who resisted him and repeatedly made sallies." Then he said in his own words:

"He gave much trouble to the hosts of Tamarlang and to his scouts, while he was besieging Bahansa, and slew a multitude of them and sent their heads to Haleb; and overthrew with shameful defeat a tuman [ten thousand men] which was sent against him, so that the most of them threw themselves into the Euphrates, and Tamarlang sent a letter to him, in which he used these words:

> I went forth from the distant country of Samarkand and none stood against me and the other kings of countries came over to me; and you send men to harass my followers and slay any that they can seize. But now we are leading our armies against you. If therefore you care for yourself and your subjects, come over to us, that you may experience pity and clemency, which we shall not proffer any further; if not, we shall come upon you and lay waste your city; and lo, Allah Almighty said that kings, when they have entered a city, lay it waste and bring low the most powerful of its people; and thus they will do. Therefore prepare for that which will befall you, if you refuse to side with me.

"But he held the envoy and threw him in chains and cared nothing for Tamarlang's words. Then the first line of his army came against him, and he went forth against it and slew and crushed them.

"And on the second day of the week when Tamarlang came to the fort of the Muslims, he went forth against him and fought fiercely with him and when the battle was at its height, Tamarlang discovered in it his resolute courage and ceased to wage war with him and strove to deceive him by presents and flattery and sought peace from him and that he should send him horses and supplies, because of his dignity, but he did not suffer himself to be bewitched by him; and when he sank to the point of asking only one slave from him, he did not gain even this, but withdrew foiled; then he attacked Tamarlang's rear and slew and plundered and took prisoners and that after leaving open the gate of his fort, which he did not shut even for one day. . . .

"But on the fifth day of the week, the ninth of the first Rabia, Tamarlang attacked Haleb, the governor of which was Al Muqar Al Saifi Tamardash and he had armies of the cities of Syria, the army of Damascus with its Governor Saidi Sudun and the army of Turabulus with its Governor Al Muqar Al Saifi Sheikh Al Khaski and the army of Hamah with its Governor Al Lear Al Saifi

Daqmaq and the army of Safad and others, and their counsels conflicted, one advising: 'Enter the city and fight from the walls,' another: 'Pitch a camp in tents outside the city.' And when Al Muqar Al Saifi saw their conflict, he let the people of Haleb leave the city empty and betake themselves where they wished; and this indeed was the best counsel, but they did not agree to it and pitched tents outside the city towards the enemy.

"And when Tamarlang's envoy had come, the Governor of Damascus ordered him to be slain and a slight skirmish happened on the day of prayer between the wings of the armies.

"But on the Sabbath, the eleventh day of the first Rabia, when Tamarlang led out his armies and his people against the enemy, the Muslims retreated towards the city and crowded in the gates and many of them met their death, the enemy slaying them from behind and making prisoners. And Tamarlang took Haleb by force with the sword, but the Governors of the kingdom and the nobles climbed to the fort, in which the people of Haleb had hidden most of their goods.

"And on the third day of the week the fourteenth of the first month Rabia, after giving a promise of safety and an oath he took the fort; nevertheless the oath was not kept; and on the next day he climbed the fort and at the close of day summoned its learned men and judges; and we appeared before him and after he had made us stand a little while, he ordered us to sit and summoned his own learned men and said to the chief of them, whom he had with him, namely Maulvi Abdul Jabar son of Ulama Namanuddin Hanifi, whose father was among the famous Ulamas of Samarkand:

Tell them that I wish to put a question to them, concerning which I have asked the Ulamas of Samarkand, Bokhara, Herat and all the cities which I have taken, but they have not found the right answer; but do not be like them, and let none reply to me except your most learned and most eminent man, who knows rightly what he says, for I am intimate with learned men, to whom I am greatly devoted and in whose company I delight and I have the ancient zeal for learning.

"And we had already learnt about him, that he troubled learned men by putting a certain question, which he used as a reason to put them to death or torture; and Qazi Sharafuddin Muse Ansari, the Shafeite, said concerning me:

'This is our Sheikh and the professor and mufti of these countries—ask him by Allah the Helper!' Presently Abdul Jabar said to me: 'Our Sultan asks: *Yesterday when some of our men and yours were slain, who were the martyrs, our slain or yours?* Then everyone was silent because of fear and we said to ourselves: 'This is the very thing, which we have heard of his harassment.' Howbeit Allah, while all kept silence, opened to me a reply ready and apt, and I said: 'This same question was put to our master, the Prophet of Allah, on whom be the favour of Allah and peace! to which he replied and I reply the same as our master, the Prophet of Allah' . . . and Tamarlang turned his ear and eye towards me and said to Abdul Jabar, gibing at my speech: *How was this question put to the Prophet of Allah, on whom be the favour of Allah and peace! And how did he reply?*

"I said: 'An Arab came to the Prophet of Allah, on whom be the favour of Allah and peace! and said: "O Prophet of Allah! One man fights to defend his own, another to show his courage, another to display his power; which of us will be in the way of Allah?" And the Prophet of Allah on whom be the favour of Allah and peace! replied: "He who fights to make strong the word of Allah, which is the highest thing, is a martyr."'

"Then Tamarlang said: *Good! Good!* . . .

"And the gate of familiarity being opened, Tamarlang said: *I am half a man and yet I have taken such and such countries,* and he numbered all the kingdoms of Persia and Irak and Hind and all the countries of the Tatars.

"Then I said: 'Give thanks for this fortune by sparing these Imams and slay none.' And he said: *By Allah! I slay no one of set purpose, but you bring death on yourselves; but I, by Allah! will slay none of you and you will be secure concerning your lives and goods.*

"And he repeatedly put fresh questions, to which we replied and with eagerness all those present skilled in the law were most ready to reply. . . .

"And the last question of Tamarlang was: *What do you say concerning Ali and Muavia and Yazid?* [This refers to a religious controversy: Shia Muslims regard Ali's sons, Hasan and Husein, as true khalifs; the Sunnis recognize Muavia and his son Yazid.]

"Then Qazi Sharafuddin, who was at my side, whispered to me: 'You should know how to reply to him, for he is a Shia.'

- 309 -

"Now I had not fully heard his words, when forthwith Qazi Alamuddin Qafsi Al Maliki replied to him, saying: that each of them fought for the faith, on account of which saying Tamarlang seized with violent anger replied: *Ali was the right successor, Muavia an usurper and Yazid wicked; but you men of Haleb join with the people of Damascus, who being followers of Yazid, slew Husein.*

"Then I began to soothe him and excuse Al Maliki, because he gave a reply, which he found in a book, not discerning its meaning; and he almost returned to his former calm.

"Then to Abdul Jabar, who asked about me and Qazi Sharafuddin, he said concerning me: *This is an excellent doctor,* and concerning Sharafuddin, *This man is a clear speaker.*

"Then Tamarlang asked me about my age; 'I was born,' I replied, 'in the year 749 and have now reached fifty-four years.'

"Then he said to Qazi Sharafuddin: *And how old are you?*

"And he replied: 'I am about one year older than he.'

Therefore, you are of the age of my sons; but I have now reached the age of seventy-five. [Actually, he was about sixty-five.]

"Then it was the time of evening prayer, which was said, Abdul Jabar leading us as Imam, and Tamarlang prayed standing at my side, prostrating himself and bowing his head. Then we departed.

"On the next day he broke faith with all who were in the fort and took all the goods, furniture and utensils therein of which the number cannot be reckoned. A certain scribe of his told me that in no city did he gain so much booty as in this fort; and most of the Muslims were subjected to various tortures, whom they kept in the fort, some bound with fetters and chains, some shut in prison or in their own houses.

"At length, leaving the fort, Tamarlang stayed in the house of the Governor and he gave a banquet in the manner of the Moghals, all the rulers and governors serving him, to whom he ordered goblets of wine to be carried; but the Muslims were wretchedly afflicted, despoiled, slain and thrown in chains, their mosques, colleges and houses destroyed, burned and laid waste and overturned up to the end of the first month of Rabia. . . .

"And on the first day of the second month of Rabia, he left the city, making for Damascus . . . which he plundered and burned and dealt worse with it than with Haleb. . . . This is what I have copied from the words of Ibn Shahana, as I [Ibn Arabshah] found it. . . ."

THE WONDERFUL GIFTS OF TIMUR AND HIS NATURE AND CHARACTER

Timur [Arabshah continues] was tall and of lofty stature as though he belonged to the remnants of the Amalekites, big in brow and head, mighty in strength and courage, wonderful in nature, white in colour, mixed with red, but not dark, stout of limb, with broad shoulders, thick fingers, long legs, perfect build, long beard, dry hands, lame on the right side, with eyes like candles, without brilliance, powerful in voice; he did not fear death; and though he was near his eightieth [actually, seventieth] year, yet he was firm in mind, strong and robust in body, brave and fearless, like a hard rock. He did not love jest and falsehood; wit and sport pleased him not; truth, though troublesome to him, pleased him; he was not sad in adversity or joyful in prosperity.

The inscription of his seal was: *Rasti, Rusti*—that is, "Truth is safety"—and for a brand on his beasts and centremark on his coins he used three rings placed in this way. He did not allow in his company any obscene talk or talk of bloodshed or captivity, rapine, plunder and violation of the harem. He was spirited and brave and inspired awe and obedience. He loved bold and brave soldiers, by whose aid opened the locks of terror and tore in pieces men like lions and through them and their battles overturned the heights of mountains. He excelled in plans that struck the mark and in wonders of physiognomy; was excellent in fortune, of diligence, firm of purpose and truthful in business. I have said:

> *How often his plans kindled the fuel of trouble,*
> *And blazed for the author of disasters and inflamed peoples.*

Johann Schiltberger

FROM *Travels and Bondage*

HOW TAMERLIN CONQUERED THE KINGDOM OF SEBAST

When Weyasit had expelled Otman from Tamast, [Otman] went to his lord named Tamerlin, to whom he was subject, and complained of Weyasit, how he had driven him away from the kingdom of Tamast, which he had conquered, and at the same time asked [Tamerlane] to help him to reconquer his kingdom. Tamerlin said that he would send to Weyasit to restore the country. This he did, but Weyasit sent word that he would not give it up, for as he had won it by the sword, it might as well be his as another's. So soon as Tamerlin heard this, he assembled ten hundred thousand men, and conducted them into the kingdom of Sebast, and lay siege to the capital, before which he remained twenty-one days, and he undermined the walls of the city in several places, and took the city by force, although there were in it five thousand horsemen sent by Weyasit. They were all buried alive in this way. When Tamerlin took the city, the governor begged that he would not shed their blood. To this he consented, and so they were buried alive. Then he levelled the city, and carried away the inhabitants into captivity in his own country. There were also nine thousand virgins taken into captivity by Tamerlin to his own country. Before he took the city, he had at least three thousand men killed. Then he returned to his own country.

WEYASIT CONQUERS LESSER ARMENIA

Scarcely had Tamerlin returned to his own country, than Weyasit assembled three hundred thousand men, and went into Lesser Armenia and took it from Tamerlin, and took the capital called Ersingen, together with its lord who was named Tarathan, and then went back to his own country. So soon as Tamerlin heard that Weyasit had conquered the said country, he went to meet him with sixteen hundred thousand men; and when Weyasit heard this, he went to meet him with fourteen hundred thousand men. They met near a city called Augury, where they fought desperately. Weyasit had quite thirty thousand men of White Tartary, whom he placed in the van at the battle. They went over to Tamerlin; then they had two encounters, but neither could overcome the other. Now Tamerlin had thirty-two trained elephants at the battle, and ordered, after mid-day, that they should be brought into the battle. This was done, and they attacked each other; but Weyasit took to flight, and went with at least one thousand horsemen to a mountain. Tamerlin surrounded the mountain so that he could not move, and took him [on July 20, 1402]. Then he remained eight months in the country, conquered more territory and occupied it, and then went to Weyasit's capital and took him with him, and took his treasure, and silver and gold, as much as one thousand camels could carry; and he would have taken him into his own country, but he died on the way. And so I became Tamerlin's prisoner, and was taken by him to his country. After this I rode after him. What I have described took place during the time that I was with Weyasit.

HOW TAMERLIN GOES TO WAR WITH THE KING-SULTAN

After Tamerlin had overcome Weyasit and returned to his own country, he went to war with the king-sultan, who is the chief king among Infidels. He took with him twenty-one hundred thousand men, went into his territory, and lay siege to a city called Hallapp, which contains four hundred thousand houses. Then the lord and governor of the city took with him eighty thousand men, and went out and fought with Tamerlin, but he could not overcome him, and fled again into the city, and many people were killed in his flight. He continued to defend himself, but Tamerlin took a suburb on the fourth day, and the people he found in it he threw into the moat of the city, put timber and mire upon them, and filled the moat in four places. The moat was twelve fathom deep, and [cut] in the solid rock. Then he stormed the city, and took it by assault and captured the governor, and fully occupied the city, and then went to another city called Hrumkula, which surrendered.

Then he went to another city called Anthap. There he lay siege for eight days, and took it on the tenth day by assault, and pillaged it, and went to another city called Wehessum. There he lay siege for fifteen days. After that they gave themselves up and he occupied it. The cities I have named are chief cities in Syria. Then he went to another city called Damaschk [Damascus]; it is the principal capital in the country. When the king-sultan heard that he was laying siege to Tamasch [Damascus], he sent and begged that he would not injure the city, and spare the temple. To this he consented, and went further on. The temple in the city of Tamasch is so large, that it has externally forty gates. Inside the temple hang twelve thousand lamps, of which number nine thousand are lit daily. But every week, on Friday, all of them are lit. Amongst these lamps are many in gold and silver, made by the order of kings and great lords. So soon as Tamerlin had gone out from the city, the king-sultan left his capital Alchei Terchei, with thirty thousand men, hoping to arrive before Tamerlin took it, and he sent twelve thousand men to Tamaschen. When Tamerlin heard this, he marched towards him, and the king-sultan returned again to his capital. Tamerlin pursued him, and where the king-sultan passed the night, there in the morning he caused the water and the grass to be poisoned; and wherever Tamerlin came, he suffered great losses amongst his people and cattle, and could not overtake him.

Then he turned again against Tamaschen and besieged it for three months, but could not take it. During those three months they fought every day, and when the twelve thousand men saw that they had no assistance from their lord, they asked Tamerlin to be allowed to pass. He consented, and they left the city at night and returned to their lord. Then Tamerlin stormed the city and took it by assault. And now, soon after he had taken the city, came to him the Geit, that is as much as to say a bishop, and fell at his feet, and begged mercy for himself and his priests. Tamerlin ordered that he should go with his priests into the temple; so the priests took their wives, their children and many others, into the temple for protection, until there were thirty thousand young and old. Now Tamerlin gave orders that when the temple was full, the people inside should be shut up in it. This was done. Then wood was placed around the temple, and he ordered it to be ignited, and they all perished in the temple.

Then he ordered that each one of his [soldiers] should bring to him the head of a man. This was done, and it took three days; then with these heads were constructed three towers, and the city was pillaged. After this he went into another country called Scherch, a country where no cattle are bred, and this country gave itself up. He ordered them to bring food for his people who were famished, although they had been before a city so rich in spices. Then he returned to his country, having left that country and occupied the cities.

HOW TAMERLIN CONQUERED BABILONI

Now when he returned from the land of the king-sultan, he took ten hundred thousand men with him and marched upon Babiloni. When the king heard this, he left a garrison in the city and went out of it. Tamerlin besieged it for a whole month, during which time he undermined the walls, took the city and burnt it. Then he had the earth ploughed and barley planted there, because he had sworn that he would destroy the city, so that nobody should know whether there had been houses or no. Then he went to a fortress; it stood in a river, and the king kept his treasure there. He could not take this fortress, across the water, so he turned away the water, and found under the water three leaden chests full of gold and silver; each chest was two fathoms long, and one fathom broad. The king sank them here, so that if the fortress was taken, the gold would remain. The chests he removed, and he took the fortress and found fifteen men in it. They were hanged. They also found in the fortress four chests full of silver and gold, which he also took away, and then conquered three cities. Then summer began, so that on account of the heat he could not remain in the country.

HOW TAMERLIN CONQUERED LESSER INDIA

When Tamerlin returned home from Babiloni, he sent word to all in his land that they were to be ready in four months, as he wanted to go into Lesser India, distant from his capital a four months' journey. When the time came, he went into Lesser India with four hundred thousand men, and crossed a desert of twenty days' journey; there, is a great want of water, and then he got to a mountain which it took him eight days, before he came out of it. On this mountain there is a path, where camels and horses must be bound to planks and lowered. Then he came to a valley where it is so dark, that people cannot see each other by the light of day, and it is of half a day's journey. Then he came to a high mountainous country, in which he travelled for three days and three nights, and then got to a beautiful plain, where lies the capital of the country. He stopped with his people in the plain, near the wooded mountain, and sent word to the king of the country: Mirttemirgilden, that is as much as to say, Give up thyself, the lord Tamerlin is come. When the king received the message, he sent word to tell him that he would settle with him with the sword. Then he marched against Tamerlin with four hundred thousand men, and with four hundred elephants trained for war; upon each elephant was a turret, in each of which were at least ten armed men. When Tamerlin heard of this, he advanced with his people to meet him; in the meantime the king placed the elephants in the front, and when they engaged, Tamerlin might easily have conquered; but he could not overcome the king, because his horses were afraid of the elephants and would not advance. This went on from morning until mid-day, so that Tamerlin retired and had his counsellors to consult, how the king and his elephants were to be overcome? One named Suleymanschach advised, that camels should be taken and wood fastened on them, and when the elephants advanced, the wood should be ignited, and the camels driven up against the elephants; thus would they be subdued by the fire and the cries of the camels, because the elephants are afraid of fire. Then Tamerlin took twenty thousand camels and prepared them as above described, and the king came with his elephants in front. Tamerlin went to meet him, and drove the camels up against the elephants, the wood on them being on fire. The camels cried out, and when the elephants saw the fire and heard the great cries, they took to flight, so that none could hold them. When Tamerlin saw this, he pursued them with all his force, and of the elephants many were killed. When the king saw this, he went back into his capital. Tamerlin followed him up and besieged the city for ten days. In the mean time the king agreed with him, to give him two zentner of gold of India, which is better than the gold of Arabia, and he also gave him many precious stones, and promised to lend him thirty thousand men whenever he might want them; and so they were reconciled with each other. The king remained in his kingdom, and Tamerlin returned to his country, and took with him one hundred elephants and the riches the king had given him.

HOW A VASSAL CARRIED OFF RICHES THAT BELONGED TO TAMERLIN

When Tamerlin returned from Lesser India, he sent one of his vassals named Chebakh, with ten thousand men, to the city of Soltania, to bring to him the five-yearly tribute of Persia and Armenia which was kept in that city. He came, and took the tribute, and loaded one thousand waggons, and then he wrote to a lord in the country of Massander, who was his friend. He came with fifty thousand men, they made an alliance with each other, and the treasure was taken to Massenderam. When Tamerlin heard of this, he sent a great many people to conquer the above-named country, and bring to him the two lords as prisoners. When the people got to the country, they could not do any harm because of the large forests which surround it, and they sent to Tamerlin for more people. He sent other seventy thousand men to clear the woods and make a road. They did so for ten miles, but could not conquer the territory. They sent to tell Tamerlin, and he ordered them to go home, which they did, without having done anything.

HOW TAMERLIN CAUSED THOUSANDS OF CHILDREN TO BE KILLED

Then he went into a kingdom called Hisspahan and made for the capital, Hisspahan, and required it to surrender. They gave themselves up, and went to him with their wives and children. He received them graciously, occupied the city with six thousand of his people, and took away with him the lord of the city, whose name was Schachister. And so soon as the city heard that Tamerlin was gone out of the country, they closed all the gates and killed the six thousand men. When Tamerlin knew this, he returned to the city and besieged it for fifteen days, but he could not take it, and made peace with them on condition that they should lend him the archers that were in the city, for an expedition; after that, he should send them back. They sent to him twelve thousand archers; he cut off all their thumbs, and forced them back into the city and himself entered it. He assembled all the citizens, and ordered all those over fourteen years to be beheaded, and the boys under fourteen years he ordered to be spared, and with the heads was constructed a tower in the centre of the city; then he ordered the women and children to be taken to a plain outside the city, and ordered the children under seven years of age to be placed apart, and ordered his people to ride over these same children. When his counsellors and the mothers of the children saw this, they fell at his feet, and begged that he would not kill them. He would not listen, and ordered that they should be ridden over; but none would be the first to do so. He got angry, and rode himself [among them] and said: "Now I should like to see who will not ride after me?" Then they were all obliged to ride over the children, and they were all trampled upon. There were seven thousand. Then he set fire to the city, and took the other women and children into his own city; and then went to his capital called Semerchant, where he had not been for twelve years.

TAMERLIN WANTS TO GO TO WAR WITH THE GREAT CHAN

At about this time, the great Chan, king of Chetey, sent an ambassador with four hundred horsemen, to demand of him the tribute which he had forgotten, and kept for five years. Tamerlin took the ambassador with him, until he came to his above-named capital, and sent him from there to tell his lord, that he would neither pay tribute nor be subject to him, and that he should himself pay him a visit. Then he sent messengers all over his country that they should prepare, as he wished to advance on Chetey, and taking eighteen hundred thousand men, he marched for a whole month. He then came to a desert that was seventy days journey across; there he travelled ten days, and lost many people there for want of water. Great harm also befell his horses and other cattle, because it was very cold in that country; and when he perceived his great losses amongst his people and cattle, he turned and went back to his capital and fell ill.

OF TAMERLIN'S DEATH

It is to be noted, that three causes made Tamerlin fret, so that he became ill, and died of that same illness. The first cause was grief that his vassal had escaped with the tribute; the other it is to be noted was, that Tamerlin had three wives, and that the youngest, whom he loved very much, had been intimate with one of his vassals whilst he was away. When Tamerlin came home, his eldest wife told him that his youngest wife had cared for one of his vassals, and had broken her vow. He would not believe it. She came to him and said: "Come to her and order her to open her trunk: you will find a ring with a precious stone, and a letter which he has sent to her." Tamerlin sent to tell her that he would pass the night with her, and when he came into her room, he told her to open her trunk. This was done, and he found the ring and the letter. He sat down near her, and asked whence the ring and letter had come to her? She fell at his feet, and begged he would not be angry, because one of his vassals had sent them to her without any right. After this he went out of the room, and ordered that she should be immediately beheaded. This was done. He then sent five thousand horsemen after this same vassal, that they might bring him as a prisoner; but he was warned by the commander who was sent after him, and the vassal took with him five hundred men, his wife and children, and fled to the country of Wassandaran. There Tamerlin could not get at him. It fretted him so much that he had killed his wife, and that the vassal had escaped, that he died, and was buried in the country with great magnificence. Be it also known that, after he was buried, the priests that belong to the temple, heard him howl every night during a whole year. His friends gave large alms, that he should cease his howlings. But this was of no use. They asked advice of their priests, and went to his son and begged that he would set free the prisoners taken by his father in other countries, and especially those that were in his capital, who were all craftsmen he had brought to his capital, where they had to work. He let them go, and so soon as they were free, Tamerlin did not howl any more. All that is written above, happened during the six years [actually, three years] that I was with Tamerlin, and I also was present.

—XV—

THE CRUSADES:
INFIDEL AGAINST INFIDEL

The Crusades: Christians warring against Muslims, and each side believed—and "believed" is the key word, not "thought"—that the other was the barbarian, the infidel, the enemy of God.

On and off, for more than three hundred years, bands of armed men made their way out of Europe toward Jerusalem: soldiers, mystics, adventurers, priests, kings, runaways, con men, mercenaries, devout peasants. It all began in 1095 with words—a speech to a multitude gathered in a field at Clermont in France. A monk named Robert, who was there, wrote in his *History of the Crusade to Jerusalem*—a portion of which is reprinted here—of Pope Urban II's call to rescue the Holy Land from the hands of "an accursed race," the Muslims. A simple slogan—"Deus vult," God wills it—inspired thousands to march into the Middle East and begin what turned out to be centuries of bloodshed.

The account here of the capture of Jerusalem by the Crusaders in 1099, at the end of the First Crusade, is a compilation by the American historian August C. Krey of two alternating—and very different—voices. Together they present a vivid portrait of an expedition that was both military and religious and was dogged from the very beginning with endless squabbling. The first voice is that of an unidentified crusader, probably a lesser Norman knight, who in 1100 or 1101 composed the first complete report of the Crusade. Known to scholars as *Gesta Francorum*, it was written, according to

Professor Krey, in a southern Italian Latin style and is completely secular in its outlook. For this anonymous crusader, the capture of the Holy City was a straightforward military problem. The other eyewitness is a French priest, Raymond, canon of Le Puy, who was chaplain to Count Raymond IV of Toulouse, the wealthiest of the Crusade leaders. Written before 1102 as a celebration of the exploits in the Holy Land of Count Raymond and Adhemar, bishop of Le Puy, it is rich in mystical visions, saintly miracles, and mentions of Peter Bartholomew, the simple foot soldier turned mystic who felt divinely inspired to find the lance that had pierced Jesus' side on the cross.

The view from the Muslim side is provided by Usamah ibn-Murshid (1095–1188), a Syrian poet and soldier, from his *An Arab-Syrian Gentleman and Warrior in the Period of the Crusades*. Usamah first tells of some skirmishes and a few more peaceful encounters he had with crusaders (whom he calls Franks) and then rather gleefully catalogs the Westerners' grotesque oddities.

Saladin won Jerusalem back for Islam in the Third Crusade (1187), but the bloody confrontations in the names of Christ and Muhammed went on for another century (for a total of Nine Crusades) until 1291, when Acre, the last Christian stronghold in the Holy Land, fell to the Muslims for the last time.

But farther north in Constantinople, the tottering Eastern Roman Empire still held on. Surviving 1,100 years since it had been founded by Constantine, it finally fell to the Ottoman Turks under Mehmed II in 1453. That last battle and the capture of the city were described a few years later by Doukas (his first name is unkown) in his *Decline and Fall of Byzantium to the Ottoman Turks*. He was not an eyewitness, but he knew many who were.

ROBERT THE MONK

"POPE URBAN II CALLS FOR A CRUSADE"

1095

I n the year of our Lord's Incarnation one thousand and ninety-five, a great
council was convened within the bounds of Gaul, in Auvergne, in the city
which is called Clermont. Over this Pope Urban II presided, with the
Roman bishops and cardinals. This council was a famous one on account of the
concourse of both French and German bishops, and of princes as well. Having
arranged the matters relating to the Church, the lord Pope went forth into a certain spacious plain, for no building was large enough to hold all the people. The
Pope then, with sweet and persuasive eloquence, addressed those present in
words something like the following, saying:

"Oh, race of Franks, race beyond the mountains [the Alps], race beloved
and chosen by God (as is clear from many of your works), set apart from all
other nations by the situation of your country, as well as by your Catholic faith
and the honor you render to the holy Church: to you our discourse is addressed,
and for you our exhortations are intended. We wish you to know what a serious matter has led us to your country, for it is the imminent peril threatening
you and all the faithful that has brought us hither.

"From the confines of Jerusalem and from the city of Constantinople a
grievous report has gone forth and has been brought repeatedly to our ears;
namely, that a race from the kingdom of the Persians, an accursed race, a race
wholly alienated from God, 'a generation that set not their heart aright, and
whose spirit was not steadfast with God' [Ps., lxxviii. 8], has violently invaded
the lands of those Christians and has depopulated them by pillage and fire.
They have led away a part of the captives into their own country, and a part

- 323 -

they have killed by cruel tortures. They have either destroyed the churches of God or appropriated them for the rites of their own religion. They destroy the altars, after having defiled them with their uncleanness. . . . The kingdom of the Greeks [the Eastern Empire] is now dismembered by them and has been deprived of territory so vast in extent that it could not be traversed in two months' time.

"On whom, therefore, rests the labor of avenging these wrongs and of recovering this territory, if not upon you—you, upon whom, above all other nations, God has conferred remarkable glory in arms, great courage, bodily activity, and strength to humble the heads of those who resist you. Let the deeds of your ancestors encourage you and incite your minds to manly achievement—the glory and greatness of King Charlemagne, and of his son Louis [the Pious], and of your other monarchs, who have destroyed the kingdoms of the Turks and have extended the sway of the holy Church over lands previously pagan. Let the holy sepulcher of our Lord and Saviour, which is possessed by the unclean nations, especially arouse you, and the holy places which are now treated with ignominy and irreverently polluted with the filth of the unclean. Oh most valiant soldiers and descendants of invincible ancestors, do not degenerate, but recall the valor of your ancestors.

"But if you are hindered by love of children, parents, or wife, remember what the Lord says in the Gospel, 'He that loveth father or mother more than me is not worthy of me' [Matt., x. 37]. 'Every one that hath forsaken houses, or brethren, or sisters, or father, or mother, or wife, or children, or lands, for my name's sake, shall receive an hundred-fold, and shall inherit everlasting life' [Matt., xix. 29]. Let none of your possessions restrain you, nor anxiety for your family affairs. For this land which you inhabit, shut in on all sides by the seas and surrounded by the mountain peaks, is too narrow for your large population; nor does it abound in wealth; and it furnishes scarcely food enough for its cultivators. Hence it that you murder and devour one another, that you wage war, and that very many among you perish in civil strife.

"Let hatred, therefore, depart from among you; let your quarrels end; let wars cease; and let all dissension and controversies slumber. Enter upon the road of the Holy Sepulcher; wrest that land from the wicked race, and subject it to yourselves. That land which, as the Scripture says, 'floweth with milk and honey' [Num., xiii. 27] was given by God into the power of the children of Israel. Jerusalem is the center of the earth; the land is fruitful above all others, like another paradise of delights. This spot the Redeemer of mankind has made illustrious by His advent, has beautified by His sojourn, has consecrated by His passion, has redeemed by His death, has glorified by His burial.

"This royal city, however, situated at the center of the earth, is now held captive by the enemies of Christ and is subjected, by those who do not know God, to the worship of the heathen. She seeks, therefore, and desires to be liberated, and ceases not to implore you to come to her aid. From you especially she asks succor, because, as we have already said, God has conferred upon you, above all other nations, great glory in arms. Accordingly, undertake this journey eagerly for the remission of your sins, with the assurance of the reward of imperishable glory in the kingdom of heaven."

When Pope Urban had skilfully said these and very many similar things, he so centered in one purpose the desires of all who were present that all cried out, "It is the will of God! It is the will of God!" When the venerable Roman pontiff heard that, with eyes uplifted to heaven, he gave thanks to God, and commanding silence with his hand, said:

"Most beloved brethren, today is manifest in you what the Lord says in the Gospel, 'Where two or three are gathered together in my name, there am I in the midst of them' [Matt., xviii. 20]. For unless God had been present in your spirits, all of you would not have uttered the same cry; since, although the cry issued from numerous mouths, yet the origin of the cry was one. Therefore I say to you that God, who implanted this in your breasts, has drawn it forth from you. Let that, then, be your war cry in battle, because it is given to you by God. When an armed attack is made upon the enemy, let this one cry be raised by all the soldiers of God: 'It is the will of God! *Deus vult!* It is the will of God!'

"And we neither command nor advise that the old or feeble, or those incapable of bearing arms, undertake this journey. Nor ought women to set out at all without their husbands, or brothers, or legal guardians. For such are more of a hindrance than aid, more of a burden than an advantage. Let the rich aid the needy; and according to their wealth let them take with them experienced soldiers. The priests and other clerks [clergy], whether secular or regular, are not to go without the consent of their bishop; for this journey would profit them nothing if they went without permission. Also, it is not fitting that laymen should enter upon the pilgrimage without the blessing of their priests.

"Whoever, therefore, shall decide upon this holy pilgrimage, and shall make his vow to God to that effect, and shall offer himself to Him for sacrifice, as a living victim, holy and acceptable to God, shall wear the sign of the cross of the Lord on his forehead or on his breast. When he shall return from his journey, having fulfilled his vow, let him place the cross on his back between his shoulders. Thus shall ye, indeed, by this twofold action, fulfill the precept of the Lord, as He commands in the Gospel, 'He that taketh not his cross, and followeth after me, is not worthy of me'" [Luke, xiv. 271].

Anonymous Norman Knight and Raymond, Canon of Le Puy

"The Capture of Jerusalem"

1099

MARCH TO JERUSALEM (May 13–June 7, 1099)

Knight:

Accordingly, we left the fortified town and came to Tripoli on the sixth day of the week on the thirteenth day of incoming May, and we stayed there for three days. At length, the [Muslim] King of Tripoli made an agreement with the leaders, and he straightway loosed to them more than three hundred [Christian] pilgrims who had been captured there and gave fifteen thousand pesants [gold coins] and fifteen horses of great value; he likewise gave us a great market of horses, asses, and all goods, whence the whole army of Christ was greatly enriched. But he made an agreement with them that if they could win the war and take Jerusalem, he would become a Christian and would recognize his land as (a gift) from them. In such manner it was settled.

We left the city on the second day of the week in the month of May and, passing along a narrow and difficult road all day and night, we came to a fortress, the name of which was Botroun. Then we came to a city called Gibilet near the sea, in which we suffered very great thirst, and, thus worn out, we reached a river named Ibrahim. Then on the eve of the day of the Ascension of the Lord we crossed a mountain in which the way was exceedingly narrow, and there we expected to find the enemy lying in ambush for us. But God favoring us, none of them dared to appear in our way. Then our knights went ahead of us and cleared the way before us, and we arrived at a city by the sea which is called Beirut, and thence we went to another city called Sidon, thence to another called Tyre, and from Tyre to the city of Acre. But from Acre we came to a fortified place the name of which was Cayphas, and then we came near Caesarea. There was celebrated Pentecost on the third day of outgoing May. Then we came to Ramlah, which through fear of the Franks the Saracens had left empty. Near it was the famous church in which rested the most precious body of St. George, since for the name of Christ he there happily received martyrdom from the treacherous pagans. There our leaders held a council to choose a bishop who should have charge of this place and erect a church. They gave tithes to him and enriched him with gold and silver, and with horses and other animals; that he might live the more devoutly and honorably with those who were with him. He remained there with joy.

Priest:

Meanwhile the Count [Raymond IV of Toulouse] and the other princes inquired of the inhabitants of that region how the march to Jerusalem might be better and more easily made. For there are the mountains of Lebanon, in which almost sixty thousand Christian men dwell. The Christians who are near the city of Tyre (now commonly called Sur, whence they are called Surians) have possessed that land and mountains for a long time. But when the Saracens and Turks arose through the judgment of God, those Surians were in such great oppression for four hundred and more years that many of them were forced to abandon their fatherland and the Christian law. If, however, any of them through the grace of God refused, they were compelled to give up their beautiful children to be circumcised, or converted to Mohammedanism; or they were snatched from the lap of their mothers, after the father had been killed and the mother mocked. Forsooth, that race of men were inflamed to such malice that they overturned the churches of God and His saints, or destroyed the images; and they tore out the eyes of those images which, for lack of time, they could not destroy, and shot them with arrows; all the altars, too, they undermined. Moreover, they made mosques of the great churches. But if any of those distressed Christians wished to have an image of God or any saint at his home, he either redeemed it month by month, or year by year, or it was thrown down into the dirt and broken before his eyes. In addition, too harsh to relate, they placed youths in brothels, and, to do yet more vilely, exchanged their sisters for wine. And their mothers dared not weep openly at these or other sorrows. . . .

When those Surians who, as we said above, come to the Count, were asked about the better route, they replied: "The way through Damascus is level and full of victuals; but you will not find water for two days. The other way through the mountains of Lebanon is safe enough and well watered, but it is very hard for the pack animals and camels. There is another way along the sea, where there are so many and such narrow passes that if fifty or a hundred Saracens want to hold them, they can do so against all mankind. And yet it is contained in the Gospel of St. Peter, which we have, that if you are the people who are to take Jerusalem, you will pass along the sea-coast, though because of the difficulty it seems impossible to us. Moreover, there is written in that Gospel among us not only what you have done, but also what you ought to do about this march and many other things."

While some were urging in this and other ways, and others were contradicting, William Hugo of Monteil returned with the Cross [belonging to the bishop of Le Puy]. Moreover, when the friends of the Count likewise beheld this Cross, they became so eager for the march that, except for the counsel of the Count and the other princes, the servants of the Count would have burned their huts and been the first to leave the siege of Archas. . . .

At this time, St. Andrew appeared to Peter Desiderius, of whom we have made mention above, and said to him, "Go and speak to the Count, saying: 'Do not molest thyself or others, for unless Jerusalem shall first have been taken, thou shalt have no help. Do not trouble thyself about the unfinished siege of Archas; let it not weigh upon thee that this city, or others which are on the journey, are not taken at present, because a fight will soon come upon thee in which these and many other cities shall be captured. Furthermore, do not trouble thyself or thy men, but distribute freely in His name whatever God shall grant to thee, and be a companion and loyal friend to thy vassals. If thou shalt do this, God will grant thee Jerusalem and Alexandria and Babylon.'"

For once, when we wanted to set out from Antioch, that priest came to me, Raymond, and said to me that a certain person had appeared to him in a vision who said to him, "Go into the church of St. Leontius, and thou wilt find there the relics of four saints; take them with thee and carry them to Jerusalem." And he showed him in that vision the relics and locations of the relics, and he taught him the names of the saints. When that priest had awakened, not fully believing in his vision, he began to urge God with prayers and entreaties to make known to him a second time if this vision was from Him. Several days later the same saint stood before him in a vision and threatened him much because he had neglected the command of God, and [said that] unless he had taken those relics away by the fifth day of the week, it would be a great hurt to him and his lord, Count Ysoard. . . .

When it became morning, we went with the priest to the places where the relics were kept, and we found everything just as it had been foretold. Moreover, these are the names of the saints: Cyprian, Omechios, Leontius, John Chrysostom. And furthermore, at the place where the relics were kept we found a little chest filled with relics. When he asked a priest about these, of which saint they were the relics, he replied that he did not know.

But the priest wished to take them up and put them with the collection of other relics. To him, I, Raymond, said angrily in the presence of all who were there, "If this saint wishes to come with us to Jerusalem, let him make known his name and wish; otherwise let him remain here. Why should we weight ourselves with unknown bones and carry them along?" Therefore on that day those relics were left behind. But when the priest had collected the other relics and had rolled them up in cloths and a covering, on the night which followed, as he lay awake, there appeared to him a youth of about fifteen years, exceedingly beautiful, who said to him, "Why didst thou this day not take any relics with the rest?"

The priest replied to this, "Who art thou?"

"Dost thou not know who is the standard bearer of this army?" he replied.

The priest answered, "I do not, Sire."

When the priest had made the same reply to the same question a second time, the youth threatened the priest terribly, saying, "Tell me the truth."

And then the priest said, "Sire, it is said of St. George that he is the standard-bearer of this army."

He replied, "Thou hast said well. I am he. Take, therefore, my relics and put them with the others."

But before we go on to the remainder, we ought not to pass over these men who did not hesitate, for love of the most holy expedition, to sail through the unknown and very long water of the Mediterranean and the Ocean. For when the Angles [the English] heard the name of the Lord's vengeance against those who unworthily occupied the birthplace of Jesus Christ and His apostles, they embarked upon the Anglican Sea. Rounding Spain, crossing the ocean, and thus ploughing through the Mediterranean Sea, with great labor they gained the port of Antioch before our army came thither by land. Their ships, as well as those of the Genoese, were of advantage to us at this time, for during the siege we had trade with the island of Cyprus and the remaining islands because of these ships and the security which they offered. Forsooth, these ships passed daily over the sea, and for this reason the ships of the Greeks were safe, since the Saracens feared to encounter them. But when the Angles saw the army setting forth for Jerusalem, and that the strength of their own ships was impaired by the long wait (for though they had thirty ships in the beginning, they now had scarcely nine or ten), some abandoned their ships and exposed them; others, however, burned theirs and hastened with us on the journey.

When our princes were entangled in delay before Tripoli, the Lord sent such great desire of going to Jerusalem that no one could there restrain himself, or another, but, setting out at evening against the decrees of the princes and the custom of our army, we walked along all that night and came on the following day to Beirut. After this, when the narrow passages which are called The Twisted Mouth had been suddenly seized in advance, we came in a few days and without baggage to Acre. The King of Acre, however, afraid that we would besiege his city, and hoping that we would withdraw, took oath to the Count that if we captured Jerusalem, or were in the region of Judaea for twenty days, and the King of Babylon did not meet us in battle, or if we were able to overcome that king, he would surrender himself and in the meanwhile he would be our friend.

Setting forth from Acre one day at vespers, we pitched camp by the swamps which are near Caesarea. And while, according to custom, some ran here and there below the camp, as need demanded, and while others were inquiring from acquaintances where their companions were lodged, a dove, mortally wounded by a hawk, fell down in the midst of those running about. When the Bishop of Agde took it up, he found a letter which it was carrying. And the sense of the letter was as follows:

The King of Acre to the Duke of Caesarea.

A canine breed, a foolish and troublesome host without order, passed me. As you love your law, try by yourselves and through others to hurt them; this you can easily do, if you wish. Send this likewise to other cities and fortresses.

In the morning, when we were commanding the army to rest, the letter was shown to the princes and to all the people, and (it was manifest) how God had been kind to us, so that not even the birds could cross through the air to harm us, and that He likewise disclosed to us the secrets of our foes. Wherefore, we rendered praise and thanks to Almighty God. And thence setting forth securely and willingly, we went forward, frequently in the front rank of the army, and also at the end.

But when the Saracens who lived in Ramlah heard that we had crossed the river near by, they left their fortifications and arms and much grain in the fields, and crops, which we gathered. And when we came to it on the next day, we found out that God was truly fighting for us. So we offered vows to St. George because he had confessed himself our guide. The leaders and all the people agreed that we should there choose a bishop, since that was the first church which we found in the land of Israel, and, also, in order that St. George might entreat God in our behalf, and might lead us faithfully through the land in which He was worshipped. Moreover, Ramlah is about fifteen miles from Jerusalem. Therefore, we there held a conference.

Some said, "Let us not go to Jerusalem at present, but towards Egypt; we will obtain not only Jerusalem, but likewise Alexandria and Babylon and very many kingdoms. If we go to Jerusalem and, failing of sufficient water, give up the siege, we will accomplish neither this nor the other afterwards."

But others said in opposition, "There are scarcely fifteen hundred knights in the army, and the number of armed men is not great; and yet it is now suggested that we go to very distant and unknown regions, where we will be able neither to get help from our people nor to place a garrison in a city, if we capture one; nor, even if it should be necessary, would we be able to return thence. But none of this; let us hold to our way, and let God provide for His servants for the siege, for thirst, for hunger, and for other things."

Accordingly, after leaving a garrison in the fortress of Ramlah with the new Bishop, we loaded our camels and oxen, and then all our baggage animals and horses, and turned our march to Jerusalem. However, the word which Peter Bartholomew [a peasant soldier who, guided by St. Andrew, had discovered the spear Crusaders believed pierced Jesus' side] had commanded us—that we should not approach Jerusalem except with bared feet—we forgot and held in low regard, each one, from ambition to occupy castles and villas, wishing to go ahead of the next. For it was a custom among us that if any one came to a castle or villa first and placed his standard there with a guard, it was touched by no one else afterward. Therefore, because of this ambition they arose at midnight and, without waiting for companions, gained all those mountains and villas which are in the meadows of the Jordan. A few, however, to whom the command of God was more precious, walked with naked feet and sighed heavily for the contempt of the Divine word; and yet no one recalled a companion or friend from that ambitious chase. Moreover, when by such arrogant procedure we had come near Jerusalem, the people of Jerusalem came forth to meet the first of our men and wounded the horses severely. Of those men three or four fell on that day, and many were wounded.

THE SIEGE (June 7-July 15, 1099)

Knight:

Rejoicing and exulting, we reached the city of Jerusalem on Tuesday, on the third day of the week, the eighth day before the Ides of June, and began to besiege the city in a marvelous manner. Robert the Norman besieged it from the north side, near the church of St. Stephen, which was built on the very spot where that first martyr won eternal happiness by being stoned in Christ's name.

Next to the Norman Count was Robert, Count of Flanders, while Duke Godfrey and Tancred besieged the city from the west. The Count of St. Gilles located himself on the south, on Mount Zion, near the church of St. Mary, the mother of the Lord, where Christ once supped with His disciples.

On the third day some of our men, namely Raymond Piletus and Raymond of Turenne, went out on a foraging expedition. They encountered a force of two hundred Arabs, and the soldiers of Christ fought these unbelievers. With the Lord's help, they fought so valiantly that they killed many of the enemy and captured thirty horses. On the second day of the following week, we made an attack on the city, and so bravely did we fight that, if scaling ladders had been ready for our use, the city most certainly would have fallen into our hands. As it was, we pulled down the outer wall and placed one ladder against the main wall, upon which some of our men ascended and fought hand to hand with swords and lances against the Saracen defenders of the city. Many of our men were killed in this attack, but more of the enemy.

For a period of ten days during the siege we were not able to buy bread at any price, until a messenger came announcing the arrival of our ships. We also suffered greatly for thirst. In fear and terror we were forced to water our horses and other animals at a distance of six miles from camp. The Pool of Siloam, at the foot of Mount Zion, sustained us, but, nevertheless, water was sold among us very dearly.

When the messenger arrived from our ships, the leaders took counsel and decided that armed men should be sent to guard the ships and sailors at the port of Joppa. So one hundred men from the army of Raymond, Count of St. Gilles, under Raymond Piletus, Achard of Montemerle, and William of Sabran, left camp in the early dawn and started confidently toward Joppa. Thirty of these knights separated themselves from the rest of the band and met seven hundred Arabs, Turks, and Saracens from the army of the Emir. The soldiers of Christ boldly attacked the enemy, whose force was so superior to ours that they soon surrounded us. Achard and some of the poor footmen were killed. While this band was completely surrounded, and all believed that they would be killed, a messenger was sent to Raymond Piletus, who said, "Why do you stand here with these knights? Lo, all of our men are in serious danger from the Arabs,

Turks, and Saracens, and may all be dead by this time. Hasten to them and aid them." As soon as they heard this, our men hastened to the scene of battle. When the pagans saw the rest of our knights approaching, they formed them-selves into two lines. Our men rushed upon the unbelievers shouting the name of Christ, each determined to bring down his man. The enemy soon realized that they would not be able to withstand the bravery of the Franks, so they turned their backs and fled in terror. Our men, pursuing them a distance of four miles, killed many of them, but kept one alive to give them information. One hundred and three horses were captured.

During this siege we were so distressed with thirst that we sewed up skins of oxen and buffalos and in these carried water for a distance of six miles. Between fetid water and barley bread we were daily in great want and suffering. Moreover, the Saracens hid in ambush at the watering places and either killed and wounded our animals or drove them away to caverns in the hills.

Priest:

Duke Godfrey and the Count of Flanders and the Count of Normandy besieged the city from the north side, that is from the church of St. Stephen, located in the center of the city, southward to the angular tower next to the tower of David. Count Raymond and his army, however, settled down on the West and besieged Jerusalem from the camp of the Duke to the foot of Mount Zion. But since his men could not come close to besiege the wall because of a gully which intervened, the Count wished to move his camp and change his position. One day, while he was reconnoitering, he came to Mount Zion and saw the church which is located on the Mount. When he heard of the miracles that God had performed there, he said to his leaders and companions, "If we neglect to take this sacred offering, which the Lord has so graciously offered us, and the Saracens there occupy this place, what will become of us? What if through hatred of us they should destroy and pollute these sacred things? Who knows that God may not be giving us this opportunity to test our regard for Him? I know this one thing for certain: unless we carefully protect this sacred spot, the Lord will not give us the others within the city." And so Count

Raymond, against the wishes of the leaders of his army, ordered his tents to be moved to that spot. As a result, he incurred such great hatred from his men that they were neither willing to encamp with him nor to do guard duty during the night; each stayed where he had first pitched his tent, with the exception of a few who accompanied the Count. However, by great rewards the Count daily induced knights and footmen to guard his camp. There are in that church these sacred treasures—the tombs of the kings, David and Solomon, as well as that of the first martyr, St. Stephen. There the Blessed Mary departed from this world; the Lord supped there and, after rising from the dead, appeared there to His disciples and to Thomas. On this spot, also, the disciples were filled with the Holy Spirit.

Thereupon, when the siege had been set, it happened one day that some of the leaders of the army met a hermit on the Mount of Olives, who said to them, "If you will attack the city tomorrow till the ninth hour, the Lord will deliver it into your hands." They replied, "But we do not have the necessary machinery for storming the walls." The hermit replied: "God is all powerful. If He wills, He will storm the walls even with one ladder. The Lord aids those who labor for the Truth." So, with such machinery as could be constructed during the night, an attack was made on the city in the early morning, and it lasted till the third hour. The Saracens were compelled to retreat behind the inner walls, for the outer wall was broken down by our men, some of whom even climbed to the top of the inner walls. Now when the city was about to be captured, in the confusion of desire and fear the attack was interrupted, and we then lost many men. On the next day no attack was attempted.

After this, the whole army scattered throughout the surrounding country to collect provisions, and nothing was even said of the necessity of preparing the machines that were needed to capture the city. Each man was serving his mouth and stomach; what was worse, they did not even ask the Lord to free them from such great and manifold evils, and they were afflicted even unto death. Just before our arrival, the Saracens had filled up the springs, destroyed the cisterns, and dammed up the brooks from the springs. And the Lord Himself had turned rivers into wilderness and water-springs into thirsty ground for the wickedness of them that dwell therein. Therefore water was obtained with great difficulty.

There is a fountain at the foot of Mount Zion, which is called the Pool of Siloam. Indeed, it is a large spring, but the water flows forth only once in three days, and the natives say that formerly it emptied itself only on Saturdays; the rest of the week it remained stagnant. We do not know how to explain this, except that the Lord willed it to be so. But when, as we have said, the water did flow forth on the third day, it was consumed with such great crowding and haste that the men pushed one another into it, and many baggage animals and cattle perished in it.

And so when the pool was filled with the crowd and with the bodies of dead animals, the stronger, even at the price of death, forced their way to the very opening in the rocks through which the water flowed, while the weak got only the water which had already been contaminated. Many sick people fell down by the fountain, with tongues so parched that they were unable to utter a word; with open mouths they stretched forth their hands toward those who had water. In the field were many horses, mules, cattle, and sheep, most of the animals without strength enough to move. And when they had become parched and died because of extreme thirst, they rotted where they had long stood, and there was a most sickening stench throughout the camp. Because of such affliction it was necessary to fetch water a distance of two or three leagues, also to drive the cattle to distant watering places.

When the Saracens noticed that our people were going unarmed to the watering places through the dangerous passes in the hills, they lay in wait for them in ambush. They killed many of them and drove away the flocks and herds. The situation was so bad that when any one brought foul water to camp in vessels, he was able to get any price that he cared to ask, and if any one wished to get clear water, for five or six *nummi* [coins] he could not obtain enough to satisfy his thirst for a single day. Wine, moreover, was never, or very rarely, even mentioned. In addition, the heat, the dust, and the wind increased their thirst, as though this was not bad enough in itself. But why say so much about these troubles? None, or few, were mindful of the Lord, or of such work as was needed to capture the city; nor did they take heed to beseech the Lord's favor. And thus we did not recognize God in the midst of our affliction, nor did He show favor to the ungrateful.

Meanwhile, messengers came to camp, announcing that our ships had arrived at Joppa and that the sailors demanded that a guard be sent to hold the tower of Joppa and to give them protection at the port; for the town of Joppa had been destroyed except the castle, and that was nearly in ruins, with the exception of one tower. However, there is a harbor there, and it is the one nearest to Jerusalem, being about one day's journey distant. All of our people rejoiced when they heard the news of the ships, and they sent out Count Galdemar, surnamed Carpinellus, accompanied by twenty knights and about fifty footmen. Later, they sent Raymond Piletus with fifty knights and William of Sabran with his followers.

As Galdemar and his contingent approached the plains that are on this side of Ramlah, they encountered a force of four hundred chosen Arabs and about two hundred Turks. Galdemar, because of the small number of his men, arranged his knights and bowmen in the front ranks and, trusting in the Lord, advanced upon the enemy without hesitation. The enemy, however, thought that they would be able to crush this band, and, rushing upon them and shooting arrows, they encircled them. Three or four of Galdemar's knights were killed, including Achard of Montemerle, a noble youth and renowned knight; others were wounded, and all our bowmen fell. However, many of the enemy were also killed. Nevertheless, the attack of the enemy did not slacken on account of all this, nor did the courage of our knights, nay God's knights, falter; though oppressed by wounds and death itself, they stood up to their enemies all the more fiercely, the more they suffered from them. But when our leaders, rather from weariness than from fear, were about to withdraw, a cloud of dust was seen approaching. Raymond Piletus was rushing headlong into the fight with his men. Moreover, his men raised so much dust that the enemy thought there were very many knights with him. Thus, by the grace of God, our men were delivered. The enemy scattered and fled, about two hundred of them were killed, and much plunder was taken. It is the custom of this people, when they flee and are hard pressed by the enemy, first to throw away their arms, then their clothes, and lastly their saddle bags. Thus it happened in this fight that our few knights continued killing the enemy until they were worn out, and they kept the spoils obtained from the rest, even of those whom they did not kill.

After the pursuit was over our men assembled, divided the spoils, and then marched to Joppa. The sailors received them with great joy and felt so secure after their arrival that they forgot their ship and neglected to place watches on the sea, but entertained the crusaders with a feast of bread, wine, and fish from their ships. The sailors, careless of their security, failed to post lookouts for the night, and in the darkness they were suddenly surrounded by enemies from the sea. When dawn came, they realized that the enemy was too strong to be resisted, and they abandoned their ships, carrying only the spoils. Thus our knights returned to Jerusalem after winning one battle and losing another. However, one of our ships which had gone on a plundering expedition was not captured. It was returning to port with the greatest plunder when it saw the rest of our ships surrounded by so great a fleet of the enemy. By the use of oars and sail it made its escape to Laodicaea and told our friends and companions at that port what had been happening at Jerusalem. We knew that we had deserved this misfortune, for we had refused to place faith in the words sent to us by the Lord. Despairing of God's mercy, the men went to the plain of the river Jordan, collected palms, and were baptized in its waters. They did so chiefly with the intention of abandoning the siege, having seen Jerusalem, and before going to Joppa, thence to return home by whatever means they could. But the Lord looked after the ships for His unfaithful.

About this time a public assembly was held, for the leaders of the army were quarreling with each other. There was dissatisfaction because Tancred had occupied Bethlehem and had placed his standard over the church of the Nativity, as though it was an ordinary house. An effort was also made to elect one of the princes king to have custody of the city, lest what had been achieved in common should be destroyed in common for want of anyone to take care of the city, if God should give it to us. The bishops and clergy replied (to this suggestion), "You ought not to choose a king where the Lord suffered and was crowned. For if a David, degenerate in faith and virtue, should say in his heart, 'I sit upon the throne of David and hold his kingdom,' the Lord would probably destroy him and be angry with place and people. Besides, the prophet proclaims, saying, 'When the Holy of Holies shall come, unction shall cease, because it will be manifest to all peoples that He has come.' But there should be an advocate to guard the city and divide the tributes and rents of the region among the guardians of the city." For this and many other reasons the election was stopped and put off until the eighth day after the capture of Jerusalem. . . .

The Bishop [Adhemar] appeared before Peter Desiderius, saying, "Speak to the princes and all the people, and say to them: 'You who have come from distant lands to worship God and the Lord of hosts, purge yourselves of your uncleanliness, and let each one turn from his evil ways. Then with bare feet march around Jerusalem invoking God, and you must also fast. If you do this and then make a great attack on the city on the ninth day, it will be captured. If you do not, all the evils that you have suffered will be multiplied by the Lord.'"

These words were pleasing to both princes and people, and it was publicly commended that on the next Friday the clergy should lead the procession with crosses and relics of the saints, while the knights and all able-bodied men, with trumpets, standards, and arms, should follow them barefooted. All this we did according to the commands of God and the princes. When we reached the spot on the Mount of Olives whence the Lord had ascended into heaven after the resurrection, the following exhortation was made to the people: "Now that we are on the very spot from which the Lord made His ascension and we can do nothing more to purify ourselves, let each one of us forgive his brother whom he has injured, that the Lord may forgive us."

Although we have passed over many matters, this one we ought to record. While we marched around the city in procession, the Saracens and Turks made the circuit on the walls, ridiculing us in many ways. They placed many crosses on the walls in yokes and mocked them with blows and insulting deeds. We, in turn, hoping to obtain the aid of God in storming the city by means of these signs, pressed the work of the siege day and night.

FINAL ASSAULT AND CAPTURE (July 15, 1099)

Knight:

At length, our leaders decided to beleaguer the city with siege machines, so that we might enter and worship the Saviour at the Holy Sepulchre. They constructed wooden towers and many other siege machines. Duke Godfrey made a wooden tower and other siege devices, and Count Raymond did the same, although it was necessary to bring wood from a considerable distance. However, when the Saracens saw our men engaged in this work, they greatly strengthened the fortifications of the city and increased the height of the turrets at night. On a certain Sabbath night, the leaders, after having decided which parts of the wall were weakest, dragged the tower and the machines to the eastern side of the city. Moreover, we set up the tower at earliest dawn and equipped and covered it on the first, second, and third days of the week. The Count of St. Gilles erected his tower on the plain to the south of the city.

While all this was going on, our water supply was so limited that no one could buy enough water for one denarius to satisfy or quench his thirst. Both day and night, on the fourth and fifth days of the week, we made a determined attack on the city from all sides. However, before we made this assault on the city, the bishops and priests persuaded all, by exhorting and preaching, to honor the Lord by marching around Jerusalem in a great procession, and to prepare for battle by prayer, fasting, and almsgiving. Early on the sixth day of the week we again attacked the city on all sides, but as the assault was unsuccessful, we were all astounded and fearful. However, when the hour approached on which our Lord Jesus Christ deigned to suffer on the Cross for us, our knights began to fight bravely in one of the towers—namely, the party with Duke Godfrey and his brother, Count Eustace. One of our knights, named Lethold, clambered up the wall of the city, and no sooner had he ascended than the defenders fled from the walls and through the city. Our men followed, killing and slaying even to the Temple of Solomon, where the slaughter was so great that our men waded in blood up to their ankles. Count Raymond brought his army and his tower up near the from the south, but between the tower and the wall there was a very deep ditch. Then our men took counsel how they might fill it, and had it proclaimed by heralds that anyone who carried three stones to the ditch would receive one denarius. The work of filling it required three days and three nights, and when at length the ditch was filled, they moved the tower up to the wall, but the men defending this portion of the wall fought desperately with stones and fire. When the Count heard that the Franks were already in the city, he said to his men, "Why do you loiter? Lo, the Franks are even now within the city." The Emir who commanded the Tower of St. David surrendered to the Count and opened that gate at which the pilgrims had always been accustomed to pay tribute. But this time the pilgrims entered the city, pursuing and killing the Saracens up to the Temple of Solomon, where the enemy gathered in force. The battle raged throughout the day, so that the Temple was covered with their blood. When the pagans had been overcome, our men seized great numbers, both men and women, either killing them or keeping them captive, as they wished. On the roof of the Temple a great number of pagans of both sexes had assembled, and these were taken under the protection of Tancred and Gaston of Beert. Afterward, the army scattered throughout the city and took possession of the gold and silver, the horses and mules, and the houses filled with goods of all kinds.

Later, all of our people went to the Sepulchre of our Lord, rejoicing and weeping for joy, and they rendered up the offering that they owed. In the morning, some of our men cautiously ascended to the roof of the Temple and attacked the Saracens, both men and women, beheading them with naked swords; the remainder sought death by jumping down into the temple. When Tancred heard of this, he was filled with anger.

Priest:

The Duke and the Counts of Normandy and Flanders placed Gaston of Beert in charge of the workmen who constructed machines. They built mantlets [protective screens] and towers with which to attack the wall. The direction of this work was assigned to Gaston by the princes because he was a most noble lord, respected by all for his skill and reputation. He very cleverly hastened matters by dividing the work. The princes busied themselves with obtaining and bringing the material, while Gaston supervised the work of construction. Likewise, Count Raymond made William Ricau superintendent of the work on Mount Zion and placed the Bishop of Albara in charge of the Saracens and others who brought in the timber. The Count's men had taken many Saracen castles and villages and forced the Saracens to work as though they were their serfs. Thus, for the construction of machines at Jerusalem fifty or sixty men carried on their shoulders a great beam that could not have been dragged by four pair of oxen. What more shall I say? All worked with a singleness of purpose, no one was slothful and no hands were idle. All worked without wages except the artisans, who were paid from a collection taken from the people. However, Count Raymond paid his workmen from his own treasury. . . .

Meanwhile, the Saracens in the city noting the great number of machines that we had constructed strengthened the weaker parts of the wall, so that it seemed that they could be taken only by the most desperate efforts. Because the Saracens had made so many and such strong fortifications to oppose our machines, the Duke, the Count of Flanders, and the Count of Normandy spent the night before the day set for the attack moving their machines, mantlets and platforms to that side of the city which is between the church of St. Stephen and the valley of Josaphat. You who read this must not think that this was a light undertaking, for the machines were carried in parts almost a mile to the place where they were to be set up. When morning came and the Saracens saw that all the machinery and tents had been moved during the night, they were amazed. Not only the Saracens were astonished, but our people as well, for they recognized that the hand of the Lord was with us. The change was made because the new point chosen for attack was more level, and thus suitable for moving the machines up to the walls, which cannot be done unless the ground is level; and also because that part of the city seemed to be weaker, having remained unfortified, as it was some distance from our camp. This part of the city is on the north.

Count Raymond and his men worked equally hard on Mount Zion but they had much assistance from William Embriaco and the Genoese sailors, who, although they had lost their ships at Joppa, as we have already related, had been able, nevertheless, to save ropes, mallets, spikes, axes, and hatchets, which were very necessary to us. But why delay the story? The appointed day moved and the attack began. However, I want to say this first, that, according to our estimate and that of many others, there were sixty thousand fighting men within the city, not counting the women and those unable to bear arms, and there were not many of these. At the most we did not have more than twelve thousand able to bear arms, for there were many poor people and many sick. There were twelve or thirteen hundred knights in our army, as I reckon it, not more. . . .

Our men began to undermine the towers and walls. From every side stones were hurled from the *tormenti* and the *petrariae*, and so many arrows that they fell like hail. The servants of God bore this patiently, sustained by the premises of their faith, whether they should be killed or should presently prevail over their enemies. The battle showed no indication of victory, but when the machines were drawn nearer to the walls, they hurled not only stones and arrows, but also burning wood and straw. The wood was dipped in pitch, wax, and sulphur; then straw and tow were fastened on by an iron band, and, when lighted, these firebrands were shot from the machines. (They were) all bound together by an iron band, I say, so that wherever they fell, the whole mass held together and continued to burn. Such missiles, burning as they shot upward, could not be resisted by swords or by high walls; it was not even possible for the defenders to find safety down behind the walls. Thus the fight continued from the rising to the setting sun in such splendid fashion that it is difficult to believe anything more glorious was ever done. Then we called on almighty God, our Leader and Guide, confident in His mercy. Night brought fear to both sides. The Saracens feared that we would take the city during the night or on the next day, for the outer works were broken through and the ditch was filled, so that it was possible to make an entrance through the wan very quickly. On our part, we feared only that the Saracens would set fire to the machines that were moved close to the walls, and thus improve their situation. So on both sides it was a night of watchfulness, labor, and sleepless caution: on one side, most certain hope, on the other doubtful fear. We gladly labored to capture the city for the glory of God, they less willingly strove to resist our efforts for the sake of the laws of Muhammed. It is hard to believe how great were the efforts made on both sides during the night.

When the morning came, our men eagerly rushed to the walls and dragged the machines forward, but the Saracens had constructed so many machines that for each one of ours they now had nine or ten. Thus they greatly interfered with our efforts. This was the ninth day, on which the priest had said that we would capture the city. But why do I delay so long? Our machines were now shaken apart by the blows of many stones, and our men lagged because they were very weary. However, there remained the mercy of the Lord which is never overcome nor conquered, but is always a source of support in times of adversity. One incident must not be omitted. Two women tried to bewitch one of the hurling machines, but a stone struck and crushed them, as well as three slaves, so that their lives were extinguished and the evil incantations averted.

By noon our men were greatly discouraged. They were weary and at the end of their resources. There were still many of the enemy opposing each one of our men; the walls were very high and strong, and the great resources and skill that the enemy exhibited in repairing their defenses seemed too great for us to overcome. But, while we hesitated, irresolute, and the enemy exulted in our discomfiture, the healing mercy of God inspired us and turned our sorrow into joy, for the Lord did not forsake us. While a council was being held to decide whether or not our machines should be withdrawn, for some were burned and the rest badly shaken to pieces, a knight on the Mount of Olives began to wave his shield to those who were with the Count and others, signalling them to advance. Who this knight was we have been unable to find out. At this signal our men began to take heart, and some began to batter down the wall, while others began to ascend by means of scaling ladders and ropes. Our archers shot burning firebrands, and in this way checked the attack that the Saracens were making upon the wooden towers of the Duke and the two Counts. These firebrands, moreover, were wrapped in cotton. This shower of fire drove the defenders from the walls. Then the Count quickly released the long drawbridge which had protected the side of the wooden tower next to the wall, and it swung down from the top, being fastened to the middle of the tower, making a bridge over which the men began to enter Jerusalem bravely and fearlessly. Among those who entered first were Tancred and the Duke of Lorraine, and the amount of blood that they shed on that day is incredible. All ascended after them, and the Saracens now began to suffer.

Strange to relate, however, at this very time when the city was practically captured by the Franks, the Saracens were still fighting on the other side, where the Count was attacking the wall as though the city should never be captured. But now that our men had possession of the walls and towers, wonderful sights were to be seen. Some of our men (and this was more merciful) cut off the heads of their enemies; others shot them with arrows, so that they fell from the towers; others tortured them longer by casting them into the flames. Piles of heads, hands, and feet were to be seen in the streets of the city. It was necessary to pick one's way over the bodies of men and horses. But these were small matters compared to what happened at the Temple of Solomon, a place where religious services are ordinarily chanted. What happened there? If I tell the truth, it will exceed your powers of belief. So let it suffice to say this much, at least, that in the Temple and porch of Solomon, men rode in blood up to their knees and bridle reins. Indeed, it was a just and splendid judgment of God that this place should be filled with the blood of the unbelievers, since it had suffered so long from their blasphemies. The city was filled with corpses and blood. Some of the enemy took refuge in the Tower of David, and, petitioning Count Raymond for protection, surrendered the Tower into his hands.

Now that the city was taken, it was well worth all our previous labors and hardships to see the devotion of the pilgrims at the Holy Sepulchre. How they rejoiced and exulted and sang a new song to the Lord! For their hearts offered prayers of praise to God, victorious and triumphant, which cannot be told in words. A new day, new joy, new and perpetual gladness, the consummation of our labor and devotion, drew forth from all new words and new songs. This day, I say, will be famous in all future ages, for it turned our labors and sorrows into joy and exultation; this day, I say, marks the justification of all Christianity, the humiliation of paganism, and the renewal of our faith. "This is the day which the Lord hath made, let us rejoice and be glad in it. . . ."

Then our leaders in council . . . ordered all the Saracen dead to be cast outside because of the great stench, since the whole city was filled with their corpses; and so the living Saracens dragged the dead before the exits of the gates and arranged them in heaps, as if they were houses. No one ever saw or heard of such slaughter of pagan people, for funeral pyres were formed from them like pyramids, and no one knows their number except God alone.

Usamah ibn-Murshid

"Encounters with Crusaders in Syria"

ca. 1150

AN ARAB-SYRIAN GENTLEMAN BATTLES AGAINST FRANKS AND MOSLEMS

Usamah's First Experience in Warfare Against the Franks

It happened that Najm-al-Din Ilghazi ibn-Urtuq (may Allah's mercy rest upon his soul!) defeated the Franks at al-Balat, on Friday, the fifth of Jumada I, in the year 513 [A.D. 1119], and annihilated them. He killed Roger, the lord of Antioch, and all his cavalry. Thereupon my paternal uncle, Iizz al-Din abu-al-Asakir Sultan (may Allah's mercy rest upon his soul!), set out to join Najm-al-Din, while my father (may Allah's mercy rest upon his soul!) remained behind in the Castle of Shayzar. My uncle had instructed my father to send me against Afamiyah at the head of the men who were with me in Shayzar, and to call out the people, together with the Arabs, for the pillage of the crops of Afamiyah. A great number of the Arabs had recently joined us.

A few days after the departure of my uncle, the public announcer called us to arms, and I started at the head of a small band, hardly amounting to twenty horsemen, with full conviction that Afamiyah had no cavalry in it. Accompanying me was a great body of pillagers and Arabs. As soon as we arrived in the Valley of Bohemand, and while the pillagers and the Arabs were scattered all over the planted fields, a large army of the Franks set out against us. They had been reinforced that very night by sixty horsemen and sixty footmen. They repulsed us from the valley, and we retreated before them until we joined those of our number who were already in the fields, pillaging them. Seeing us, the

Franks raised a violent uproar. Death seemed an easy thing to me in comparison with the loss of that crowd in my charge. So I turned against a horsemen in their vanguard, who had taken off his coat of mail in order to be light enough to pass before us, and thrust my lance into his chest. He instantly flew off his saddle, dead. I then faced their horsemen as they followed, and they all took to fight. Though a tyro in warfare, and having never before that day taken part in a battle, I, with a mare under me as swift as a bird, went on, now pursuing them and plying them with my lance, now taking cover from them.

In the rear guard of the Franks was a cavalier on a black horse, large as a camel, wearing a coat of mail and the full armor of war. I was afraid of this horseman, lest he should be drawing me further ahead in order to get an opportunity to turn back and attack me. All of a sudden I saw him spur his horse, and as the horse began to wave its tail, I knew that it was already exhausted. So I rushed on the horseman and smote him with my lance, which pierced him through and projected about a cubit in front of him. The lightness of my body, the force of the thrust and the swiftness of my horse made me lose my seat on the saddle. Moving backward a little, I pulled out my lance, fully assuming that I had killed him. I then assembled my comrades and found them all safe and sound.

In my company was a young mameluke holding the halter of an extra black mare which belonged to me. Under him was a good female riding mule with a saddle the tassels of which were silver. The mameluke dismounted from the mule, left it by itself and jumped on the back of the mare, which flew with him towards Shayzar.

On my return to my comrades, who had caught the mule, I asked about that boy. They said, "He's gone." I immediately knew that he would reach Shayzar and cause anxiety to my father (may Allah's mercy rest upon his soul!). I therefore called one of the soldiers and said to him, "Hasten to Shayzar and inform my father of what has happened."

In the meantime the boy had arrived and my father had him brought before him and asked, "What things have ye met?" The boy said, "O my lord, the Franks have set out against us with a thousand men, and I doubt if any of our men would escape with the exception of my master." "But how would thy master," asked my father, "of all the men, escape?" "Well," replied the slave, "I have seen him covered with full armor riding on a green mare." Here he was interrupted in his conversation by the arrival of the horseman whom I had sent. The horseman related to my father the facts. I arrived right after him, and my father (may Allah's mercy rest upon his soul!) questioned me. So I said to him, "O my lord, that was the first fight in which I took part. But the moment I saw that the Franks were in contact with our men, then I felt that death would be an easy matter for me. So I turned back to the Franks, either to be killed or to protect that crowd."

My father (may Allah's mercy rest upon his soul!) quoted the following verse as illustrating my case: "The coward among men flees precipitately before danger facing his own mother. But the brave one protects even him whom it is not his duty to shelter."

In Flight Before the Franks of Antioch

The army of Antioch made an incursion on us. Our comrades met their vanguard and were retreating before them. I posted myself on their route, expecting their arrival and hoping thereby to be able to get an opportunity to attack the enemy. Our comrades began to pass by me in defeat. Among those who thus passed was Mahmud ibn-Jum'ah. I said, "Halt, O Mahmud!" He stopped for an instant; then he spurred his horse and left me. By that time the vanguard of the Frankish horsemen had reached me, so I retired before them, turning back my lance in their direction and my eyes towards them lest some one of their horse should prove too quick for me and pierce me with his lance. In front of me were some of our companions, and we were surrounded by gardens with walls as high as a sitting man. My mare hit with its breast one of our companions, so I turned its head to my left and applied the spurs to its sides, whereupon it leaped over the wall. I so regulated my position until I stood on a level with the Franks. The wall only separated us. One of their horsemen hastened to me, displaying his colors in a green and yellow silk tunic, under which I thought was no coat of mail. I therefore let him alone until he passed me. Then I applied the spurs to my mare, which leaped over the wall, and I smote him with the lance. He bent sideways so much that his head reached his stirrup, his shield and lance fell off his hand, and his helmet off his head. By that time we had reached our infantry. He then resumed his position, erect in the saddle. Having had linked mail under his tunic, my lance did not wound him. His companions caught up with him, all returned together, and the footman recovered his shield, lance and helmet.

When the battle was over and the Franks withdrew, Jum'ah (may Allah's mercy rest upon his soul!) came to me apologizing on behalf of his son, Mahmud, and said, "This dog fled away while in thy company!" I replied, "What of it?" He said, "He flees from thee and what of it?" "By thy life, O abu-Mahmud," said I, "thou wilt also flee away while in my company." To this he replied, "O what shame! By Allah, my death would verily be easier for me than to flee away and leave thee."

Only a few days passed after that when the horsemen of Hamah made an incursion on us. They took a herd of cattle which belonged to us and shut it up in an island under the Jalali Mill. Their archers mounted on the mill in order to defend the herd. I went to them with Jum'ah and Shuja' al-Dawlah Madi, one of our adopted men who was a man of valor. I said to the two with me, "We will cross the water to the other side and take our animals." So we crossed. Madi's mare was hit with an arrow which caused its death. The mare carried him back to his companions with great difficulty. As for me, an arrow struck my mare at the nape of its neck and entered a span deep in it. But by Allah, my mare neither kicked nor was disturbed, but it went on as though it felt no cut. As regards Jum'ah, he went back, fearing for his horse. When we returned I said, "O abu-Mahmud, did I not tell thee that thou wouldst flee away from me, when thou wert blaming thy son Mahmud?" "By Allah," he replied, "I feared for nothing except for my mare. It is so dear to me." And he apologized. . . .

Usamah Ransoms Captives

I used to visit frequently the king of the Franks [Fulk V of Anjou, king of Jerusalem] during the truce [June 1139–March 1140] on account of the fact that King Baldwin, father of the wife of King Fulk, was under obligation to my father (may Allah's mercy rest upon his soul!). During these visits the Franks used to bring before me their captives so that I might buy them off, and I would buy off those of them whose deliverance Allah (exalted is he!) would facilitate.

Once a devil of a Frank named William Jiba set out in his vessel for a piratical raid, and captured a vessel in which were Maghribi pilgrims numbering about four hundred souls, men and women. Now some of these Maghribis would be brought to me and I would buy from among them those whom I could buy. One of the captives was a young man who would salute and sit without uttering a word. I inquired about him and was told that he was an ascetic owned by a tanner. So I said to the tanner, "For how much wilt thou sell me this one?" The tanner replied, "By the truth of my religion, I will not sell him except in conjunction with this sheikh, and that for the same price that I paid for them, namely forty-three dinars." I bought them both, and I bought for my own use a few others. I also bought for the Amir Mu'in-al-Din (may Allah's mercy rest upon his soul!) a few others costing one hundred twenty dinars. I paid the money that I had with me and offered a bond for the balance. . . .

There remained with William Jiba thirty-eight of the captives, among whom was the wife of one of those whom Allah had delivered through my hand. So I bought her off without paying her price on the spot. Soon after, I rode to Jiba's home (may Allah's curse be upon him!) and said, "Wilt thou sell me ten of the captives?" "By my religion," he replied, "I won't sell them but all together." "I haven't got on my person the price of them all," I replied. "So I will now buy some, and then another time I will buy the rest." "I will not sell them to thee but all together," he repeated. So I departed. But Allah (worthy of admiration is he!) decreed and they fled away that very night, all of then. The inhabitants of the villages of Akka being all Moslems, whenever a captive came to them they would hide him and see that he got into Moslem territory. That accursed one sought his runaways, but succeeded in capturing none, for Allah (worthy of admiration is he!) made their deliverance good.

The second morning he began to demand from me the price of the woman whom I had purchased but whose price I had not paid and who was one of those who had fled away. I said to him, "Deliver her to me and then take her price." He replied, "Her price is mine by right since yesterday before she fled away." And he forced me to pay her price. So I paid it and considered it an easy thing since I was so happy at the deliverance of those miserable ones.

Cases of miraculous escape

An unsuccessful attempt at Amid: The following is a case of miraculous escape due to the intervention of destiny and the previous decision of divine will.

Al-Amir Fakhr-al-Din (may Allah's mercy rest upon his soul!) made a number of attempts on the city of Amid, while I was in his service, without accomplishing his object. In the course of the last attempt he made on it, a Kurdish amir, who was in charge of the register at Amid, heading a group of followers, entered into correspondence with Fakhr-al-Din and agreed with him that on a certain night, which they appointed, the army of Fakhr-al-Din would arrive near his place and he would help them climb [the walls of the city] by means of ropes, and thus Fakhr-al-Din would come into possession of the city.

Fakhr-al-Din intrusted the execution of this momentous plan to a Frankish servant of his, named Yaruq, whom the whole army hated and despised because of his evil character.

Yaruq rode forward at the head of some troops. The rest of the amirs rode behind him. Then he began to slow down. So the rest of the amirs got to Amid ahead of him. That Kurdish amir with his companions looked down upon them from the tower and suspended the ropes to them saying, "Climb." But not one of them did climb. So they descended from the tower and broke the locks of the city gate and said, "Enter." But they would not enter. All this was due to the fact that Fakhr-al-Din intrusted the execution of his momentous plan to an ignorant lad instead of intrusting it to the great amirs. . . .

The inhabitants of the city and the army knew of the treachery. They fell upon the conspirators and killed some of them; others threw themselves over the walls. Some of them they seized. As one of those who threw themselves over was falling down through the air, he stretched out his arm, as if seeking something to take hold of, and his hand fell upon one of those ropes which had been suspended in the early part of the night and up which nobody climbed. So he clung to it and escaped alone of all the company. But the skin of his two palms was stripped off from contact with the rope. All this took place in my presence.

A Frank and His Children Revert to Christianity

Among the Frankish captives who were carried into my father's home was an aged woman accompanied by her daughter—a young woman of great beauty—and a robust son. The son accepted Islam, and his conversion was genuine, judging by what he showed in the practice of prayer and fasting. He learned the art of working marble from a stonecutter who had paved the home of my father. After staying for a long time with us my father gave him as wife a woman who belonged to a pious family, and paid all necessary expenses for his wedding and home. His wife bore him two sons. The boys grew up. When they were five or six years old, their father, young Ra'ul, who was very happy at having them, took them with their mother and everything that his home contained and on the second morning joined the Franks in Afamiyah, where he and his children became Christians, after having practiced Islam with its prayers and faith. May Allah, therefore, purify the world from such people!

AN APPRECIATION OF THE FRANKISH CHARACTER

Their Lack of Sense

Mysterious are the works of the Creator, the author of all things! When one comes to recount cases regarding the Franks, he cannot but glorify Allah (exalted is he!) and sanctify him, for he sees them as animals possessing the virtues of courage and fighting, but nothing else; just as ants have only the virtues of strength and carrying loads. I shall now give some instances of their doings and their curious mentality.

In the army of King Fulk, son of Fulk, was a Frankish reverend knight who had just arrived from their land in order to make the holy pilgrimage and then return home. He was of my intimate fellowship and kept such constant company with me that he began to call me "my brother." Between us were mutual bonds of amity and friendship. When he resolved to return by sea to his homeland, he said to me, "My brother, I am leaving for my country and I want thee to send with me thy son (my son, who was then fourteen years old, was at that time in my company) to our country, where he can see the knights and learn wisdom and cavalry. When he returns, he will be like a wise man."

Thus there fell upon my ears words which would never come out of the head of a sensible man; for even if my son were to be taken captive, his captivity could not bring him a worse misfortune than carrying him into the lands of the Franks. However, I said to the man, "By thy life, this has exactly been my idea. But the only thing that prevented me from carrying it out was the fact that his grandmother, my mother, is so fond of him and did not this time let him come out with me until she exacted an oath from me to the effect that I would return him to her."

Thereupon he asked, "Is thy mother still alive?" "Yes," I replied. "Well," said he, "disobey her not."

Their Curious Medication: A Case Illustrating Their Curious Medicine Is the Following:

The lord of al-Munaytirah [in Lebanon] wrote to my uncle asking him to dispatch a physician to treat certain sick persons among his people. My uncle sent him a Christian physician named Thabit. Thabit was absent but ten days when he returned. So we said to him, "How quickly hast thou healed thy patients!" He said:

> They brought before me a knight in whose leg an abscess had grown; and a woman afflicted with imbecility. To the knight I applied a small poultice until the abscess opened and became well; and the women I put on a diet and made her humor wet. Then a Frankish physician came to them and said, "This man knows nothing about treating them." He then said to the knight, "Which wouldst thou prefer, living with one leg or dying with two?" The latter replied, "Living with one leg."
>
> The physician said, "Bring me a strong knight and a sharp ax." A knight came with the ax. And I was standing by. Then the physician laid the leg of the patient on a block of wood and bade the knight strike his leg with the ax and chop it off at one blow. Accordingly he struck it—while I was looking on—one blow, but the leg was not severed. He dealt another blow, upon which the marrow of the leg flowed out and the patient died on the spot.

He then examined the woman and said, "This is a woman in whose head there is a devil which has possessed her. Shave off her hair." Accordingly they shaved it off and the woman began once more to eat their ordinary diet—garlic and mustard. Her imbecility took a turn for the worse. The physician then said, "The devil has penetrated through her head." He therefore took a razor, made a deep cruciform incision on it, peeled off the skin at the middle of the incision until the bone of the skull was exposed and rubbed it with salt. The woman also expired instantly. Thereupon I asked them whether my services were needed any longer, and when they replied in the negative I returned home, having learned of their medicine what I knew not before.

I have, however, witnessed a case of their medicine which was quite different from that. The king of the Franks had for treasurer a knight named Bernard, who (may Allah's curse be upon him!) was one of the most accursed and wicked among the Franks. A horse kicked him in the leg, which was subsequently infected and which opened in fourteen different places. Every time one of these cuts would close in one place, another would open in another place. All this happened while I was praying for his perdition. Then came to him a Frankish physician and removed from the leg all the ointments which were on it and began to wash it with very strong vinegar. By this treatment all the cuts were healed and the man became well again. He was up again like a devil.

Another Case Illustrating Their Curious Medicine Is the Following:

In Shayzar we had an artisan named Abu-al-Fath, who had a boy whose neck was afflicted with scrofula. Every time a part of it would close, another part would open. This man happened to go to Antioch on business of his, accompanied by his son. A Frank noticed the boy and asked his father about him. Abu-al-Fath replied, "This is my son." The Frank said to him, "Wilt thou swear by thy religion that if I prescribe to thee a medicine which will cure thy boy, thou wilt charge nobody fees for prescribing it thyself? In that case, I shall prescribe to thee a medicine which will cure the boy." The man took the oath and the Frank said: "Take uncrushed leaves of glasswort, burn them, then soak the ashes in olive oil and sharp vinegar. Treat the scrofula with them until the spot on which it is growing is eaten up. Then take burnt lead, soak it in ghee butter and treat him with it. That will cure him."

The father treated the boy accordingly, and the boy was cured. The sores closed and the boy returned to his normal condition of health.

I have myself treated with this medicine many who were afflicted with such disease, and the treatment was successful in removing the cause of the complaint.

Newly Arrived Franks Are Especially Rough: One Insists That Usamah Should Pray Eastward

Everyone who is a fresh emigrant from the Frankish lands is ruder in character than those who have become acclimatized and have held long association with the Moslems. Here is an illustration of their rude character.

Whenever I visited Jerusalem I always entered the Aqsa Mosque, beside which stood a small mosque which the Franks had converted into a church. When I used to enter the Aqsa Mosque, which was occupied by the Templars, who were friends, the Templars would evacuate the little adjoining mosque so that I might pray in it. One day [about 1140] I entered this mosque, repeated the first formula, "Allah is great," and stood up in the act of praying, upon which one of the Franks rushed on me, got hold of me and turned my face eastward saying, "This is the way thou shouldst pray!" A group of Templars hastened to him, seized him and repelled him from me. I resumed my prayer. The same man, while the others were otherwise busy, rushed once more on me and turned my face eastward, saying, "This is the way thou shouldst pray." The Templars again came in to him and expelled him. They apologized to me, saying, "This is a stranger who has only recently arrived from the land of the Franks and he has never before seen anyone praying except eastward." Thereupon I said to myself, "I have had enough prayer." So I went out and have ever been surprised at the conduct of this devil of a man, at the change in the color of his face, his trembling and his sentiment at the sight of one praying towards the qiblah [in the direction of Mecca].

Another Wants to Show to a Moslem God as a Child

I saw one of the Franks come to al-Amir Mu'in-al-Din (may Allah's mercy rest upon his soul!) when he was in the Dome of the Rock and say to him, "Dost thou want to see God as a child?" Mu'in-al-Din said, "Yes." The Frank walked ahead of us until he showed us the picture of Mary with Christ (may peace be upon him!) as an infant in her lap. He then said, "This is God as a child." But Allah is exalted far above what the infidels say about him!

Franks Lack Jealousy in Sex Affairs

The Franks are void of all zeal and jealousy. One of them may be walking along with his wife. He meets another man who takes the wife by the hand and steps aside to converse with her while the husband is standing on one side waiting for his wife to conclude the conversation. If she lingers too long for him, he leaves her alone with the conversant and goes away.

Here is an illustration which I myself witnessed:

When I used to visit Nablus, I always took lodging with a man named Mu'izz, whose home was a lodging house for the Moslems. The house had windows which opened to the road, and there stood opposite to it on the other side of the road a house belonging to a Frank who sold wine for the merchants. He would take some wine in a bottle and go around announcing it by shouting, "So and so, the merchant, has just opened a cask full of this wine. He who wants to buy some of it will find it in such and such a place." The Frank's pay for the announcement made would be the wine in that bottle. One day this Frank went home and found a man with his wife in the same bed. He asked him, "What could have made thee enter into my wife's room?" The man replied, "I was tired, so I went in to rest." "But how," asked he, "didst thou get into my bed?" The other replied, "I found a bed that was spread, so I slept in it." "But," said he, "my wife was sleeping together with thee." The other replied, "Well, the bed is hers. How could I therefore have prevented her from using her own bed?" "By the truth of my religion," said the husband, "if thou shouldst do it again, thou and I would have a quarrel."

Such was for the Frank the entire expression of his disapproval and the limit of his jealousy.

Another illustration: We had with us a bath-keeper named Salim, [who] related the following story:

I once opened a bath in al-Ma'arrah in order to earn my living. To this bath there came a Frankish knight. The Franks disapprove of girding a cover around one's waist while in the bath. So this Frank stretched out his arm and pulled my cover from my waist and threw it away. He looked and saw that I had recently shaved off my pubes. So he shouted, "Salim!" As I drew near him he stretched his hand over my pubes and said, "Salim, good! By the truth of my religion, do the same for me." Saying this, he lay on his back and I found that in that place the hair was like his beard. So I shaved it off. Then he passed his hand over the place and, finding it smooth, he said, "Salim, by the truth of my religion, do the same to madame," referring to his wife. He then said to a servant of his, "Tell madame to come here." Accordingly the servant went and brought her and made her enter the bath. She also lay on her back. The knight repeated, "Do what thou hast done to me." So I shaved all that hair while her husband was sitting looking at me. At last he thanked me and handed me the pay for my service.

Consider now this great contradiction! They have neither jealousy nor zeal but they have great courage, although courage is nothing but the product of zeal and of ambition to be above ill repute.

Here is a story analogous to the one related above:

I entered the public bath in Sur [Tyre] and took my place in a secluded part. One of my servants thereupon said to me, "There is with us in the bath a woman." When I went out, I sat on one of the stone benches and behold! The woman who was in the bath had come out all dressed and was standing with her father just opposite me. But I could not be sure that she was a woman. So I said to one of my companions, "By Allah, see if this is a woman," by which I meant that he should ask about her. But he went, as I was looking at him, lifted the end of her robe and looked carefully at her. Thereupon her father turned toward me and said, "This is my daughter. Her mother is dead and she has nobody to wash her hair. So I took her in with me to the bath and washed her head." I replied, "Thou hast well done! This is something for which thou shalt be rewarded [by Allah]!"

Another Curious Case of Medication

A curious case relating to their medicine is the following, which was related to me by William of Bures, the lord of Tabarayyah [Tiberias], [who] related to us the following story in these words:

> We had in our country a highly esteemed knight who was taken ill and was on the point of death. We thereupon came to one of our great priests and said to him, "Come with us and examine so and so, the knight." "I will," he replied, and walked along with us while we were assured in ourselves that if he would only lay his hand on him the patient would recover. When the priest saw the patient, he said, "Bring me some wax." We fetched him a little wax, which he softened and shaped like the knuckles of fingers, and he stuck one in each nostril. The knight died on the spot. "We said to him, 'He is dead.'" "Yes," he replied, "he was suffering great pain, so I closed up his nose that he might die and get relief."

A Funny Race Between Two Aged Women

We shall now leave the discussion of their treatment of the orifices of the body to something else. I found myself in Tabarayyah at the time the Franks were celebrating one of their feasts. The cavaliers went out to exercise with lances. With them went out two decrepit, aged women whom they stationed at one end of the race course. At the other end of the field they left a pig which they had scalded and laid on a rock. They then made the two aged women run a race while each one of them was accompanied by a detachment of horsemen urging her on. At every step they took, the women would fall down and rise again, while the spectators would laugh. Finally one of them got ahead of the other and won that pig for a prize.

A Duel

I attended one day a duel in Nablus between two Franks. The reason for this was that certain Moslem thieves took by surprise one of the villages of Nablus. One of the peasants of that village was charged with having acted as guide for the thieves when they fell upon the village. So he fled away. King Fulk sent and arrested his children. The peasant thereupon came back to the king and said,

"Let justice be done in my case. I challenge to a duel the man who claimed that I guided the thieves to the village." The king then said to the tenant who held the village in fief, "Bring forth someone to fight the duel with him." The tenant went to his village, where a blacksmith lived, took hold of him and ordered him to fight the duel. The tenant became thus sure of the safety of his own peasants, none of whom would be killed and his estate ruined.

I saw this blacksmith. He was a physically strong young man, but his heart failed him. He would walk a few steps and then sit down and ask for a drink. The one who had made the challenge was an old man, but he was strong in spirit and he would rub the nail of his thumb against that of the forefinger in defiance, as if he was not worrying over the duel. Then came the viscount (i.e., the seignior of the town) and gave each one of the two contestants a cudgel and a shield and arranged the people in a circle around them.

The two met. The old man would press the blacksmith backward until he would get him as far as the circle, then he would come back to the middle of the arena. They went on exchanging blows until they looked like pillars smeared with blood. The contest was prolonged and the viscount began to urge them to hurry, saying, "Hurry on." The fact that the smith was given to the use of the hammer proved now of great advantage to him. The old man was worn out and the smith gave him a blow which made him fall. His cudgel fell under his back. The smith knelt down over him and tried to stick his fingers into the eyes of his adversary, but could not do it because of the great quantity of blood flowing out. Then he rose up and hit his head with the cudgel until he killed him. They then fastened a rope around the neck of the dead person, dragged him away and hanged him. The lord who brought the smith now came, gave the smith his own mantle, made him mount the horse behind him and rode off with him. This case illustrates the kind of jurisprudence and legal decisions the Franks have—may Allah's curse be upon them!

Ordeal by Water

I once went in the company of Al-Amir Mu'in-al-Din (may Allah's mercy rest upon his soul!) to Jerusalem. We stopped at Nablus. There a blind man, a Moslem, who was still young and was well dressed, presented himself before Al-amir carrying fruits for him and asked permission to be admitted into his service in Damascus. The amir consented. I inquired about this man and was informed that his mother had been married to a Frank whom she had killed. Her son used to practice ruses against the Frankish pilgrims and cooperate with his mother in assassinating them. They finally brought charges against him and tried his case according to the Frankish way of procedure.

They installed a huge cask and filled it with water. Across it they set a board of wood. They then bound the arms of the man charged with the act, tied a rope around his shoulders and dropped him into the cask, their idea being that in case he was innocent, he would sink in the water and they would then lift him up with the rope so that he might not die in the water; and in case he was guilty, he would not sink in the water. This man did his best to sink when they dropped him into the water, but he could not do it. So he had to submit to their sentence against him—may Allah's curse be upon them! They pierced his eyeballs with red-hot awls.

A Frank Domesticated in Syria Abstains from Eating Pork

Among the Franks are those who have become acclimatized and have associated long with the Moslems. These are much better than the recent comers from the Frankish lands. But they constitute the exception and cannot be treated as a rule.

Here is an illustration. I dispatched one of my men to Antioch on business. There was in Antioch at that time al-Ra'is Theodoros Sophianos, to whom I was bound by mutual ties of amity. His influence in Antioch was supreme. One day he said to my man, "I am invited by a friend of mine who is a Frank. Thou shouldst come with me so that thou mayest see their fashions." My man related the story in the following words:

> I went along with him and we came to the home of a knight who belonged to the old category of knights who came with the early expeditions of the Franks. He had been by that time stricken off the register and exempted from service, and possessed in Antioch an estate on the income of which he lived. The knight presented an excellent table, with food extraordinarily clean and delicious. Seeing me abstaining from food, he said, "Eat, be of good cheer! I never eat Frankish dishes, but I have Egyptian women cooks and never eat except

their cooking. Besides, pork never enters my home." I ate, but guardedly, and after that we departed.

As I was passing in the market place, a Frankish woman all of a sudden hung to my clothes and began to mutter words in their language, and I could not understand what she was saying. This made me immediately the center of a big crowd of Franks. I was convinced that death was at hand. But all of a sudden that same knight approached. On seeing me, he came and said to that woman, "What is the matter between thee and this Moslem?" She replied, "This is he who has killed my brother Hurso." This Hurso was a knight in Afamiyah who was killed by someone of the army of Hamah. The Christian knight shouted at her, saying, "This is [a merchant] who neither fights nor attends a fight." He also yelled at the people who had assembled, and they all dispersed. Then he took me by the hand and went away. Thus the effect of that meal was my deliverance from certain death.

DOUKAS

"THE FALL OF CONSTANTINOPLE"

1453

When all preparations had been completed according to plan, Mehmed [commander of the Ottoman Turks] sent an envoy to the emperor [Constantine] inside the City with the following message: "The preparations for the assault have been concluded. It is now time to consummate what we planned long ago. Let us leave the outcome of this undertaking to God. What say you? Do you wish to quit the City and go wherever you like together with your officials and their possessions, leaving behind the populace unharmed by us and by you? Or do you choose to resist and to lose your life and belongings, and to have the Turks take the populace captive and scatter them throughout the earth?" The emperor and the senate answered, "If you so wish, as your fathers did before you, you too, by the grace of God, can live peacefully with us. . . . Keep the fortresses and the lands which have been unjustly seized from us as justly yours. Extract as much tribute annually as we are able to pay you, and depart in peace. Can you be certain that victory instead of defeat awaits you? The right to surrender the City to you belongs neither to me nor to anyone who dwells therein. Rather than to have our lives spared, it is our common resolve willingly to die."

When the tyrant heard this reply, he despaired of a peaceful surrender of the City. He therefore instructed the heralds to announce to the entire army the day on which the assault would be launched. He also affirmed on oath that he desired for himself no gain other than the buildings and walls of the City. As for the treasures and captives to be taken, he declared, "Let those be your reward." The troops shouted their approval.

As night fell, he sent heralds around the camp with instructions that large torches and fires should be lighted at every tent. And once the torches were burning, they were all to chant and shout in their foul and impious tongue. This strange spectacle was indeed incredible. As the torches poured their light over land and sea, brighter than the sun, they illuminated the entire City, Galata, all the islands, ships and boats as far as Skutari. The entire surface of the water flashed so brightly that it was like lightning. Would that it had been lightning, the lightning which not only produces light but also burns and utterly consumes everything! The Romans thought that fire had fallen on the camp and ran up to the breach in the wall. When they saw the Turks dancing and heard their joyous shouts, they foresaw the future. With a contrite heart they prayed to God, "Spare us, O Lord, from Thy just wrath and deliver us from the hands of the enemy." The spectacle and din affected the citizens so much that they appeared to be half-dead, unable to breathe either in or out. . . .

On Sunday, the tyrant began to engage in full scale warfare. Right into the evening and through the night he gave no rest to the Romans. That Sunday was the Feast of All Saints, the twenty-seventh day of May.

From daybreak he engaged in light skirmishes until the ninth hour [3 P.M.], and after the ninth hour he arrayed the army from the palace to the Golden Gate. He also deployed the eighty ships from the Xyloporta Gate to the Plataea Gate. The remaining ships, which were stationed at the Double Columns, began an encircling maneuver, starting from the Horaia Gate and continuing past the Acropolis of Demetrios the Great and the small postern located at the Hodegetria monastery. Sailing past the Great Palace and crossing the harbor, they completed the encirclement as far as Vlangas. In addition to all kinds of equipment, each vessel carried a scaling ladder equal to the height of the walls.

Just as the sun set, the call to battle rang out. The battle array was most formidable indeed! The tyrant himself was on horseback on Monday evening. Exactly opposite the fallen walls he gave battle with his faithful slaves, young and all-powerful, fighting like lions, more than ten thousand of them. To the rear and on both flanks there were more than one hundred thousand fighting cavalrymen. To the south of these and as far as the harbor of the Golden Gate there were another hundred thousand troops and more. From the spot where the ruler was standing to the extremities of the palace there were another fifty thousand soldiers. The troops on the ships and at the bridge were beyond number.

The City's defenders were deployed in the following manner: The emperor and [his general] Giovanni Giustiniani were stationed at the fallen walls, outside the stockade in the enclosure, with about three thousand Latins and Romans. The grand duke was posted at the Imperial Gate with about five hundred troops. At the sea walls and along the battlements from the Xyloporta Gate to the Horaia Gate, more than five hundred crossbowmen and archers were arrayed. Making the complete circuit from the Horaia Gate to the Golden Gate there was stationed in each bastion a single archer, crossbowman, or gunner. They spent the entire night on watch with no sleep at all.

The Turks with Mehmed rushed to the walls, carrying a great number of scaling ladders which had been constructed beforehand. Behind the lines, the tyrant, brandishing an iron mace, forced his archers to the walls by using both flattery and threats. The City's defenders fought back bravely with all the strength they could muster. Giovanni and his men, supported by the emperor in arms, together with all his troops, fought back courageously.

But just as Fortune's feats of arms were about to snatch victory from Turkish hands, from the very middle of the embattled Roman troops, God removed their general, a mighty warrior of gigantic stature. He was wounded just before dawn by lead shot which went through the back of his arm, penetrating his iron breastplate which had been forged in the manner of Achilles' weapons. Unable to relieve the pain of the wound, he cried out to the emperor, "Stand your ground bravely, and I will retire to the ship to attend to my wound. Then I will quickly return." When the emperor beheld Giovanni in retreat he lost heart and so did his companions. Yet they continued the fight with all their strength.

The Turks gradually made their way to the walls, and, using their shields for cover, threw up their scaling ladders. Thwarted, however, by stone-throwers from above, they achieved nothing. Their assault, therefore, was repulsed. All the Romans with the emperor held their ground against the enemy, and all their strength and purpose were exerted to prevent the Turks from entering through the fallen walls. Unbeknown to them, however, God willed that the Turks would be brought in by another way. When they saw the sallyport open, some fifty of the tyrant's renowned slaves leaped inside. They climbed to the top of the walls and zealously slew anyone they met and struck down the sentinels who discharged missiles from above. It was a sight filled with horror! Some of the Romans and Latins who were preventing the Turks from attaching scaling ladders to the walls were cut to pieces, while others, closing their eyes, jumped from the wall and ended their lives horribly by smashing their bodies. Unimpeded, the Turks threw up the scaling ladders and ascended like soaring eagles.

The Romans and the emperor did not know what had happened because the entry of the Turks took place at a distance; indeed, their paramount concern was the enemy before them. The fierce Turkish warriors outnumbered the Romans twenty to one. The Romans, moreover, were not as experienced in warfare as the ordinary Turks. Their attention and concern, therefore, were focused on the Turkish ground attack. Then suddenly arrows fell from above, slaughtering many Romans. When they looked up and saw the Turks, they fled behind the walls. Unable to enter through the Gate of Charisios because of the press of the multitude, only those got through who were stronger and able to trample down the weaker. When the tyrant's troops witnessed the rout of the Romans, they shouted with one voice and pursued them inside, trampling upon the wretches and slaughtering them. When they reached the gate, they were unable to get through because it was blocked by the bodies of the dead and the dying. The majority entered through the breaches in the walls and they cut down all those they met.

The emperor, despairing and hopeless, stood with sword and shield in hand and poignantly cried out, "Is there no one among the Christians who will take my head from me?" He was abandoned and alone. Then one of the Turks wounded him by striking him flush, and he, in turn, gave the Turk a blow. A second Turk delivered a mortal blow from behind and the emperor fell to the earth. They slew him as a common soldier and left him, because they did not know he was the emperor.

Only three Turks perished and all the rest made their way inside. It was the first hour of the day [6 A.M.], and the sun had not yet risen. As they entered the City and spread out from the Gate of Charisios to the palace, they slew those who resisted and those who fled. Some two thousand fighting men were slaughtered. The Turks were apprehensive because they had estimated that within the

City there must be at least fifty thousand soldiers. Consequently, they slew the two thousand. Had they known that the total number of armed troops did not exceed eight thousand men, they would not have killed any of them. This nation is a lover of money and if a patricide fell into their hands, they would release him for gold. . . . After the conflict I met many Turks who related the following to me, "Fearful of those ahead of us, we slew as many as we met. Had we known that there was such a dearth of men in the City, we would have sold them all like sheep."

Some of the Azabs, that is, the tyrant's retinue who are also called Janissaries, overran the palace. Others swarmed over the Monastery of the Great Forerunner called Petra and the Monastery of Chora in which was found the icon of my Immaculate Mother of God. O tongue and lips, how can I relate what happened there to the icon because of your sins? While the apostates were anxious to go elsewhere for more plunder, one of the infidels, extending his befouled hands, hacked the icon into four pieces with an axe. Casting lots, each received his equal share and its accompanying ornament. After they seized the monastery's precious vessels, they rode off. . . .

Then a great horde of mounted infidels charged down the street leading to the Great Church. The actions of both Turks and Romans made quite a spectacle! In the early dawn, as the Turks poured into the City and the citizens took flight, some of the fleeing Romans managed to reach their homes and rescue their children and wives. As they moved, bloodstained, across the Forum of the Bull and passed the Column of the Cross [in the Forum of Constantine], their wives asked, "What is to become of us?" When they heard the fearful cry, "The Turks are slaughtering Romans within the City's walls," they did not believe it at first. They cursed and reviled the ill-omened messenger instead. But behind him came a second, and then a third, and all were covered with blood, and they knew that the cup of the Lord's wrath had touched their lips. Monks and nuns, therefore, and men and women, carrying their infants in their arms and abandoning their homes to anyone who wished to break in, ran to the Great Church. The thoroughfare, overflowing with people, was a sight to behold!

Why were they all seeking refuge in the Great Church? Many years before they had heard from some false prophets that the City was fated to be surrendered to the Turks who would enter with great force, and that the Romans would be cut down by them as far as the Column of Constantine the Great. Afterwards, however, an angel, descending and holding a sword, would deliver the empire and the sword to an unknown man, extremely plain and poor, standing at the Column. "Take this sword," the angel would say, "and avenge the people of the Lord." Then the Turks would take flight and the Romans would follow hard upon them, cutting them down. They would drive them from the City and from the West, and from the East as far as the borders of Persia, to a place called Monodendrion. Because they fully expected these prophecies to be realized, some ran and advised others to run also. This was the conviction of the Romans who long ago had contemplated what their present action would be, contending, "If we leave the Column of the Cross behind us, we will avoid future wrath." This was the cause then of the flight into the Great Church. In one hour's time that enormous temple was filled with men and women. There was a throng too many to count, above and below, in the court-yards and everywhere. They bolted the doors and waited, hoping to be rescued by the anonymous savior. . . .

Pillaging, slaughtering, and taking captives on the way, the Turks reached the temple before the termination of the first hour. The gates were barred, but they broke them with axes. They entered with swords flashing and, beholding the myriad populace, each Turk caught and bound his own captive.

There was no one who resisted or who did not surrender himself like a sheep. Who can recount the calamity of that time and place? Who can describe the wailing and the cries of the babes, the mothers' tearful screams and the fathers' lamentations? The commonest Turk sought the most tender maiden. The lovely nun, who heretofore belonged only to the one God, was now seized and bound by another master. The rapine caused the tugging and pulling of braids of hair, the exposure of bosoms and breasts, and outstretched arms. The female slave was bound with her mistress, the master with his slave, the archi-mandrite with the doorkeeper, tender youths with virgins, who had never been exposed to the sun and hardly ever seen by their own fathers, were dragged about, forcibly pushed together and flogged. The despoiler led them to a cer-tain spot, and placing them in safekeeping, returned to take a second and even a third prize. The abductors, the avengers of God, were in a great hurry. Within one hour they had bound everyone, the male captives with cords and the women with their own veils. The infinite chains of captives who like herds of kine and flocks of sheep poured out of the temple and the temple sanctuary made an extraordinary spectacle! They wept and wailed and there was none to show them mercy.

What became of the temple treasures? What shall I say and how shall I say it? My tongue is stuck fast in my larynx. I am unable to draw breath through my sealed mouth. In that same hour the dogs hacked the holy icons to pieces, removing the ornaments. As for the chains, candelabra, holy altar coverings, and lamps, some they destroyed and the rest they seized. All the precious and sacred vessels of the holy sacristy, fashioned from gold and silver and other valuable materials, they collected in an instant, leaving the temple desolate and naked; absolutely nothing was left behind. . . .

The frightful day on which the City fell was the Feast Day of the Holy Martyr Theodosia. It was a very popular festival and on its eve many men and women kept an all night vigil at the saint's sepulcher. In the morning, as many women with their husbands set out to venerate the saint in her church, carrying beautifully embellished and adorned candles and incense, they suddenly fell into the trap of the Turks. How were they to know that such wrath could instantly spill over the whole City? They who had seen its magnitude, however, knew full well!

This menace, of which we have spoken, took fire and burned from the Gates of Charisios and St. Romanos to the environs of the palace. The resistance from the ships and along the harbor did not allow the Turks to throw up their scaling ladders on the walls. The Romans were superior to the Turks, discharging stones and missiles until the third hour [9 A.M.] of the day. About this time in the morning, a number of looters gained entrance into the City. Observing the Romans giving battle to the Turks outside the walls, the looters shouted with all their might and rushed to the top of the walls. When the Romans saw that the Turks were already inside the City, they emitted the anguished cry of woe and threw themselves off the wall. The strength and might of the Romans were exhausted. When the Turks in the ships saw their comrades inside the City, they knew that the City had fallen. They quickly threw up scaling ladders and climbed over the wall; then they broke down the gates and all rushed inside.

When the grand duke, who was guarding the Imperial Gate with five hundred troops, saw the Turks approaching his post, he abandoned the defense of the Gate and set out for his home with a few companions. All the Romans had dispersed. Some were captured before they could reach their homes. Others, on reaching their homes, found them robbed of children, wife, and belongings. Before they had time to groan and wail, their hands were bound behind them. Still others, on reaching their homes and finding their wives and children already abducted, were themselves bound and fettered with their closest friends and their wives. The old men and women who were unable to leave their houses, either because of infirmity or old age, were slaughtered mercilessly. The newborn infants were flung into the squares.

The grand duke, returning home to find that his daughters, sons, and sick wife had taken shelter in the tower and had blocked the Turks from gaining entry, was taken captive with his companions. The tyrant dispatched soldiers to guard him and his entire household, and gave an ample sum of silver coins to the Turks who had besieged and surrounded his house in payment for their ransom according to the oath he had sworn. The grand duke and his entire household were placed under guard.

As the Turks entered the City, they all—even the muleteers and cooks—carried their plunder with them.

As soon as Giovanni Giustiniani, who in our last report was going back to his ship to dress his wound, reached the harbor, several of his men who had taken flight reported that the Turks had entered the City and that the emperor was slain. On hearing this most bitter and harsh news, he instructed his heralds to recall his adjutants and marines by bugle call.

The remaining ships also prepared to depart. Most of them had lost their captains through capture. It was a pitiful sight to behold at the harbor's edge men, women, monks, and nuns crying out piteously and beating their breasts, pleading with those in the ships to come to their rescue. But that was impossible. It was foreordained, once and for all, that they must drink to the dregs the cup filled with the Lord's wrath. Even if the ships had wanted to help, they could not. And had the tyrant's ships not been occupied with looting and plundering the City, not one vessel would have escaped. The Turks had left their ships and were all inside the City. Consequently, finding their passage clear, the Latins sailed out of the harbor. The tyrant gnashed his teeth but was unable to stop them and endured the situation unwillingly. . . .

All these events took place between the first hour of the day and the eighth hour [6 A.M. to 2 P.M.]. Setting aside his suspicions and fears, the tyrant made his entry into the City with his viziers and satraps, preceded and followed by his fire-eating slaves, all of whom were archers superior to Apollo, youthful Herakleidae eager to challenge ten men. Proceeding to the Great Church, he dismounted from his horse and went inside. He marveled at the sight! When he found a Turk smashing a piece of marble pavement, he asked him why he was demolishing the floor. "For the faith," he replied. He extended his hand and struck the Turk a blow with his sword, remarking "You have enough treasure and captives. The City's buildings are mine." When the tyrant beheld the treasures which had been collected and the countless captives, he regretted his compact. The Turk was dragged by the feet and cast outside half dead. He summoned one of his vile priests who ascended the pulpit to call out his foul prayer. The son of iniquity, the forerunner of Antichrist, ascending the holy altar, offered the prayer. . . .

The Temple of the Holy Trinity, and Great Church and New Sion, today has become an altar of barbarians, and has been named and has become the House of Muhammad. Just is Thy judgment, O Lord.

When Mehmed left the sanctuary, he asked for the grand duke, who was immediately brought forth. He approached and made obeisance, and then Mehmed spoke to him, "Did you do well not to surrender the City? Behold the damage and ruin! Behold the captivity of so many!" The duke replied, "Lord, we did not have the authority to give you the City. The emperor himself did not have that authority. Moreover, some of your own officials urged the emperor to do otherwise by writing such words as: 'Fear not. He will not prevail against you.'" The tyrant assumed that this was Halil Pasha against whom he nursed a grudge. When he heard the name of the emperor, he asked if he had escaped in the ships. The duke replied that he did not know because he was posted at the Imperial Gate when the Turks, who entered by the Gate of Charisios, encountered the emperor. Two youths from the army now stepped forward. The first informed the tyrant, "Lord, I slew him. I was in a hurry to enter the City with my companions to search for plunder, so I left him behind dead." The second youth added, "I struck him the first blow." The tyrant ordered both men to bring back the emperor's head. Running swiftly, they found him, and cutting off his head, they presented it to the ruler.

The tyrant inquired of the grand duke, "Tell me truthfully if this is the head of your emperor." Upon careful examination, he answered, "It is his, Lord." Others saw it too and recognized it. Then they affixed it to the Column of the Augustaion, and it remained there until evening. Afterward, the skin was peeled off and stuffed with straw, and Mehmed sent it around, exhibiting the symbol of his triumph to the chief of the Persians and Arabs, and to all the other Turks. . . . The morning following the black day on which the utter destruction of our nation took place, the tyrant entered the City. . . . Within, neither man nor beast nor fowl was heard to cry out or utter a sound. Only they were left who were too weak to pillage. Many were killed as one dragged away the spoils of another. He who was able seized, and he who was unable to resist, received a mortal blow and succumbed. On the second day, the thirtieth of May, the Turkish troops entered and collected whatever had been abandoned.

After the tyrant had traversed most of the City, he celebrated by holding a banquet on the palace grounds. Full of wine and in a drunken stupor, he summoned his chief eunuch and commanded him, "Go to the home of the grand duke and tell him, 'The ruler orders you to send your younger son to the banquet.'" The youth was handsome and fourteen years old. When the boy's father heard this, his face turned ashen as though he had been struck dead. He protested to the chief eunuch, "It is not our custom to hand over my own child to be despoiled by him. It would be far better for me if the executioner were sent to take my head." The chief eunuch advised him to surrender his child for otherwise the tyrant would be wrathful. But the grand duke was unconvinced, and said, "If you want him you will have to seize him. I could never willingly surrender him to you." The chief eunuch reported to the ruler all that had been said by the grand duke and that he refused to hand over the child. In a rage, the tyrant commanded the chief eunuch, "Take the executioner with you, and bring me back the boy. Let the executioner bring the duke and his sons."

When they had arrived and the duke learned of the command he embraced his wife and children and set out with the executioner, his son, and son-in-law, Kantakouzenos. The chief eunuch took the boy with him. He entered the palace to show the boy to the ruler and to inform him that the others were standing at the palace gate. Mehmed ordered the executioner to cut off their heads with the sword. The executioner took them a little way below the palace and told them the decision. When the duke's son heard they were to be slaughtered, he wept. His courageous father gave strength and support to the youths . . . bolstered with these sentiments, and they were ready to die. To the executioner he said, "Carry out your instructions, beginning with the youths." Complying with the request, the executioner beheaded the youths while the grand duke stood by and mummured, "I thank Thee Lord," and, "Thou art just, Lord." He then spoke to the executioner, "Brother, grant me a little time to go inside and pray." There was a small chapel in that place. Permission being granted him, he went inside and prayed. Afterward, as he exited through the chapel gate—the bodies of his sons were still twitching there—and offered up, once more, a doxology to God, his head was cut off. The executioner picked up the heads and resumed to the banquet, presenting them to the bloodthirsty beast. He had abandoned the bodies where they lay naked and uninterred.

Mehmed sent the chief nobles and palace officials whom he had redeemed to the executioner, and they also were slaughtered. From among their wives and children, he selected the beautiful maidens and handsome boys, and entrusted them to the watchful care of the chief eunuch. The remaining captives he entrusted to the care of others until they could be taken to Babylon, that is, Adrianople.

To behold the whole City in the tents at the fosse was indeed a spectacle. And the City was desolate, lying dead, naked, soundless, having neither form nor beauty.

O City, City, head of all cities! O City, City, the center of the four corners of the earth! O City, City, the boast of Christians and the ruin of barbarians! O City, City, a second Paradise planted in the West and containing within many plants, laden with spiritual fruits.

Where is your beauty, O Paradise?

— EPILOGUE —

As we've seen, one of the great turning points in the balance of power between Romans and barbarians came at Hadrianople in 378 when the Goths routed the legions and killed Valens, the emperor whose body was never found. Let us close by returning to those city gates about a thousand years later for a scene actually witnessed by Doukas. With an earth-shaking bang, barbarians—and surely the last defenders of the Roman Empire in the East considered Mehmed and his Ottoman Turks barbarians—entered the modern world.

DOUKAS "AT THE GATES OF HADRIANOPLE," 1453

In January Mehmed came to Adrianople from Didymoteichos. Since every piece of military equipment was ready, he wished to test the cannon which the technician had constructed. Placing it skillfully before the great gate of the courtyard of the palace buildings which he had built that year, inserting the stone carefully and measuring out the powder, he planned to discharge it the next day. All of Adrianople was notified that the impending blast and crash would be like thunder from the heavens so that the sudden shock would not leave some speechless or cause pregnant women to abort. In the morning when he ignited the powder and the air became heated, the stone when discharged, was propelled from the cannon with a piercing air-rending sound, and the air was filled with smoke and haze. The explosion could be heard over ten miles away. The stone landed one mile from the point of departure and the hole it made where it fell was one fathom deep. Such was the power of the gunpowder which propelled the stone.

By the time Mehmed fired his cannon and Constantinople fell, it no longer made sense to divide the world between civilized folk and barbarians. Former barbarian nations, such as France and England, were now thoroughly respectable. Descendants of former barbarians ruled all of Europe and much of the East as well. From now on the notion of barbaric behavior—which was always, of course, what you claimed your enemy was doing—was a matter of political philosophy, moral outrage, or simple name-calling.

At its blandest, there is this definition by Julius Charles Hare, an early-nineteenth-century English clergyman: "A barbarian is a person who does not talk as we talk, or dress as we dress, or eat as we eat; in short, who is so audacious as not to follow our practice in all the trivialities of manners." That is droll enough to raise a chuckle in the vicarage, but a more extreme example of demonizing the stranger—the enemy—was the common World War I custom, which Winston Churchill carried on into World War II, of calling Germans "Huns" or, more often, "filthy Huns."

Which of course they weren't—Huns, that is. The Huns had originated farther east than Germany. "Goths" would have been more on the mark, but "Gothic" had over the years—thanks to art and architecture—lost its barbarous connotations, while the very word "Hun" cannot be mentioned without thinking of mindless slaughter and Attila, a name that after a millennium can still be used as a bogeyman.

It is curious which words associated with barbarism have come into common use and which have not. Attila has, but not Alaric, who actually sacked Rome. The name "Vandal" is perhaps best remembered (it has even been adopted by American street gangs), but who remembers their leaders? "Vandalism," in fact, entered the English language at the end of the eighteenth century. It came across the Channel from France, so the British etymologist C. T. Onions believes, where it had been coined, significantly enough, in the violent aftermath of the French Revolution.

And some names have undergone interesting changes. Gothic architecture has been mentioned, but "gothic" has also taken on an almost comically romantic quality because of the elaborately sinister school of novels that has appropriated its name. The Celts not only are not remembered as barbarians but are now thought of as the people who, in their remote Irish monasteries, actually "saved" or at least preserved Western civilization during the Dark Ages. Genghis Khan, for hundreds of years a synonym for terror in the West, has, since the fall of the Communist regime in Mongolia, become the father of his country. His statue is replacing Lenin's in village squares, and his picture appears not only on the country's currency—the thousand-tugrik bills—but on the labels of a local brand of vodka. Tamerlane's tomb in Samarkand has become a tourist attraction.

Barbarians have even been made to seem like a fun crowd. There are now barbarian comic strips—*Hagar the Horrible* (who appears to be a Viking) and *Asterix* (definitely a Gaul)—and television shows that feature characters who seem to spend a good deal of time taking care of their hair, such as "Xena: Warrior Princess." *Conan the Barbarian* has been on the big screen, just as Tamerlane and Genghis Khan were in the movies before him. What are Wagner's *Ring* operas but inflated and tidied up barbarian tales? And in professional sports, there are the Celtics and the Vikings.

With all these cosmetic changes, one word has not evolved: "barbarian." Whether it is used trivially (for some poor soul who doesn't know the proper wine to order with fish) or seriously (for the ethnic cleansers in the Balkans), even if it is used by someone who in another's eyes is himself a barbarian, it never has a positive connotation. It is our way of telling ourselves that in this barbaric world, we still have our standards, our culture, our way of separating ourselves from the others, from strangers we hope are our inferiors.

The modern Greek poet C. P. Cavafy wrote a poem entitled "Waiting for the Barbarians." In it citizens gather in the city forum, having heard rumors that the barbarians are coming. But after a long wait, the bewildered crowd melts away. Someone says there are no barbarians anymore. Someone else (in this translation by Edmund Keeley and Philip Sherrad) says: "Now what's going to happen to us without them?/ The barbarians were a kind of solution."

They both built our world and serve as scapegoats for its imperfections.

SOURCES

Chapter I: Barbarians on the Landscape

1). From Strabo, *Geography*, translated by H. C. Hamilton and W. Falconer, London: George Bell & Sons, 1892.

Chapter II: The Greeks' Barbarians

1). From Herodotus, *The History*, translated by Henry Cary, New York: Harper & Brothers, 1873.

Chapter III: Rome Encounters the Celts

1). From Diodorus Siculus, *Library of History*, Vol. VI, translated by C. H. Oldfather, Cambridge, Mass.: Harvard University Press, 1904. Reprinted by permission of the publishers and the Loeb Classical Library.

2). From Livy, *History*, Vol. III, translated by B. O. Foster, Cambridge, Mass.: Harvard University Press, 1924. Reprinted by permisson of the publishers and the Loeb Classical Library.

3). From Polybius, *The Histories*, Vol. I, translated by W. R. Paton, Cambridge, Mass.: Harvard University Press, 1922. Reprinted by permission of the publishers and the Loeb Classical Library.

Chapter IV: Gaul

1). From Julius Caesar, *The Gallic War*, translated by W. A. McDevitte, New York: Vincent Parke and Co., 1909.

2). From Diodorus Siculus, *The Library of History*, Vol. III, translated by C. H. Oldfather, Cambridge, Mass.: Harvard University Press, 1939. Reprinted by permission of the publishers and the Loeb Classical Library.

3). From Julius Caesar, *The Gallic War*, translated by H. J. Edwards, Cambridge, Mass.: Harvard University Press, 1917. Reprinted by permission of the publishers and the Loeb Classical Library.

Chapter V: Germany

1). From Julius Caesar, *The Gallic War*, translated by W. A. McDevitte, New York: Vincent Parke and Co., 1909.

2). Tacitus, *Germania*, translated by A. J. Church and W. J. Brodribb, London: Macmillan, 1868.

Chapter VI: Britain

1). From Julius Caesar, *The Gallic War*, translated by W. A. McDevitte. New York: Vincent Park and Co., 1909.

2). From Diodorus Siculus, *The Library of History*, Vol. III, translated by C. H. Oldfather, Cambridge, Mass.: Harvard University Press, 1939. Reprinted by permission of the publishers and the Loeb Classical Library.

3). From Tacitus, *Agricola*, translated by A. J. Church and W. J. Brodribb, London: Macmillan, 1868.

Chapter VII: The Goths Turn South to Rome

1). From Ammianus Marcellinus, *History*, translated by C. D. Yonge, London: Bohn's Classical Library, 1862.

2). From Procopius, *The History of the Wars*, Vol. II, translated by H. B. Dewing, Cambridge, Mass.: Harvard University Press, 1916. Reprinted by permission of the publishers and the Loeb Classical Library.

3). From Edward Gibbon, *The History of the Decline and Fall of the Roman Empire*, London, 1781.

Chapter VIII: The Huns

1). Claudian, "The Huns," translated by Thomas Hodgkin, Oxford: Oxford University Press, 1880.

2). From Priscus, *Exc. de. Leg.*, translated by J. B. Bury, London: Macmillan, 1923.

3). From Jordanes, *The Origins and Deeds of the Goths*, translated by C. C. Mierow, Princeton, N.J.: Princeton University Press, 1915.

Chapter IX: The Vandals

1). From Edward Gibbon, *The History of The Decline and Fall of the Roman Empire*, London, 1781.

Chapter X: The Vikings

1). "The Battle of Maldon," translated by R. K. Gordon, London: J. M. Dent & Sons, 1926.

2). From *The Annals of St. Bertin*, New York: The American Book Co., 1909.

3). From *The Anglo-Saxon Chronicle*, translated by Benjamin Thorpe, London: Rolls Series, Vol. 1, 1861.

4). From Ibn Fadlan, *Risala*, translated by H. M. Smyser in *Francipelegius*, ed. by J. B. Bessinger and R. P. Creed, New York: New York University Press, 1965. Reprinted by permission of the publisher.

5). From Procopius, *The History of the Wars*, Vol. III, translated by H. B. Dewing, Cambridge, Mass.: Harvard University Press, 1916. Reprinted by permisson of the publishers and the Loeb Classical Library.

Chapter XI: Ireland

1). From Giraldus Cambrensis, *The Typography of Ireland*, translated by T. Wright, London: George Bell & Sons, 1881.

2). "Bricriu's Feast," from *Cuchulain of Muirthemne*, translated by Lady Gregory, New York, Scribners, 1903.

Chapter XII: Genghis Khan

1). From Ata-Malik Juvaini, *The History of the World Conqueror*, edited and translated by John Andrew Boyle, Manchester, England: Manchester University Press in association with the University of Washington Press, 1958. Reprinted by permission of the University of Washington Press and Manchester University Press.

2). From *The Secret History of the Mongols*, translated by F. W. Cleaves, Cambridge, Mass.: The Harvard-Yenching Institute, 1982. Reprinted by permission of the Harvard-Yenching Institute.

Chapter XIII: Mongols and Tartars

1). From C. de Bridia, *The Tartar Relation*, translated by George D. Painter, from *The Vinland Map and the Tartar Relation* by R. A. Skelton, Thomas E. Marston, and George D. Painter, New Haven: Yale University Press, copyright © 1965 by Yale University Press. Reprinted by permission of the publisher.

2). From *The Chronicle of Novgorod*, translated by Robert Mitchell and Nevil Forbes, London: Royal Historical Society, 1914.

3). From Matthew Paris, *Chronicles*, translated by R. A. Giles, London: H. G. Bohn, 1852.

Chapter XIV: Tamerlane

1). From Ahmed ibn Mohammed Ibn' Arabshah, *The Life of Timur*, translated by J. H. Sanders, London: Luzac and Co., 1933.

2). From Johann Schiltberger, *Travels and Bondage*, translated by J. B. Telfer, London: The Hakluyt Society, 1879.

Chapter XV: The Crusades

1). From Robert the Monk, *The History of the Crusade to Jerusalem*, translated by Dana C. Munro, New York: The American Book Co., 1909.

2). From D. C. Krey, *The First Crusade: The Accounts of Eye-witnesses and Participants*, Princeton, N.J.: Princeton University Press, 1921.

3). From Usamah ibn-Murshid, *An Arab-Syrian Gentleman and Warrior in the Time of the Crusades*, translated by Philip K. Hitti, copyight © 1929 by Columbia University Press. Reprinted with permission of the publisher.

4) and 5). From Doukas, *The Decline and Fall of Byzantium to the Ottoman Turks*, translated by Harry J. Magoulias, Detroit: Wayne State University Press, 1975. Copyright © 1975 by Wayne State University Press. Reprinted by permission of the Wayne State University Press.

Bury, J. B. *History of the Later Roman Empire.* 2 vols. London: Macmillan, 1923.

_____ *The Invasion of Europe by the Barbarians.* New York: W.W. Norton, 1967.

Cavafy, C. P. *The Essential Cavafy.* Translated by Edmund Keeley and Philip Sherrard. Princeton: Princeton University Press, 1967.

Cunliffe, Barry. *Rome and Her Empire.* New York: McGraw-Hill, 1978.

Ferrill, Arthur. *The Fall of the Roman Empire.* New York: Thames and Hudson, 1988.

Fletcher, Richard. *The Barbarian Conversion.* New York: Henry Holt, 1998.

Gordon, C. D. *The Age of Attila.* Ann Arbor: The University of Michigan Press, 1960.

Grun, Bernard. *The Timetables of History.* 3rd ed. New York: Simon & Schuster, 1991.

Heather, Peter. *The Goths.* Oxford: Blackwell, 1996.

Herm, Gerhard. *The Celts.* New York: St. Martin's Press, 1977.

Hookham, Hilda. *Tamburlaine the Conqueror.* London: Hodder and Stoughton, 1962.

Howarth, Peter. *Attila, King of the Huns.* London: Constable, 1994.

Jones, Gwyn. *A History of the Vikings.* Oxford: Oxford University Press, 1968.

McEvedy, Colin. *The New Penguin Atlas of Medieval History.* New York: Penguin Books, 1992.

Morgan, David. *The Mongols.* Oxford: Blackwell, 1968.

Ogg, Frederic Austin. *A Source Book of Medieval History.* New York: The American Book Company, 1907.

Page, R. I. *Chronicles of the Vikings.* London: British Museum Press, 1995.

Randers-Pehrson, Justine Davis. *Barbarians and Romans.* Norman, Okla.: University of Oklahoma Press, 1983.

Runciman, Steven. *The First Crusade.* Cambridge: Cambridge University Press, 1952.

Schama, Simon. *Landscape and Memory.* New York: Knopf, 1995.

Vaughan, Richard. *Matthew Paris.* Cambridge: Cambridge University Press, 1958.

Fletcher, Richard. *The Barbarian Conversion.* New York: Henry Holt, 1998.

INDEX

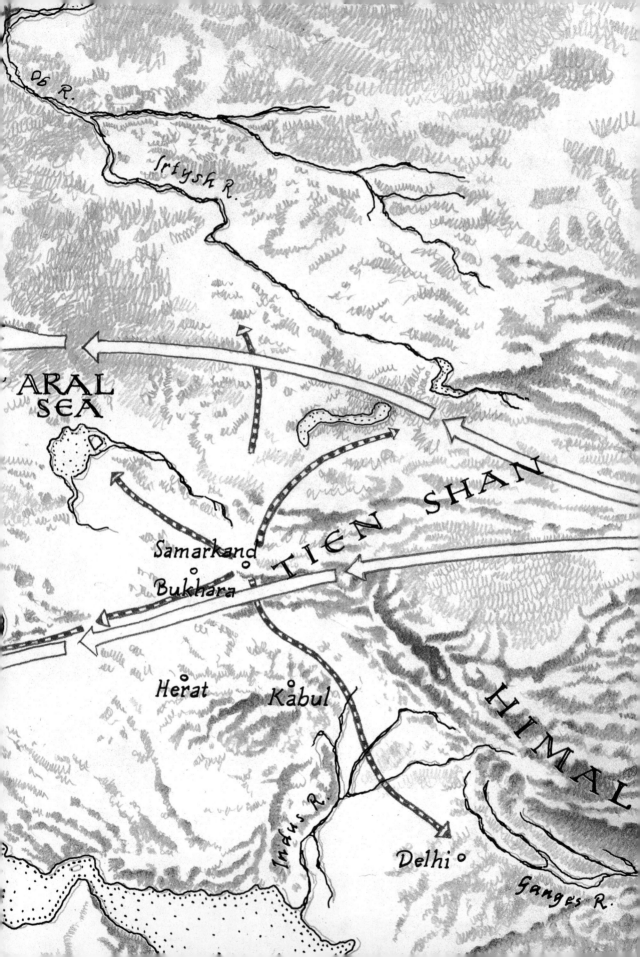

Ob R.

Irtysh R.

ARAL
SEA

TIEN SHAN

Samarkand
Bukhara

Herat   Kabul

HIMAL

Indus R.

Delhi

Ganges R.